Autism Spectrum Disorders:
Psychological Theory and Research

D1260192

Autism Spectrum Disorders: Psychological Theory and Research

DERMOT M. BOWLER
Department of Psychology
City University
London

BICENTENNIAL
1807
⊛WILEY
2007
BICENTENNIAL

John Wiley & Sons, Ltd

Published 2007   John Wiley & Sons Ltd
The Atrium, Southern Gate, Chichester,
West Sussex PO19 8SQ, England
Telephone (+44) 1243 779777

Email (for orders and customer service enquiries): cs-books@wiley.co.uk
Visit our Home Page on www.wiley.com

Other Wiley Editorial Offices

John Wiley & Sons Inc., 111 River Street, Hoboken, NJ 07030, USA

Jossey-Bass, 989 Market Street, San Francisco, CA 94103-1741, USA

Wiley-VCH Verlag GmbH, Boschstr. 12, D-69469 Weinheim, Germany

John Wiley & Sons Australia Ltd, 42 McDougall Street, Milton, Queensland 4064, Australia

John Wiley & Sons (Asia) Pte Ltd, 2 Clementi Loop #02-01, Jin Xing Distripark, Singapore 129809

John Wily & Sons Canada Ltd, 6045 Freemont Blvd, Mississauga, Ontario, L5R 4J3, Canada

Library of Congress Cataloging-in-Publication Data

Bowler, Dermot M.
  Autism spectrum disorders : psychological theory and research /
Dermot M. Bowler.
  p. ; cm.
  Includes bibliographical references and index.
  ISBN -13: 978-0-470-02686-1 (pbk. : alk. paper)
  ISBN -10: 0-470-02686-3 (pbk. : alk. paper)
  1. Autism. 2. Autism–Patients–Mental health. 3. Psychology,
Pathological. I. Title.
  [DNLM: 1. Autistic Disorder. 2. Psychological Theory.
WM203.5 B787a 2007]
  RC553. A88B694 2007
  616.85′882–dc22
                             2006026238

A catalogue record for this book is available from the British Library

ISBN -13   978-0-470-02686-1
ISBN -10   0-470-02686-3

Printed and bound in Great Britain by TJ International Ltd, Padstow, Cornwall

To:
Ciss
Pidgeon
Michael

Ba mhaith liom breith ar eireaball spideóige.

Contents

Preface

A reasonable reaction on picking up this volume might be 'not *another* book on autism!', to which my response would be, as you might expect, that this book is different. Although many books have been written about autism spectrum disorders (ASD), most consist either of descriptions of these conditions with a view to developing understanding and dispelling myths; others present more or less detailed accounts of their authors' own ideas with only passing reference to those of other scientists. Those that do present overviews of different positions tend to be edited volumes where experts in the field present up-to-date reviews of the state of play in their own corner of the field, with little attempt at painting a broader picture. What seems to be missing is a work that provides an overview from a single perspective of the main currents of thought. My first aim in writing this volume is to provide such an overview. I present a summary of the main psychological ideas that have been brought to bear on ASD in recent years and where possible, try to identify actual or potential common themes. The reviews of research are not meant to be exhaustive, but I hope that the selections I have made give a fair reflection of the state of current thinking in each domain. My second aim is to highlight the strengths and limitations of the different approaches and to develop a critical stance in readers that will help them evaluate new material as it appears. Finally, I aim to set out some of my own thoughts about how we should take our ideas forward. Insofar as such a thing is possible, I have tried to present the different theoretical systems in a dispassionate manner and to view my own ideas and those of others in the same critical light. But as the former *Observer* television critic, Clive James, once put it, the ego tends to adjust the light to suit its purposes. My ego is no exception.

No piece of academic work is ever the sole work of its author. Ideas always develop in the context of discussion, debate and collaboration. The thoughts expressed in this book, although my own, have been heavily influenced by encounters with a large number of colleagues and friends, to whom I must express my gratitude. First, I must give equal thanks to Chris Kiernan for giving me my first job as a researcher and for taming my rather adolescent approach to critical evaluation, and to Lorna Wing, who introduced me to the fascinating world of ASD and Asperger's syndrome. Lorna was among the first to advocate a spectrum (and more latterly, a dimensional) view of what was then referred to simply as 'autism'. Her tenacious defence against considerable opposition of this once highly unpopular but now widely accepted idea is an inspiration. Throughout my career as a scientist, I have worked alongside many other remarkable colleagues, including Sarah Lister Brook, Gillian Baird, Jill Boucher and John Gardiner. My ideas also owe a great deal to the discipline offered by gifted research assistants and students among whom I can count Jackie Briskman, Sarah Grice, Sebastian Gaigg, Jonathan Martin, George Berguno, Dianne Gumley, Paul Holland, Catherine Molesworth, Sophie Lind, Niki Daniel and Esther Strom. On the wider ASD front, I would also like to thank Tony Charman, Uta Frith, Francesca Happé, Pam Heaton, Peter Hobson, Chris Jarrold, Sue Leekam, Peter Mitchell, Derek Moore, Kate Plaisted, Michelle O'Riordan and John Swettenham. And from outside the field of ASD, Barbara Reid, John Versey, Donald Peterson, Marie Poirier, Alan Porter, Zofia Kaminska, James Hampton, Evelyne Thommen and Charles Legg. A special thanks goes to the Wellcome Trust, the Medical Research Council of the United Kingdom and the Department of Psychology at City University, without whose generous support many of my ideas would never have been subjected to the rigours of empirical test. I should also particularly like to thank the Department of Educational and Counselling Psychology, McGill University and the Clinique spécialisée des troubles envahissants du développement, Hôpital Rivière-des-Prairies, Montréal for generously accommodating me during a period of sabbatical leave during which the bulk of the book was written, and of course, my hosts Jacob Burack and Laurent Mottron, who provided insightful comments and encouragement during this process. And finally, thanks to Robert, for his endless patience, love and understanding.

ACKNOWLEDGEMENTS

The cover illustration is *Drawing 11* by Geoff Catlow, 2003, reproduced by kind permission of the artist.

The quotation on p. v is from the poem *Adhlacadh mo Mháthar* in the collection *Eireaball Spideóige* by Seán Ó'Ríordáin (1953). Baile Átha Cliath (Dublin): Sáirséal agus Dill. Reproduced by kind permission of Sáirséal·Ó Marcaigh Tta.

The description of the *Wisconsin Card Sorting Test* given on p. 71 is reproduced by special permission of the Publisher, Psychological Assessment Resources, Inc. 16204 North Florida Avenue, Lutz, Florida 33549, from the Wisconsin Card Sorting Test by David A. Grant., PhD and Esta A. Berg, PhD, Copyright 1981, 1993 by Psychological Assessment Resources, Inc. (PAR). Further reproduction is prohibited without permission of PAR.

1 Identifying Autism: From Discrete Entity to Multidimensional Spectrum

In one respect there is no need to write this chapter at all. As this is a book about psychological research and theoretical approaches *to* autism spectrum disorders (ASD), it is tempting to adopt the stance of the mathematician and to say something analogous to 'there exists the set of positive integers 1, 2, 3, 4, ..., n, ..., $n + 1$..., which have the following properties ...'; in other words, to assume that such disorders exist and to leave debates about the whys and wherefores of their existence for others, choosing to concentrate instead on their properties. But matters are not that simple. A complex behavioural syndrome is not quite so easily described as the set of positive integers, and definition and explanation are perhaps more closely intertwined in the field of psychopathology than they are in mathematics. Moreover, a grasp of what we mean when we use terms like 'autism', 'autism spectrum', 'pervasive developmental disorder' or whatever is crucial to the development of a critical understanding of the psychological research into these conditions. We need not only to be clear about what is currently understood by these terms, but also to have some idea of how this understanding has evolved over time as well as how such evolution impacts upon and nuances our current conceptualisation of the conditions. What is proposed in this chapter is a discussion of the historical development of the concept of autism followed by an overview of the diagnostic systems currently in use together with a discussion of some of the issues that remain controversial. This will include some consideration of characteristics of the condition that fall outside the strict parameters of the diagnostic systems but which are nonetheless important to understanding them. Finally, there will be some material on early detection of autism and its implications for other areas of research.

EARLY CONCEPTIONS: THE 'AUTISTIC CHILD'

In the 1940s, in the middle of World War II, two clinical descriptions of psychopathological conditions appeared in the literature, one written in

English and the other in German. The first was by Leo Kanner (Kanner, 1943) in which he described a series of 11 children whom he had seen in his clinical practice, and who were characterised by what he called 'autistic disturbances of affective contact'. This description laid the foundation for all the work that forms the basis of the remainder of this book and brought to general awareness the notion of 'the autistic child'. Kanner was not the first to describe children like these. Wing (see e.g. Wing, 1993) has long argued that Victor, the 'Wild Boy of Aveyron' first described by Itard (Lane, 1977), may have had the condition described by Kanner, and U. Frith (2003) provides an insightful survey of a number of historical figures, including Victor (and a fictional one – Tommy from the 1970s rock musical by The Who), who in all probability had autism. Hobson (1990b) cites a description by Melanie Klein of a young boy called Dick. She describes him as being devoid of affect, undisturbed at being separated from his nurse, showing no desire to be comforted. He did not play and '. . . several times ran round me, just as if I were a piece of furniture . . .' (Klein, 1930/1975, cited in Hobson, 1990b). Klein's description resembles that given by Kanner, but although Klein provided some important observations about Dick's condition (most notably that she thought it was constitutional in origin, and that it involved disruption of interpersonal processes), her account was of a single case, and so did not carry with it the notion of a syndrome – a cluster of symptoms that can be identified in different cases – and so did not enter the scientific literature in the same way that Kanner's observations did. It was Kanner's terminology and the condition he described that gradually became widely known, and both his description and the diagnostic scheme he proposed have formed the basis of our conception of autism ever since. The beauty of Kanner's account is that it captures very concisely the picture of a child with what we now sometimes call 'Kanner-type autism' and who would probably meet currently accepted criteria for autistic disorder.

The children described by Kanner were characterised by a failure to develop the kinds of emotionally charged interpersonal relations that usually become part of a child's behavioural repertoire. They tended to treat other people as objects rather than as human beings like themselves. They also showed characteristic patterns of speech and language use, being either mute or having delayed language development. And they also often displayed what he called immediate and delayed echolalia. Immediate echolalia is the tendency to repeat back what has just been heard or, in the case of a longer sentence, just the last few words. Delayed echolalia is the repeated use of a phrase such as 'go for a walk now' that was heard some time previously and that appears to bear no relation to the current context. A marked, and important, aspect of these children's use of language was the tendency to reverse pronouns. In normal conversation, when I speak about myself, I call myself 'I' or 'me', and refer to my interlocutor as 'you'. The other person, by contrast, does the reverse, referring to me as 'you' and to him/herself as 'I' or 'me'. Such adjustments of pronoun use according to the role of the speaker are hard for many individuals with autism, who tend to refer to themselves consistently as 'you' and to others as 'I' or 'me'. It is as if they regard words like 'I', 'me' and 'you' as names or labels rather than as role-determined attributions. Kanner also noted what he called an 'obsessive insistence on sameness', where children would attempt to return a changed situation to its original state and often became quite distressed when a well-practised routine was altered in some way, such as when they were taken to school by a different route. A related characteristic was a tendency for the behaviour of his children to be repetitive and lacking in imagination. When given a toy car, for example, children like those he described often prefer to turn it over and repeatedly make the wheels spin rather than to enact a car-related scenario or, rather than pretending that a set of wooden blocks are characters and props in a story, they prefer to line the blocks up or repetitively build and demolish towers.

Two other features observed by Kanner were that the children he described had good rote memory, that is to say that they could recall material without really understanding what it meant, and that they were of normal appearance. This last observation seems an unusual one to make, but the prevailing psychiatric climate of Kanner's time paid a great deal of attention to documenting psychopathological syndromes that were accompanied by characteristic facial features. In that context, it was striking that children who exhibited such markedly atypical behaviour should not be in any way unusual in their physical appearance. The topic of memory will be dealt with in more detail in Chapter 7.

Thus, the picture we get from Kanner's clinical description is of a child who is unremarkable in appearance but who seems indifferent to other people, often interacting with them only to obtain something he cannot get for himself. Spontaneous behaviour is markedly repetitive, with the child preferring to impose his own routines, which lack spontaneity and imagination. Language sometimes fails to develop, but when it does, it has the particular characteristics of immediate and delayed echolalia and pronominal reversal described above, and is often used in a way that has no obvious communicative function.

Most research into autism carried out in the 1950s, 1960s and 1970s recruited samples of children who more or less fitted the clinical picture of the syndrome described by Kanner. This work attempted to refine his descriptions with the aims of gaining greater understanding of underlying difficulties and of providing a richer description in the hope of improving diagnosis and treatment. Particular patterns of cognitive processing were demonstrated in a series of experimental investigations conducted by Hermelin, O'Connor and colleagues (see Hermelin & O'Connor, 1970), who observed difficulties in cross-modal processing and processing of temporally patterned material as well as difficulties in encoding and using meaningful aspects of information. The methods used to arrive at this conclusion were drawn from mainstream experimental psychology and involved precise experimental manipulation of variables in order to tap processing that was hypothesised to be spared or impaired.

Other approaches to assessing autism-specific aspects of cognitive processing employed standardised tests of intellectual function where profiles of performance across subtests are evaluated. Among the most widely used tests of intellectual functioning are the scales of intelligence known as the Wechsler scales – the Wechsler Pre-School and Primary Scale of Intelligence (WPPSI), Wechsler Intelligence Scale for Children (WISC) and Wechsler Adult Intelligence Scale (WAIS). All these tests consist of sets of subscales, which can be grouped into those that measure verbal skills or non-verbal (or 'performance' in the Wechsler terminology) skills. Level of achievement on these tests is usually expressed not in terms of raw numbers of test items passed, but in normative terms, i.e. how an individual's performance compares with that of an appropriate sample taken from the typical population. Thus, the performance of a child aged 5 years 5 months would be compared to that of a random sample of children of that age recruited from the general population. A characteristic of intelligence tests like these is that typically, for any one individual, normed scores tend to be rather similar across individual subtests. So someone who scores highly on one subtest will tend to score highly on all the others. This is usually not the case for children with autism. Atypical profiles across Wechsler subtests were reported by Bartak, Rutter and Cox (1975) who compared children with a diagnosis of autism but who had non-verbal IQs greater than 70 to dysphasic children who had problems with language. The difference in levels of attainment between verbal and performance tests was greater for the children with autism than the comparison children, and, moreover, the former group were observed to perform significantly less well than the latter on the Comprehension, Similarities and Vocabulary subtests of the WISC and better (but just short of statistically significantly so) on the Block Design subtest. This discrepancy between verbal and performance IQ in the children with autism but not the comparison children was also found for the results of the Peabody Picture Vocabulary Test (a test of receptive vocabulary) and the Coloured Progressive Matrices (a test of non-verbal intelligence, see Raven, 1996). Similar findings to these have been reported since the original study of Bartak et al. (see Manjiviona & Prior, 1999), with minor differences in emphasis depending on the overall level of functioning of the ASD participants being tested. With the advent of a broader conception of autism (see below), intellectual profiles have been used in an attempt to differentiate subgroups in the autism spectrum. But for individuals who fit the picture of autism presented by Kanner, it remains true that relatively enhanced performance can be found on tasks such as Block Design or matrices-type tests, which are visuo-spatial in nature (see Figure 5.2 for an example from the Block Design Test).

FROM DISCRETE ENTITY TO SPECTRUM OF RELATED CONDITIONS

The widespread consensus that prevailed up until the late 1980s – that the syndrome described by Kanner was a distinct psychopathological entity with a prevalence of about 4 per 10 000 children (Lotter, 1966; 1967) – was first challenged in an epidemiological study of the school-age population of the Metropolitan Borough of Camberwell in south London by Wing and Gould (1979). They found a 'history of typical autism' in 4.9 out of 10 000 children, but with a broader definition of impaired reciprocal social interaction ('social impairment' in Wing & Gould's terminology), the prevalence rate rose to 21.2 per 10 000. Two related developments followed from these observations. The first was that, far from being a discrete entity with clear boundaries, the syndrome described by Kanner represented a particular manifestation of a wider set of conditions that shared certain features even if they did not all express all of them in the same way. The second development was an attempt to characterise the factors unifying the different manifestations of this wider set of conditions. To this end, Wing & Gould proposed that autism was one of a spectrum of conditions, all of which were characterised by a triad of impairments in social, imaginative and symbolic functioning accompanied by repetitive behaviours. The identification of a broader set of parameters within which to conceptualise the syndrome described by Kanner led Wing and her colleagues to search for other conditions, which although not identical to Kanner's, could nonetheless be considered as other manifestations of impairments of elements of the triad. It was this search that raised the profile of what has now become known as Asperger's syndrome or Asperger disorder.

The next observer after Kanner to use the term 'autistic' in the context of child psychopathology was Hans Asperger (Asperger, 1944/1991). His paper was in German and unsurprisingly did not receive much attention in the English-speaking world until Wing's (1981) clinical account of what she termed 'Asperger's syndrome' (although see Bosch, 1970; Van Krevelen, 1971). Asperger described four cases of adolescents whom he described as having 'autistic psychopathy'. Although the cases he described were in many respects quite different from those described by Kanner, most notably in the domain of language and communication as well as in overall level of intellectual functioning, the common thread linking the two was the characteristic disconnectedness from other people to which both authors gave the term 'autism', a term first employed by Bleuler (1911) to describe the retreat into a world of their own that he observed in people with schizophrenia. Both Kanner and Asperger noted that their patients were curiously disconnected from other people; Kanner's children often treating others like objects and Asperger's adolescents being wrapped up in their own interests, with little care whether or not another person shared their fascination. Although Asperger did not list specific criteria for the diagnosis of the condition he described, Wing (1981) identified eight points in his account. These are listed in Box 1.1 and paint a picture of an individual of normal intelligence with good verbal communication skills but with a long-winded and pedantic style and odd intonation. There was also evidence of circumscribed interests on odd topics, the pursuit of which took up much of the individual's time. Asperger also noted impaired gross motor functioning and a lack of common sense. But the most striking feature of the condition remains the social oddity and lack of empathic reciprocity with others and it is this characteristic that led Wing and colleagues to consider that the conditions described by Kanner and by Asperger to be facets of a common underlying set of factors.

Box 1.1. Characteristics of Asperger's syndrome as listed by Wing (1981)

- More common in boys
- Normal age of onset of speech
- Impaired non-verbal communication
- Flat intonation and absent or large, clumsy gestures
- Impairment of two-way social interaction
- Repetitive activities and resistance to change
- Poor motor coordination
- Clumsy, odd gait and posture
- Circumscribed interests with good rote memory for facts on narrowly defined or unusual topics
- Bullied at school because of perceived eccentricity

Reproduced by kind permission of Cambridge University Press.

Although Asperger's syndrome and autism of the kind described by Kanner are perhaps the most widely known forms of ASD, there are other conditions that have been described in the literature and which overlap to a greater or lesser extent with the other conditions in the autism spectrum. These include dementia precocissima (De Sanctis, 1906; 1908), dementia infantalis (Heller, 1908), childhood schizophrenia (Bender, 1947) and childhood psychosis (Creak, 1963). More recently, Rourke (1989) identified a syndrome characterised by good rote memory that was used to cope with complex social and non-social situations, unusual prosody in speech and impaired social judgment. As well as attributing this condition to damage to the right hemisphere, Rourke gave it the name non-verbal learning disability (NLD), which is related to developmental learning disability of the right hemisphere (Weintraub & Mesulam, 1983). Wolff and colleagues have described a group of children and adults to whom they have given the label *schizoid personality disorder* (Wolff, 1995; Wolff & Barlow, 1978; Wolff & Chick, 1980). These individuals were characterised by solitariness, lack of empathy, emotional detachment, mental rigidity and single-minded pursuit of specialised interests, and language difficulties in the area of understanding linguistic devices such as metaphor. In later writings, Wolff acknowledges the overlap between the individuals she described and those described by Asperger. Gillberg and colleagues (Gillberg, 1983) have identified a group of children whose symptomatology overlaps with that of the autism spectrum, whose condition they have labelled *deficits in attention, motor control and perception (DAMP)*. As the term implies, children who are given this label are of normal IQ, have difficulty focusing their attention, are hyperactive and impulsive, experience gross motor difficulties and may show features of other developmental psychopathological conditions including those from the autism spectrum. A further group of individuals from what Bishop (Bishop, 1989; Bishop & Norbury, 2002) has called 'the borderlands of autism' are those described as having semantic–pragmatic disorder or semantic–pragmatic syndrome, and who now tend to be described as having pragmatic language impairment (PLI). The initial published descriptions of such children led Lister Brook and Bowler (1992) to conclude that they were probably a manifestation of the autism spectrum, but more recent studies have shown that although some children whose language is pragmatically impaired meet current criteria for autistic disorder or pervasive developmental disorder, many do not (Bishop & Norbury, 2002). All these conditions overlap to some extent with the autism spectrum, and the extent of their overlap will provide clues not only to a finer delineation of the necessary factors for a diagnosis of autism but also for a better understanding of the mechanisms underlying its development. But both because of the relatively small amount of research into these conditions, and because they are on the periphery of the autism spectrum, they will not be considered in any detail here.

Wing and Gould's characterisation of autism as a spectrum of conditions (later to include Asperger's syndrome) was initially controversial, but has now entered into mainstream thinking where the term *broader phenotype* is currently used to describe individuals who may not meet strict criteria for autistic disorder or Asperger's syndrome but who nevertheless show sufficient features of these conditions to suggest that they share an underlying pathology. Such acceptance of a broader spectrum of autism-related conditions has had repercussions not only on how we think about explaining their underlying characteristics, but also on how common these conditions are in the general population. We have already seen that early studies of what proportion of the population might have autism gave a prevalence rate of about 4 per 10000 (Lotter, 1966; Wing & Gould, 1979). However, as Rutter (2005) points out, these early studies had a number of shortcomings, principally that they were conducted on relatively small samples, that they used a fairly strict definition of autism based on Kanner's criteria (although Lotter acknowledged that he did encounter individuals who did not exactly fit this picture), and that standardised instruments were not used in making the diagnoses. In a review of more recent epidemiological studies that have tested larger samples using current diagnostic criteria and assessment instruments, Rutter (2005) concludes that most well-conducted epidemiological studies of autism spectrum disorders cite a prevalence of somewhere between 30 and 60 cases of autism spectrum disorder per 10000 of the population. This figure is considerably higher than that reported in earlier epidemiological studies and is in part a reflection of the broadening of diagnostic criteria and improved methods for assessing these criteria. Whether this increase is a reflection of a true increase in incidence or of more effective diagnosis remains uncertain.

In addition to forcing us to revise our estimates of the incidence of ASD in the general population, the shift in conceptualisation from discrete entity to spectrum of conditions also prompts a reconsideration of their broader symptomatology. Symptoms need to be described in terms that are applicable to all manifestations of the spectrum. Such descriptions need to be sufficiently precise in order to enable all manifestations of the spectrum to be readily identifiable, but also because they form the starting point for many of the theoretical accounts that will be discussed later in this book. Furthermore, the revised prevalence estimates represent a shift in our thinking about the relationship between autism spectrum disorder and global intellectual disability. When the earlier prevalence figures were currently accepted, it was widely held that about 75% of individuals labelled autistic also had some degree of global intellectual impairment or mental retardation (Wing & Gould, 1979). However, with the shift to a broader, spectrum conceptualisation of autism, this proportion is estimated at about 25%, meaning that the majority of people with an autism spectrum diagnosis have normal levels of intellectual functioning.

The most striking feature of individuals from any part of the autism spectrum remains what Wing (Wing & Gould, 1979) refers to as social impairment. This can range from an almost total disconnectedness from other people, who are treated almost like pieces of furniture (so-called 'aloof' children), to those who passively accept the social overtures of others but rarely if ever initiate interaction and those whose behaviour consists of repetitive approaches centred on the individual's own concerns or obsessions rather than those of the person they are approaching ('active-but-odd'). More subtle interpersonal difficulties are often noted, such as insensitivity to the feelings of others or a failure to understand the reasons why people might act the way they do in certain situations. Attempts to explain social impairment have dominated research into ASD from the mid 1980s until the beginning of the present century and are dealt with in Chapters 2 and 3 of this book.

A second notable feature is the characteristic difficulty with imaginative and symbolic behaviours seen in individuals with ASD. We have already noted that since Kanner's first description, children with autistic disorder were described as not playing with objects in the way typical children of similar developmental level do. Rather than pretend that one object is another (e.g. acting towards a brick as if it were a car or a boat), or acting out scenarios using miniature objects, they prefer to engage in repetitive and stereotyped object-related activities. Although older and more able children with ASD may develop some apparently symbolic routines with objects, these are often centred on one or two themes and repeated over and over again. Individuals with Asperger's syndrome often show little interest in more adult forms of imaginative activity such as fiction or televised drama, often reporting difficulties in following plots. More controlled observations have confirmed Kanner's initial observation (Baron-Cohen, 1987; Charman, Swettenham, Baron-Cohen, Cox et al., 1997; Wing, Gould, Yeates & Brierly, 1977; Wolff, 1985, see Jarrold, Boucher & Smith, 1993 for a review). Jordan (2003) observes that play is at once a transparently simple concept, yet one that is quite difficult to pin down in terms of precise and comprehensive definition. Behaviourally, it entails manipulation of objects in a way that is systematic yet flexible and that relates that object to some sort of context. The context is often social in nature, and much play in typical development occurs in social interactions, often with more able, older individuals, such as siblings or caregivers and, as we shall see in Chapter 2, psychological theories of social impairment closely link the development of the capacity to pretend with the ability to understand other people, especially the fact that other people have minds. Play, as has long been noted (see Piaget, 1962 and Vygotsky, 1962), has a symbolic component, in that attributes of the manipulated object, or, as in the example of using a brick as a car given above, another, absent object are evoked by means of relevant action sequences, which from Vygotsky's point of view, develop in a social context. Thus, impairments of play can result from difficulties with one or more of a number of components. There may be difficulties in imagining alternative uses for an object, or in evoking absent properties of an object (see Harris, 2000), or in the structuring of flexible action sequences (see Chapter 4 on impairments in executive functioning) or in social interaction.

Most of the studies that demonstrated impaired play in children with ASD nevertheless engage in some activity that could be coded as pretend or symbolic play, leading some researchers (such as Lewis & Boucher, 1995) to argue that given appropriate prompts, increased play activity could be induced in these children. In a review of the studies of prompting and play, Jarrold (2003) concludes that although some studies have demonstrated that children with ASD can be prompted to engage in pretend play, these children remain impaired in their overall level of play compared to matched comparison children. Jarrold also reviews studies that show that children with ASD are able to override the functional properties of props in a play scenario and use the props for a different purpose (e.g. using a pencil as a pretend toothbrush). The overall conclusion is that children with ASD can understand and produce pretend acts but experience difficulty in organising these acts into more complex imaginative sequences. Jarrold also highlights a problem that is a recurring theme across almost all domains of psychological inquiry into ASD, namely that it is difficult to extrapolate from behavioural measures of play to the actual experience of the child who is playing. We need to be cautious drawing conclusions from task performance and when making inferences about underlying capacities or mechanisms.

Impaired symbolic and play behaviours seem to be related to impairments in the ability to generate novel approaches to solving problems. Such impairment tends to lead to repeated attempts to use unsuccessful strategies, giving the appearance of a repetitive behavioural repertoire. Repetitive behaviour constitutes one of the core diagnostic features of ASD and, like other features, manifests itself differently depending on the context of the wider symptomatology, especially level of overall cognitive ability. Together, impaired imagination and generativity coupled with a tendency to engage in repetitive behaviour has led to developments of accounts of ASD in terms of impairments in the so-called *executive functions*. These accounts will be explored in greater detail in Chapter 4.

Kanner's original account gives us a picture of language that is sometimes absent and often delayed in its development. When it does develop, it has the characteristic qualities of immediate or delayed echolalia and pronominal reversal. But these characteristics tend to be found in individuals who fit the Kanner picture and who have some degree of global intellectual impairment. Language impairments in people with ASD who are not globally cognitively impaired tend to be subtler and may relate more to their social impairments rather than language difficulties *per se*. We have already seen that Asperger observed that his patients had odd intonation and a tendency to engage in monologues about their specific interests. And more controlled investigations have discovered difficulties in organising discourse and in generating coherent narratives. For example, Losh and Capps (2003) compared the performance of children with high-functioning ASD (including some with a diagnosis of Asperger disorder) and matched typical children on a range of narrative tasks including personal and picture-book-based narratives. Although there were many similarities between the groups on measures such as length of narrative and numbers of personal narratives, the ASD group showed less thematic integration and coherence in their accounts, especially of their own personal experience. Whereas earlier studies of narrative production in more globally impaired children with ASD tended to show impairments in narrative length and numbers of narratives produced (see Tager-Flusberg, 1995), Losh and Capps' findings seem to suggest that even in the absence of global cognitive impairment, individuals with autism experience difficulties in organising their recall of experience in a way that enables them to provide a coherent account of it. This is a theme that will be taken up in the discussion of memory in Chapter 7.

DIAGNOSTIC SYSTEMS AND INSTRUMENTS

It was not until 1980 that autism-related conditions were included in the third revision of the *Diagnostic and Statistical Manual* of the American Psychiatric Association (DSM-III, American Psychiatric Association, 1980), which included a category of *infantile autism*, later changed to *autistic disorder* in the revised DSM-IV (American Psychiatric Association, 1987). Since then, the shift in the conceptualisation of autism from a single entity to a spectrum of related conditions has been reflected in later revisions of this manual as well as in the procedures employed to make diagnoses. The current reference for diagnosing autism spectrum disorder is the text revision of the fourth version of DSM (DSM-IV TR, American Psychiatric Association, 2000), which, under the heading *Disorders usually first diagnosed in infancy, childhood or adolescence*, lists the category of *Pervasive Developmental Disorders* (PDD), which includes the conditions listed in Box 1.2. Inspection of this table shows that 'autism' consists of not one but a range of conditions that are assumed to be linked in some way. This immediately poses a problem: what terms do we use to describe the set of conditions set out in Box 1.2? Describing the individual elements is less problematic, in that the DSM-IV TR terms can be used, but choice of a collective term is more difficult. One possibility would be to opt for the DSM-IV TR term of PDD. But, although this may well (and probably should) become the case in the medium to long term, terms such as 'autism', 'autism spectrum' and 'autistic (or autism) spectrum disorder' have become so entrenched in the literature that changing terminology at this stage might be more confusing than enlightening. Moreover, using a term like PDD to cover all the conditions listed in Box 1.2 might confuse some readers into thinking that what was being referred to was pervasive developmental disorder not otherwise specified (PDD-NOS), which, because it is grouped along with atypical autism, gives the impression that it applies to atypical rather than typical manifestations. Because this book deals primarily with autistic disorder, Asperger disorder and PDD-NOS, I have decided to use the term *autism spectrum disorder* (usually abbreviated to ASD) when speaking of these conditions collectively. On occasions, especially where the literature under discussion warrants it, I use the term *autism* to refer to autistic disorder that is accompanied by some degree of global intellectual disability and *high-functioning autism* when no global disability is present. Because the term 'autism' has been used to describe a set of conditions as well as a set of symptoms, it will sometimes be used here to refer to the cluster of symptoms that are thought to underlie all manifestations of the autism spectrum. The terms *Asperger's syndrome* and *Asperger disorder* are used synonymously. In relation to the nomenclature of individuals (whether with autism or without) whose global level of development lags behind that of their age peers, the term *intellectual disability* is used, although on occasions where the research being described uses terms such as 'mental handicap', 'mental retardation' or 'global cognitive impairment', then these are also used. All these terms are treated as synonyms.

Box 1.2. Conditions listed under the heading Pervasive Developmental Disorders in the DSM-IV TR (American Psychiatric Association, 2000)

- Autistic disorder
- Rett's disorder
- Childhood disintegrative disorder
- Asperger's disorder
- Pervasive developmental disorder not otherwise specified (including atypical autism)

Reproduced by permission of the American Psychiatric Association.

The criteria listed in DSM-IV TR to determine whether an individual can be said to have autistic disorder or Asperger's syndrome are set out in Box 1.3. Inspection of the table shows that the key impairments in both conditions occur in the domains of social interaction and the flexible patterning of behaviour, reflecting the initial clinical descriptions of Kanner and Asperger. The major distinction between the two conditions on these criteria lies in the domains of communication, general cognitive delay and imaginative activities. For a diagnosis of autism, there must be evidence that at least one of social interaction, communicative use of language and symbolic or imaginative play were impaired before the age of 3 years, but there is no requirement for impaired communication or for general cognitive delay in order to make a diagnosis of Asperger disorder. Indeed, on these criteria such a diagnosis is reserved for those who show no clinically significant delay in language. In addition to the criteria for these two disorders, DSM-IV also allows for a diagnosis of PDD-NOS, which is characterised by a 'severe and pervasive impairment in the development of reciprocal social interaction . . .'. This may be accompanied by other features similar to those described for autism and Asperger disorder, but to an extent insufficient to meet the criteria for these and a range of other conditions.

Box 1.3. DSM-IV TR diagnostic criteria

Autistic disorder

A A total of six (or more) items from (1), (2), and (3), with at least two from (1), and one each from (2) and (3):
(1) qualitative impairment in social interaction, as manifested by at least two of the following:

   (a) marked impairment in the use of multiple non-verbal behaviours such as eye-to-eye gaze, facial expression, body postures, and gestures to regulate social interaction

   (b) failure to develop peer relationships appropriate to developmental level

   (c) a lack of spontaneous seeking to share enjoyment, interests, or achievements with other people (e.g. by a lack of showing, bringing, or pointing out objects of interest)

   (d) lack of social or emotional reciprocity

(2) qualitative impairments in communication as manifested by at least one of the following:

   (a) delay in, or total lack of, the development of spoken language (not accompanied by an attempt to compensate through alternative modes of communication such as gesture or mime)

   (b) in individuals with adequate speech, marked impairment in the ability to initiate or sustain a conversation with others

   (c) stereotyped and repetitive use of language or idiosyncratic language

   (d) lack of varied, spontaneous make-believe play or social imitative play appropriate to developmental level

(3) restricted repetitive and stereotyped patterns of behavior, interests, and activities, as manifested by at least one of the following:

   (a) encompassing preoccupation with one or more stereotyped and restricted patterns of interest that is abnormal either in intensity or focus

   (b) apparently inflexible adherence to specific, non-functional routines or rituals

   (c) stereotyped and repetitive motor mannerisms (e.g. hand or finger flapping or twisting, or complex whole-body movements)

   (d) persistent preoccupation with parts of objects

B Delays or abnormal functioning in at least one of the following areas, with onset prior to age 3 years: (1) social interaction, (2) language as used in social communication, or (3) symbolic or imaginative play.

C The disturbance is not better accounted for by Rett's disorder or childhood disintegrative disorder.

Asperger's disorder

A Qualitative impairment in social interaction, as manifested by at least two of the following:

(1) marked impairment in the use of multiple non-verbal behaviours such as eye-to-eye gaze, facial expression, body postures, and gestures to regulate social interaction

(2) failure to develop peer relationships appropriate to developmental level

(3) a lack of spontaneous seeking to share enjoyment, interests, or achievements with other people (e.g. by a lack of showing, bringing, or pointing out objects of interest to other people)

(4) lack of social or emotional reciprocity

B Restricted repetitive and stereotyped patterns of behaviour, interests, and activities, as manifested by at least one of the following:

(1) encompassing preoccupation with one or more stereotyped and restricted patterns of interest that is abnormal either in intensity or focus

(2) apparently inflexible adherence to specific, non-functional routines or rituals

(3) stereotyped and repetitive motor mannerisms (e.g., hand or finger flapping or twisting, or complex whole-body movements)

(4) persistent preoccupation with parts of objects

C The disturbance causes clinically significant impairment in social, occupational, or other important areas of functioning.

D There is no clinically significant general delay in language (e.g. single words used by age 2 years, communicative phrases used by age 3 years).

E There is no clinically significant delay in cognitive development or in the development of age-appropriate self-help skills, adaptive behaviour (other than in social interaction), and curiosity about the environment in childhood.

F Criteria are not met for another specific pervasive developmental disorder or schizophrenia.

From DSM-IV TR (American Psychiatric Association, 2000). Reproduced by permission of the American Psychiatric Association. Copyright © 2000 American Psychiatric Association. All rights reserved.

Although widely and increasingly employed, DSM-IV is not the only diagnostic system that has been used by clinicians or researchers. Another major framework is the tenth edition of the International Classification of Diseases (ICD-10; World Health Organization, 1993). The criteria used in this system show a remarkable similarity with those of DSM-IV. Other, less widely used criteria are those of Gillberg and colleagues (Ehlers & Gillberg, 1993), Szatmari, Bremner and Nagy (1989) and Wing (Wing & Gould, 1979), although they differ in certain respects, and although these differences have generated considerable debate (see Mayes, Calhoun & Crites, 2001), they share the notion that the core features of the condition hinge on impairments in reciprocal social interaction and the presence to some extent of repetitive behaviours of some kind.

The first observation to make about all the diagnostic schemes just described is that they specify *behavioural* criteria for the identification of ASD. Despite widespread consensus that ASD has a biological basis reflected in brain pathology, as yet there exist no biological or neurobiological markers to identify these conditions. Second, the criteria often refer not just to the presence or absence of particular behaviours but to their *patterning*. This patterning occurs both over the short term (i.e. that can be observed in a single encounter), such as repetitive or stereotyped activities, or over the longer term, such as atypical developmental trajectories in the area of social and communicative development. As a consequence of these two factors, any attempt at diagnosis must elicit evidence of behavioural indices for the diagnostic criteria and, where appropriate, their patterning over time.

Although the diagnostic systems themselves provide some indication of the kinds of behaviours to look for when deciding whether or not a diagnosis of ASD should be made, the descriptions are vague and can only be interpreted in the context of training under the supervision of someone experienced in making such diagnoses. In order to bring some standardisation to the process of making the behavioural observations needed to make a diagnosis, a number of formal assessment instruments have been developed, the most widely used of which are the Autism Diagnostic Interview – Revised (ADI-R, Lord, Rutter & Le Couteur, 1994; LeCouteur, Lord & Rutter, 2003) and the Autism Diagnostic Observation Schedule (ADOS-G, Lord, Risi, Lambrecht et al., 2000). Other instruments, such as the Childhood Autism Rating Scale (CARS; Schopler, Reichler & Renner, 1986) or the Diagnostic Interview for Social and Communicative Disorders (DISCO; Wing, Leekam, Libby et al., 2002) and the Developmental, Dimensional and Diagnostic Interview (3di; Skuse, Warrington, Bishop et al., 2004) also exist, the last two share with the ADI and the ADOS the requirement that users undergo formal training. Systems such as ADI, ADOS, DISCO or 3di represent codifications and standardisations of good clinical diagnostic practice. As such, they build on, rather than completely supersede, methods of diagnosis that have been used in the past and are to some extent still widespread. The purpose of all these instruments is to provide descriptions of the behaviours that need to be present to make a diagnosis of ASD, as well as to specify standardised methods for assessing the presence of these behaviours. The purpose of training is to ensure that the person using the instruments can make reliable and valid evaluations of whether or not specific behaviours are or have been exhibited and whether or not the diagnostic criteria are met. The process of making a diagnosis involves a trained observer recognising a particular pattern of symptoms. This implies that the observer must have encountered similar patterns in the past and, with the guidance of a trained supervisor, learn to distinguish them from other, similar patterns. It is this pattern-recognition process that is at the heart of the diagnostic process (for any condition, not just for autism) and it can only be mastered by exposure to a range of patterns that do and do not fit the diagnostic entity of interest. This exposure to actual cases is at the heart of the process and is not made redundant by the use of more explicit procedures such as those embodied in the ADI or other measures. All that these measures do is to make explicit the criteria on which a particular diagnosis has been made and the manner in which those criteria were assessed with the overall aim of giving us greater confidence when comparing findings across different investigations that the participants in those investigations are similar in terms of their symptomatology. This point is important when we come to compare studies that have recruited participants using different diagnostic systems and different methods of assessment for diagnosis. It is always possible that participants in a study who were described merely as having 'a diagnosis of Asperger's syndrome' may not be directly comparable to those who 'met DSM-IV criteria for Asperger disorder on the basis of the ADI', although, as we shall see, it is likely that the latter are a subset of the former. But it is perhaps going too far to suggest, as does Mottron (2004, p. 21) that the findings of all investigations conducted before the advent of instruments like the ADI or the ADOS are unreliable because the diagnostic criteria and assessment processes used were not clearly specified, and threfore we can have no confidence in whether or not the participants did in fact have the disorder claimed by the investigator. The utilisation of a standardised instrument does not guarantee that the procedures and criteria specified by that instrument have been rigorously applied, any more than the non-use of such an instrument implies that they have not.

DIMENSIONS VERSUS ENTITIES: 'LUMPING' VERSUS 'SPLITTING'

Despite the widespread acceptance of the existence of an autism spectrum comprising a range of different conditions, the historical legacy of the two original clinical accounts remains, fuelling a debate about whether the syndrome described by Asperger is a qualitatively different psychopathological condition from that described by Kanner, especially when the latter is not accompanied by global intellectual impairment. Moreover, current diagnostic schemes tend to encourage the assigning of individuals to categories, rather than thinking of dimensions of impairment. These two processes have contributed to the question of whether or not we should lump the different conditions from the autism spectrum together under a common heading or split them under different ones. This is a question that needs to be tackled both at a conceptual and an empirical level. Conceptually, we need to ask what we are trying to achieve by having a diagnostic system. The purpose of any diagnostic and classification system is to reduce the complexity and diversity encountered in clinical practice into a smaller set of categories, the members of which have features in common and who do not share features with members of other categories. So, for example, people who complain of abdominal pain can be divided into those who have upper abdominal pain and lower abdominal pain, and each of these categories can be further subdivided, so that we eventually speak of inflammation of the stomach or inflammation of the appendix, each of which will have a set of symptoms that does not overlap with the other, and which will call for a different treatment strategy. The important point here is that the different symptoms actually do reflect different disease processes. In the context of abdominal pain, it is possible to draw up symptom sets that do not do this. If we were, for example, to have a scale of severity of pain, then this would not distinguish between stomach and appendix disease, since both can produce pain that is mild or severe. Patients could be reliably classified on this dimension, but whether this would be clinically useful, or whether it would tell us anything about the underlying reality of their disease would be questionable. In the context of diagnosing autism or Asperger disorder, we need to determine whether or not the differentiations required by DSM-IV or ICD-10 reflect different underlying dysfunctions. This is a question that can only be tested empirically.

Macintosh and Dissanayake (2004) identify two broad strategies for empirically determining whether Asperger's syndrome can be differentiated from high-functioning autism. The first is to take a large group of individuals and administer a number of measures, including a diagnostic assessment such as one of those described earlier on in this chapter. Cluster analysis is then applied to the data in order to see first whether subgroups of individuals can be identified, and then to see how these subgroups map onto the categories generated by the diagnostic system. For example, Prior, Eisenmajer, Leekam, Wing et al. (1998) applied cluster analysis to a group of 135 individuals who had been given a diagnosis of high-functioning autism, Asperger's syndrome or PDD according to DSM-III (an earlier version of DSM-IV) criteria. Measures used in the cluster analysis came from a questionnaire measure, the Autism Spectrum Disorders Checklist (Rapin, 1996) from which measures of social impairment, impairments in communication and imagination and repetitive behaviours were derived. Application of cluster analysis yielded three clusters (which they labelled A, B and C), with a majority of individuals (46%) with a diagnosis falling into cluster A, a majority of those with a diagnosis of Asperger's syndrome (58%) falling in cluster B and a majority of those with another PDD (56%) falling in cluster C. Prior et al. conclude from these observations that although the characteristics measured by the checklist they use do cluster into groups that resemble the DSM-based diagnostic categories, there is considerable overflow across the boundaries of these categories. In each of the three empirically derived clusters, almost half the participants came from one or other of the non-majority diagnosis for that group. Prior et al. argue that such observations support a spectrum view of ASD, which sees impairment as occurring along a number of dimensions, each of which may be impaired independently of the others.

The notion of a spectrum reflecting different dimensions of behaviour that can be independently impaired to a greater or lesser extent, with the resulting cluster of impairments defining the clinical picture presented by the individual is seductive. However, such a conceptualisation begs a number of questions. First, how do we define what the dimensions of behaviour are? In Prior et al.'s study, they were derived from the Autism Spectrum Disorders Checklist, which as we have seen, seeks information about behaviours in the domains of social interaction, communication and imagination, and repetitive activities. But such a framework makes the questionable assumption that these dimensions are independent. There may well be, for example, a relation between repetitive behaviours and lack of imaginative activities (someone who is compelled in some way to repeat actions over and over may thus be prevented from engaging in more flexible behaviours that marks the existence of an imaginative capacity and help its further development). In short, we need a theory of what the dimensions mean and of what psychological processes might underlie their behavioural manifestations. Nevertheless, the approach of studies such as that of Prior et al. (1998) marks an important step in helping us to do just that. By showing that individuals can vary along behavioural dimensions that can be measured reliably, we have a basis for exploring underlying processes that goes beyond simple group classification. This process will be aided by the development of assessment instruments such as the 3di (Skuse et al., 2004), which provide quantitative estimates along dimensions of impairment as well as assignment of cases to diagnostic categories.

Macintosh and Dissanayake (2004) take issue with clustering studies for a number of reasons other than those just outlined. They identify several flaws in the sampling of some of the investigations that have used this method. For example, they argue that as the children who were diagnosed with Asperger's syndrome in the Prior et al. (1998) study also met criteria for autism, we cannot be certain whether the claimed qualitative similarity between the two conditions is not an artefact of poor sample selection. By labelling at the outset children with autism as Asperger children, it is perhaps not surprising that the cluster analysis came up with clusters that were quantitatively but not qualitatively different. Macintosh and Dissanayake further argue that cluster analysis ends up in assigning individuals to clusters in ways that can yield groups that are not matched on chronological or mental age, making it likely that the differences between the groups may be a result of differences on these measures rather than on more directly autism-related measures. However, this last point is valid only if the resultant clusters do differ on these measures, and even then it would be necessary to show that the differences were in a range of magnitude that was in some way related (either conceptually or on the basis of empirical evidence) to autistic symptomatology.

A second way to address the question of whether the different categories of ASD should be thought of as a single entity or several different entities is to recruit groups of people who meet criteria for the different subgroups and who are carefully matched on a number of variables such as IQ and age. These individuals are then tested on a range of measures that do not form part of the diagnostic criteria (although they may be related to them) to see if any differences emerge. This establishes what Miller and Ozonoff (2000) call *external validity*, i.e. an indication of how the groups might differ on measures that do not form part of the procedures used for diagnosis. Many of the early studies that took this approach (e.g. Klin, Volkmar, Sparrow et al., 1995; Ozonoff, Rogers & Pennington, 1991b) did not use the more recently developed DSM-IV criteria and thus it is likely that many of the participants described as having Asperger's syndrome would also have met criteria for autism. But one study that did recruit participants on the basis of the application of DSM-IV and ICD-10 criteria was that of Manjiviona and Prior (1999). They took children and adolescents who had a clinical diagnosis of either autism or Asperger's syndrome, and administered a battery of intelligence and neuropsychological tests. Group comparisons were made both on the basis of clinical diagnosis and of the application of DSM-IV or ICD-10 categories. On the basis of clinical diagnosis, the Asperger group showed higher overall IQ, which resulted from better performance on verbal tasks. When the groups were defined by DSM or ICD criteria, no such differences emerged. Whichever way the groups were defined, no differences in neuropsychological performance or in Wechsler subtest profile emerged. Manjiviona and Prior concluded that their observations did not support the case for differentiating Asperger's syndrome from high-functioning autism and that in practice, such a differentiation is often based on considerations of high IQ. Another study that used DSM-IV criteria for diagnosis was that of Ozonoff, South & Miller (2000). They compared a group of high-functioning children and adolescents with autism and a group of children and adolescents with Asperger disorder, all of whom were selected on the basis of DSM-IV criteria. A battery of intelligence and neuropsychological tests was administered as well as assessments of current symptomatology and early history using the ADI and the ADOS. The two groups were found to differ on early history (which is not surprising, given the diagnostic criteria), and the Asperger group showed less severe symptoms and a developmental trajectory that was less impaired than the autism group. Ozonoff et al. conclude that their observations make it unlikely that there are any meaningful differences between high-functioning autism and Asperger's syndrome over and above the diagnostic criteria used to differentiate them. They do express caution, however, and point out that the differences in imagination and repetitive behaviour (which relate to the diagnostic criteria and therefore do not contribute to external validity) merit further exploration, and that a final judgment on whether or not to aggregate the two conditions should await further research in these two domains.

The fact that earlier studies have reported more differences between Asperger's syndrome and high-functioning autism whereas later studies have not is, as we have seen, due to the fact that the former tended not to use DSM criteria whereas the latter did. This raises the question of what kind of findings might emerge if systematic comparisons were made among groups defined by a strict application of other diagnostic schemes. When Ghaziuddin, Tsai and Ghaziuddin (1992) applied six different sets of criteria to a group of individuals with a diagnosis of PDD, only half met criteria for all six schemes. This would suggest that we might find differences in measures of external validity when some schemes were used to classify individuals. Proposing such a thought experiment is useful in that it prompts us to reflect on what we mean when we attempt to divide a group of individuals into diagnostic categories on the basis of a set of criteria. In the present discussion, we have seen that some sets of criteria yield groups that differ on measures external to those criteria and others do not. Which raises the question of why we should prefer one set of diagnostic criteria to another. Moreover, even within a scheme like DSM-IV, two individuals can be given the same diagnosis, even though the criteria that they met are, although overlapping, not identical (see Box 1.3). It is worth reflecting on what might emerge if we were to compare groups based on precisely the same sets of criteria using a design like that of Ozonoff et al. (2000). If differences were to emerge, exactly how would we interpret them? These reflections prompt us to think carefully about the way we have approached autism research in terms of group comparisons rather than variations along dimensions. In much of the research reported in this book, the strategy has been to select groups according to sets of criteria and then to compare these groups with others who do not meet these criteria. As we shall see in later chapters, there is some inconsistency of findings across studies that have adopted this research strategy. It is tempting to speculate that such differences might be a consequence of undue adherence to diagnostic categories, rather than a more dimensional view of ASD.

As well as considering the conceptual validity of diagnostic criteria, we also need to bear in mind the way in which the differentiations between autism and Asperger disorder have come about historically. Our current diagnostic schemes still reflect an historical happenstance, namely the fact that two clinicians made important observations about two groups of patients. It is legitimate to ask had Kanner or Asperger seen a different caseload, would they have come up with precisely the same observations, or had a third clinician written a clinical account of cases in their experience, would we now be talking of three rather than two conditions? Indeed, as we have seen, there are other conditions such as schizoid personality disorder and semantic–pragmatic disorder that some investigators have argued are part of the autism spectrum, and it is possible to imagine a diagnostic scheme akin to DSM-IV or ICD-10 that would make further differentiations, which would raise the question of whether these conditions were separate entities or facets of the same underlying disorder. The point to take away from all this is not that we should abandon diagnosis or classification but that we should take a critical and questioning approach to them. Just because we have a set of criteria that can be applied to a group of cases in a way that enables the cases to be subdivided reliably does not mean that the subdivisions make any sense or that they have the same meaning intended by their eponymous progenitor. An interesting illustration of this point can be found in a study by Miller and Ozonoff (1997), in which they subjected the original case descriptions given by Asperger to the criteria of DSM-IV. They found that none of his cases would fit current criteria for Asperger disorder, but rather would have been classified as having autism.*

The foregoing paragraphs show that although current diagnostic systems can be used to identify individuals as having pervasive developmental disorder and to place those individuals into the subcategories of autistic disorder, Asperger disorder and PDD-NOS, it is clear that the results of research involving either regression or cluster analysis, or group comparison approaches have not yielded convincing evidence that these conditions can be qualitatively differentiated (see Macintosh & Dissanayake, 2004 for a review). As a consequence, we should regard such subclassifications with a degree of suspicion. The evidence shows a great deal of symptomatological overlap between the different categories, overlap that has important implications both for clinical management of these conditions as well as for scientific investigations aimed at identifying underlying causal processes. The assumption made in this book is that although the different categories of ASD can be differentiated quantitatively along a number of dimensions, the factors that give rise to the autistic component of these different conditions (e.g. social impairment, repetitive activities), although as yet poorly understood, are common to all the subcategories. Their manifestation and operation may differ because of interaction with variability on other dimensions such as global cognitive ability or language level in a way that produces a range of clinical pictures that are ultimately different end points of similar underlying impairments.

EARLY DETECTION

As we have seen, ASD is now thought of as a set of pervasive *developmental* disorders, that is to say, that it is a group of conditions in which the typically expected developmental trajectory is disrupted in particular and characteristic ways. Implicit in this formulation is the idea that there must be some starting point for this abnormal trajectory. Put another way, what are the earliest signs that give a clue to a later developmental trajectory that is characteristic of ASD? As we have seen above, ASD can be accompanied by greater or lesser levels of overall global cognitive impairment (sometimes referred to as mental or intellectual retardation). But impairments like these are not necessarily different from those seen in individuals without ASD. What is of greater interest

---

* There is a problem with the DSM-IV rules for deciding between autistic disorder and Asperger disorder. If a child meets criteria for both disorders (including the lack of clinically significant language delay) then a diagnosis of autistic disorder must be given. Wing (2006) quite rightly calls this illogical.

are those behaviours that are delayed or never develop in ASD individuals without global intellectual impairment, or which develop in people with such impairment but not ASD. Given that ASD is characterised by impairments in social interaction, imagination and communication, it makes sense to look for behavioural markers of these functions in typical development and to examine their developmental trajectory in individuals with ASD. This can be done in a number of ways. One is to look at those who already have received a diagnosis of ASD. If these developmentally typical behaviours are diminished in frequency or absent (assuming the child has reached the developmental level at which they typically first appear), then we can conclude that these behaviours are more likely to be attributable to ASD rather than to general developmental delay. A second strategy is to carry out a prospective study, in which target behaviours are assessed in a large group of infants who are then followed up to see which children develop ASD and which do not. And a third is to analyse home movies and videos taken during infancy of children who later received a diagnosis of ASD.

There is now a large body of research that shows that certain kinds of preverbal communicative behaviour emerge at specific points in the developmental trajectory of typically developing children. One such behaviour is what Bruinsma, Koegel and Koegel (2004) refer to as *initiation of joint attention* (IJA), in which a child draws the attention of an adult to an object of interest by pointing, vocalising and alternating gaze between the adult and the object. The work of Bates and her colleagues (Bates, 1979) established that these behaviours typically emerged at about 9 months of age, and made the distinction between *protoimperative* and *protodeclarative* behaviours. Both involve the child's pointing towards an object and vocalising, but the latter crucially involves gaze alternation, in which the child repeatedly looks back and forth from the object of interest to the caregiver. The achievement of this latter milestone is generally taken as marking the beginning of the child's understanding that others can be as interested in surrounding objects and events as they themselves are, and that the dawn of such understanding forms the bedrock of the later development of higher forms of social cognition, interpersonal skill and cultural practice (see Tomasello & Rakoczy, 2003). There is also a growing body of research that shows particular patterns of impairment in IJA behaviours in children with ASD, even those whose overall developmental level would predict that such behaviours would have emerged (see Mundy, Sigman & Kasari, 1993 for a review). In a study that observed children with autistic disorder and matched children with intellectual disabilities aged between 38 and 75 months and mean verbal age of about 25 months (i.e. older than that at which IJA typically emerges), Mundy, Sigman, Ungerer and Sherman (1986) observed fewer IJA behaviours, especially eye contact, in children with ASD than the comparison children. Baron-Cohen (1989a) found that in children with ASD, whilst unimpaired in their use of protoimperative pointing, their use of protodeclarative pointing was impaired.

The most widely known prospective studies of the development of ASD are those based on the Checklist for Autism in Toddlers (CHAT) developed by Baird, Baron-Cohen, Charman and colleagues (Baird, Charman, Baron-Cohen et al., 2000; Baird, Charman, Cox et al., 2001; Baron-Cohen, Allen & Gillberg, 1992). This is a brief screening device designed for administration to children at 18 months of age. The items in the checklist were designed to assess behaviours that previous research had demonstrated as being impaired in children with ASD (see Box 1.4). Baird et al. (2000) screened 16 235 18 month old infants, and those in whom the initial screen revealed problems were tested again 1 month later. Children were classified into those deemed to have a high risk for ASD (12 children), who failed items measuring pointing, gaze following and play on both tests and those deemed to have a moderate risk (22 children) who failed the pointing items. The children identified as at risk were followed up until 7 years of age, at which time only one of the high-risk children and 2 of the medium risk were found to have a clinically normal developmental trajectory. Thus, the CHAT had good specificity, i.e. when it identified a child as having particular problems there was a good chance that those problems were predictive of the development of a pervasive developmental disorder of some kind. Yet the instrument lacks sensitivity, in that it missed quite a number of children in the screened population who later turned out to have ASD (40 were missed) or pervasive developmental disorder (34 were missed). As Sigman, Dijamco, Gratier and Rozga (2004) put it, abnormalities on the CHAT are predictive of an ASD trajectory, but lack of abnormalities does not put a child in the clear.

Box 1.4. The Checklist for Autism in Toddlers (CHAT)

Section A: Ask parent:

1 Does your child enjoy being swung, bounced on your knee, etc.? YES/NO
2 Does your child take an interest in other children? YES/NO
3 Does your child like climbing on things, such as up stairs? YES/NO
4 Does your child enjoy playing peek-a-boo/hide-and-seek? YES/NO
5 Does your child ever PRETEND, for example, to make a cup of tea using a toy cup and teapot, or pretend other things? YES/NO
6 Does your child ever use his/her index finger to point, to ASK for something? YES/NO
7 Does your child ever use his/her index finger to point, to indicate INTEREST in something? YES/NO
8 Can your child play properly with small toys (e.g. cars or bricks) without just mouthing, fiddling or dropping them? YES/NO

9 Does your child ever bring objects over to you (parent) to
  SHOW you something?   YES/NO

Section B: GP or Health Visitor observation:

i During the appointment, has the child made eye contact
  with you?   YES/NO
ii Get child's attention, then point across the room at an
   interesting object and say 'Oh look! There's a (name of
   toy!)' Watch child's face. Does the child look across to see
   what you are pointing at?   YES/NO
iii Get the child's attention, then give child a miniature toy
    cup and teapot and say 'Can you make a cup of tea?'
    Does the child pretend to pour out tea, drink it, etc.?   YES/NO
iv Say to the child 'Where's the light?', or 'Show me the
    light'. Does the child point with his/her index finger at
    the light?   YES/NO
v Can the child build a tower of bricks? (If so, how many?)
  (Number of bricks:.............)   YES/NO

From Baron-Cohen et al. (1992). Reproduced by kind permission of the BMJ
Publishing Group.

Several studies have examined home movies and videos taken of children
when they were in their first year and who were later given a diagnosis of ASD.
The best controlled of these studies are those that used raters who were blind
to the diagnosis of the children, standardised the timing of the making of the
video, such as at first birthday parties, and included a comparison group of
children who later developed intellectual retardation but not ASD (see
Baranek, 1999; Osterling, Dawson & Munson, 2002). Behaviours that were
found to distinguish children who went to develop ASD from those who did
not were increased mouthing of objects, increased aversion to social touch,
diminished responses to own name and diminished looking at others. These
are behaviours that echo the impaired social responsiveness and impaired
imaginative activities that have been a feature of descriptions of autistic disorders from the outset. A recent study by Baranek, Barnett, Adams, Wolcott
et al. (2005) analysed videos of 9–12 month old children who subsequently did
or did not develop ASD. They reported few differences in functional or relational play between the groups, although the children who subsequently
showed developmental delay or ASD, in contrast to the typical children, did
not exhibit functional play by the age of 12 months. This finding is important
in that it shows that behavioural atypicalities that are characteristic of ASD
do not become evident until the child's second year.

The general conclusion that can be drawn from studies of autistic features in infants is that the absence of certain behaviours is likely to indicate an autistic developmental trajectory, but that later development of ASD need not be preceded by obvious evidence of such deficits. Why some children should fail to develop behaviours like protodeclarative pointing and others develop them but later go on to develop ASD is as yet poorly understood. This is partly because we as yet have underdeveloped theoretical systems for explaining how particular behaviours at one stage in development causally contribute to later development of others (although see Hobson, 2002 and Chapter 9 of this book for more on developmental approaches to ASD). This last observation nuances a conclusion made by Sigman et al. (2004) that early identification is important in that it allows us to intervene in ways that enable the developing child to 'overcome its self-imposed social deprivation' (p. 221) and thereby avoid an autistic developmental trajectory. There is much we do not understand about how psychological development comes about, and what mechanisms underlie particular patterns of overt behaviour. In the current state of knowledge, it is perhaps premature to leap from the patterning of behavioural trajectories to underlying processes to the consequences of intervention.

CONCLUSION

The concept of ASD as a set of different developmental trajectories that compromise an individual's interpersonal relations and tend to produce behaviour that is rigid and repetitive has evolved considerably over the last five decades. It is now accepted that there is a spectrum of conditions, the most commonly occurring of which are (in DSM terminology), autistic disorder, Asperger disorder and PDD-NOS. Although individuals can readily be identified who fit the criteria for each of these conditions, the boundaries between the categories are not always clear, and assigning a particular individual to one or other category is often a matter of judgment, which like all human judgment is prone to error. Nevertheless, we can provisionally conclude that there exists in nature a group of individuals whose development differs from the typical trajectory in that they experience particular kinds of difficulties in relating to and understanding other people and who have impoverished imagination and a behavioural repertoire that tends to be repetitive and stereotyped in nature. The trajectory may or may not be accompanied by global intellectual impairment, which can range from mild to profound. The combination of social and cognitive impairment may inhibit the development of verbal communication, but even in non-intellectually disabled individuals, language and communication are marked by particular characteristics. Thus we have a basis for the work that will be described in the rest of this book; we have a natural phenomenon that we can attempt to explain.

2 Understanding Other Minds: Cognitive Approaches

Although it is widely thought that conceptions of ASD in terms of impaired understanding of others began sometime in the 1980s, in fact, this way of thinking about these conditions goes back much further. The very title of Kanner's original paper (1943) indicates a disturbance in interpersonal relatedness, and a reading of his case descriptions reveals that for him, this failure to treat others as persons was one of the most striking aspects of the condition. Wing and Gould, too, emphasised what they referred to as 'social impairment' (see Wing & Gould, 1979), which they classified into three subgroups – 'aloof', 'passive' and 'active-but-odd'. What happened in the mid 1980s was the start of a series of attempts to provide an explanatory framework to try to account for why individuals with ASD experience the difficulties in interactions with people that they do. From a historical perspective, these attempts can be considered under two broad but overlapping headings, the first of which – those considered in this chapter – are based on cognitive or computational approaches to understanding mind and centre around the so-called '*theory of mind deficit*' account of ASD. The second approach – dealt with in the next chapter – sees ASD as a deficit in the patterning of emotional relatedness between individuals and the regulation of other behaviour on the basis of such patterning. More recently, emphasis has been placed on the overlap between the two approaches. This, too, will be dealt with in the next chapter. The cognitive accounts discussed here aim to elucidate those psychological and computational mechanisms that are thought to mediate our understanding of other minds. Some are modular or domain-specific in approach; others are very definitely domain-general or non-modular. All approaches – those in this chapter and the next – take the view that the core of ASD can be characterised in terms of some kind of disrupted interpersonal relatedness.

UNDERSTANDING FALSE BELIEF: A SPECIFIC MENTAL MODULE?

In 1985, Baron-Cohen, Leslie and Frith published a paper that has become one of the seminal works of the experimental psychology of ASD. They reported an apparently simple study in which they showed that children with ASD had more difficulty than comparison children in understanding that the beliefs that someone else holds about the world can be false, that is different from what the child him or herself knows to be truly the case. Baron-Cohen et al. adapted a technique first developed by Wimmer and Perner (1983; the 'Maxi and the chocolate scenario') to study typical children's development of an understanding of mind. In Baron-Cohen et al.'s version, two dolls, Sally and Anne, were made to act out a scenario in which Sally hid her marble in a basket and then left the scene. While she was out, Anne moved the marble from the basket to a box. Sally then returned and the child was asked 'Where will Sally look for her marble?' Wimmer and Perner (1983) had already shown that between the ages of 4 and 6 years, typical children developed the capacity to predict correctly that Sally would look in the basket – i.e. in the location that did *not* contain the marble. Yet only 20% of Baron-Cohen et al.'s children with ASD could do this, despite their having an average verbal mental age of 5 years 5 months. Baron-Cohen et al. took great care to include adequate control procedures to ensure the reliability of the findings of this experiment. The first control centred on the question of low IQ. As we have seen in Chapter 1, the majority of children with Kanner-type autism have IQs below 70; that is to say, they are in the range described as having intellectual disabilities. So in an experiment such as this, we need to show that any differences between the groups are due to ASD and not to low IQ. Baron-Cohen et al. did this by including a group of children with Down syndrome, who are characterised by low IQ but usually not by autistic social impairment. The performance of the participants with Down syndrome (85%) was similar to that of typical comparison children (80%) and significantly better than that of the children with ASD (20%), indicating that a failure to understand Sally's false belief was disproportionately common in the children with ASD. The second control procedure consisted of additional questions to test the child's memory for the initial and final location of the marble. Only children who answered both these questions correctly were included in the study. So it was unlikely that the children with ASD were performing poorly on the Sally–Anne task because of low IQ or because they could not follow the story. The most likely conclusion was that they had difficulty in understanding false belief – the fact that Sally could hold a belief about the location of the marble that was different from the child's own.

This study by Baron-Cohen et al. forms the cornerstone of nearly 20 years of research into impaired theory of mind in individuals with ASD, and has generated a body of work that has until recently dominated psychological research into the condition (see, for example Baron-Cohen, Tager-Flusberg & Cohen, 1993; 1999). To understand why the findings of such an apparently simple experiment should have such a broad impact, we need to consider some of the related currents of thought in philosophy as well as in the psychology of typical children's development of an understanding of mind drawn upon by this approach.

A question that has preoccupied philosophers for centuries, and which more recently has attracted the attention of psychologists, computer scientists and neuroscientists, is that of 'other minds'. How do we know what goes on inside the head of another person? Although we have direct access to what goes on inside our own heads (so-called 'first person access'), we have only indirect access to and can only guess at what, if anything, goes on inside someone else's. Indeed, some philosophers would argue (e.g. Ryle, 1949) that we are not justified in making any speculations about the contents of other minds. This position lies at the heart of behaviourist approaches to psychology and philosophy and eschews any reference to unobservable or 'private' events that might influence behaviour (see, for example Skinner, 1938). Yet in our everyday lives, we regularly say things like *'I looked everywhere for my glasses. I thought they were in the kitchen, but I couldn't find them there. My partner knew that I had left them in the garage, and if I had known he knew where they were, then I would have asked him'.* Words like 'thought' and 'knew' are part of the everyday language we use to describe our own behaviour and that of others (try gossiping about friends and acquaintances without using such terms). Such everyday, mentalistic explanations of behaviour are often referred to as *folk psychology* and the mental state terms used in folk psychology are referred to as *propositional attitudes.* Propositional attitudes have a number of interesting properties, the most striking of which is that they refer to things that we cannot see, feel or touch; we can only infer their existence in others by looking at behaviour in context. So when we see Sally look for her marble in a place where we know the marble is not (say, the basket), we describe Sally as 'thinking the marble is in the basket'. Similarly, the fact that we know that Sally has not witnessed Anne's transfer of the marble from the basket allows us to predict accurately where Sally will look for her marble. It is this ability to infer unseen entities by looking at behaviour (Sally did not see the marble being moved, so her knowledge of where the marble is located remains unchanged), and to understand that these entities can influence behaviour (Sally will act in accordance with what she knows) that led researchers such as Premack and Woodruff (1978) and others to propose that we possess a *theory of mind.*

Inferring the existence of hypothetical, unseen entities from observed regularities in behaviour and the subsequent use of the properties of these hypothetical entities to predict future behaviour is known as the hypothetico-deductive method of theory construction and is one that is widespread in scientific enquiry. Think of a chemist who mixes up liquids of different colours, heats the mixtures to certain temperatures, bubbles gases through the mixture and records what happens. One way to describe the behaviour of the material manipulated by the chemist is to say 'a white powder x was mixed with clear liquid y, the mixture bubbled strongly and a sediment settled out. Some of the clear liquid was then drained off and some colourless gas was bubbled through it. The contents of the flask turned milky and another sediment settled out'. This is one way to describe a chemical procedure, and is somewhat akin to a behaviourist's account of a person's actions. But chemists do not usually stop at this kind of description, but re-formulate it in terms like the following:

$$CaO + H_2O = Ca(OH)_2$$

$$Ca(OH)_2 + CO_2 = CaCO_3 + H_2O$$

This re-description of the behaviour of the substances manipulated by the chemist is not simply a re-description; it goes beyond observable events and tries to explain what is happening in terms of unseen, hypothetical entities called atoms and molecules, which combine and recombine according to certain laws and principles.*

There are considerable advantages to this kind of re-description. In the case of chemistry, it allows us to predict what might happen in certain circumstances (for example, that the quantity of Ca that can combine with a given quantity of O is half the quantity of H that will combine with the same quantity of O). In psychology, postulation of hypothetical entities like 'thought', 'knowledge', 'belief', etc. helps us to explain why, for example, Sally will go to look for her marble where we know there is no marble. In this respect, 'theory-theorists' argue that what we do when confronted by seemingly bizarre behaviour (Sally looking in the obviously wrong place for her marble) is to develop a theory in which behaviour is caused by hypothetical mental states that have certain properties. Many philosophers (e.g. Carruthers, 1996), as well as developmental psychologists (see Gopnik, 1993), argue that our understanding of mind develops in this way, a position that is often referred to as the *theory-theory* account of an understanding of mind (see Russell, 1992 for a critical review). What is important in the present context is that failure on a false-belief task such as the Sally–Anne test is taken as an index of impaired ability to generate hypothetical entities that can be used to explain behaviour.

An alternative to the theory-theory position on the understanding of other minds is that of simulation theory, which proposes that when we see someone behave in an unusual manner, such as Sally looking for her marble in a place where we know there is no marble, we explain Sally's behaviour by simulating – or imagining – what we would be doing if we were in Sally's shoes. A theory-theorist, by contrast, argues that when people make statements like 'Sally went over to the basket to look for her marble; she must think her marble is there', they are behaving like scientists constructing a theory and eventually come up with entities like 'thought' to explain Sally's behaviour. Proponents of simulation theory (e.g. Harris, 2000) argue that passing false-belief tasks and engaging in pretend play capitalise on the same underlying

---

*Atoms and molecules can now be seen with electron microscopes, but at the time this method of re-description was developed, they could not. Their existence was therefore a matter of conjecture. Chemists at that time had a theory of atoms.

process of imagination. In the case of pretence, the child has to imagine that
a toy brick is a car and behave accordingly. In false-belief tasks, the child has
to imagine what it is like to be Sally and accordingly decide where to look for
the marble. In this view, impairment in the capacity to imagine or to generate
alternative scenarios will impact adversely on a child's capacity both to engage
in pretend play and to pass false-belief tasks. This is an observation that has
resonances in other theoretical systems, as we shall see later. Although considerable debate has surrounded the question of whether our understanding
of other minds develops by means of mental simulation or the use of a theory
(interested readers can consult a pair of articles by Gopnik, 1993 and by
Goldman, 1993), this is not a debate that has had much impact on the field of
ASD (although see Gopnik, 2003). Yet the theory-theory/simulation debate is
important, since the two positions tell us different things about what is happening when a child fails a false-belief task. The simulationist position argues
that such a child has difficulties in imagining what it is like to be in the position of the protagonist with the false belief. The theory-theorist argues that
the problem lies in understanding that there are entities that lie behind behaviour (thoughts, beliefs) that can direct that behaviour in ways that are not
obvious from a reading of the world the way it actually is.

Another particular property of mental states like 'thinks' or 'believes' – the
so-called *epistemic mental states* – is that they are what philosophers refer to
as 'intentional', which in this context means that they have content, i.e. they
are 'about' something. So when we say 'John thinks', we must complete the
sentence with the content of John's thought: *John thinks it is raining.* Moreover, when deciding whether or not this statement is true, it does not matter
what the weather is actually like. John can think it is raining (and take his over-
coat and umbrella when going outside) even though the sun is shining, and is
forecast to go on shining for the whole week. This observation demonstrates
another interesting aspect of mental-state, propositional attitude language,
namely that mental states are not reflections of the way the world is, but are
representations of it. That is to say, they can stand in true or false relation to
reality. It was this analysis of the capacity of representations that formed the
basis of Wimmer and Perner's (1983) development of the Maxi and the chocolate scenario, which in turn formed the basis of the Sally–Anne task used by
Baron-Cohen et al. (1985) to test children with ASD (see Perner, 1991 for a
full discussion). For Perner, at the heart of understanding representations was
the ability to grasp that they can be true *or* false. In other words, the child has
to represent in her own mind the representational relationship between John's
thought and the actual state of the weather. Fully understanding this relationship involves accepting that John can think it is raining when it is, in fact,
not or vice versa. The term given by Perner to this capacity was *metarepresentation*, a capacity that does not, on the basis of Wimmer and Perner's (1983)
findings, fully develop until a typical child's fifth year. Thus, on the basis of
Perner's analysis, the results of Baron-Cohen et al.'s (1985) Sally–Anne study

show that children with ASD have a metarepresentational deficit – they fail to grasp the notion that Sally's belief about the location of her marble can be, by virtue of its being a representation, false.

Although the experimental basis of Baron-Cohen et al.'s (1985) Sally–Anne experiment was derived from the work of Perner, its theoretical impetus came from a different source. Working within the tradition of cognitive science, which attempts to derive computational algorithms that can simulate the workings of the human mind, Leslie (1987) developed a computational account of how we develop an understanding of pretence and of representations. He was struck by the similarity of the task facing an observer who tries to understand, or a computer scientist who tries to write a program to implement, the following two sentences:

John thinks it is raining

and

Mary pretends this brick is a car.

For Leslie, both sentences contain terms ('thinks', 'pretends') that have contents, and both contain statements that can conflict with the actual state of the world (it may not be raining, and the brick is not a car). For these reasons, Leslie argued that, both statements posed a common computational problem, which suggested that they were driven by a common underlying computational mechanism.

Briefly put, Leslie argues that when we encounter the world, we build up what he refers to as *primary representations*, which stand for objects as they are in the world. In the second sentence above, a primary representation of a brick would be of a small cube of wood or plastic. But from the age of about 18 months, we typically also begin to construct what he refers to as second-order representations. The example he uses is of a child watching her mother playing with a banana as if it were a telephone. To understand this scenario, the child must not only grasp what a banana is (a yellow, elongated fruit), and also (at least in some rudimentary sense) what a telephone is. But to understand her mother's behaviour, the child must be able to represent the banana in a way that allows it to be treated as if it were a telephone. These second-order representations are *decoupled* from the primary representations by a modular mechanism (see Fodor, 1983 for an explanation of modularity) that was triggered by the behaviour of others towards objects for which the child already possesses primary representations. These second-order, or agent-centred, representations were given the name *metarepresentations* (subsequently modified to 'M-representations', see Leslie & Roth, 1993, p. 91) by Leslie. Leslie called the mechanism responsible for the decoupling of primary representations the *theory of mind mechanism* (ToMM), intact functioning of which is a prerequisite for an ability to engage in pretence and to understand false beliefs in others. Thus, an intact capacity to pretend or to understand mental states depends on the decoupling of primary representations by the theory of mind mechanism.

The important point that emerges from Leslie's writing is that he established a common, modular, mechanism that drives both an understanding of mental states and an understanding of pretence. So if someone is impaired in one, then they should be impaired in the other. Since people with ASD are known to be impaired in their understanding of pretence (Jarrold, 2003), then it follows that they should have difficulties in understanding representational mental states, which is exactly what Baron-Cohen et al. (1985) demonstrated in their seminal Sally–Anne study. Moreover, they concluded that this impairment resulted from damage to a specific mechanism – the theory of mind mechanism.

It is unfortunate, and confusing for newcomers to the field, that Leslie and Perner used the same term (metarepresentation) for two quite different phenomena, each of which develops in children at quite different ages. Grasping the potentially false nature of the representational relation between objects and their representations does not begin to develop until around a child's fourth birthday; the ability to generate agent-centred representations of objects and to use these in the service of pretence typically develops by about 18 months. As a consequence, when speaking about purported psychological deficits in ASD it is important to be clear about which sense of the term is being used. Further discussion of the differences between the two conceptions of metarepresentation can be found in Leslie and Roth (1993) and Perner (1993).

This observation that children with Kanner-type ASD experienced difficulty in predicting the behaviour of another person on the basis of that person's false belief unleashed a plethora of research into how and why this should be the case. Much of this research was admirably theory-driven, testing propositions derived from the theoretical positions from which the original study emerged. So, for example, Baron-Cohen, Leslie and Frith (1986) used the ideas of the philosopher Daniel Dennett (see Dennett, 1987) to make predictions about how children with ASD might behave. Dennett proposed that when we describe the behaviour of different systems, we adopt three different 'stances': the *mechanical*, the *behavioural* and the *intentional*. The mechanical stance is used to describe machines, or events, such as the wind blowing a door closed, where things happen without the action of an agent. When someone carries out an action, such as getting into their car to drive to the shops, we adopt the behavioural stance. But when we explain Sally's search for the marble in the empty location in terms of her falsely believing that that is where the marble is, we are using the intentional stance. Note, we can (and often do) use the intentional stance to describe mechanical situations, such as attributing malice to our car when it won't start in the morning. Baron-Cohen et al. (1986) asked children to place sets of four line drawings in sequence in order to tell a story representing either a mechanical, a behavioural or an intentional scenario.

Their findings showed that the children with ASD, whilst better than controls on mechanical sequences, and equivalent to controls on behavioural sequences, performed significantly worse on the intentional sequences, reflecting their impaired theory of mind.

A large number of other investigations have demonstrated that children with classic, Kanner-type autism are impaired or seriously delayed in their ability to predict someone's behaviour on the basis of that person's having a false belief. Happé (1995), in a meta-analysis of this research, reports that whereas 50% of typical children pass false-belief tasks when they reach a verbal mental age of 4 years, it is not until they reach a verbal mental age of 9 years 2 months that 50% of children with ASD pass the same tests. The emerging picture is that individuals with ASD have an impaired understanding of false belief that is not due to low IQ and appears to be limited to their grasp of mental states and that this results from impairment in a modular system responsible for the development of a theory of mind.

The claim that there is a modular system that is damaged in ASD has given rise to two further sets of assertions. The first is that this pattern of impairment is specific to ASD; the second is that the damaged system specifically mediates the understanding of mental states. Although the initial study by Baron-Cohen et al. (1985), which showed unimpaired theory of mind in children with Down syndrome, provides evidence for the first claim, two strands of evidence appear to contradict it. The first comes from a meta-analysis of existing studies of false belief in children with ASD by Yirmiya, Erel, Shaked and Solomonica-Levy (1998). They concluded that although rates of failing false-belief tasks were not as high in children with mental retardation but without ASD as in children who did have ASD, they were nonetheless higher than those seen in typical comparison groups, thus casting doubt on the specificity claim. Other evidence comes from the work of Siegal and Peterson (see Peterson & Siegal, 2000 for a review) who report marked delay in passing false-belief tasks in deaf children who are raised by hearing parents in a non-signing environment. Deaf children raised by deaf parents in a signing environment do not show this delay.

Evidence for the second claim comes from a range of studies that tested the development of children's grasp of mental and non-mental representations. If, as Perner (1991) points out, children develop an understanding that minds are representational, then it is plausible to argue that they should also develop an understanding that other media, such as drawings or photographs, are representational as well. This conjecture was first tested out by Zaitchik (1990), who presented children with a scenario in which an object was photographed in one location and then moved to another. Children were asked (without ever seeing the photograph) where the object was located in the photograph. Zaitchik found that the pass rates for this task were slightly lower than those in false-belief tasks of the Sally–Anne type and concluded that the two measures tapped the same underlying phenomenon, namely an understanding that representational media (minds or photographs) could misrepresent as well as represent reality.

However, when Zaitchik's paradigm was used to test the understanding of false non-mental representation by children with classic, Kanner-type autism (see Charman & Baron-Cohen, 1992; Leekam & Perner, 1991; Leslie & Thaiss, 1992), all the investigations showed that whereas false-belief understanding is impaired in this group, understanding of false non-mental representations is not, thus lending support to the notion that the deficit found in children with ASD is specific to mental states – i.e. that they lack a theory of *mind*.

Part of the success of the mental state-specificity argument was due to its consistency with the notion of ASD as being primarily a set of conditions involving social impairment as well as being consistent with a number of observations of behavioural deficits in the early development of children with ASD. Early clinical observations (e.g. Wing, 1966) as well as later, more controlled observational studies found that children with ASD are considerably less likely than controls matched for developmental delay to point out objects that they are interested in to other people. From the age of 10–12 months, if a typically developing child sees something she is interested in, she will point to it, sometimes vocalise, and then shift her gaze back and forth from the object to her caregiver in an attempt to get the caregiver to focus attention on the object (Carpenter, Nagell, Tomasello et al. 1998). This phenomenon was labelled *protodeclarative pointing* by Bates, Camaioni and Volterra (1975), and implies a capacity for *joint attention* (Bruner, 1983), involving *triadic deployment of attention* (Loveland & Landry, 1986) on the part of the child. In other words, the child has to coordinate her attention between herself, her caregiver and an object, being aware both of her own directedness towards the object and of that of another person. This behaviour is one of the earliest markers of a child's awareness of others and, has been shown to be deficient in children with ASD (Sigman, Mundy, Sherman & Ungerer, 1986). We have also seen that the absence of such behaviours is a strong predictor of an autistic developmental trajectory (see Charman, Taylor, Drew et al., 2005). It is worth noting at this point the conceptual resonance between the idea of a child's ability to grasp the difference between her own relation to an object and that of another person to the same object and Leslie's idea of agent-centred representations as being crucial to an initial understanding both of mind and (later on) of the representational nature of mental states. The development of pretence and the development of protodeclarative pointing behaviours emerge in tandem in the typical child and are both notably absent in children with ASD. This convergence of theoretical speculation and empirical evidence lends support to Leslie's theoretical position.

In the context of the findings on impaired protodeclarative pointing and impaired false belief understanding, Baron-Cohen (1995) further refined the idea that autistic social impairment could be explained by damage to a dedicated modular system. Baron-Cohen's revised system consisted of a modular theory of mind mechanism (ToMM) (a term borrowed from Leslie, 1987) served by other modular subsystems, namely the shared attention mechanism (SAM), intentionality detector (ID) and eye direction detector (EDD). Modular systems are triggered automatically by appropriate environmental input, and if damaged, systems higher up in the cognitive system fail to function properly because they lack input from the relevant modular systems lower down. The elaboration of this multi-module theory of social functioning was underpinned by a number of experimental studies. Baron-Cohen and Cross (1992) showed children with and without ASD photographs of people either looking straight at the camera or directing their gaze somewhere above and behind the observer. Children with ASD were significantly worse at deciding which of the two people was thinking. Baron-Cohen, Campbell, Karmiloff-Smith, Grant and Walker (1995) used stimuli like the one illustrated in Figure 2.1 and asked children with and without ASD either which object the character was looking at or which object the character wanted. Children with ASD were impaired on the latter but not the former question. These kinds of observations led to the development of an account that emphasised the role of the eyes in understanding other minds, and in turn led to the development of tests of mental state understanding (such as the Reading the Mind in the Eyes Test) that will be discussed later.

Other evidence consistent with the notion of an SAM–ID–EDD system comes from studies that show that children with ASD, when learning language, seem to behave differently from children with typical development. Scientists such as Tomasello (1988) and Baldwin (1993) observed typical children

Figure 2.1. Stimuli used by Grant et al. (1995, cited in Baron-Cohen et al., 1995) to assess children's sensitivity to eye gaze direction. Reproduced by permission of the British Psychological Society.

interacting with adults in situations where from time to time the adults named objects that the children had not seen before. They found that from about 18 months of age, children tended to attach a new name to whatever object was being looked at by the adult rather than the object the child was looking at. In other words, children used a *speaker's direction of gaze* (SDG) rather than a *listener's direction of gaze* (LDG) strategy to acquire new vocabulary. On the basis of the 'theory of mind deficit' account of ASD, and more specifically on observations of impaired joint attention in ASD, Baron-Cohen, Baldwin and Crowson (1997a) predicted that such children would be more likely to use LDG rather than SDG when in situations used by Tomasello and Baldwin in their experiments. This prediction was supported by their findings, suggesting that either a difficulty in understanding the significance of the directedness of another person's gaze or problems in disengaging one's own attention from an object is important for an autistic child's development of language. Although Baron-Cohen et al. (1997a) tend to favour the former over the latter explanation, the evidence from studies of executive function in ASD is consistent with the latter (see Chapter 5).

The acquisition of vocabulary is not the only aspect of language that has been argued to reflect impaired understanding of mind in individuals with ASD. They have been shown to have difficulties in separating out mental state terms such as 'think' or 'want' from other behavioural or body-related descriptors such as 'walk' or 'face' (Baron-Cohen, Ring, Moriarty, Schmitz, Costa & Ell, 1994). And Baron-Cohen (1997a), Happé (1994) and Kaland, Møller-Nielsen, Callesen et al. (2002) have shown that children with ASD experience difficulties in understanding figures of speech, sarcasm, metaphors and humour. Studies of the pragmatics of language (the socially appropriate use of language) have also revealed difficulties in children with ASD, and as we have seen in Chapter 1, there is an ongoing debate as to whether or not individuals with ASD can be described as having a pragmatic language disorder. The presence of pragmatic impairment – using language in socially inappropriate ways – is clearly consistent with difficulties in understanding mental states in others.

Still further evidence that can be argued to be consistent with a 'theory of mind deficit' account comes from studies such as that of Frith, Happé and Siddons (1994) who found that individuals with ASD who fail false-belief tasks are also more severely impaired on those aspects of social functioning that appear to depend more on an understanding of mind, such as keeping secrets, than on those aspects that do not, such as keeping the rules of the house. There are, however, important issues to bear in mind when thinking about studies like these: for example, when interpreting the correlations reported in these studies to presuppose that 'theory of mind deficits' in some way *cause* deficits in other areas of functioning. Although such an interpretation may be justified by a particular theoretical position, methodologically, it is not legitimate to draw causal inferences from correlational findings. It is just as likely that the direction of cause is in the other direction, or that a third factor is common to both the 'theory of mind' measure and the other variable of interest.

The question of what valid conclusions to draw from correlational data is not the only one to raise about those investigations that claim to provide evidence linking false-belief task performance or 'theory of mind' to other domains of psychological functioning. They also often make presuppositions about the measures they use, specifically about what is actually assessed by false-belief tasks and appropriate control tasks. Research into deception is illustrative here. The ability to deceive others requires the deceiver to understand that another person does not know something that they themselves do know – a knowledge of the contents of another person's mind. Investigations into the understanding of deception in children with ASD have revealed that they find it hard both to deceive others and to detect situations where they themselves are being deceived (Baron-Cohen, 1992; Sodian & Frith, 1992; Yirmiya, Erel, Shaked & Solomonica-Levi, 1998). But if we look, for example at the detail of Sodian and Frith's deception study, we see that perhaps what is being measured is something other than what the experimenters had in mind. They compared performance on a sabotage and a deception task. In both tasks, a thief was coming to take valuables from a box belonging to a friend of the child being tested. In the sabotage test, the box has a lock, and the child is asked what they would do if a friend or a thief was approaching the box. Children with and without ASD performed similarly on this task – they could say that the box should be locked if the thief was coming and left open if the friend was coming. In the deception condition, the thief or the friend would ask the child from a distance whether the box was open or closed. Children with ASD had greater difficulty in telling the thief that the box was closed when in fact it was open. These findings were interpreted as reflecting a relative difficulty with the concept of deception in the ASD children. But the two tasks ask different things of the child. On the one hand, s/he has to perform an action on the box. In the second, s/he has to describe the state of the lock on the box, which in the case where the thief was approaching, would be a counterfactual description. It would be useful to replicate this study by having the child tell the experimenter what to do to the box in the sabotage condition or what to say to the friend/thief in the deception condition. This would at least equalise the tasks in terms of the act the child has to perform.

UNDERSTANDING MINDS: A SPECIFIC PROCESS OR SOMETHING ELSE?

The observations made at the end of the last paragraph serve to remind us that whatever an investigator thinks a particular task might be measuring, there is always the possibility that it is in fact measuring something else. The assumption underlying the use of Sally–Anne type tasks is that they tap the functioning of an underlying system, however differently it might be conceptualised by different theorists, that mediates a child's understanding of belief. For some theorists (Baron-Cohen, Leslie) such understanding is mediated by a mechanism dedicated to this task – the theory of mind mechanism. This is a conclusion that hinges crucially on differential performance on control tasks (false-photograph tasks in this case). But as with the deception study just described, these control tasks also merit a closer look. Bowler, Briskman, Gurvidi and Fornells-Ambrojo (2005) took as their starting point the fact that children with ASD characteristically perform better on tasks of non-mental representation such as Zaitchik's (1990) false-photograph task than they do on tasks measuring false belief (Charman & Baron-Cohen, 1992; Leekam & Perner, 1991; Leslie & Thaiss, 1992). The theory that ASD results from a specific impairment in understanding mental representations stems directly from this difference in performance between the two tasks and hinges on the assumption of equivalence between them. The two tasks are argued to be equivalent in all respects except their mental state content. Bowler et al. (2005) questioned this assumption by arguing that tasks of the false-photograph type were simpler than false-belief tasks. The former had one central character, who could be in one of two locations, and a photograph, which could either truly or falsely represent the location of the character. The scenario involved the object being placed in one location where its photograph was taken. The object was then moved to another location and the child was asked about the contents of the photograph. False-belief tasks involve two protagonists, an object which could be in two locations and observations about the behaviour of each protagonist towards the object. The scenario involves one protagonist leaving an object in one location and leaving the scene. The other protagonist displaces the object and on the return of the first protagonist, the child is asked to predict where she will look for the object. Bowler et al. argued that because false-belief scenarios are more complex than false-photograph ones (they have more elements and more episodes), a proper test of the mental-state specificity hypothesis of ASD required a non-mental-state task that was equivalent to false-belief tasks in every respect except mental state content. False-belief tasks contained the goal (marble)-directed actions of an agent (Sally). The goal can be in one of two locations, each of which is indicated by one of two states of a signal (Sally's mental state). It is the state of the signal and not the location of the goal that determines the agent's behaviour towards the goal, so in cases where the signal state conflicts with the location of the goal, the agent will act according to the former. To perform correctly on these tasks, children need to understand goal-directed action of agents, mediation of action by signals, and the possibility that signals can be false. To test their conjecture that the difficulties that children with ASD experience in understanding mental states may be but one aspect of a wider problem with these other factors, Bowler et al. developed the scenario illustrated in Figure 2.2.

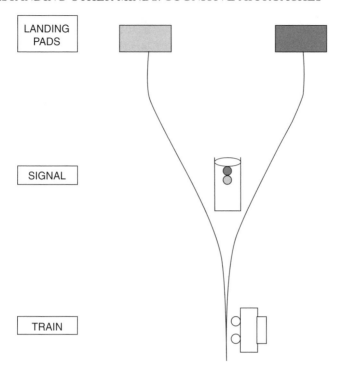

Figure 2.2. Mechanical analogue of the Sally–Anne false-belief task developed by Bowler et al. (2005). Reproduced by kind permission of Lawrence Erlbaum Inc.

The apparatus consisted of a model airport in which an automatic, driver-less shuttle conveyed goods from an aeroplane to a terminal. Planes could land on either a blue or yellow landing pad, and when a plane landed, its location was signalled to the train by a blue or yellow signal lamp. Once children had shown that they reliably understood that when the plane landed on blue (or yellow), the blue lamp came on and the train went to the blue (or yellow) pad, a false-belief analogue test trial was given. In this, the plane started to land on one pad (say the blue), but was beaten to it by a bird, whose descent triggered the blue lamp. The plane then landed on yellow, and the bird flew away. The blue signal remained lit. When children (with ASD and comparison partici-pants matched on verbal mental age) were asked to predict the destination of the train on these trials, in all groups, children who passed a Sally–Anne task predicted that the train would follow the light and children who failed the Sally–Anne task predicted that it would go to the pad on which the plane had landed. This result was found irrespective of whether the participating children had ASD, intellectual disabilities without ASD or were typically developing. The findings suggest that rather than being a failure to understand the mental realm, failure on false-belief tasks may simply be a reflection of a difficulty in grasping certain kinds of complex events of which mental states are but one example among many others.

The precise nature of the complex reasoning that needs to be available is not elucidated by the findings of Bowler et al. (2005), but a number of speculations can be made. The first relates to an analysis of false-belief tasks made by Zelazo and colleagues (Frye, Zelazo & Burack, 1998; Frye, Zelazo & Palfai, 1995; Zelazo, Burack, Benedetto & Frye, 1996; Zelazo, Burack, Boseovski, Jacques & Frye, 2001; Zelazo & Frye, 1998) in which they argue that an important capacity that develops in typical children is the ability to reason using 'if–then' rules. This can be illustrated in their Dimensional Change Card Sorting Task (DCCS), in which children are asked to sort red and blue circles and triangles according to either their shape or their colour. Typical 3 year old children have little difficulty in sorting using pairs of rules such as 'if this is a triangle, it goes in the triangle pile; if this is a circle, it goes in the circle pile'. They can also sort according to a pair of colour rules. But they experience difficulty in switching flexibly between pairs of rules. So if, after sorting according to shape, the experimenter then explains that the game is now a colour game, and that the colour rules must be used, a toddler confronted with a red triangle will place it with the triangles – i.e. she will perseverate on the old rule. According to Zelazo and colleagues, what needs to develop is a domain-general capacity to embed 'if–then' rules. So to switch rules flexibly, a child must be able to handle statements like 'if this is the colour game, and this is a red triangle, then it should go in the red pile'. This capacity develops some time after a child's fourth birthday and, according to Zelazo and colleagues, underpins the ability to pass tasks such as Sally–Anne tasks that assess a child's understanding of false belief. From this perspective, to solve false-belief tasks, a child, when asked where Sally will look for her marble, has to reason that if the question is about the protagonist, then the answer will be in the location where she left it, but if the question is about me (the child), then the answer will be where the marble is. Zelazo, Jacques, Burack and Frye (2002) found that performance on the DCCS and false-belief tasks correlated strongly in typical children, a finding that was replicated in children with ASD by Colvert, Custance and Swettenham (2002).

Similar correlations have been reported between performance on false-belief tasks and other tasks that involve embedded 'if–then' reasoning. Zelazo et al. (1996) tested typical children and children with Down syndrome using a task where a child had to predict the trajectory of a marble rolling down a ramp on the basis of whether a lamp was or was not lit. Younger children always made their predictions on the basis of gravity, whereas older or more able children tempered their predictions according to the state of the light. Zelazo et al. (2002) also reported correlations between the ramp task and false-belief tasks for children with ASD.

Another example of research that has taken a general rather than a specific approach to mental state understanding is that of Peterson and colleagues (see

Riggs, Peterson, Robinson & Mitchell, 1998), who took a fresh look at the Sally–Anne false-belief task. Rather than conceptualising the task as a test of a child's ability to understand the behavioural consequences of someone's holding a false belief, Peterson argued that what was involved was a particular kind of counterfactual reasoning problem. Peterson and Riggs (1999) argued that cognitively, this counterfactual reasoning process involved subtracting from the premises involved in solving the problem the fact that Anne had moved the marble – hence the term *subtractive reasoning*. Testing a child's ability to engage in subtractive reasoning involves scenarios that are identical to the Sally–Anne or Maxi and the chocolate scenarios discussed earlier. One of two protagonists places an object in one location and leaves the scene. The other protagonist then moves the object and the first protagonist returns. But instead of asking 'Where will [protagonist 1] look for the object?' the child is asked 'If [protagonist 2] had not moved the object, where would it be now?'. Peterson and Riggs (1999) found that performance on false-belief tasks and subtractive reasoning tasks were highly correlated in typical children, suggesting that the two measures tapped a common psychological mechanism. This mechanism could not involve understanding mental states, since the subtractive reasoning question made no reference to them. On these findings, theory of mind, far from being a specific capacity to reason about propositional attitudes, representational relations or intentionality, was just a specific case of a capacity to engage in a certain kind of reasoning.

Two studies have used the subtractive reasoning paradigm with children with ASD. Peterson and Bowler (2000) recruited children with ASD, with intellectual disabilities and with typical development and presented them with false-belief and subtractive reasoning scenarios. Apart from replicating the findings of earlier studies by finding a significantly lower false-belief pass rate in the children with ASD when compared to the children with typical development, and that the two types of task correlated in the latter group, Peterson and Bowler also found that although both tasks were of equal difficulty in the typical children, the subtractive reasoning task was significantly easier than false belief for the children with ASD. A similar correlation between performance on false belief and counterfactual reasoning tasks was reported by Grant, Riggs and Boucher (2004) with a more able sample of children with ASD.

To explain the discrepancy in performance between two tasks that purportedly embody the same logical form, Peterson and Bowler (2000) argued that the subtractive reasoning task provided the child with information that the standard false-belief scenario did not. The former provided the child explicitly with the counterfactual supposition 'if the marble had not been moved', whereas in the latter, the children had to generate this for themselves. They argued that this capacity for generativity might be impaired in children with ASD. This is a conjecture that has empirical support from behavioural observations in the domains of pretence, repetitive behaviour and memory and is, incidentally, in line with a simulationist account of the development of 'theory of mind'. Grant et al. give a more cautious interpretation of their findings, based on their replication of some work by Sparrevohn and Howie (1995) on belief understanding in ASD. Both Sparrevohn and Howie and Grant et al. found that children with ASD and matched comparison children, although impaired on 'standard' false-belief scenarios, were unimpaired on tasks which required the prediction of a protagonist's behaviour on the basis of in inferred belief, a belief which was not the child's own or a false belief that was made explicit to the child. These observations suggest that it is not belief *per se* that poses problems for most children with ASD, but rather, certain aspects of the particular tasks that have become the 'gold standard' for testing what is loosely referred to as 'theory of mind' – false-belief tasks of the Sally–Anne type. What these aspects consist of remains an open question.

As we have seen, Peterson and Bowler (2000) suggested that the ability to generate possible solutions to a problem or to select appropriately from a range of such possibilities may lie at the heart of successful false-belief understanding. We have also seen that theorists such as Frye, Zelazo and colleagues have produced evidence consistent with a difficulty in embedding 'if–then' conditional rules, and that this difficulty presents itself in all children who have difficulty with false-belief tasks, irrespective of diagnosis. A related possibility is the contention by Halford and colleagues (see Halford, 1992) that certain tasks (including, but not limited to, unexpected transfer false-belief tasks) are characterised by a certain kind of relational complexity, where information from a variety of independent sources (in this case, three) has to be manipulated in order to be solved successfully. Such an account echoes an early suggestion by Minshew and colleagues (see Minshew, Johnson & Luna, 2001) that characterises ASD as a difficulty in processing complex information. More specifically, de Villiers and colleagues (de Villiers, 2000) have developed a model in which mastery of particular linguistic structures – the ability to embed sentential complements – is necessary for passing false-belief tasks. Smith, Apperly and White (2003) further refined this position by reporting a correlation in typically developing children between ability to pass Sally–Anne type false-belief tasks and ability to understand sentences, such as '*The girl kicked the man that jumped over the wall*' in which two events are described and where the object of the event described first is the subject of the event described second. Interestingly for our present discussion, Smith et al. are quite explicit about the issue of causality and readily acknowledge that both their measures might be correlated with development in another set of variables.

What is becoming clear in this discussion is the idea that the initial picture of impaired 'theory of mind' in ASD as resulting from damage to a dedicated modular mechanism is open to question. Although much of the empirical data that gave rise to the 'modularist' account still stands, the way in which this evidence is interpreted differs. Shifting the interpretational framework raises a whole new set of empirical questions but more importantly, it changes the way we think about the patterning of behaviour in ASD both within and across individuals and over time. But before attempting to deal with these issues, one other important aspect of the literature on impaired theory of mind in ASD needs to be discussed. This aspect relates particularly to individuals from the higher functioning part of the autism spectrum, including those with Asperger's syndrome.

The empirical bedrock of the 'theory of mind deficit' account of ASD remains those studies that have shown difficulties in understanding false belief. As we have seen, the data from the original Baron-Cohen et al. (1985) study are clear; whereas about four-fifths of the control children passed the Sally–Anne task, only one fifth of the children with ASD did. Indeed, Happé (1995) found that pass rates for autistic samples in published studies ranged from 15% to 60%, suggesting that a substantial minority (and sometimes a majority) of samples of children with ASD respond as if they possessed a theory of mind. Observations such as these pose a problem. Strictly speaking, if a group of people are supposed to have an impaired psychological mechanism that drives passing false-belief tasks, then they all should fail. Admittedly, in a task where there are only two possible answers (the child can only respond 'box' or 'basket'), some children will answer at random, and produce the correct answer even when they do not understand the question. But 20% (or more, on the basis of Happé's review) is a rather large proportion to attribute to random error.

In response to the findings that a substantial majority of children with ASD could pass first-order false-belief tasks, Baron-Cohen (1989a) argued that even if a subset of children with ASD were able to pass first-order tests of false belief (i.e. those that test the child's grasp of statements like 'Sally *thinks* her marble is in the basket . . .'), they would be impaired on second-order tasks (where the child must grasp 'John *thinks* that Mary *thinks* that the ice-cream van is in the park). This conjecture was tested in a study by Baron-Cohen (1989b), who adapted a second-order false-belief task developed by Perner and Wimmer (1986) in the context of typical children's development. The 'ice-cream van' story tests children's understanding of how one person will act on the basis of a false belief about another person's true belief about an aspect of current reality. Put another way, children are asked about how Mary will act on the basis of her false belief about John's belief about the location of the ice-cream van. Perner and Wimmer demonstrated that typical children could solve tasks like this from about the age of 7 years. Baron-Cohen (1989b) tested a group of adolescents with ASD, all of whom had passed a first-order, Sally–Anne-type task, and found that they all failed the second-order task. The conclusion was that although a minority of individuals with ASD could pass simpler, first-order tests of false belief, they continued to have an impaired theory of mind because they could not pass more difficult second-order tasks. However, when Bowler (1992; 1997) used Perner and Wimmer's task to test a group of adults with Asperger's syndrome, their performance was found to be identical to that of two matched control groups. These observations suggested that for older, and more intellectually and linguistically able individuals with ASD, manifestations of impaired 'theory of mind' become more subtle and harder to detect.

In addition to asking the test question ('Where does Mary think John has gone to buy his ice cream?'), Bowler (1992) also asked participants to justify their responses and coded their justifications according to whether they made no reference to mental states, referred only to one or other of the protagonists' mental states, or embedded one protagonist's mental state within that of the other. But all three groups of participants showed similar distributions of responses across the three categories. Even when the story was changed to prompt greater use of mental state explanations, similar results emerged, suggesting that, for adults with Asperger's syndrome at least, theory of mind seemed not to be a problem. Yet Bowler pointed out that despite showing quite a sophisticated grasp of false belief, adults with Asperger's syndrome remain socially impaired in real life. Similar findings to those of Bowler (1992; 1997) have been reported by Bauminger and Kasari (1999), Dahlgren and Trillingsgaard (1996) and Tager-Flusberg and Sullivan (1994).

Nevertheless, the observations that false-belief understanding was relatively unimpaired in individuals from the higher-functioning end of the autism spectrum led to further attempts to demonstrate impaired theory of mind in this population. Building on the logic of earlier false-belief tasks, namely that someone acts on the basis of a false representation of the world, Happé developed a series of measures that have become formalised in what is now known as the Strange Stories Test (Happé, 1994; Jolliffe & Baron-Cohen, 1999). Starting from the argument that false-belief tasks are not good models of the uses of theory of mind skills that are needed in real life, Happé developed a series of vignettes that were argued to be more realistic. These tested participants' understanding of verbal expressions of Lie, White Lie, Joke, Pretend, Misunderstanding, Persuade, Appearance/Reality, Figure of Speech, Sarcasm, Forget, Double Bluff and Contrary Emotions. The story embodying sarcasm was about Sarah and Tom who were going on a picnic on Tom's suggestion. When, on the day, it poured with rain, Sarah became angry. She then says, 'Oh yes, it's a lovely day for a picnic', and participants are asked whether or not what she says is true. They are also asked to explain why she said it. An example of a physical (control) story is of two armies, Red and Blue, the former with stronger infantry power and the latter with stronger air power. At the final, decisive battle, the weather is very foggy, resulting in the Blue army winning. Participants are asked to say why this would have happened. Performance on these stories was compared with that on stories describing outcomes of scenarios that involved physical rather than psychological components. Overall, the performance of the children with ASD (all of whom had some global cognitive impairment) was worse than that of comparison participants on the 'mental' stories but not on the 'physical' ones. Moreover, Happé observed an association between performance on the 'mental' stories and performance on second-order false-belief tasks, suggesting that the two measures were tapping a similar underlying ability. The same procedure was administered to high-functioning adults with ASD and Asperger's syndrome by Jolliffe and Baron-Cohen (1999), with similar results.

Although Happé has clearly demonstrated that individuals with high-functioning ASD and Asperger's syndrome are impaired on tasks that share the logic of earlier false-belief tasks, two important observations need to be made. The first is that we must look carefully both at the control and the experimental tasks to make sure that they do what they are supposed to do. In the first case, they mirror the mental state task in all respects except mental state content and in the second, they must be a test of mental state under-standing and not of something else. In the examples given above, the Sarcasm story involves an utterance that flatly contradicts the actual state of affairs, whereas in the second case, although inferences have to be drawn from prior information, there is no actual state of affairs that is contradicted. This makes the second task easier than the first, even if we accept that knowing about mental states (and the complexities of other people) makes the first story easier to comprehend. The second observation is that if we accept the rea-soning behind the original findings of difficulty with false belief in children with ASD, then the argument is that there is a system that develops in typical children that enables them to understand mental states in other people and, as a consequence, enables them to pass tasks such as (first-order) false belief. This transition from inability to grasp false belief and its implications to a state of understanding false belief is behaviourally indicated by the transition from failing to passing Sally–Anne-type tasks. Typical children then go on to develop more sophisticated understanding of mental states, as evidenced by their mastery of second-order false belief. However, the transition from an understanding of zero-order to an understanding of first-order false belief is qualitatively quite different from the transition from first- to second-order understanding. The first transition marks the dawn of understanding of the representational nature of mind and as such is a critical transition, the failure of which is profoundly significant. The second transition merely marks an increase in the ability to handle cognitive complexity and, from the point of view of developing – or failing to develop – a theory of mind, is relatively trivial. As a consequence, it is hard to see how failure to pass higher-order false-belief tasks can be taken as evidence for an impaired theory of mind, at least within the parameters of the theoretical framework from which this account of ASD was drawn.

In parallel with Happé's work on strange stories, Baron-Cohen and his col-leagues developed a different set of measures, which he argued were more appropriate measures of theory of mind in older and more able individuals. Arguing that it was not surprising that higher-functioning people with ASD could pass second-order false-belief tasks as such tasks are appropriate for children aged 7 years or over, Baron-Cohen asserted that what was needed were more age-appropriate tests of mental state understanding. Starting from some early observations that children with ASD seem to look differently at people's eyes (e.g. Hutt & Ounsted, 1966; Sigman, Mundy, Sherman & Ungerer, 1986, but see Hermelin & O'Connor, 1970) and from some work that suggests that they have difficulty in grasping that visual access leads to knowing about something (and, more crucially, that not seeing may mean *not* knowing (Baron-Cohen & Goodhart, 1994; Leslie & Frith, 1988), Baron-Cohen developed, in addition to his ID–EDD–ToMM theory outlined earlier, a number of experimental investigations (Baron-Cohen & Cross, 1992; Baron-Cohen, Campbell, Karmiloff-Smith, Grant & Walker, 1995) into how children can infer thoughts and other mental states from an appraisal of eye direction. On the basis of these findings, Baron-Cohen (Baron-Cohen, Jolliffe, Mortimore & Robertson, 1997b, see also Baron-Cohen, Wheelwright, Hill, Raste & Plumb, 2001b) developed a test called the Reading the Mind in the Eyes Test in which participants are shown a series of pictures of the eye regions of faces and asked to select which of a number of mental states was being expressed by the eyes. Baron-Cohen et al. (2001b) found that whereas adults with high-functioning ASD or Asperger's syndrome were as likely as matched controls to identify the gender of person whose eyes were being rated, they were significantly less likely to identify the mental state expressed by the eyes. On the basis of these findings, Baron-Cohen argues that people from the high-functioning end of the autism spectrum, although able to solve problems of higher-order false belief, remain impaired on more advanced tests of theory of mind, thus justifying the claim that they have fundamentally the same impairments as individuals with more classic ASD.

The first observation that must be made regarding the 'theory of mind deficit' account of ASD is that it has provided a major breakthrough in our understanding of the condition. Being able to explain the odd, bizarre, dangerous or rude behaviour of a child in terms of his having difficulty in grasping 'what is going on in other people's heads' not only makes sense of what hitherto seemed inexplicable, but also provides a potential way to develop successful interventions. Parents, caregivers and friends who are aware that certain situations and certain kinds of language are understood very differently by an individual with ASD can find alternative ways of communicating and can ensure help is at hand in those situations that are known to engender difficulties. But however successful the 'theory of mind deficit' account might be in the contexts just described, we need to evaluate how good an explanation it is of autistic symptomatology. That is to say, does it give us clues to the causes of ASD? Science is about more than just providing solutions that work (although that is one of its important functions). Science also aims to simplify the diversity of phenomena we see in the world by means of explanations in terms of lawful interactions among entities whose properties may not exactly mirror those of the phenomenon of interest, and are also likely to play a wider explanatory role. So, for example, although splints and plaster casts are invaluable in helping broken legs to mend, a science of broken bones, to be maximally effective, must go beyond attempts to develop better splints or stronger, longer-lasting, quicker-setting plaster. We need to understand why bones break and under what circumstances they mend and fail to mend. The diversity under investigation in this example ranges from age-related changes in bone hardness (osteoporosis), to cross-species differences (horse bones mend less easily than human ones) and so on. Ultimately, we enter the territory of biomechanics, cell biology, genetics and biochemistry. Working out why things happen the way they do often involves shifting the way we conceptualise the problem, as in the chemistry example given earlier on, and using language and conceptual structures that are sometimes far removed from the phenomenon we are trying to explain.

One of the most important steps a scientist must take when, in the phrase of the philosopher Immanuel Kant, 'putting nature to the question', is to be clear about what the question is. When we ask 'do people with ASD lack a "theory of mind"?' we need to be clear exactly what a theory of mind is. Readers who have made it this far will already have a feeling that the apparently simple term can mean radically different things to different people. As we have seen, to some (e.g. Gopnik, 1993) it refers to a hypothetico-deductive system for inferring mental states on the basis of behaviour; to others (e.g. Goldman, 1993) it stands for the system by which we can simulate in our own minds what is happening in the minds of others. To researchers such as Perner (1991), it specifically refers to an ability to grasp the representational nature of beliefs. Many of these different accounts come from philosophers, who are interested in how it is possible to characterise the possession of an understanding of another mind, and from developmental psychologists who are concerned with documenting when and how children come to understand that people have internal mental lives like their own.

In the context of ASD research, it is already apparent that there is a certain lack of clarity about what exactly is deficient in the mental state understanding of individuals with ASD. From an operational point of view, much of the research uses paradigms (false-belief tasks) that were developed in the theoretical context of representational theory of mind. However, although the theoretical impetus for the initial experimental work came from a different source – one that sought to identify a modular system dedicated to the understanding of both pretence and of mental states in others (see Leslie, 1987), only some of the later empirical investigations (e.g. those of Happé, 1994) stayed within the theoretical frameworks of metarepresentationalism. Others (e.g. Baron-Cohen et al. 1997b; 2001) transcended these constraints and have used measures of mental state understanding that would not typically be understood as testing representational aspects of mind. So, whereas a test of a child's understanding a white lie or a double-bluff can be thought of as assessing a grasp of what one person might think about a situation that another person knows more about, a child's ability to detect a person's gender or whether that person is thinking, concerned or happy just by seeing their eyes is testing something different. In this context, Bowler (2001) borrowed a distinction made by Cromer (1974) in relation to children's development of language. In his discussion of the relation between language and thought, Cromer identified 'strong' and 'weak' arguments. The former posited a strict necessity of dependence between language and thinking – the development of thought structures always preceded the development of corresponding linguistic structures. The latter argued for a looser relation between the two domains. In the case of theory of mind impairment in ASD, Bowler argues that strong formulations of the 'theory of mind deficit' account of ASD should take the strict implications of the theoretical position on board when evaluating evidence in relation to the theory. So to make the strong argument that impaired theory of mind in ASD results from impairment in a modular system that mediates understanding pretence and understanding false belief (whether first- or second-order) entails arguing, for example, that someone who passes false-belief tasks cannot also have impaired pretence. Yet Bowler (1992) found that of their participants who showed impaired pretend play and impaired protodeclarative pointing as infants and toddlers, all passed second-order false-belief tasks – an observation that is inconsistent with a strong version of the 'theory of mind deficit' account. We have already encountered one explanation of inconvenient findings like these – namely that the tasks used by Bowler (1992) were appropriate for typical 7–8 year olds and that it was not surprising therefore that they should be passed, even by individuals with a deficient theory of mind module. The findings have also prompted a range of alternative explanations.

The first of these hinges on the argument that individuals with ASD who have intellectual functioning within the normal range and who have good language develop alternative strategies to solve tests of false belief. Hermelin and O'Connor (1985) introduced the term *logico-affective state* to account for the way individuals with ASD might use cognitive routes to solve problems or deal with situations that were typically solved or dealt with using emotional capacities and systems. Bowler (1992) argued that this 'hacking out' (Happé, 1995) of solutions to false-belief tasks would slow reactions in social situations, making such individuals appear odd. However, when tested experimentally, individuals with Asperger's syndrome were found to be slower than comparison participants in their responses to all questions in false-belief tasks, not just those with a mental state component (Bowler, 1997). These findings pose a challenge to the idea that the impairments found in individuals from the autism spectrum result from damage to a specific mechanism that handles mental state reasoning. In a more recent study, Kaland, Møller-Nielsen, Callesen et al. (2002) claim to have found specific slowing of responses to mental state questions in children and adolescents with Asperger's syndrome.

However their study is marred by a number of methodological weaknesses: groups are poorly matched on IQ, the method for measuring reaction time was unreliable and the performance of the comparison group approached ceiling in a number of conditions, potentially obscuring important group differences. Thus it remains a possibility that what appears to be a specific deficit in the understanding of mind is in fact due to more general impairments.

PROVISIONAL CONCLUSIONS

As befits the paradigm that has dominated ASD research for nearly two decades, this has been a long chapter. It has dealt with a range of theoretical positions as much from philosophy as from developmental psychology. Against these theoretical issues has been set a range of disparate findings from populations widely spaced on the autism spectrum. A reasonable question, then, would be whether we are any closer to answering the question of whether people from the autism spectrum have an impaired theory of mind. It should be clear by now that no answer to this question can be entirely straightforward. It depends as much on which 'kind' of ASD is being referred to as on what exactly is meant by the term 'theory of mind'. Clearly, a mute child with some degree of global intellectual disability and dominated by repetitive behaviours, who appears far more interested in objects than in people, who never seems to look someone in the eye, and only interacts with others to satisfy needs, is very unlikely to have the same grasp of what is going on in another person's head as a typical child of comparable developmental level. But what of an adult with Asperger's syndrome? Someone, perhaps with an IQ of 130 (found in less than 2.5% of the population) who perhaps lives in a relationship and holds down a job, but who has no friends, is considered emotionally cold by his partner, spends most of his spare time gathering and cataloguing information about mobile phone masts, and tries to bring all conversations round to this topic? This man would have no difficulty working out that John falsely thinks that Mary truly thinks that Peter has been misinformed about some circumstance that has changed in a way unbeknownst to all of them. Yet those around him who are not on the autism spectrum find him odd, self-centred and sometimes even callous. Both individuals seem to have difficulties in understanding and relating to others albeit in very different ways. Are we justified in thinking that these extremes are conceptually related in some way? And if they are, just how should this relation be formalised?

In this chapter we have examined the development of the idea that such difficulties should be thought of as resulting from an impaired understanding of mental states in other people, and more particularly from impairment in a cognitive system that is specific to mental state understanding. Although the early evidence lent promising support to this formulation, more recent work has nuanced the picture considerably. It now seems that many of the tasks that were thought to measure mental state understanding may have been measuring other aspects of cognition, such as embedded conditional reasoning or specific kinds of linguistic complexity. And other, more recently developed tasks measure a wider range of mental states than just those that are representational in nature. These observations make it increasingly likely that mental state understanding, far from being the result of the operation of a specific component of the human cognitive system, is but one facet of the coordinated functioning of a range of diverse systems. Such considerations limit the utility of terms like 'mental state understanding' or 'theory of mind' to not much more than vague shorthand descriptions of a range of abilities that enable one individual to 'get inside the head of another'. And so we are left with the very real phenomenon of autistic social impairment and how to explain it.

3 Understanding Other People: Emotion and Interaction

Alongside the evolution of the explanations of ASD explored in the last chapter has been a parallel strand of research that, although placing equal emphasis on the importance of social impairment, has taken a radically different view of its underlying nature. Rather than seeing impaired sociability as the result of damaged computational mechanisms that mediate an understanding of other minds, proponents of the alternative view argue for an impairment in the processes that constitute a direct perception of *persons* and the fact that such persons – such 'others' – are fundamentally like the child's own experiencing self. In recent years, there have been some attempts to bring these two strands of work together. The question remains, however, as to whether such divergent viewpoints can feasibly be reconciled, and whether any such reconciliation can offer genuine enhancement of our understanding of ASD.

Although the term 'theory of mind' has been used differently by different investigators, during the early period of the 'theory of mind deficit' account of ASD, the general consensus was that the difficulties faced by people from the autism spectrum were due to problems in understanding mental states in others, i.e. in generating the hypothetical entities such as thoughts and beliefs that are typically used to explain and predict other people's behaviour. The first serious criticism of this view in the context of ASD came from Hobson (see Hobson, 1993; 2002). Hobson's critique, and the empirical approaches derived from it, are rooted in two distinct philosophical and psychological perspectives. The first of these reflects his training as a psychoanalyst and echoes the very title of Kanner's (1943) original article by emphasising the emotional or affective nature of the disorder. For Hobson, the *sine qua non* of ASD is the fact that people with the condition do not engage in affectively charged interactions with other people. Hobson's explanation for this deficit is rooted in his theory that people with ASD lack a capacity to perceive other people as persons like themselves. Drawing on theories of perception like those of Gibson (1968), Hobson argues that such person-perception is direct and not the consequence of inferential processes. These arguments are developed in two ways: through his theoretical work on the role of affective interchange in the cognitive and social development of children both with and without ASD, and by means of his empirical work on the perception of emotions and on self-other understanding.

Underlying Hobson's theory of ASD is a particular view of typical development that sees engagement with other people as crucial to the child's developing understanding both of the social and the non-social world. Central to this view is the question of how an infant comes to understand that other people are experiencing beings like themselves. Everything else that develops in a child's understanding of others (being able to appreciate that they have mental states and, eventually, that these mental states may differ from the child's own) flows from this basic ability. Even the capacity to 'put oneself in another person's shoes' that simulation theorists argue is at the heart of the development of an understanding of mind, or the generation of conjectures about mental contents that are to be tested against evidence that 'theory-theorists' argue as being important, all presuppose this ability to engage with other people.

On this view, explaining the development of an understanding of other minds requires answers to two related questions: what is the nature of initial forms of inter-subjective experience, and how do these 'primordial sharing situations' (Werner & Kaplan, 1963) enable infants to differentiate themselves from the person with whom they initially engage? Hobson answers these questions by appealing to the philosophical arguments of (among others) Bechtel (1988), Hamlyn (1974) and Strawson (1962) and by concluding that infants have a hard-wired capacity to perceive the directedness of another's body towards the external world. Additionally, he argues that it is in the interactional context of typical caregiving, infants come to grasp commonalities between their own directedness and that of others, that gives rise to a concept of the other as person. Related to the directly perceived aspect of the behaviour of others is the fact that much object- and person-directed behaviour also incorporates an emotional component, which is also directly perceived. In this respect, Hobson's ideas mirror those of Merleau-Ponty (1964) and Wittgenstein (1980) on the nature of our understanding of other people. Thus, Hobson's answer to the first question is that initial subjective experience depends on an innately specified capacity to perceive directedness (both affective and non-affective) in the behaviour of others.

In attempting to answer the second question – that of development and differentiation – Hobson draws heavily on experimental literature that documents children's increasing use of the attitudes of others towards the world to regulate their own behaviour towards that world. For example, he cites the work of Campos and colleagues who carried out a series of studies exploring how infants use the emotional reactions of their mothers in order to decide what to do in a dangerous situation. The apparatus used was the 'visual cliff' developed by Gibson and Walk (1960) to study infant perception. It consists of a checkerboard-patterned surface, which drops off at one edge and continues some distance below, creating a 'cliff' over which the child can fall. The level of the top surface continues past the drop-off by means of a sheet of glass, over which the infant can choose to move. As soon as they can crawl, infants typically stop at the edge of the 'cliff', and do not crawl out on to the glass. But by 12 months of age, if the infant's mother is placed at the other side of the apparatus, infants will look at the mother and either move back or crawl on to the glass depending on the emotional expression on the mother's face (Campos & Sternberg, 1981). Hobson argues that this 'social referencing' marks the beginnings of the child's understanding that others have relatedness to an environment and that this environment is the same as that to which the child itself can relate. This concordance between the child, another person and the environment is another aspect of what Loveland and Landry (1986) call *triadic deployment of attention*, and which underpins behaviours like pointing to share interest in an object or event (protodeclarative pointing; Bates, 1979) and alternating gaze between object and caregiver (Bretherton, McNew & Beeghly-Smith, 1981). In this particular context, it is infants' use of their mothers' *emotional* expression in relation to the world in order to regulate their own behaviour to the same world that is important.

APPRAISAL OF EMOTION IN OTHERS

Given the importance of the ability to use the emotional expressions of other people to regulate behaviour, Hobson undertook a programme of research designed to demonstrate deficiencies in this domain in the autistic population. These experiments are worthy of close scrutiny because they form the major empirical justification for what is to a large extent a set of philosophical arguments about the autistic person's relation to other people.

If, as Hobson argues, children with ASD experience difficulty in 'reading' emotions from facial and bodily expressions, then they should perform less well on tasks that require the evaluation of such expressions. This difficulty was demonstrated in an early study (Hobson, 1986a) in which children with ASD and typical comparison children, matched on either verbal or non-verbal mental age, were shown short video clips or asked to listen to short audio clips. The video sequences were of a person with a blurred face engaging in actions that were typical of the emotions of anger, sadness, happiness or fear; the audio clips were of someone making non-verbal sounds typical of these emotions. Children had to select the appropriate depiction of emotion from a set of five schematic drawings of faces (the five emotions just described plus a neutral expression). The results showed that all groups of children performed at a level that showed that they were unlikely to be responding at random. But the children with ASD were significantly worse than the comparison children on this task, suggesting that they were experiencing difficulty in matching facial to bodily or to vocal expressions of emotion.

What is noteworthy about Hobson's study is the inclusion of control tasks that help to rule out possible alternative explanations in terms of non-emotional effects. The first control procedure consisted of ensuring that the process of matching did not in itself pose problems for any of the children. In a pre-test, children had to match pictures of a train, a bird, a dog, a car and an aeroplane to short video clips of these items in motion. To ensure that matching of facial expressions of emotion did not pose problems for participants, children were asked to match drawings of facial expressions of emotion with videotaped sequences of the same emotions. Although children from all groups performed well on the first task, the children with ASD required more training on the second, already indicating that they had some difficulty with emotional stimuli.

In addition to the pre-experiment control procedures, Hobson also included a control condition within the experiment itself. In the control condition, children were shown blurred video tapes of a moving dog, car, bird or train and asked to select a picture of the object represented in the video. In a second control condition, children had to choose which of the pictures just described went with a video of a dog kennel, a train station, a bird's nest or a garage. Levels of performance on the control tasks were comparable across groups, thus strengthening the conclusion that the difficulty experienced by the children with ASD on the experimental task resulted from its emotional content. It is worth noting that the group differences remained even when those children with ASD who needed extra training on the pre-experimental control task were taken out of the analysis. So it cannot be argued that the ASD-related deficit results from the poor performance of a few children who may have more basic, matching-related difficulties. To counter the argument that the difficulty demonstrated in the children with ASD resulted from problems with schematic drawings and not emotion *per se*, Hobson replicated the study using photographs of a human face depicting the various emotions. The findings were similar to those of the first study, thus reinforcing the conclusion that it is emotion and not some other aspect of the experimental procedure that generates difficulty for the children with ASD.

The findings just described were replicated in a further study by Hobson (1986b) in which children with and without ASD were asked to select drawings of postures typical of the kinds of emotions used in the previous studies to 'go with' videotaped sequences of facial expressions of these emotions or audio-taped sequences of vocal expressions of emotions. As in the previous studies, the children with ASD, while performing similarly to comparison children on the control tasks, showed poorer performance on the emotion-matching tasks. Also, as in the previous study, the performance of the children with ASD on the emotion-matching task was correlated with their performance on the test measuring their verbal mental age, thus suggesting, as Hobson points out, that verbal ability may be an important factor in mediating the performance of children with ASD on tasks such as these. Moreover, Hobson

(1986b) concludes that, since performance on emotion recognition tasks correlates with both verbal and non-verbal mental age, these children may come to understand expressions of emotion in a radically different way from typical children.

Further studies have attempted to determine which aspects of emotional expression are most problematic for individuals with ASD. Weeks and Hobson (1987) hypothesised that it may be facial expressions that prove particularly difficult for this group. They asked children with ASD and comparison children matched on chronological age and verbal IQ to sort pictures of faces according to age, gender, type of hat worn and emotional expression. They found that the children with ASD chose emotion as a sorting criterion at a later stage than did the comparison children and that they more often required an explicit cue to sort by emotion. These observations further support the idea that facial expressions of emotion are not as salient for these children as for children in the comparison group. Hobson, Ouston and Lee (1988a) asked participants to match photographs of facial expressions of emotion with tape recordings of non-verbal emotional expressions or of short stories read in emotionally different tones of voice. The children with ASD performed better on the non-emotional matching tasks and worse on the emotional tasks, confirming earlier findings. And in a further series of studies, Hobson, Ouston and Lee (1988b) asked children with ASD and comparison children matched on verbal mental age to sort faces according to identity or according to emotional expression. Faces were presented either complete, or with the mouth, or the mouth and forehead areas blanked off (see Figure 3.1). In separate

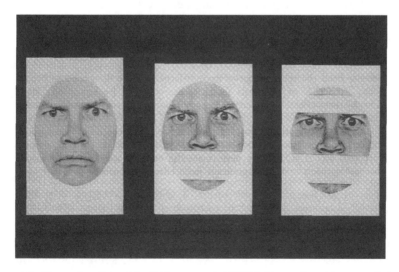

Figure 3.1. Face stimuli used by Hobson et al. (1988b). Reproduced by permission of the British Psychological Society.

experiments, the faces to be sorted were either the right way up or upside-down. The results showed that while on the identity sorting tasks, progressively blanking off facial features attenuated the performance of both groups to the same extent, the drop-off was much greater for the children with ASD on the emotion-sorting task. Moreover, turning the faces upside-down had a less detrimental effect on the performance of these children than on the comparison children. But perhaps most interestingly, whereas for the children with ASD, performance levels on the emotional and non-emotional tasks were correlated, this was not the case for the comparison children. This observation suggests that the latter group were using similar and possibly inappropriate processing strategies to solve both the emotional and the non-emotional tasks.

Evidence of impaired appraisal of expressions of emotion in ASD has also been reported by other investigators. For example, although Ozonoff, Pennington and Rogers (1990) failed to find emotion-specific differences on a range of tasks similar to those described in the experiments reported above, this was only apparent when participants were matched on verbal mental age. ASD-related impairments became more evident when matching was done on non-verbal measures, which, as Burack, Iarocci, Flanagan & Bowler (2004) argue, tend to underestimate the cognitive ability of individuals with ASD, especially those from the Kanner part of the spectrum. Emotion-perception deficits were also found in high-functioning individuals with ASD (Ozonoff, Pennington & Rogers, 1991a) and Asperger's syndrome (Ozonoff, Rogers & Pennington, 1991b). The latter researchers also found that emotion perception deficits and measures of executive dysfunction were better than advanced measures of false belief at discriminating high-functioning adolescents with ASD from those with Asperger's syndrome. In a study where pictures of faces were presented for brief periods (780 ms) and the target and matching pictures did not appear together on the screen, Celani, Battacchi & Arcidiacono (1999) found diminished accuracy of emotion recognition in children who had ASD and retardation in comparison to children with retardation only. Because this study required participants to hold representations of pictures in memory when making judgments, the findings suggest that part of the problem facing the autistic participants may lie in their poorer memory for faces or, more generally, for configural aspects of complex visual stimuli.

The investigations described so far have used methods that involve matching sounds and actions to facial or bodily expressions of emotion. But impaired understanding of emotion has also been demonstrated using other paradigms. Hobson and Lee (1989) observed that adolescents with ASD were poorer than matched controls with retardation at correctly identifying pictures corresponding to emotional words on the British Picture Vocabulary Scale (BPVS, Dunn, Dunn, Whetton & Burley, 1997). This was despite the two groups being matched on overall BPVS performance and showing similar performance on words rated as abstract by independent raters. In a study that used point-light displays of the human body as stimuli, Moore, Hobson and Lee (1997) also showed that children with ASD were impaired in recognising bodily expressions of emotion. This study is particularly interesting because the children with ASD were able to identify the point-light displays as people and not just as patterns of moving lights, a capability that is present in typical babies as young as 5 months (Bertenthal, Proffitt, Kramer & Spetner, 1987). What poses difficulty for the children with ASD in the Moore et al. study is the capacity to detect emotion in such displays. This study is also interesting in that it does not involve facial expressions of emotion, thus reinforcing Hobson's conjectures that emotion is also directly perceived through whole body expressions.

Work by Dissanayake, Kapps, Sigman and Yirmiya has consistently shown that children with Kanner-type ASD are less responsive to displays of emotional distress in others. Typically, tasks involve asking participants to watch an experimenter who is made to appear to experience something unpleasant such as when she (pretends to) hit her finger while hammering a nail. Using this and other scenarios, Sigman, Kasari, Kwon and Yirmiya (1992) found that the children with ASD looked less often at the face of the distressed adult than did comparison children matched on developmental level. Similarly attenuated responses have been observed by Kasari, Sigman, Baumgartner and Stipek (1993) in situations where positive feedback was provided, demonstrating that lack of behavioural responsiveness to expressions of emotion is not limited to negative situations. Such lack of responsiveness was found to persist for up to 5 years in a study by Dissanayake, Sigman and Kasari (1996), who also reported strong correlations between level of empathic responsiveness and mental age. Although Dissanayake et al. report verbal mental age data, they do not report separate correlations between these data and measures of empathic ability. Corona, Dissanayake, Arbelle et al. (1998) report similar rates of cardiac indices of arousal (increased heart rate) in response to another person's distress in children with ASD and comparison children. But the former group showed fewer indices of cardiac orienting response (slowing of heart rate) compared to the latter group. These findings indicate that expressions of emotion in others are less likely to capture the attention of children with ASD. Sigman, Dissanayake, Corona and Espinosa (2003) did not replicate this finding, although they did replicate the finding of no arousal responses to distress, and also observed that children with ASD differed from comparison children by not showing cardiac orienting responses to the presence of strangers when they were separated from their mothers. These findings show that at the level of physiological response, other people appear very different to children with ASD and to typical individuals.

Most of the work just described has tested individuals with ASD who have accompanying retardation in the mild or moderate range. The fact that in most studies impairments can be seen even when compared to non-autistic participants of similar level strongly suggests that the difficulties reported are due to ASD and not some other factor. More recently, some investigations of individuals from the higher-functioning end of the ASD spectrum have been carried out, but with mixed results. A case report of two adolescents with Asperger's syndrome, while finding no impairment in recognising expressions of emotion, found that they were unable to integrate this knowledge into a wider context (Shamay-Tsoory, Tomer, Yaniv & Aharon-Peretz, 2002). In an investigation of brain regions involved in emotional processing, Piggot, Kwon, Mobbs et al. (2004) found no difference in accuracy of emotional labelling or matching pictures of facial expression of emotions in adolescents with Asperger's syndrome but did find that they took longer to perform the emotion-matching task than did controls. Taken together with the finding of a strong correlation in children with more classic forms of ASD between emotion-processing skills and verbal ability, it seems likely that the mixed findings from individuals from the higher-functioning end of the spectrum are due to emotional perception being masked by greater verbal intelligence in this group. This conjecture is borne out by a study by Grossman, Klin, Carter and Volkmar (2000) who found that adding mismatching emotional labels to pictures of facial expressions of emotion selectively disrupted the emotional-labelling ability of children and adolescents with Asperger's syndrome. The possible role of language in emotional processing may also help to explain a body of findings that report no impairment of perception of emotional expression in individuals with ASD. Studies by Braverman, Fein, Lucci and Waterhouse (1989), Gepner, Deruelle and Grynfeltt (2001) and Ozonoff et al. (1990) have all reported relatively unimpaired performance in this domain. However, in all these experiments, matching of groups was based on verbal measures and as we have seen, typical patterns of performance are more likely when groups are matched on verbal rather than non-verbal ability, suggesting that when individuals with ASD process emotional stimuli, they do so using different strategies from those employed by typical individuals or individuals with retardation but without ASD. These observations echo a theme that emerged in the last chapter in the discussion of factors contributing to the passing of false-belief tasks. In that domain also, verbal ability appears to play a role in the successful performance of some individuals with ASD.

A second body of evidence that can potentially cast doubt on an emotion-perception deficit account of ASD consists of findings showing that this deficit is not unique to these conditions. An early study by Gray, Fraser and Leudar (1983) reported high levels of confusion in the recognition of the basic emotions of happiness, surprise, anger, sadness, fear and disgust by young adults with mild or severe retardation. The degree of emotion recognition was correlated with IQ. However, there was no control group in their study and no indication was given of whether verbal or non-verbal IQ measures were employed. Similarly, Maurer and Newbrough (1987) report impaired identification of emotion in a group of individuals with mild to moderate retardation, but their procedure did not embody any control tasks to rule out difficulties with the non-emotional aspects of the tasks. Mueser, Doonan, Penn et al.

(1996) report impaired recognition in people with schizophrenia in receipt of medication. But in that study, unlike those reported above on autistic samples, the clinical group was also impaired on non-emotional control tasks, suggesting that either the clinical condition or the medication used to treat it was affecting performance in a manner that was not specific to emotion. For studies like these to be used to disconfirm the emotion-perception deficit account, we need to show that individuals with some form of non-autistic, lifelong developmental psychopathology are selectively impaired on emotion recognition tests.

A final sceptical point relates to the methods used in the original studies that demonstrate diminished appraisal of emotion in ASD. The experimental studies of Hobson and his colleagues are important, not just because of the information they give us on emotional understanding in ASD, but also because of the high degree of experimental rigour and precise control procedures that they embody. But readers will remember from Chapter 2 that the validity of any experiment hinges crucially on the adequacy of the control tasks used. A sceptical reader should always cast a cold eye on the validity of control procedures used in any experiment. The participant-related control procedures used in the studies described earlier on are about as good is it is possible to be. Great care is taken to ensure individual matching on a measure (usually Raven's Matrices; Raven, 1996) that does not underestimate the ability of the children with ASD (see Burack et al., 2004). But the control tasks that are designed to make similar demands on children in every respect except that of emotional appraisal are more open to criticism. Can we really say that matching a blurred film of a dog running about with a picture of a dog kennel is similar in every respect to a blurred video of someone (with their face blanked off) engaging in fear-related movements being matched with a facial expression of fear? Both procedures require the participant to infer something from the patterns of movement and the shapes in the film, and then to use this information to choose from a range of pictures. However, in the case of emotion, the participant has to identify a transient state of the person on the basis of the film and match it to a photograph of a transient state (we assume that the person in the photograph does not permanently have the displayed emotion). But in the case of the dog, it is the permanent identity of the content of the film that has to be matched with an occasional use of the item depicted in the photograph (we assume that the dog is in the kennel only some of the time). In this example, the pictures seem to be reasonably well matched (both show entities which have to be chosen on the basis of transient properties). But the films are less well matched, in that in the case of the emotion, what must be identified is a transient aspect of the entity (the person), whereas in the case of the dog, it is a permanent attribute. It may well be that it is this difference, and not the emotional–non-emotional difference that poses problems for the children with ASD. These observations are made as much to nuance the conclusions we might draw from the studies discussed so far, as to point out the difficulty in devising adequate control procedures for experimental investigations. Readers interested in further discussion of the difficulties inherent in this area should read Hobson (1991a) or Burack et al. (2004).

These methodological caveats aside, most investigations into appraisal of expressions of emotion present a reasonably coherent picture of impairment right across the autism spectrum. It is also clear that in those instances where there is some evidence of intact ability (it should be kept in mind that what is documented is *diminished* not *absent* ability), it seems that the participants with ASD may be performing the tasks in a manner that is different from that of typical comparison groups, with the strong possibility that verbal ability seems to play a greater role in their success on such tasks.

UNDERSTANDING THE DIRECTEDNESS OF BEHAVIOUR

Appraisal of emotion is only part of the developmental account proposed by Hobson. He also argues for the importance of an understanding of the directedness of the behaviour of others. But to date, the evidence on impaired perception of directedness of behaviour is limited. Hobson and Lee (1999) asked children who had ASD and retardation and matched children with retardation only to imitate a series of movements performed by an experimenter using a set of objects (for example a stick rubbed along a pipe rack). As well as the object-oriented movement, the experimenters varied the style of the action – the stick was moved gently or firmly along the pipe rack; and on some trials, objects were directed towards the experimenter while on others they were not. The results showed that although the children with ASD were comparable to the comparison group in their rate of correct imitation of the actions, they were significantly less likely either to imitate the style or the self–other directedness of the action. The authors interpret these findings as supporting the conjecture that as well as being impaired in their ability to see emotional expressions in others, children with ASD are also impaired in their perception of the self- or other-directedness of the actions of self or of others. They speculate that this deficit may be linked to impairment in self-understanding and self-perception. This conclusion is echoed in a review of studies of imitation in ASD by Williams, Whiten and Singh (2004), and is further supported by a study by Lee, Hobson and Chiat (1994) in a study of the use of personal pronouns in adolescents with ASD and mild to moderate retardation and comparison participants without ASD. Although that study did not find much evidence of pronoun reversal, the children with ASD were more likely to use the pronoun 'I' than 'me' to refer to themselves, and participants with lower verbal ability were more likely to refer both to themselves and the experimenter by using proper names rather than pronouns. Lee et al. interpret these findings as reflecting an impaired sense of self in individuals with ASD. This theme of an impaired sense of self was taken up by Lee and Hobson

(1998), who administered Damon and Hart's (1982) self-understanding interview to a group of adolescents with ASD and retardation and a matched comparison group without ASD. They found that although the participants with ASD produced similar numbers of statements that referred to the self in psychological (rather than physical) terms, they made fewer self-descriptions that were social or interpersonal in nature and used a more restricted range of emotions to describe themselves. This restricted emotional range and lack of groundedness of interpersonal experience is taken by the authors as evidence in support of Hobson's theoretical position on the importance of interpersonal affectivity and its impairment in the development of ASD.

Two points need to be made in relation to the studies just described. The first relates to the pipe-rack study (Hobson & Lee, 1999), in which participants with ASD were found to be less likely to imitate self–other and emotional aspects of an experimenter's actions. Another interpretation of these findings is in terms of source memory impairment, which is sometimes seen in individuals with ASD (see Bowler, Gardiner & Berthollier, 2004). It could be argued that the tasks used by Hobson and Lee represent a target memory (the *core* action) and a context, akin to the source of the memory (the self–other orientation or the *tone* of the action). Individuals with ASD may fail to imitate the latter components because of a failure of source memory, rather than for reasons related to deficits in emotional perception or self–other understanding. The observation by Lee and Hobson of impaired self-concept may also be due to an impairment of memory rather than a damaged concept of self. High-functioning individuals with ASD and Asperger's syndrome have been found to have an impairment in the kind of conscious awareness that accompanies memories of personally experienced events (Bowler, Gardiner & Grice, 2000a). Instead of recalling such events as having been personally experienced by them, they experience them as 'timeless facts' (Tulving, 2001), as part of their store of general knowledge, such as capital cities of countries or the names of planets. In this respect, it is worth noting that several of Lee and Hobson's autistic participants spoke about themselves when they were babies, whereas none of the comparison participants did so. This suggests that the individuals with ASD knew facts about themselves that had equal status with things they came to know through personal experience. The issue of the role of self-awareness in memory will be dealt with in greater detail in Chapter 6, but considering Lee and Hobson's findings in the context of what we do know about memory in ASD suggests that we may be able to unravel the processes that underlie the kinds of deficits that Hobson claims are characteristic of ASD.

All these experimental studies of emotion in ASD have without doubt deepened our understanding of the condition. But we should, nonetheless, ask ourselves some difficult questions. For example, is Hobson's theoretical position, namely that the atypical developmental trajectories to which we give the label ASD are caused by a disruption of the *affectively patterned* interchanges with others, unequivocally supported by the empirical findings just summarised? This observation splits into two parts. First, whether or not it has been demonstrated that perception of emotion is something irreducible to other psychological processes and second, even if it is, has its *necessity* or its causal role in typical development been demonstrated?

Although Hobson draws on a wide range of arguments to support the contention that the perception of emotions in others is a process of direct perception (Gibson, 1968) and that it is a hard-wired predisposition in all humans, this set of assertions does not rule out the possibility that the process cannot be analysed into subcomponents. It seems almost simplistic to say that in order to detect object-directed attitudes and accompanying facial expressions in others, we must have a relatively intact visual system that must be structured in some way to detect certain configurations of objects and components of objects as well as the patterning of movements over time. To suggest that much of the neural 'hardware' that accomplishes such processes is innately specified is nowadays hardly controversial. Yet it is not incompatible with this view to state that these hardware systems are in some way componential, that is to say that they are made up of subsystems that, when damaged, partly or completely compromise the working of the whole system. Accordingly, even if individuals with ASD can be shown to have impaired perception of facial expressions of emotion, it does not follow that this cannot be the result of some process that is both a subcomponent of this overall capacity and can also contribute to impairment in other areas. To support such a conjecture, we need to establish patterns of correlations and associations among measures of face processing, understanding emotion and other measures of adaptive functioning. There is now considerable evidence (summarised in more detail in Chapter 7) that individuals from the autism spectrum process faces in general – not just emotional faces – in a manner that is different from that of typical individuals. In a recent study, Mottron, Dawson, Soulières et al. (2006) report that in a face recognition test, whereas comparison participants without ASD need to be primed by at least two facial components in order for recognition to improve, those with ASD show improved recognition with only one prime. Exactly how such altered face-processing impacts on emotion perception remains to be demonstrated, but observations like these suggest that impairments that may underlie emotion perception deficits may go beyond the specific domain of emotion. A similar argument can be made in relation to the operation of systems that mediate the directedness of affective expression. The functioning of such systems may extend beyond emotional stimuli and encompass other aspects of the directedness of an individual's activity. For example, Bowler and Thommen (2000) report a study in which children with ASD and comparison children matched on chronological or verbal mental age were asked to describe a short film of animated shapes developed by Heider and Simmel (1944). Most notable about the descriptions provided by the children with ASD was that they were delayed in the extent to which they described the actions of an agent on an inanimate object, and deficient (i.e. impaired relative to the comparison children matched on chronological *and* verbal mental age) in their descriptions of actions between two agents when the two agents were not in contact (as when one agent chased another). These observations suggest that it may be agent–object and agent–agent directedness in general that pose problems for children with ASD and not specifically emotional directedness. But whether or not the processes of appraisal of emotion or directedness of behaviour are driven by specific or more general mechanisms, there remains the question of their necessity for typical development, and by implication, of the causal role of their impairment in ASD.

In order to establish that impairment of the systems that appraise emotion in others is causal of ASD, we need some sort of investigation that manipulates exposure to such expressions across development. To carry out such investigations in a systematic and controlled manner would be unethical to say the least, but there are some situations that have provided us with 'natural experiments' in this domain. Studies of the prevalence of autistic-like symptoms in blind children can arguably be taken as evidence of the necessity of an emotional component to the understanding of others. Because of their visual handicap, blind children have attenuated exposure to expressions of emotion, and very little exposure to the directedness of the behaviour of others. They show some autistic behavioural features that diminish over time, suggesting that their limited emotional exposure is eventually sufficient to bring about more typical patterns of social and emotional relatedness and thus overcome their lack of experience of directedness. Brown, Hobson, Lee and Stevenson (1997) report an observational study of children who had been blind from birth. They found that the proportion of children meeting diagnostic criteria for ASD in this group was 400 times greater than in the general population. But when compared with sighted children with ASD, matched on age and IQ, they observed that the blind children were less severely autistic and were more likely to show some rudimentary symbolic play. Hobson (2002) reports that on a 5 year follow-up, the relationships with other people of the blind children who met the criteria for ASD had improved compared with the sighted autistic children. Hobson concludes from this that the blind children have available to them pathways towards interpersonal relatedness that children with typical ASD do not.

Further support for the conjecture that experience of emotional expressions and directedness of actions may be necessary components of an understanding of other people and their minds comes from a study of false-belief understanding by Minter, Hobson and Bishop (1998). They used two tasks, based on the 'deceptive box' paradigm developed by Perner, Leekam & Wimmer (1987) and another that was an adaptation of the Sally–Anne type false-belief task. In the first task, children were asked what they thought was inside a warm teapot.

When children responded 'tea', some sand was then poured out of the teapot, and the child was asked two questions: what they thought was in the teapot when they were first asked, and what a friend who was outside the room would think was in the teapot. The blind children were more likely than sighted comparison children to give a response that was based on the actual contents of the teapot, which is also what children with ASD tend to do (Perner, Frith, Leslie & Leekam, 1989). Similarly, on the task modelled on the Sally–Anne procedure, a significantly higher proportion – about 20% – of the blind children responded on the basis of the actual location of the hidden object rather than where the protagonist thought it was. These findings have been replicated by Green, Pring and Swettenham (2004), and are very similar to what is found in children with ASD. They support the notion that deprivation of access to aspects of emotional expression and directedness of the actions of others can yield social-cognitive symptomatology that mirrors that of ASD. Hobson and his colleagues take such observations as supporting their conjecture that ASD results from similar informational deprivation, albeit using processes that are different from those that operate in blindness. What remains to be demonstrated, however, is whether or not the consequences of blindness extend to tasks such as the Train Task (Bowler et al., 2005), or the Dimensional Change Card Sorting Task (Hongwanishkul, Happeney, Lee & Zelazo, 2005) that correlate with false-belief tasks in typical children and children with ASD.

   The other natural experiment in this domain is the tragic case of children who were abandoned in Romanian orphanages, some of whom were subsequently adopted into typical caregiving environments (see, for example Beckett, Bredenkamp, Castle et al., 2002; Rutter, Anderson-Wood, Beckett et al., 1999; Rutter, Krepner & O'Connor, 2001). These children experienced major deprivation early in childhood, but were placed in typical caregiving environments in the UK before the age of 42 months. The consequences of such deprivation were manifold, including cognitive delay and attachment difficulties. But what was also noticed was that about one child in eight showed autistic-like behaviours that ranged from mild to severe in extent. From the perspective of Hobson's theory, it seems reasonable to assume that these children could see plenty of examples of directedness of other people's behaviour, even of acts directed towards themselves, but that there was little in the way of affectively patterned *interchanges* between them and their caregivers. It can be argued that the fact that some of these children showed ASD-like behaviours suggests that it is the absent emotional patterning that impacted on their development and resulted in autistic-like symptomatology.

   We must be extremely careful, however, in drawing conclusions about the nature and causes of ASD from investigations such as the Romanian orphan studies. Although it is legitimate to use such findings in the way Hobson does, to support a case for the necessary role of affectively charged interpersonal interchanges in typical social development – and by extension, their absence as a cause of ASD – it is not legitimate to conclude that ASD is caused by early deprivation. All the Romanian orphan studies published to date document qualitative differences between the autistic features seen in the orphan samples and those who develop ASD without having had a history of deprivation. It is an error in logic to conclude that because some children with extreme deprivation develop autistic-like behaviour, all children with ASD have suffered extreme deprivation. What appears to be happening is that certain forms of extreme physical and social deprivation can produce behaviours that closely resemble, but do not exactly mirror 'typical' ASD. In cases of ASD that occur in the absence of deprivation, children may well have constitutional impairments that severely restrict their capacity to 'see' those aspects of their social and interpersonal environment that were absent from the environments of the Romanian children and that blind children literally cannot see. What Hobson's theory does is to use these different findings to support an account that implicates affective and interpersonal factors in the development of ASD without concluding that ASD is necessarily caused by deprivation.

Although the evidence from the two natural experiments just described – blindness and extreme early deprivation – do not completely settle the question of what determines the development of typical sociability, it seems that the child's appraisals both of affectivity and of directedness of action play an important part in the social and cognitive development in children and that constitutional factors in children with ASD seem to compromise the ability to make such appraisals. What is less certain is whether the constitutional impairment is limited to these capacities or spreads its damage more widely. This criticism echoes a similar one raised in the context of the specificity argument in relation to understanding mental states discussed in the previous chapter. Both in that case, and in the case of Hobson's theory, ASD is seen as the result of damage to a system that processes particular kinds of psychological phenomena; understanding of mental states in others on the one hand, and on the other, appraisal of emotional directedness of the actions of other people. In both cases it can be argued that whilst either or both of these sets of processes can be dysfunctional, the underlying system or systems that drive them need not be specific to them, either in whole or in part.

There has been a widespread tendency – in part engendered by the authors themselves (see Hobson, 1990a; Leslie & Frith, 1990a) – to regard Hobson's work in strict opposition to that of the proponents of one or other form of 'theory of mind deficit' as the cause of ASD. The differences between the two positions hinge to a large extent on terminology. Hobson's position (Hobson, 1990a; 1991b) takes issue with the notion that the child's understanding of others constitutes a *theory* of mind. He argues that understanding others begins with a capacity to appreciate directedness of others' actions and gradually becomes differentiated to a point where theory construction becomes possible. That is to say, this capacity has to emerge before the point at which the child can make conjectures about possible contents of another person's mind, which can then be tested against evidence. So a *theory* of mind, according to Hobson, is the end point and not the start of interpersonal understanding. Leslie (1987) uses the term *theory* in a rather different sense. The theory of mind mechanism, which becomes active in the child's second year of life, automatically generates certain outputs (M-representations) when certain inputs (object-incongruent acts) are presented to it. In this respect, theory of mind mechanism has a theory of behaviour in the same way as chlorophyll has a theory of gases.* But neither in the infant nor in the leaf of a plant is there a conscious evaluation of the evidence leading to a conjecture followed by a search for confirming or refuting evidence. Hobson, by restricting the term *theory* to a deliberate process of conscious conjecture, clearly differentiates himself from those who propose that ASD results from an impaired theory of mind.

Yet despite these differences, there are striking similarities between the two positions. This observation may seem odd to readers who have followed some of the debate in this area, but if we take, for example, the two issues of system-specificity and directedness of behaviour, we can see some major points of similarity. Leslie (1987) and Baron-Cohen (1995) advocate an innately specified modular system or set of systems that is dedicated to an understanding of mind in others. Hobson, although not explicitly advocating a modular system, also proposes innately specified systems that mediate the appraisal of emotional expression and its directedness. Although his analysis does not concentrate on the mechanics of such a system, and does not explicitly rule out the possibility that it may consist of dissociable subprocesses, he nevertheless argues strongly against any notion that appraisals of emotion and the directedness of attitudes of persons are the result of inferential processes. In this respect he subscribes, however inadvertently, to the notions of informational encapsulation and automatic triggering that are considered by Fodor (1983) to be essential characteristics of modular systems. Leslie's modular theory of mind mechanism is a system that detects actions of agents directed towards objects in such a way as to contradict the properties of the primary representations of those objects, resulting in a decoupled or 'agent-centred' metarepresentation (or latterly M-representation) of that object. Hobson, although not employing the metaphor of modularity, also implicates the necessity of an understanding of the directedness of action in order for psychological development to take place.

Thus, on the one hand we have a set of systems that enable the child to detect bodily expressions of emotion and the directedness of actions in

---

*Chlorophyll is the green pigment in the leaves of plants. When water and sunlight are present, it treats carbon dioxide gas differently from other gases. In the presence of carbon dioxide, it manufactures carbohydrate to build the plant; in the presence of other gases, it does nothing.

others and to recognise the other person as being like the child's own self. These systems enable the child to engage in and profit from affectively charged interchanges with other people that gradually become anchored in the surrounding world of objects and events, eventually leading to a shared understanding of self and other in relation to the world. On the other hand, we have a cluster of hypothetical modular systems dedicated to the understanding of mental states, which may comprise subsystems that detect eye direction and intentional behaviour and which manifest themselves differently at different points in development. During the second year of life, these systems enable the infant to engage in symbolic play and to share experiences by pointing and shifting gaze between the object pointed at and the person with whom the infant wishes to share the experience. By the fifth year, they enable the child to pass first-order false-belief tasks and by the eighth or ninth year to pass second-order tasks. Later on, the capacity to discern mental states from the eye region of the face alone becomes apparent. In ASD, disruption to the systems that subtend this constellation of behavioural indices results either in total absence of or a marked delay in the emergence of some or all of these behavioural markers. Those that do emerge are thought to do so by means of some process or set of processes that differs markedly from the typical case, and which is of no assistance in enabling the individual to navigate the social world (see Tager-Flusberg, 2001 for a thoughtful exposition of this interpretation of the 'theory of mind deficit' account of ASD). This change in emphasis as to what constitutes a theory of mind has led to developments such as the Reading the Mind in the Eyes Test, which includes emotional as well as epistemic mental states and has yielded an account that resembles Hobson's theory in that it argues for an understanding of directedness (by means of ID, the intentionality detector), even if it differs from his account in attaching greater importance to an appraisal of the direction of the eyes. These developments mark a subtle shift away from the contention that the underlying cause of autistic social impairment is simply a failure to develop an understanding of epistemic mental states that can be used in a hypothetico-deductive manner to predict and explain the behaviour of others.

UNDERSTANDING OTHERS IN AUTISM: FINAL CONCLUSIONS

Much of what has been covered in this chapter and in the previous one is history. But, because of the need to understand the intellectual background to a terminology that is widespread when describing and explaining autistic social impairment, it is important history. The term *theory of mind* has emerged out of a rich theoretical background in philosophy and comparative psychology. But its use in autism research has shifted from something in which the logic of particular experimental procedures was firmly anchored to a particular theoretical framework, to a vague description of how one individual comes to understand the inside of another person's head. Procedures used to measure mental state understanding now seem to be developed on an ad-hoc basis, more designed to demonstrate impairment rather than to refine a particular set of theoretical underpinnings.

Two issues are clear, however. The first is that it is now best to restrict use of the term 'theory of mind' to a description rather than an explanation of the difficulties faced by individuals with autism. Understanding of mind, however we might conceive it, is clearly a more complex affair than the hypothetico-deductive process of working out when someone might be holding a false belief about the world. Children younger than 4 years of age are not able to do this, yet they are not socially impaired; individuals with ASD often can learn to do this, yet they remain socially impaired. As Tager-Flusberg (2001) points out, having a theory of mind should not be reduced to a categorical capacity to pass or fail false-belief tasks. Understanding people begins with early social interchanges and develops into a sophisticated grasp of others that includes an ability to understand representational mental states, and to use this understanding to understand complex situations. But by acknowledging the complexity, diversity and developmental nature of understanding people, we must surely also acknowledge that recourse to a single construct – theory of mind – is inappropriate as an explanation of its delayed or impaired development. The second issue follows from the points just made. Precisely because the term 'theory of mind' can now only be used descriptively, and precisely because the tests used to demonstrate autistic social impairment at different ages and different levels of ability vary radically in terms of their underlying theoretical constructs, we must look elsewhere for an explanation of what confronts the observer as impairment in the social domain.

To an outsider, many of the critical observations made in these chapters may seem to be examples of the worst kind of academic nitpicking. But the kinds of sceptical points made throughout these two chapters must be made if we want to go beyond mere re-description of what we already know. For example, we shall see in a later chapter that brain-scanning studies of ASD rely on many of the kinds of tasks that have been described here. The patterns of brain activation seen in such studies are interpreted in terms of the theoretical constructs that the tasks are meant to test, and conclusions are drawn about what brain systems are implicated in particular psychological processes. But what happens when we can interpret the meaning of the tasks differently? Or when the developmental patterning of success on these tasks is different in ASD from the typical case? Or when performance on these tasks correlates differently with other tasks in individuals with ASD than in typical individuals (see Brent, Rios, Happé & Charman, 2004 for an illustration of this last point)? Considerations like these, all of which have been documented in the literature, profoundly affect not only the way we conceptualise the difficulties embodied in ASD, but also the interpretations we place on findings that use these procedures in the first place. What we need to do is to move beyond the most striking aspect of ASD from the perspective of a person without these conditions; to move beyond social impairment and to consider psychological functioning on a wider front. Only when we map this set of domains can we begin to put together a picture of the autism spectrum that encompasses all its manifestations.

4 Beyond Social Impairment: Difficulties with Executive Functions

It will be remembered from Chapter 1 that the symptomatology of ASD includes impairments across a wide range of behaviours, not all of which are limited to social interaction, imagination or communication. The most common of the non-social impairments are those that come under the heading of repetitive and stereotyped behaviours, which are often the most striking characteristic of an individual with ASD at first meeting. As with attempts to understand the triad of social, imaginative and communication impairments, theoretical and empirical paradigms from other areas of psychology and other psychopathological conditions have been brought to bear on repetitive behaviour. Many of these paradigms were developed in particular contexts to deal with particular clinical issues but whether or not their adaptation to the context of ASD has turned out to be enlightening remains a matter of debate. This chapter will provide an overview of the findings of one of these areas – executive functions – many measures of which have been employed with this population. The aim is both to elucidate spared and impaired functions and to evaluate the utility of concepts such as executive dysfunction to an understanding of ASDs. Readers interested in further detail should look at reviews of the area by Hill (2004a, b) and Pennington and Ozonoff (1996) as well as a book edited by Russell (1997a).

The term 'executive functions' has its origins in a series of observations of the behaviour of individuals who had suffered damage to the frontal lobes of the brain. Every undergraduate psychologist learns about the case of Phineas Gage, a railway worker in the nineteenth century who was involved in an accident in which a tamping iron flew upwards, entering under his lower jaw and exiting through the top of his skull. In the process, most of the left frontal lobe of his brain was destroyed. The effects of this dramatic brain injury were interesting for two reasons. Although Gage was unable to return to his old job of foreman, he continued to function adaptively, albeit at a lower level than before, working in jobs such as farm labouring. Yet his personality was changed completely. From being an astute, capable manager of staff, he became capricious, profane and irreverent and was unable to settle on one activity or to plan activities for the future. It was these observations of 'disinhibited' behaviour, coupled with an impaired ability to plan for the future, that led clinicians to look for other behavioural indicators that were specific to frontal lobe damage (see for example Fuster, 1997; Luria, 1966). Out of this clinical work emerged a body of procedures designed to systematise behavioural observations of patients with brain damage, and out of these procedures arose the concept of 'executive function', which broadly refers to those capacities that enable an individual to adapt better to their environment by adopting a greater distance from the here-and-now of the situation. Such distancing enables attention to be shifted across different aspects of the task in hand, inhibition of responses that are no longer appropriate and the planning of response strategies.

Perhaps the best way to get a flavour of the kinds of processes grouped under the rubric of executive functions is to consider what behaviours are required by one of the most widely used measures in this domain, namely the Wisconsin Card Sorting Test (WCST). The WCST (Heaton, Chelune, Talley et al., 1993) presents participants with four target cards, the first showing a red triangle, the second two green stars, the third three yellow crosses and the fourth four yellow circles. Participants are presented with additional cards one by one, and given the task of matching a presented card (say, two red crosses) with one of the top four. The example card just described could be matched with the red triangle on the basis of colour, with the two green stars on the basis of number or with the three yellow crosses on the basis of shape. In fact, the experimenter has in mind (unbeknown to the participant) a colour match. When the participant makes a choice, feedback is given and another card is presented (e.g. one with three red circles). This can match with either the first, the third or the last target card on the basis of colour, number or shape respectively. A participant who scored correctly on the first trial is likely to match this new card with the red triangle, whereas someone who matched on the basis of number might make a correct choice based on number or an incorrect one based on shape. Once again, feedback is provided and a new card is presented. Once a participant has made 10 consecutive correct responses, the tester, without telling the participant, then changes the criterion to that of shape. So, faced again with a card showing two red crosses, the correct match would, under the new criterion, be with the second target card. Once again, when the participant has made 10 consecutive correct responses, the criterion is changed again and the participant must sort the presented items differently. This technique provides a measure of how long it takes the participant to learn what the new criterion is, as well as any tendency to perseverate, that is, to continue responding according to a criterion that is no longer valid. The test as a whole also provides a measure of how many different categories or dimensions of the stimuli the participant becomes aware of.

Taken overall, the majority of investigations that have used the WCST with individuals from the autism spectrum have shown some degree of impairment relative to comparison participants (see Hill, 2004a,b for detailed reviews).

Impairments have been observed not only in children with Kanner-type autism, accompanied by some global cognitive impairment, but also in individuals of normal intelligence who may or may not meet the criteria for Asperger's syndrome (Ozonoff et al., 1991a). Moreover, impairments have been shown not only in comparison to individuals with typical development but also to those with other psychopathological conditions such as attention deficit hyperactivity disorder (ADHD) and dyslexia or reading/writing difficulties (Nyden, Gillberg, Hjelmquist & Heiman, 1999). Comparing the performance of people with ASD against that of individuals with other psychopathological conditions is important because as Pennington and Ozonoff (1996) point out, executive dysfunction is not specific to ASD and is particularly prevalent in the groups just listed. Merely demonstrating that individuals with ASD have executive impairments when compared to typical controls, although informative, does not tell us much about the specifics of autistic psychological functioning if other groups without ASD show similar deficits. If we can show impairments in certain functions relative to these other groups, then we are going some way to a more refined understanding of ASD.

Although most investigations of WCST performance of people with ASD have shown some degree of impairment, there are some studies that have reported no deficits. Contrary findings like these need careful consideration, as they may provide insights that can constrain any conclusions we might draw about the causal role of executive functions in ASD. Minshew, Goldstein, Muenz and Payton (1992) found no statistically significant difference in the number of perseverative errors on the WCST between a group of autistic adolescents and adults and typical comparison participants. All participants had IQs greater than 70 and were matched on chronological age, IQ, gender and ethnicity. However, despite the lack of statistical significance, close inspection of Minshew et al.'s data shows that the number of perseverative errors made by the ASD group was 50% higher than that of the comparison group and, as the authors themselves point out, the mean value for the ASD group was outside the range given in normative tables (that is, they scored unusually highly by comparison with a large sample drawn from the typical population), whereas that of the comparison group was within the normal range. Nyden et al. (1999) reported no difference between a group of children with Asperger's syndrome, and comparison participants with ADHD and reading/writing difficulties. But their sample size was small ($N = 10$ in each group) and they used number of categories completed rather than perseverative errors as their measure of impairment on this test. These two measures are related (the more one perseverates the fewer categories one can complete) but nevertheless, the use of a different measure makes comparison between these findings and those of other studies difficult.

Given that the general tendency of findings is that individuals from the autism spectrum show some impaired performance on the WCST, the question arises as to what this means in terms of impaired psychological functioning. It must constantly be borne in mind that tests such as the WCST arose out of an ad-hoc analysis of the clinical picture presented by individuals with frontal lobe damage. Moreover, these tests are not 'pure', in that they make demands on a range of different psychological processes only some of which may be impaired in ASD. Once having determined that individuals with ASD are impaired on such tests, the necessary next step is to try to determine which components of psychological functioning contribute to poor performance. An obvious candidate for explaining perseverative responding on WCST-type tasks is the notion of inhibition. Initiation of a correct response strategy when the rule changes requires the inhibition of a previously learned response strategy, and individuals who experience difficulties with inhibiting well-learned responses will perseverate on the task.

Numerous measures of inhibition have been developed, most notably the Colour Stroop task (Stroop, 1935), the Go/No-Go task (Drewe, 1975) and tasks involving negative priming (Tipper, 1985). The Colour Stroop task involves asking participants to read out a set of colour words presented one at a time. Each word is printed in a colour that is different from the word itself, so the word RED would be printed in blue ink or the word YELLOW might be printed in green ink. On some trials, participants are asked to call out the colour in which the word is printed rather than the name. This procedure requires the participant to inhibit the prepotent response of reading the word name and to respond with the word's colour instead. It is a task on which people with frontal lobe damage as well as certain developmental psychopathologies such as ADHD and obsessive-compulsive disorder (OCD) (Lavoie & Charlebois, 1994; Martinot, Allilaire, Mazoyer & Hantouche, 1990) perform poorly. The Go/No-Go task typically presents participants with one or other of a pair of stimuli (e.g. a red square and a blue circle). The instruction is to respond to one but not to the other. After a number of trials where, say, the circle is the target, the response requirement is reversed and participants have now to respond to the square. On later trials, the choice of which stimulus to respond to is determined randomly by the experimenter, thus testing participants' flexibility of inhibition of response. Ozonoff, Strayer, McMahon and Filloux (1994) reported impaired performance on this task by a group of high-functioning children with ASD when compared to children with Tourette's syndrome or typical development, matched on chronological age and verbal and performance IQ. The children with ASD performed worse than both comparison groups only in the conditions where inhibition of well-learned, prepotent responses, or where flexibility of inhibitory response were required. But, as Ozonoff et al. point out, these findings do not allow us to determine whether the problem experienced by the autistic participants is one of inhibition, flexibility of response or ability to disengage from an object. This last capacity is a likely candidate in view of the findings of Hughes and Russell which will be reported later. Negative priming tasks involve presenting participants with sequences of letters such as F T F T F and asking them whether or not letters 2 and 4 in the sequence are the same or different. It is typically observed that reaction times are slower on trials where these target letters had been present in positions 1, 3 and 5 of the previous trial. Ozonoff and Strayer (1997) used this task with high-functioning children with ASD and typical comparison children and were unable to demonstrate impaired inhibition in the participants with ASD.

Virtually all studies using the measures of inhibition just described have found no evidence of impairment in participants from any part of the autism spectrum, suggesting that inhibition of prepotent or well-learned but now inappropriate responses to stimuli is not a problem for such individuals. This may seem odd as people with ASD, particularly those from the Kanner part of the spectrum, can appear quite impulsive at times. The findings are also counterintuitive in the light of the typically perseverative response patterns seen on tests like the WCST. This discrepancy between everyday behaviour and WCST performance on the one hand and performance on canonical tests of inhibition may occur for a number of reasons. It could be the case that what we call 'inhibition' is in fact a heterogeneous set of capacities, not all of which are tapped by the tests discussed so far. Or it may be the case that the cause of perseverative responding in the WCST is not an impaired ability to inhibit responses but some other factor, perhaps related to the capacity to disengage attention from one set of stimuli (or dimension of a complex stimulus) and re-direct attention to another set or dimension. This is a topic that will be taken up in greater detail in Chapter 5.

One study that explored the capacity of children with ASD to shift attention from one dimension of a complex stimulus to another is that of Hughes, Russell and Robbins (1994). They argued that the WCST was a complex task and that poor performance could result from a number of factors, which they attempted to elucidate using an intradimensional/extradimensional shift (ID/ED) task. They administered a graded series of tasks to test the understanding of children with ASD and a typical comparison group matched on chronological age and moderate intellectual disability using stimuli similar to those shown in Figure 4.1. Children had first to determine which of the first pair of pink shapes was the correct one by touching it. Correct and incorrect responses were indicated on the screen. In the second phase, the reward contingencies for the two shapes were reversed. The third phase required the same discrimination and reversal of the pink shapes, but this time with the inclusion of patterns of white lines, which were presented beside the pink shapes. These white line patterns were randomly paired with the pink shapes, and were not relevant to optimal performance on the discrimination task. Phase four was similar to phase three except that the irrelevant white lines were superimposed on the pink shapes; phase five involved reversal of the contingencies. Phases six and seven required participants to shift their attention from one set of pink shapes (shown as dark grey in the figure) to another set, all of which were presented randomly paired with superimposed white lines. This intradimensional shift (ID) phase measured

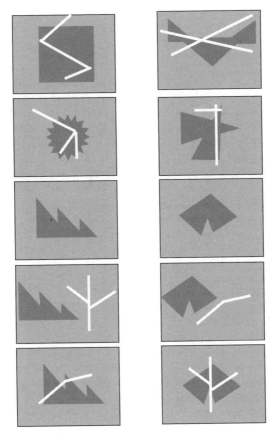

Figure 4.1. Intradimensional/extradimensional shift stimuli used by Hughes et al. (1994). Reproduced by kind permission of Elsevier.

participants' ability to shift their attention from one set of stimuli (pink shapes, dark grey in Figure 4.1) to another, similar set (other pink shapes). Phases eight and nine tested ability to engage in extradimensional shift (ED), that is, to shift responding from pink shapes to white lines and back. On these trials, participants had now to disengage attention from stimuli that had hitherto been rewarded and to shift attention to stimuli that up to this point had been ignored – the white line patterns. In general, children with ASD were unimpaired on simple discriminations and reversals, moderately impaired (along with the learning difficulties group) on ID shift and severely impaired on ED shift trials. This pattern of differences was found on the number of trials to criterion and the number of errors to criterion. It is worth noting that both the children with ASD and those with intellectual disabilities made similar numbers of perseverative errors at a significantly greater rate than did comparison children, indicating that perseveration *per se* was not specific to ASD.

The ID/ED study is an important example of how to take an existing set of observations and methodically and systematically rule out a range of explanations for their occurrence. Since participants could only move to a higher stage in the test after having successfully completed the preceding stage, impaired performance on later stages could not be attributed to difficulties with the processes measured by earlier ones. So an ED shift impairment could not be due to inability to discriminate or to reverse discriminations or to transfer learning to new situations. Ruling out these possible explanations allowed Hughes and her colleagues to conclude that the poor performance of people with ASD on tests like the WCST results not so much from a general failure in inhibition but from a more specific difficulty in disengaging attention and shifting set.

Continuing with the theme that individuals with ASD have difficulty inhibiting prepotent responses under certain circumstances, Russell and colleagues (see Russell, 1997b) have argued that failure on the kinds of false-belief tasks described in Chapter 2 is not due to a lack of mental state understanding but rather to an inability either to inhibit prepotent responses triggered by a salient reality (the actual location of the hidden object in Sally–Anne type tasks), to disengage attention from this salient reality, or both. As we have seen above, other studies have shown that inhibition of prepotent responses seems not to pose problems for individuals with ASD. But disengagement might prove difficult. In their Windows task, Russell, Mauthner, Sharpe and Tidswell (1991) argued that the difficulty that younger typical children and children with ASD experience on tests of deception could result not from an inability to understand the mind of an opponent, but simply an inability to engage in the behavioural strategies necessary for deception. In the first phase, they tested children on a task in which both a child and an opponent first closed their eyes while the experimenter placed a chocolate in one of two opaque boxes. The child was then asked to guess which box contained the chocolate. If the child chose the empty box, then the child won the chocolate. If the box containing the chocolate was chosen, then the opponent won. The aim of this phase was to teach children that it was in their interest to choose the empty box. In the second phase, the boxes used had transparent windows on the side facing the child, so that she could see which box contained the chocolate. Three-year-old typical children as well as children with ASD were found to continue to point to the box with the chocolate, whereas older typical children as well as children with intellectual disabilities pointed to the empty box, thus showing that they had grasped the principle of the task. Russell et al. also found that performance on the Windows task correlated well with that of a Sally–Anne type false-belief task. A similar pattern of results was observed in a study by Hughes and Russell (1993), who added a condition in which the opponent was removed from the scenario and the child received the chocolate only when she pointed to the empty box.

To counter the objection that even in the 'no opponent' condition children might have construed the experimenter as an opponent, and that children (e.g. younger typical children and those with ASD) who tended to choose the baited box did so because they failed to understand deception, Russell et al. developed a second task in which they asked children to retrieve a marble by reaching through an opening in the front of a metal box. The apparatus was set up in such a way that a direct reach broke an infrared beam across the opening, causing the platform holding the marble to move, and thereby making the marble drop out of reach. In order to disable the beam, participants had to do one of two things. They could either turn a knob on the side of the apparatus, which caused the platform to tilt forward and project the marble down a chute into a container where it could be retrieved, or they could throw a switch on the side of the box, which turned off the beam, thereby permitting a direct reach for the marble. Green and yellow lights on the apparatus indicated which of the knob or the switch procedure should be used to retrieve the marble. The results showed that the knob task posed no difficulty for either the children with ASD, typical development or intellectual disabilities. But the switch task was particularly difficult for the children with ASD. This finding poses a problem for any theory that proposes that individuals with ASD have difficulty in disengaging from salient reality, since they readily disengage from a direct reach towards the ball in order to turn the knob to get the ball. Russell and Hughes explain this difference between performance on the knob and the switch conditions in terms of the arbitrariness of the latter compared to the former condition. This conjecture was further tested in a series of experiments by Biró and Russell (2001) in which children with ASD and comparison children had to retrieve a ball from an apparatus similar to that developed by Hughes and Russell (1993). A direct reach through the aperture without any prior action interrupted an infrared beam, which always resulted in the ball's falling through a trapdoor out of the child's reach. However, the ball could be successfully retrieved in one of three different ways: by either raising a screen by means of a lever (least arbitrary), pressing a switch to turn off the infrared beam (more arbitrary) or turning over a cup on the table beside the apparatus, which signalled to the experimenter surreptitiously to cause the screen to be raised (most arbitrary). The results of the study showed that the children with ASD, by contrast with those in the comparison groups, made most errors on the switch task and fewest on the lever task. Performance on the cup task, although significantly impaired, lay between that of the other two. Clearly these results do not fit with Biró and Russell's initial analysis of the three types of task in terms of arbitrariness, but they argue that in fact, the switch task can be thought of as the most arbitrary because it has the least visible consequence of all three. Both the lever and the cup tasks require an action that has an immediate and visible consequence (the lifting of the screen that blocks access to the ball) whereas throwing the switch has no visible consequence – the infrared beam is invisible and so the child cannot see whether it is on or off. This argument, whilst plausible, has a slightly uncomfortable post-hoc feel to it and attempts to account retrospectively for theoretically inconvenient findings. To settle the issue, what is needed is a further study that systematically manipulates the variables of arbitrariness of action and visibility of consequence. We will return to the question of arbitrariness as an explanation for executive dysfunction in ASD in the final section of the chapter.

So far, the picture that emerges is that individuals with ASD experience particular difficulties when required to disengage attention from a salient aspect of reality, possibly in the context of the execution of an apparently arbitrary rule. This conceptualisation of autistic executive dysfunction fits with a series of observations of poor performance on the second most widely used set of tasks employed to evaluate executive capabilities in clinical groups – the so-called *tower tasks*. These are commonly regarded as tests of planning ability. Perhaps the most famous of these tests is the Tower of Hanoi task illustrated in Figure 4.2. This consists of a baseboard with three vertical pegs on which can be placed three disks of different colours and sizes. Variations of the task include the Tower of London (Shallice, 1982) and Stockings of Cambridge (Hughes, Russell and Robbins, 1994). All versions involve providing participants with a start state and an end state together with a set of rules for changing the apparatus from one to the other. In the case of the Tower of Hanoi, participants are given the apparatus shown in Figure 4.2a and asked to reproduce the configuration of disks shown in Figure 4.2b. They are told that only one disk may be moved at a time and that a larger disk may not be placed on top of a smaller one. The aim is to perform the task with a minimum number of moves.

The first rule makes redundant the most obvious solution to the problem, which is to lift all three disks from the left-hand to the right-hand peg,

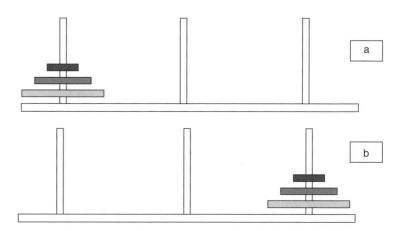

Figure 4.2. Tower of Hanoi apparatus showing start state (a) and goal state (b).

and forces the participant to reflect on other possible ways to proceed. One possibility might be to place the smallest disk on the middle peg and then place the middle disk on the right-hand peg. But this would lead to a problem, because to go any further, the smallest disk would then have to be moved to the right-hand peg in order to make space for a legitimate move of the largest disk to the middle peg. Using this strategy, we would have used four moves and not have got very far (in fact, the test can be solved in seven moves). What is required is for the participant first to place the smallest disk on the right-hand peg and then place the middle disk on the middle peg. The smallest disk can then be moved to the middle peg leaving space for the large disk to be placed on the right-hand peg. Thus the rules of the task require the participant to reflect and take stock of the situation, evaluate the validity of projected moves in relation to the rules, and to inhibit what might appear at first sight to be valid solutions to the problem.

Studies using tower-type tasks have almost universally shown deficits in individuals from across the autism spectrum. Using three- and four-ring versions of the Tower of Hanoi test illustrated in Figure 4.2, impaired planning was reported by Benetto, Pennington and Rogers (1996), Ozonoff and Jensen (1999), Ozonoff and McEvoy (1994) and Ozonoff, Pennington and Rogers (1991a). It is worth noting that in many of these studies, the performance of the participants was found to be impaired not only in relation to typical comparison groups, but also in relation to that of other groups with different psychopathologies known to have executive impairments, such as ADHD, dyslexia and Tourette's syndrome. Thus it would seem that planning impairments are common everywhere on the autism spectrum and are thus the most likely explanatory constructs to emerge in an executive dysfunction account of ASD.

However, tower-type tasks, and the executive function of 'planning' that they purport to measure are subject to a similar set of conceptual caveats to those that apply to performance on tests like the WCST. The process of planning a set of moves in a tower task involves a number of component processes. Possible moves have to be generated, and the consequences of each possible move have to be evaluated both in terms of its appropriateness to achieving the desired goal as well as its conformity with any constraining rules. Obvious solutions often have to be ruled out or inhibited because of the constraints of the rules of the task. Thus, the test measures a heterogeneous set of capacities, failure on any one of which can result in failure on the task. We have already seen that some functions, such as inhibition, which undoubtedly contribute to successful performance on tower-type tasks, are not problematic for individuals with ASD. But there are other aspects, such as the requirement to plan a certain number of moves ahead, that may pose difficulties. With these arguments in mind, Hughes, Russell and Robbins (1994) used the Stockings of Cambridge version of the Tower of London task, which allowed problems of differing levels of complexity to be presented. An important methodological aspect of their procedure is that they included a set of yoked control procedures that enabled baseline measures of time taken to initiate and execute the motor responses required by the Stockings task. Hughes et al.'s results showed that their participants with ASD, whether or not this was accompanied by cognitive impairment, experienced difficulties relative to comparison children on problems that required four or more moves for successful completion. Simpler tasks, with two or three moves, were problematic only for lower-functioning participants. Moreover, inclusion of the yoked control tasks allowed the investigators to rule out explanations in terms of motor planning or execution, which were found not to differ across groups. Yet motor planning has been shown to have some impairment in ASD. Hughes (1996) has shown that even high-functioning children with ASD have motor planning problems. Hughes's task involved asking children to pick up a rod and insert it into a disk. On some trials, in order to insert the rod with a comfortable 'thumbs-up' rather than an uncomfortable 'thumbs-down' hand position, the child had to pick up the rod with an underhand rather than an overhand action. Children with ASD engaged in this kind of motor planning significantly less often than did comparison children, suggesting that they experienced difficulties in planning goal-directed actions. Hughes speculates that these difficulties may result from impaired sequencing ability and an impaired capacity to predict the consequences of a sequence of actions, echoing the finding that higher-functioning children with ASD experience difficulties on tower-type tasks only when such tasks embody more than two or three moves. What seems to pose problems for individuals with ASD is the systematic manipulation of more than a certain number of items of information in the context of goal-directed action. It is also noteworthy that these observations mirror those of Bowler et al.'s (2005) analysis of false-belief tasks in terms of relational complexity outlined in Chapter 2.

At the start of this chapter, it was mentioned that one of the reasons that executive dysfunction became a candidate for explaining ASD was the fact that all manifestations of the autism spectrum are characterised to some extent by behaviour patterns that are repetitive and limited in repertoire. From a developmental perspective, the most obvious example of such deficits is the lack of imagination and creativity that characterises the impaired symbolic play patterns seen in this population. An important component of imagination is the ability to generate new approaches to a problem (Jarrold, Boucher & Smith, 1996) and to select from these responses in a manner that fosters new adaptive behaviours. The consensus of experimental investigations of generativity in individuals with ASD is that they are impaired in tasks such as symbolic play, where they have to generate novel ways of using objects (Jarrold, Boucher & Smith, 1993), category fluency, where they have to provide as many exemplars as possible of a category (e.g. colours or animals) in a fixed time period (Spreen & Benton, 1977), letter fluency, which requires generation of words beginning with a given letter (Rosen, 1980), and design fluency, where a sequence of different drawings is requested (Jones-Gotman & Milner, 1977). In an important and well-controlled study, Turner (1999) not only demonstrated such deficits in higher-functioning individuals with ASD, but also observed that such deficits correlated strongly with measures of repetitive behaviour in everyday life, suggesting that the laboratory-based measures were tapping similar processes to those driving day-to-day activity.

Both the findings on impaired generativity and those on impaired planning of complex sequences of goal-directed action suggest that individuals with ASD may experience difficulty in regulating self-initiated behaviour. A number of experimental investigations have been carried out using a range of tasks thought to tap participants' ability to monitor and evaluate their own adaptive behaviour in relation to a goal. For example, Philips, Baron-Cohen and Rutter (1998) found that children with ASD and moderate cognitive impairment were more likely than comparison children to attribute their success on a target-shooting task to themselves only when they were successful. However, when Russell and Hill (2001) repeated the study with non-cognitively impaired children with ASD, the finding was not replicated, suggesting that the self-monitoring impairment is due in part to a combination of ASD and global cognitive deficits. Other investigators have used tasks such as error-correction and memory for card placement (Russell & Jarrold, 1998; 1999) and action memory tasks (Hill & Russell, 2002). On all such tasks, participants with ASD accompanied by cognitive impairment experienced difficulties. However, because of the scarcity of studies that have been carried out on higher-functioning individuals from the autism spectrum, the question of whether self-monitoring is impaired on all parts of the spectrum remains an open one. As we saw in the last chapter, and will see again in Chapters 7 and 10, the question of the self and self-awareness in ASD is an important one. Diminished self-awareness appears to be associated with a range of difficulties in other domains including those discussed here.

IMPLICATIONS OF THE EXECUTIVE DYSFUNCTION ACCOUNT FOR OUR UNDERSTANDING OF ASD

At least four broad areas need to be considered when attempting to evaluate whether the 'executive function deficit' account furthers our understanding of ASD. The first of these concerns what is often called the discriminant validity question, that is, to what extent executive dysfunctions are unique to ASD. The second relates to the extent to which any coherent theoretical framework can emerge from the pattern of findings described above. Related to this is the question of whether it is at all meaningful to use conceptual categories such as executive function or dysfunction when trying to explain ASD. And finally, we need to consider a broader set of theoretical issues surrounding the concept of executive function, especially what has often been called the 'homunculus problem' – the question of who or what does the controlling or takes the executive decisions in executive function tasks.

The question of discriminant validity – the extent to which executive dysfunctions uniquely characterise ASD – has been thoroughly dealt with by Ozonoff and colleagues (Ozonoff, 1997; Pennington & Ozonoff, 1996). In a comprehensive review of the area, these researchers conclude that although deficits on executive functioning tasks can be found across a range of psychopathological and developmental psychopathological conditions, the patterning of the deficits seen in the various conditions differs. For example, whereas individuals with ASD are impaired on tasks that involve cognitive flexibility, those with Tourette's syndrome are not, yet the reverse pattern is found for negative priming. Ozonoff (1997) argues that sets of findings like these should eventually yield executive 'fingerprints' (her quotes) for different disorders. Such fingerprints would eventually play an important role in differential diagnosis. But from a scientific perspective too, the observation that different clinical groups yield particular patterns of performance across tasks that are labelled 'executive function tasks' is important. Different executive tasks embody different underlying psychological processes, and the identification of patterns of spared and impaired function is an important first step in establishing links between functions usually referred to as 'executive' and other areas of functioning, with a view towards developing a comprehensive explanatory model of ASD.

Yet in the current state of our understanding, there is considerable overlap between the patterns of executive functioning seen in ASD and other conditions and, as a consequence, the discriminant validity argument continues to be made. It seems to me that these criticisms have a clinical or diagnostic, rather than a scientific or explanatory, focus (insofar as these distinctions can be neatly made). The overriding imperative in clinical practice is to make an accurate diagnosis of an individual's condition and to rule out competing diagnoses. In a case where a tentative diagnosis of ASD is being made, then the knowledge that ASD is characterised by 'executive dysfunction' can be useful in that the administration of an 'executive test' can provide information to help decide the matter. However such an approach is only valid if we can be sure that evidence of dysfunction provided by a particular test is particular to ASD and is not shared by other conditions. As we have seen, the evidence on impairment of any of the myriad measures of executive function in ASD is not entirely unequivocal – for almost every measure there are studies that show unimpaired performance. And impairment on almost all measures overlaps to some extent with other disorders. These two factors limit the utility of executive dysfunction as a diagnostic tool. They also limit the explanatory power of measures of executive dysfunction, at least insofar as we regard these as different facets of some common, underlying process.

When considering the range of spared and impaired executive functions that have been documented in individuals from different parts of the autism spectrum, it is tempting to draw up a list and to leave it at that. But scientists feel an obligation to do more than just catalogue patterns observed in nature. There is an impulse to try to see causal processes that might lie behind such patterns with a view to explaining complex, observed diversity in terms of interactions among a smaller set of underlying mechanisms. It is therefore legitimate to ask whether or not the diversity of findings on executive functions in ASD can be re-conceptualised in some way that might enhance our understanding of the condition. To date, the only theorist to attempt such an ambitious exercise in the context of ASD has been Russell (1996; 1997a), who has hinged his analysis around the twin concepts of 'agency' and 'arbitrariness'. Russell's contention is that the particular difficulty experienced by people with ASD is on tasks where responses have to be made to prepotent stimuli in the context of arbitrary rules. This contention arose out of an analysis of their patterns of spared and impaired performance on executive functioning tasks. In particular, Russell contrasts performance on tasks such as the 'tubes' and 'day/night' tasks used by Russell, Jarrold & Hood (1999) on which performance is unimpaired and those such as tower tasks, on which individuals from all parts of the autism spectrum are impaired. The idea was further developed in the context of the reaching task experiments by Hughes and Russell (1993) and Biró and Russell (2001) as well as in the context of an attempt to provide an executive explanation for impaired performance on false-belief tasks and especially the discrepancy seen in children with ASD between their performance on false-belief and false-photograph tasks. As we have seen in Chapter 3, children with ASD find false-photograph tasks easier than false-belief tasks, even though some commentators argue that they both tap a child's understanding of the concept of representation. Russell contends that the rules linking the elements of these two experimental scenarios do not bear an arbitrary relationship to the events narrated, thereby lessening the executive demands of the tasks. Moreover, although both tasks contain aspects that might elicit prepotent responses (i.e., there is a current reality that conflicts with a representation of a past reality), this conflict is stronger in the case of false-belief than false-photograph tests. It is this weaker conflict between actual and represented reality that explains why children with ASD are typically more successful on false-photograph tasks. A similar analysis can be applied to the Train Task developed by Bowler et al. (2005) and described in Chapter 2. In this task, the child has to disengage from a salient reality (the actual location of the plane) in the context of an arbitrary rule (if the light is yellow, then go to the yellow pad . . .). Bowler et al. (2005) argued that if this analysis is true, then manipulations of the arbitrariness of the link between the location of the plane and the signal light should affect the performance of children with ASD on the task, while leaving that of comparison children without ASD unchanged. This conjecture was tested in a study by Holland (Holland, 2005; Holland & Bowler, 2005), which used the apparatus illustrated in Figure 4.3. The apparatus was a modification of the Train Task used by Bowler et al.

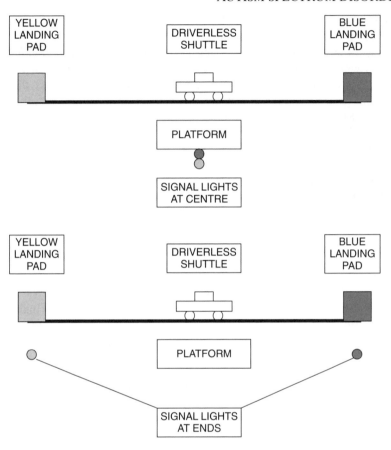

Figure 4.3. Train task used by Holland (2005).

(2005) and consisted of a model airport, with two landing pads at either end of a straight length of railway track. In the middle of the track was a terminal and a platform, which on each trial provided the starting point for an automatic train that collected goods from planes that landed on one or other of the two landing pads. Typically, when a plane landed on either the blue or the yellow pad then the corresponding coloured signal lit up, indicating to the train where it should go. Children from all participating groups (with and without ASD) quickly grasped the operation of the system. However, on experimental trials, the experimenter arranged for the contingency between the lights and the location of the plane to change, so that when a plane landed on yellow, the blue lamp lit, and vice versa. Arbitrariness was manipulated by having the lights either at the central platform (arbitrary condition) or next to the corresponding landing pad (less arbitrary) and it was hypothesised that the children with ASD should outperform the typical children in the latter but not in the former condition. However, the findings yielded a more complicated picture. When the lights were located at the landing pads (the ostensibly less arbitrary condition), half of the typical children who failed the Sally–Anne task correctly indicated that the train would follow the signal. Only 2 out of 16 children (13%) with ASD did the same. When the lights were placed near the central platform (arguably a more arbitrary condition), 3 of the 11 typical children (27%) who failed the Sally–Anne task correctly indicated that the train would follow the signal, whereas 7 out of 16 children with ASD (44%) did so. These findings show that the operationalisation of arbitrariness in terms of relative locations of signals and goals used in this study was validated by the performance of the typical children only. The children with ASD found the 'less arbitrary' condition (locating the signal beside the landing pad) harder than the 'more arbitrary' one, suggesting that what constitutes arbitrary relations for typical individuals may not be so for people with ASD. Although further research is needed to explore the implications of Holland's findings further, it is clear that concepts like 'arbitrariness' cannot be considered as properties of the world that exist independently of the observers of that world. Such a conclusion should prompt us to consider how individuals with ASD organise their experiences in ways that lead to radically different responses to relations among events.

Another problematic area for theories of executive function – the so-called 'homunculus' question – centres on the age-old issue of who exactly is doing the execution or taking the decisions when executive function tasks are being performed. Theoretical accounts of the operation of executive functions have been developed by, among others, Shallice and colleagues (Norman & Shallice, 1986; Shallice, 1988; 1994; Shallice & Burgess, 1991), Baddeley (1986; Baddeley & Hitch, 1974) and Pennington (1994). At the core of such accounts lies the question of how an individual decides among competing responses in a given situation. As Welsh and Pennington (1988) point out, we need to posit some kind of central executive because of the fact that the human information processing system has limited capacity, necessitating decisions about which information is relevant and which is irrelevant to the task in hand. Shallice uses the term 'contention scheduling' to refer to the process of deciding among courses of action and proposes that this process is controlled by a supervisory attentional system (SAS), which represents the goals that the individual must achieve. The SAS formulates its plans of action on the basis of monitoring the person's internal and external states. Baddeley's account is more focused on questions of how it is possible to solve complex problems given the limited capacity of the human memory system to store information over the short term. His working memory model proposes two modality-specific, short-term memory systems that liaise closely with a central executive, which in turn manipulates the contents of the two stores in a manner that enables problem solving to take place. Both Shallice's and Baddeley's models have given rise to a great deal of research, much of it aimed at elucidating the role of the frontal lobes in modulating behaviour (see Stuss & Knight, 2002), and much of the research into executive dysfunction in ASD has been interpreted in terms of altered frontal lobe function. The question of interpretation of the behavioural findings and their implications for understanding ASD are the main focus of the present chapter; a detailed consideration of brain dysfunction in ASD will be taken up in Chapter 8.

The executive components of these models can be considered guilty of what Pennington and Ozonoff (1996, p. 55) call 'the embarrassment of invoking a homunculus' by pushing the question of control of action into a system which itself remains unanalysed. The question then reduces to one of 'who controls the controller?'. The formulation of an account of how the brain regulates goal-directed behaviour without positing some aspect of the system that knows the solutions in advance represents one of the greatest challenges to psychology, and is a challenge that has not gone unanswered. Pennington (1994), for example, has attempted to sketch an outline of how a brain system might regulate itself in response to competing demands both from within and outside the organism in order to engage in goal-directed activity that necessitates selection from competing response alternatives. Pennington starts his analysis with a particular conception of working memory, which he sees

> ... [as] a computational arena, in which information relevant to a current task is both maintained on line and subjected to further processing. Because it is a limited capacity system, inhibition or interference control is intrinsic to its operation ... So the same mechanism both maintains some information and inhibits other information (Pennington, 1994, p. 246).

The purpose of this limited-capacity working memory system, according to Pennington, is to enable action selection by means of transient and context-specific constraint satisfaction. That is, it makes use of highly changeable information available in the here-and-now to limit the behavioural possibilities available to the organism. The homunculus problem is avoided by an appeal to anatomy. The system he proposes requires inputs from a wide range of sources of information, and needs to output to an equally wide range of destinations. Borrowing from the work of Goldman-Rakic (1988) he argues that although the prefrontal cortex is probably the locus of the system he describes, the high degree of connectivity of this part of the brain implies that activity in the prefrontal cortices entails coordinated activity across a range of other brain sites and that the patterning of this activity will differ at any particular time, being determined by the problem-solving state of the organism. Thus, he suggests that it makes little sense to argue that the prefrontal cortices are the 'seat' of executive control or of consciousness. These things are located differently depending on the current activity of the organism.

Pennington develops his analysis by drawing from two influential accounts of brain function, that of neural selection (Edelman, 1987) and that of connectionism, and uses both in the context of non-linear dynamic systems theory (more detailed accounts of connectionist models and non-linear dynamic systems can be found in Chapters 8 and 9). Connectionist (or neural network) models represent an attempt to model brain function computationally in a manner whereby aspects of past and current experience are represented by the entire network, which is in a constant state of dynamic change. Changes in the network's representation of the world are marked by changes in the weights and number of connections among the elements of the system. Thus, experience affects a network over time by strengthening some connections and weakening or eliminating others by a process akin to Darwinian natural selection. Edelman (1987) argues that processes like these operate both over the lifetime of the individual, and across evolutionary time. Non-linear dynamic systems represent an attempt to model behaviour in terms of its pat- terning over time. The most common non-mathematical metaphor used in this approach is based on Waddington's (1957) concept of *epigenetic landscape*, which is illustrated in Figure 9.4. This is a hypothetical surface, which contains depressions of varying depth and shape, referred to as *attractors* or *attractor states*. A behavioural trajectory is represented by a ball rolling across the land- scape. Sometimes the ball will roll into (or be attracted by) a shallow depres- sion or groove and then out again, but occasionally one of the depressions is sufficiently deep to maintain the ball along a given path, or to stop it com- pletely. The patterning of these depressions or attractors is determined partly by genetics, partly by past experience and partly by the current environment or problem faced by the organism, and is in a state of constant dynamic change. The topological configuration of the attractor set at any one time depends on the number of information sources available to it, and Pennington argues that an attractor set defined in the prefrontal cortex, because of the latter's high level of connectivity with other brain regions, allows for a more comprehen- sive representation of the problem space facing the organism. Moreover, the availability of information from a range of sources allows the system to detect covariances among different sources that can be used to alter temporarily the topological configuration of the landscape. Thus, shallow attractors can be tem- porarily deepened in the context of activities that are detected by the system in other areas of the landscape. Such temporary deepening of some attractors can temporarily divert behaviour from being directed into other, deeper attractors.

To illustrate these rather abstract ideas, Pennington takes Cohen and Servan-Schreiber's (1992) connectionist analysis of the Stroop test as an example. In this task, the normal deep attractor would be to read the printed word, the colour of the ink forming a very shallow attractor. But elsewhere in the system, there is activity, generated by the demands of the task, which is temporally correlated with representations of the task and that indicates that ink colour is something that should be attended to. The temporal correlation of these two activations results in a deepening of the 'ink colour' attractor, thus temporarily directing behaviour in this direction. Pennington's one criticism of this account is that in Cohen and Servan-Schreiber's connectionist network, units to detect task demands are explicitly built in by the designers of the network. But he argues that it is possible in principle to envisage a system where such units emerge epigenetically as the result of problem solving experiences. From our perspective, the Stroop test is perhaps not the best example of the application of this kind of analysis to an executive function task, because it is a task on which individuals with ASD do relatively well. But it is possible to see perseverative behaviour, for example in terms of deeper grooves in the 'landscape' that constrain behavioural trajectories.

The great advantage of Pennington's approach is that rather than seeing executive function in terms of control being exercised by some omniscient system that then begs the question of further explanation, the control is seen as emerging from the properties of a system with sufficient complexity to allow this to happen. Moreover, although his analysis posits the most likely location of this emergence in the prefrontal cortex, he argues that this area's extensive links with other areas of the brain should caution against thinking of executive control as an entirely frontal phenomenon.

CONCLUSION

Attempting to answer the question of whether ASD is a set of executive disorders is somewhat similar to answering the question of whether or not ASD results from a deficient theory of mind. It all depends on what we mean by the term executive, and how we understand the interdependence of the different measures of executive function. But whereas the concept of theory of mind arose from some fairly specific theoretical formulations in philosophy and cognitive science, the idea of executive function does not carry the same integrated conceptual baggage. Even if theorists such as Baddeley or Shallice have invoked terms such as 'central executive' or 'supervisory attentional system', these have tended to be seen as clusters of processes that exerted executive control over behaviour and served as a tool in the analysis of that behaviour. Explicitly or otherwise, it was acknowledged that that these high-level executive systems might consist of a number of different behavioural strategies (inhibition, shifting or disengagement of attention, planning etc.), each of which in turn could be driven by one or more underlying, more basic processes. At the level of global executive function, therefore, ASD can be seen as a form of executive impairment, as evidenced by the difficulties shown by individuals from across the autism spectrum on some executive tasks.

On many executive measures (inhibition, for example), people with ASD show no impairment, which makes us question the utility of considering ASD as an executive disorder. But intact areas of executive function should also prompt us to question the utility of the notion of executive dysfunction, at least as an explanation of ASD. At the level of description, it seems entirely appropriate to say that ASD is a set of conditions characterised by executive deficits on tasks such as planning and shifting of attention. Perhaps it would be simpler to drop the word 'executive' from this last sentence, and just describe the deficits. If we are to keep the term in place, then we should constantly be aware that we are using it descriptively rather than as an explanation. The component impairments can then be used to generate hypotheses about how, for example, difficulties in shifting attention might bring about problems with interpersonal sharing that might in turn yield autistic-like social impairment. Such a scenario implicates a process that is often considered to be 'executive' in the development of social impairment. But adding the term 'executive' to the mix seem to contribute nothing, except perhaps confusion, since it might be taken to imply that other executive processes such as those that are not impaired in ASD might also contribute to social impairment in some way. In this respect, Ozonoff's (1997) concept of 'executive fingerprint' is useful, in that it explicitly acknowledges that there are patterns of impairment on different executive tasks that vary across psychopathological conditions. Here again, it might be argued that the word 'executive' could be dropped, except that in this context, the notion of variability of profile and selectivity of impairment scotches any notion that there is a necessary unity among the so-called executive functions. Indeed, in this context, the retention of the term 'executive' is useful, because it adds a descriptive gloss. It marks out the tasks listed in the 'fingerprint' as being involved in some way (consciously or unconsciously) in selecting and sorting information and in using the selections as a basis on which to decide to act or not to act. In this respect, executive dysfunction accounts of ASD are helpful in that they provide a snapshot of patterns of spared and impaired processes, even if this snapshot has limited explanatory power.

5 Building a Coherent Picture of the World

The previous chapter marked a break with so-called domain-specific accounts by introducing the idea that the characteristic behaviour patterns seen in individuals with ASD were particular aspects of the operation of more general processes acting across a range of psychological functions and adaptive behaviours. Weak central coherence (WCC) theory represents another domain-independent approach that attempts to account for the behavioural phenomena of ASD in terms of higher-level processes. Unlike the theories discussed so far, WCC theory has the added advantage that it attempts to explain not only the deficits but also the enhanced performance of people with ASD on certain tasks. Some of the phenomena that led to the development of WCC theory have also spurred research into atypical attentional and enhanced perceptual processes in this population. Altered discrimination learning, diminished perception of similarity and imbalances between local and global processing of complex stimulus events have also been invoked as explanations of the kinds of phenomena that WCC theory seeks to explain. Research into this last set of topics will be dealt with in this chapter. The topic of attention will be covered in the next chapter, followed by a return to a consideration of those perceptual phenomena that might play a role in the modulation of attentional processes in terms of potential knock-on effects on the unity of higher-level cognition. The overall theme unifying the work discussed in this chapter and the next is the idea that ASD may result from difficulties in integrating the details of an experience in order to derive a more global experience of the world.

People with ASD often show a characteristic profile of strengths and weaknesses across the subtests of psychometric tests. Individuals with Kanner-type autism characteristically show a peak on the Block Design subtest of the Wechsler tests of intelligence. People with Kanner ASD and those with Asperger's syndrome also tend to show a trough on the Comprehension subtest. The Comprehension test involves answering questions about why certain things are done in a certain way (for example, why marriages have to be registered), and requires not only the possession of factual information, but also a capacity to use this information in a socially defined scenario. Poor performance on the test is usually taken as evidence of the social impairment that is considered to be characteristic of ASD, which was discussed at length in Chapters 2 and 3. By contrast, the peak on the Block Design test has long been interpreted as evidence that individuals with ASD can be characterised by their having an advantage for processing material that is visual and organised spatially (DeMeyer, Barton, Alpern et al., 1974; Lincoln, Allen & Kilman, 1995), and their preferring problems that require little reference to prior knowledge or outside context for their successful resolution. Higher-functioning individuals, including those with Asperger's syndrome, as well as showing the peak on Block Design, may also show a contrast between performance on the Comprehension and the Information or Vocabulary subtests. Because the last two tests require the recall of isolated pieces of factual information while the first requires knowledge to be integrated into a context, this discrepancy can also be viewed as a counterpart of superior Block Design performance but at a more conceptual level. On this view, ASD appears to be the result of difficulties with the application of information that the individual already possesses to a particular situation, whether at the perceptual or the conceptual level.

The observation of enhanced performance on tasks like the Block Design test led to attempts to demonstrate relatively strong performance on a range of other tasks that were thought to draw on similar processing strategies. One of the earliest controlled demonstrations was Shah and Frith's (1983) illustration of enhanced performance on the Children's Embedded Figures Test (EFT; Witkin, Oltman, Raskin & Karp, 1971, see Figure 5.1) on which participants are asked to identify a small geometric figure that is embedded in a larger, more

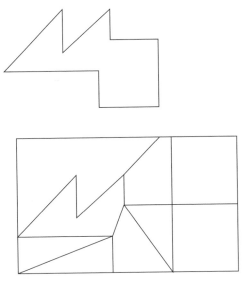

Figure 5.1. Type of stimulus used in Embedded Figures Tests.

complex and meaningful configuration. Shah and Frith found that children with Kanner autism showed faster performance than matched comparison participants, a finding that has been replicated by the majority of studies that have used this task, whether with children or adolescents (Mottron, Burack, Iarocci et al., 2003; Ropar and Mitchell, 2001) or adults with Asperger's syndrome (Jolliffe & Baron-Cohen, 1997). Shah and Frith concluded that the enhanced ability to detect parts within wholes evidenced by enhanced EFT performance could account for the tendency often seen in individuals with ASD to spot details that are usually overlooked by typical individuals, such as a change in an adult's jewellery or threads on a patterned carpet.

In an attempt to find reasons behind the greater accuracy and faster performance of individuals with ASD on block design tasks, Shah and Frith argued that if enhanced performance resulted from a piecemeal approach to processing visual stimuli and a relative neglect of the whole configuration, then they should benefit less from manipulations of the task that would favour a bit-by-bit approach. They asked high- and low-IQ children with and without ASD to complete block design problems using either the standard, unsegmented procedure or by presenting the design to be copied in a segmented form (see Figure 5.2) and found that segmenting the design improved the performance of the typical children as well as those with intellectual disabilities. The performance of the children with ASD, by contrast, did not improve. These observations were interpreted as supporting the piecemeal processing hypothesis in that they are consistent with the notion that the children with ASD were already segmenting the design.

U. Frith (1989; 2003), in a review of findings such as those just described, argued that they provided evidence for WCC in individuals with ASD. According to Frith, all of us possess a drive for central coherence, which is '. . . a strong force pulling all the information in the picture together' (U. Frith, 2003, p. 154), or '. . . pulling information together for higher-level meaning – often at the expense of memory for detail' (Happé, 1999, p. 217). Possession of this force has the advantage of enabling us to see a collection of individual trees as a wood, but can be disabling in circumstances (such as the Embedded Figures Test) where we quickly have to pick out a particular tree. For Frith and for Happé, people with ASD, because their drive for central coherence is supposedly weak, suffer in the opposite way; they have problems seeing the wood but little difficulty in identifying individual trees. Thus, children with ASD perform better on block design, embedded figures and tests of factual knowledge because they can adopt a piecemeal, detail-oriented strategy and are not distracted by the overall configuration or meaningfulness of the bigger picture. Thus any task that sets detail-oriented processing against processing of configurations should show opposite patterns of performance in typical individuals and those with ASD.

The observation of superior performance on embedded figures tasks led Happé to consider other tasks on which individuals with ASD might show

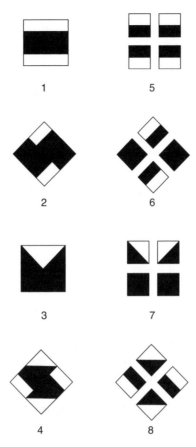

Figure 5.2. Segmented and non-segmented block design stimuli used by Shah and Frith (1993). Reproduced by kind permission of Blackwell Publishing.

enhanced performance. On the presupposition that there is a tendency to focus on the detail of visual stimuli to the relative exclusion of the wider context, Happé argued that people with ASD might be less susceptible to visual illusions. Illusions, examples of which are shown in Figure 5.3, constitute a very striking example of how our perceptual system gives a misleading impression of the way the world is actually structured. They have been investigated since the dawn of experimental psychology, and the general consensus is that we experience them as illusions because we are fooled into 'seeing' objects differently because of the context in which they are presented. In the Müller–Lyer illusion, the lengths of the two horizontal lines are perceived as being different because of the context consisting of the inward- and outward-pointing arrowheads. In the Titchener Circles illusion, the size of the dark, central circle is perceived differently depending on the size of the

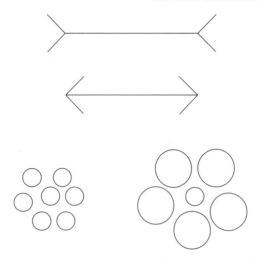

Figure 5.3. Examples of Müller–Lyer and Titchener Circles visual illusions.

surrounding circles. If individuals with ASD either focus unduly on the detail of the part of the stimulus of interest (the horizontal lines in the first example and the dark circles in the second), or experience difficulty in integrating the context with the material on which attention is focused, then they should be less likely to experience the illusion. Happé's findings showed that children and adolescents with ASD succumbed less often to illusions than did comparison children with typical development or intellectual disabilities. The effect was not found for all illusions, however. Whereas it was quite strong for the Titchener Circles, it was absent for the Müller–Lyer illusion. Happé concluded that these findings supported WCC theory by demonstrating that the children with ASD were less prone to the effects of inducing context when viewing illusions. The findings on the Müller–Lyer illusion are explained by arguing that in this case, it is harder to separate out the inducing context from the line to be judged. However, the same could be said of the Hering and Poggendorf illusions, to which the children with ASD did not succumb.

The predictions of WCC theory are not necessarily limited to visuo-spatial tasks of the kinds first described by Shah, Frith and colleagues. Difficulties in integrating information into context experienced by some individuals with ASD can also occur at a conceptual rather than a perceptual level. Many languages, including English, contain words such as BOW, TEAR, LEAD – homographs – which have two different pronunciations despite being written the same way. Which of the two pronunciations to adopt is usually determined by the context in which the word occurs, as in:

The farmer picked up the bag of grain and went to the field to sow the crop.

and

The farmer picked up the bag of grain and went to the pen to give the sow some food.

WCC theory predicts that individuals with ASD, because they have difficulties in seeing the larger, more meaningful picture, will be less likely to use context in situations like this to disambiguate the pronunciation of the homographs.

Starting from Kanner's (1943) observation that for children with ASD 'a sentence is not regarded as complete if it is not made up of exactly the same elements that were present at the time the child first confronted it' (pp. 37–8), Happé (1997) used a task developed by Frith and Snowling (1983) to test the capacity of hyperlexic children with ASD to use sentence context to disambiguate the pronunciation of homographs. Frith and Snowling found that these children were less likely to use sentence context to help decide on pronunciation of the target words. However, in a later study Snowling and Frith (1986) manipulated the relative positions of the context and the homograph in the studied sentence and found that context could help facilitation if participants were alerted before testing to the different pronunciations of the homographs. They also found that the tendency not to use context was associated with low verbal mental age both in the ASD and in the comparison groups, suggesting that failure to disambiguate was not an ASD-specific phenomenon. Happé (1997) hypothesised that individuals with ASD would show no context disambiguation effects if they had not first been prompted about the different pronunciations of the homographs, and that this effect would be found irrespective of their performance on false belief or 'theory of mind' tasks. She tested children on sentences where the context occurred after ('There was a big tear in her dress') or before the disambiguating context ('The girls were climbing over the hedge. Mary's dress remained spotless, but in Lucy's dress there was a big tear'). Her results confirmed the hypothesis. Although overall performance was lower in children who failed 'theory of mind' tasks, all of the participants with ASD used context to disambiguate pronunciation less often than the typical comparison group, even when the homograph occurred after the disambiguating context. Happé (1999) commented that as Snowling and Frith (1986) had found that the effect disappeared when participants were instructed to read for meaning, the weak central coherence (WCC) demonstrated by her own and by other findings may well be more of a cognitive style – a habitual choice of processing strategy from among a range of available strategies – rather than the only approach available.

The findings on homograph disambiguation were replicated and extended in a series of studies by Jolliffe and colleagues (Jolliffe & Baron-Cohen, 1999; 2000). Jolliffe and Baron-Cohen (1999) reported similar effects to those found by Happé and by Snowling and Frith with a group of adults with high-functioning ASD, Asperger's syndrome or typical development. They also demonstrated ASD-related impairment in the ability to select sentences on the basis of an inference drawn from previously presented sentences. Participants were shown sentences such as 'Albert said he wouldn't return to the restaurant' and 'He left without giving a tip'. They were then told:

Albert didn't leave a tip because . . .

and to choose from among:

. . . he only had enough money for the meal
. . . he was dissatisfied with the service
. . . the restaurant was closed when he arrived.

In a further experiment, participants were presented with auditory sentences the first of which contained disambiguating information for an ambiguous word contained in the second. So having heard:

The woman liked to keep her house tidy

followed by:

She said that visiting relatives can be a nuisance,

when asked 'What did she mean?' participants had to choose from:

Having relatives visit can be a nuisance
Having relatives was a nuisance
Having to visit relatives was a nuisance.

Participants with ASD and, to a lesser extent, Asperger's syndrome, were impaired on this type of task especially when the second of the two auditorily presented sentences involved a rarer interpretation of that sentence's meaning. In a further pair of studies, Jolliffe and Baron-Cohen (2000) found that adults with high-functioning ASD and Asperger's syndrome were less accurate and took longer than a typical comparison group to rearrange sentences according to a coherent theme. They were unimpaired on a task that required rearrangement of sentences according to temporal markers contained within the sentences. The two clinical groups were also impaired on a task that required the extraction of a globally coherent inference from a short written narrative.

The investigations based on WCC theory described so far suggest that individuals with ASD have difficulty in disambiguating ambiguous stimuli on the basis of context and that this difficulty goes beyond visual-perceptual material and extends 'up' the information-processing chain to conceptual processes. ASD, in this account, appears to embody a general difficulty with integrating the elements of a complex stimulus to generate a context that can be used to modulate judgments of stimuli or to regulate behaviour. However, as the findings of many other investigations show, the picture is not that simple. Not all investigations of WCC phenomena have produced the same patterns of observations. Neither Ozonoff, Pennington & Rogers (1991a) with a group of high-functioning adolescents with ASD, nor Ropar and Mitchell (2001) with a group of adolescents with Asperger's syndrome, found enhanced performance on the EFT. But it is worth noting that Ropar & Mitchell do not report the criteria on which their Asperger group was selected. This, coupled with the small group size ($N = 11$) may have resulted in a sufficient number of non-criterial Asperger cases to be included in their sample to obscure any differences in performance. Plaisted (2001) observed that the children with ASD in Shah and Frith's (1993) Block Design study were already performing close to the highest score possible, and therefore had little room to improve when patterns were presented in segmented form. And in their investigations of susceptibility to visual illusions, Mitchell and colleagues (Ropar & Mitchell, 1999) noted that Happé's procedure involved asking children to state whether the lines or the circles in the illusion were the same or different, with a response of 'different' always being scored as incorrect (since the lines and circles in the two illusions are always the same). Moreover, they also noted that Happé's participants had been told about illusions and thus may have responded on the basis of what they knew rather than what they saw. Ropar and Mitchell argued that the participants with ASD may have had a response bias in favour of saying the word 'different', or that they were less likely to give accurate verbal responses. To overcome these difficulties, Ropar and Mitchell carried out a study in which they asked children and adults with ASD and Asperger's syndrome to adjust line lengths and circle sizes on a computer screen until they judged that the line or circle in one context was the same as the line or circle in the other. They also included a condition in which verbal responses were required, but where correct responses involved giving the answer 'different'. Their results showed that the participants with ASD were as likely as controls to adjust the lines and circles in a manner that suggested that they sometimes succumbed to the illusions, even when a verbal response was required. Thus, it would seem that individuals with ASD are, in some circumstances, 'fooled' by the immediate perceptual context into judging that line lengths and circle circumferences are different from what they really are. This finding in itself is problematic for the WCC account of ASD, but Ropar and Mitchell, although they replicated earlier findings on block design and EFT performance, also found that performance on the different illusions did not correlate, suggesting that they did not tap a common factor in the way that WCC theory would suggest. Using multiple regression analysis, they found that a combined measure of visuo-spatial task performance predicted susceptibility to some illusions, a finding that goes against the predictions of WCC theory that increased visuo-spatial ability should result in *lower* susceptibility to illusions.

There is also some evidence to suggest that, in some respects, conceptual coherence might be intact in people with ASD. It has been known for some time that when typical individuals study lists of strongly associated items in the knowledge that they will be tested for memory of these items later, they will often falsely recall or recognise non-studied items that are conceptually or associatively related to the studied items (such as when 'bed', 'blanket', 'snooze', 'slumber', 'night' are studied, the word 'sleep' is often falsely recognised; Deese, 1959; Roediger & McDermott, 1995). WCC theory would predict that individuals with ASD would be less likely to exhibit this illusory memory effect because they are less oriented to the semantic context generated by the studied material. However, Bowler, Gardiner, Grice and Saavalainen (2000b) found that adults with Asperger's syndrome were subject to this effect in both recall and recognition, suggesting that they were sensitive to the associative structure of the studied material. Although this finding was not replicated by Beversdorf, Smith, Crucian, Anderson et al. (2000) who reported increased discrimination by high-functioning adults with ASD of words such as 'sleep' in the example given above, there were methodological differences between the two investigations in terms of modality of presentation of stimuli, responses required of the participants and the kinds of data analysis. Similar illusory memory effects to those of Bowler et al. (2000b) have been demonstrated with perceptual prototype materials (Molesworth, Bowler & Hampton, 2005) suggesting that in this respect, people with Asperger's syndrome are subject to associative links among studied material in memory tests, a phenomenon that WCC theory predicts should not occur.

Further doubt on the validity of the concept of WCC comes from a recent study comparing the performance of high-functioning children with ASD and typical children (Hoy, Hatton & Hare, 2004). These investigators replicated Happé's (1996; 1997) homograph but not her illusion findings. However, when receptive verbal ability was controlled statistically, the difference between the groups on the homograph task was eliminated, suggesting, as Frith and Snowling (1983) and Snowling and Frith (1986) concluded, that context-related homograph disambiguation was a function of intellectual ability rather than the presence or absence of ASD. This pattern of inconsistent findings has led researchers to explore alternative explanations of why individuals with ASD can sometimes show impaired processing of configurations and sometimes not, or why they sometimes show an awareness of context and sometimes not. It is to these accounts that we now turn.

ALTERNATIVE EXPLANATIONS OF WCC PHENOMENA

Further experimental investigations of WCC theory have hinged on three possible explanations for the phenomena just described. It is possible that WCC results from an enhanced ability to pick out the details of complex stimuli causing an overfocus on components to the detriment of seeing the larger pattern. Or it may be the case that there is a difficulty in integrating elements of a stimulus into an overall configuration. Finally, knowledge of the larger configuration, if it exists at all, may not drive processing of local detail in a way that causes perception of the global stimulus to predominate, i.e. top-down processing may not operate in a manner that enables detail to be integrated into configurations.

ENHANCED DISCRIMINATION

Despite the demonstrations that susceptibility to visual illusions appears intact in ASD, there are some aspects of visuo-perceptual performance that are atypical in that performance appears to be more focused on the details of a complex stimulus at the expense of the overall configuration. Mottron and his colleagues (Mottron & Belleville, 1993) studied a savant draughtsman with ASD, and found that he could copy so-called 'impossible' figures, such as the Penrose triangle (see Figure 5.4). Unlike the typical participants, he did not notice the impossibility of the figure when asked to make a possible/impossible judgment at a short tachistoscopic exposure. Impossible figures such as these only appear impossible if an observer can integrate all the parts of the figure in a way that tries to generate a coherent whole. Moreover, our judgment of their impossibility also results from our understanding of how the world actually is – our prior knowledge – through what is often called 'top-down' processing. This contrasts with 'bottom-up' processing, whereby what we see influences what we know. Similar findings were obtained with a group of high-functioning adolescents and adults with ASD by Mottron, Belleville & Ménard (1999a). On the basis of Mitchell and Ropar's work on illusions, it seems less likely that Mottron and Belleville's 'impossible figure' findings result from a perceptual difficulty with the integration of the components of a complex figure and may therefore be more a failure of top-down processing. Individuals with ASD may experience difficulty in using what they know about what they see in order to regulate actions that are based on what they

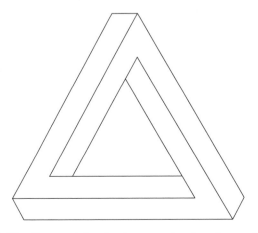

Figure 5.4. The Penrose triangle. An example of an 'impossible' figure.

see, thus producing the particular, locally focused patterns of performance seen in the experiments reviewed here.

A different explanation for enhanced Block Design and Embedded Figures performance was offered by Plaisted, O'Riordan and Baron-Cohen (1998b). Their analysis of the Embedded Figures task posited that the embedded figure to be identified had two characteristics. It contained a combination of features shared by other components of the larger, complex configuration and it also contained unique properties not shared by any of the other components. On this basis Plaisted et al. argued that the test was analogous to feature and conjunctive search tasks employed by experimental psychologists. Examples of these two kinds of task are presented in Figure 5.5. In the left hand panel we have a feature task in which participants are asked to identify the letter 'A', which shares one feature (curly font) with the two letters 'P', and has one unique feature (the fact that it is an 'A' and not a 'P' or a 'Q'). In the right hand panel, participants have to identify the 'Q' in curly font. This letter combines the letter feature of the non-curly 'Q's and the font feature of the curly 'P's, i.e. it represents a conjunction of features of the other two classes of distractor element and can be correctly identified only if the participant can integrate these two features. The findings showed that whereas typical children were slower on the conjunctive than the feature task, children with ASD were not slower on the conjunctive task and were actually faster on it than the comparison children. The only way participants can successfully perform the conjunctive search task is to integrate features of the two classes of distractors and to use this integration to identify the target item. Possession of such an ability is not consistent with the prediction by WCC theory that postulates an undue focus on detail and an inability to see more global configurations made up of combinations of these details. If this were the case, then performance on conjunctive search tasks would be compromised.

Although these experiments demonstrate superior visual search in ASD, as O'Riordan and Plaisted (2001) point out, they offer no explanation of why this should be the case. In an attempt to discover such an explanation, O'Riordan

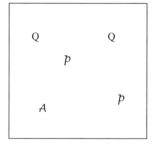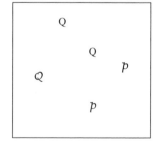

Figure 5.5. Feature and conjunctive search tasks used by Plaisted et al. (1998b). Reproduced by kind permission of Blackwell Publishing.

and Plaisted carried out a further series of experiments designed to decide between two competing accounts of superior visual search. Enhanced performance can result either from a more accurate discrimination of targets from distractors or from a superior capacity to integrate disparate features of a target. In their first experiment, O'Riordan and Plaisted tested children with and without ASD on two- and three-feature conjunctive search tasks on which targets and distractors could differ by one or two features. Their results showed that for both groups of children, increasing the similarity between targets and distractors increased the time taken to identify targets but that the rate of increase in response time was less for children with ASD. This replicates the findings of their earlier studies and supports the notion that individuals with ASD have an enhanced ability to discriminate stimulus features. Moreover, because responding was slower when target–distractor similarity was high, O'Riordan and Plaisted argued that feature integration could not be the driver of search performance. If feature integration did drive such performance, then increasing the number of features required to identify a target should slow down responding. In fact, the reverse was the case for both groups. Similar findings were found with a sample of high-functioning adolescents and young adults with ASD by O'Riordan (2004), suggesting that enhanced feature discrimination and impaired feature integration are characteristic of all conditions on the spectrum.

Enhanced discrimination has also been demonstrated by Plaisted, O'Riordan and Baron-Cohen (1998a) in an investigation designed to explain poor generalisation of learning in individuals with ASD. A widely noted feature of ASD is that learning acquired in one context does not readily generalise to similar, but not identical contexts (Mirenda & Donellan, 1987). The analysis offered by Plaisted et al. is that different contexts will have some features in common (shared features) and other features that are unique to that context (novel or unique features). Circumstances can occur where two stimuli or situations which, although they are not identical in terms of their component parts, initially appear identical, i.e. they have many common and few unique features. But on repeated presentation, participants come to recognise the difference between them by means of identifying common and unique features. Plaisted et al. use the example of a novice birdwatcher to illustrate this phenomenon of *perceptual learning*. Initially, many birds look very much alike but with repeated exposure, a birdwatcher begins to discriminate between two species that at first appear highly similar. Perceptual learning can be demonstrated experimentally by examining the extent to which prior exposure to discrimination between two stimuli that have a high proportion of elements in common enhances subsequent discrimination learning of a similar pair of stimuli that also have a large number of elements in common. Plaisted et al. tested high-functioning adults with ASD on a perceptual learning task in which participants had to learn which computer key corresponded to one or other random dot pattern presented on the computer screen. Participants would

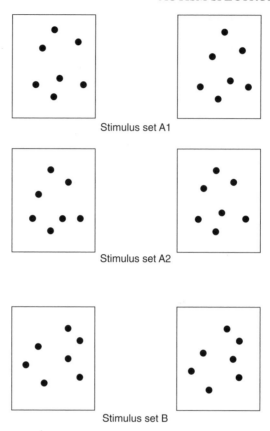

Stimulus set A1

Stimulus set A2

Stimulus set B

Figure 5.6. Discrimination learning stimuli used by Plaisted et al. (1998a). Reproduced by kind permission of Blackwell Publishing.

initially learn to discriminate the two patterns labelled A1 in Figure 5.6. Having learned this discrimination, they would then learn to discriminate a further related pair (labelled A2) and an unrelated pair (labelled B). The hypothesis was that the prior exposure to the A1 set would facilitate learning of the A2 but not the B discrimination, thus showing generalisation of learning from one set of stimuli to a related set. Plaisted et al.'s results showed that towards the end of prior exposure training, participants with ASD performed more accurately than the comparison participants. Moreover, on the main discrimination test, whereas typical participants performed better when they had undergone pre-exposure training, the reverse was true of the participants with ASD. These results are interpreted as showing that whereas typical individuals learned to process the features that were common to the stimuli in sets A1 and A2 and thereby treated these stimuli as being in some way similar (and consequently different from the stimuli in set B), the participants with ASD focused on the unique features of each stimulus, treating each stimulus as novel. This has the result of limiting generalisation and attenuating the effects of prior exposure on later learning.

It could be argued that these findings support WCC theory, because performance on the perceptual learning task depends on perceiving the overall configuration of the dot configurations. Individuals with ASD are poor at perceiving global configurations and as a consequence perform poorly on tasks that rely on such processing. But Plaisted et al. (1998a) disagree with this argument for two reasons. First, they argue that perceptual learning cannot rely on perception of a global pattern because each stimulus in a given series (A or B in Figure 5.6) has a different configuration and that perception of any common layout would require focusing on a restricted area of the overall pattern. Their second argument is that perception of global configurations would actually reduce the enhancement due to pre-exposure seen in the typical individuals because each configuration would be seen as completely novel. There is, however, another way of looking at Plaisted et al.'s stimuli. The manner in which the dot patterns were constructed consisted of fixing the positions of three of the seven dots within a set of stimuli, and varying the positions of the other four (close examination of Figure 5.6 shows that there are three dots in all the set A1 and A2 stimuli that always occupy the same position; similarly for set B), albeit for different positions. This provides a common partial configuration across stimuli and within sets, which would help individuals learn to make faster discriminations under pre-exposed conditions than under non-exposed conditions. An individual who experienced difficulty in processing configurations or whose generally intact information-processing abilities tended to be disrupted by intrusions from the individual elements would therefore be at a disadvantage on this task, especially in the pre-exposed condition. What is needed is a replication of Plaisted et al.'s study with stimuli in which the elements common to the pre-exposure and the test stimuli are defined in a way that does not confound commonality with configuration. Such a procedure would allow us to disentangle the influence of these two effects on the perceptual learning of individuals with ASD.

The studies described so far have demonstrated the enhanced processing of local elements of complex stimulus configurations. We now turn to those that have explored difficulties with global processing.

IMPAIRED GLOBAL PROCESSING

As part of a series of attempts to test the WCC theory of ASD, several researchers borrowed a paradigm from mainstream cognitive research that evaluated people's capacity to identify local and global aspects of complex stimuli. One of the most widely used tasks in this research is one developed by Navon (1977) in which individuals are presented with stimuli like those shown in Figure 5.7. These stimuli consist of large letters that are made up of

```
  AAAA          HH      HH
 AA  AA         HH      HH
 AA    AA       HH      HH
 AA    AA       HH      HH
AAAAAAAAAA      HHHHHHHHHH
AAAAAAAAAA      HHHHHHHHHH
AA      AA      HH      HH
AA      AA      HH      HH
AA      AA      HH      HH


  HHHH          AA      AA
 HH  HH         AA      AA
 HH    HH       AA      AA
 HH    HH       AA      AA
HHHHHHHHHH      AAAAAAAAAA
HHHHHHHHHH      AAAAAAAAAA
HH      HH      AA      AA
HH      HH      AA      AA
HH      HH      AA      AA
```

Figure 5.7. Hierarchical stimuli developed by Navon (1977). Reproduced by kind permission of Elsevier.

arrangements of smaller letters, which can be the same as or different from the large letter (in fact, any large configuration that can be made up of smaller components, such as a large square made up of smaller triangles, will do). When typical participants are presented with a sequence of such stimuli and asked to name either the global letter or the local letter, in cases where there is incongruity between the two levels (e.g. when a letter A made up of small letters H is presented), then naming is slower for the local letter than for the global one. This *global interference* is characteristic of the performance of typical individuals on tests like this. Because WCC theory posits that people with ASD tend to engage in more detail-focused processing and tend to overlook larger, more meaningful configurations, it would predict that they would not be subject to this global interference effect, and might possibly show a reverse, local interference effect, in which naming of the global configuration of an incongruous stimulus would be slower than naming the local element.

Several investigators have employed Navon-type tasks to test local and global interference in the performance of individuals with ASD. As one might expect, the results are not entirely clear-cut. The earliest such investigation was that of Mottron and Belleville (1993), who compared the performance of a savant artist with ASD with that of three comparison participants matched on age and gender. They found that their savant participant showed similar global interference to that seen in the comparison group, but that he also showed interference by local stimuli on global performance. Mottron and

Belleville concluded that rather than showing impaired global processing, people with ASD, unlike typical individuals, do not exhibit *global precedence*, i.e. they do not preferentially process global over local information. But two subsequent investigations, although they found global interference on identification of local stimuli in high-functioning adolescents with ASD, did not find the absence of global precedence identified by Mottron and Belleville in their case study (see Mottron, Burack, Stauder & Robaey, 1999b; Ozonoff et al., 1994). The discrepancy between the two sets of findings was resolved by Plaisted, Swettenham and Rees (1999) who observed that Mottron and Belleville (1993) used a divided attention method, whereas Ozonoff et al.'s (1994) procedure was one of selective attention. Plaisted et al. combined these two procedures in a single experiment and found that when the task required participants to look for a target at either the local or the global level, i.e. when their attention was divided, children with ASD made more global errors in contrast to the typically developing children. By contrast, when children were instructed to attend to just one of the levels (selective attention), more errors were made at a local level in both groups, thus replicating earlier studies of global interference (Mottron et al., 1999b; Ozonoff et al., 1994). However, Rinehart, Bradshaw, Moss et al. (2000) reported local interference on a selective attention task given to children and adolescents with high-functioning ASD and a separate group diagnosed with Asperger disorder according to DSM-IV criteria. To explain these discrepant findings, Rinehart et al. highlight the difference between the stimuli they used (numbers) and those by Plaisted et al. that may have contributed to the discrepant findings. They also point to a difference between their study and that of Mottron et al. (1999b). Whereas Rinehart et al. used the numbers 1 and 2 as local or global elements, Mottron et al. used the letters A and S, but also the letter E as a local element, even though the only response available to participants was either A or S. Rinehart et al. argue that this procedure compromises the degree of interference in the task, thereby diminishing the likelihood of observing local interference effects.

Despite the discrepancies in findings between the different studies, the picture that seems to emerge is that given the appropriate testing conditions, individuals with ASD can process stimuli at the global level. Plaisted et al. (1999) argue that it is this requirement for some kind of priming or cueing to the appropriate level of attention for successful performance of the task that makes global processing (or 'coherence' in Frith's terminology) weak rather than absent in this population. What also appears to be the case is that local rather than global processing appears to be the default option for individuals with ASD, by contrast with typical individuals, who characteristically adopt a global strategy. In this respect, these findings resonate with those described earlier that have employed other paradigms, namely that the capacity for global processing is weakened rather than absent in ASD. This argument is further supported by the finding by Wang and Mottron (2005) who asked participants with ASD and typical development to name local and global aspects of Navon stimuli presented at different sizes. The ASD participants were faster than comparison participants at naming the local elements but were equally accurate at naming the local and global levels. Moreover, when the global stimulus was presented at low visual angle (i.e. appeared small on the screen, thus promoting global processing), there was an enhanced global advantage only for the comparison participants.

The studies of local and global processing described so far have all been in the visual modality, but investigators have also investigated hierarchical phenomena using auditory stimuli. Heaton and her colleagues (Heaton, 2003; Heaton, Hermelin & Pring, 1998) drew an analogy between identifying individual notes in musical chords and the disembedding capacity needed for successful performance on embedded figures and block design tasks. However, Heaton et al. found no difference in ability to recognise changed notes between an ASD group and matched comparison individuals, and conclude that global auditory processing is intact in ASD. A similar finding is reported for chords (harmonious combinations of notes) and discords (disharmonious combinations) by Altgassen, Kliegel and Williams (2005), although they report a marginal superiority at disembedding local elements by individuals with a diagnosis of Asperger's syndrome. Mottron, Peretz and Ménard (2000) argued that music can be processed on at least three levels from the absolute pitch of the notes (the most local) through the relative pitches of pairs of notes to the most global level of melody contour. They asked participants with and without ASD to judge whether sequentially presented pairs of melodies were the same or different. Melodies were changed either by transposition to another key (local change) or by changing the pitch of one note either in a way that violated the melodic contour or maintained it (global and local changes respectively). The ASD participants were as good as the comparison group at recognising transposed melodies but were better than them at identifying melodies where the contour was preserved in the absence of transposition. Thus they showed the same combination of intact global and enhanced local processing in the auditory modality as was documented earlier for vision. However, Foxton, Stewart, Barnard et al. (2003) question Mottron et al.'s assumption that melodic contour results from global processing, arguing that it could equally well result from local attention to sequential pairs of notes. Foxton et al. argue that true global processing involves the integration of these local elements into a larger whole or gestalt (see Brosnan, Scott, Fox & Pye, 2004). They asked high-functioning adolescents with ASD and matched controls to judge pairs of melodies as being the same or different. Pairs of melodies were either exactly the same or differed by transposition of one internal pair of notes (local pitch interference) or differed by changing the direction of one internal pair of notes (local pitch and timing interference). Whereas performance of the typical group deteriorated over each of these three conditions, reflecting the additive influence of interfering features, that of the ASD participants did not, suggesting that their locally based judgments were not affected by changes to the global whole. The contrast between the findings of Mottron et al. and of Foxton et al. seems to hinge on the way global processing is conceptualised, with Foxton et al. emphasising the necessity for local features to be integrated into a higher-order whole that is more than simply the sum of its parts. This is an important point and will be taken up in a later section.

The investigations described up to now have all involved so-called hierarchical stimuli that consist of a large, global stimulus made up of much smaller local stimuli that come from the same category (e.g. letters or numbers). Experimental procedures are designed to assess which aspect of the stimulus, the local or the global, is more readily processed by the participant. Although the observation that individuals with ASD contrast with the typical case by tending to opt for local rather than global processing is interesting, Mitchell and Ropar (2004) raise the question of whether such phenomena are a consequence of the hierarchical nature of the stimuli used, or whether they would hold for any stimulus that can be responded to in two different ways. Ambiguous figures such as those illustrated in Figure 5.8 can be thought of as non-hierarchical analogues of Navon-type stimuli. Typical individuals readily acknowledge seeing both interpretations but also report being able to see only one of them at any particular time. If the bias towards local processing of hierarchical, Navon-like stimuli is due to a tendency not to be able to see both aspects of a complex stimulus, then we would expect to observe a diminished capacity to see alternative interpretations of ambiguous figures. However, Ropar, Mitchell and Ackroyd (2003) found that this was not the case for children with ASD. Thus, the local preference seen with hierarchical stimuli is not necessarily due to an inability to see both aspects of the stimulus configuration but rather to an atypical way of managing the processing of information at local and global levels which, in the context of certain testing procedures, will yield patterns of performance that are consistent with the

Figure 5.8. Example of 'snail/whale' and 'swan/cat' ambiguous stimuli used by Ropar et al. (2003). Reproduced by permission of the British Psychological Society.

WCC account, and which in real life will produce characteristic patterns of behaviour.

Two further experiments by Plaisted, Saksida, Alcántara and Weisblatt (2003) claim to show intact integration of features coupled with enhanced processing of individual features in high-functioning children with ASD. In their first experiment, participants had to learn which of a left or a right computer key was associated with stimuli that were either a red or a blue bar or a red or a blue circle. The left key was assigned to the red bar and the right key to the blue bar. Similarly the right key was assigned to the red circle and the left key to the blue circle. Thus both keys were associated with all four stimulus components (red, blue, bar, circle), so responding on the basis of one component only would not yield learning across trials. To perform correctly, participants had to become aware that left and right were associated with *combinations* of components. In a parallel feature discrimination task, participants had to learn which of a right or left key press was associated with either a pink star, an orange square, a yellow triangle or a purple cross. The left key was associated with the first two stimuli and the right key with the second two. Here, unlike in the first task, participants could successfully learn the association by concentrating on one or other dimension of the stimuli (if pink or orange or star or square, then left; if yellow or purple or triangle or cross, then right). The results revealed comparable performance by the two groups on the first task, but enhanced performance by the children with ASD on the second, thus confirming enhanced featural discrimination in the latter group.

In a second experiment, Plaisted et al. (2003) asked participants to determine which of two computer keys was associated with random dot patterns presented on the screen. Some patterns consisted of either pink or blue dots (feature trials) and some contained pink and blue dots (configural trials). All patterns contained some yellow and green dots as distractors. To score correctly, a participant had to learn to press the left key on all feature trials (i.e. those that contained only blue or pink dots) and the right key on trials with blue and pink dots (configural trials). To learn this response strategy, a child had to learn to associate a particular response with the *combination* of pink and blue dots. Responding to pink or to blue alone would yield the wrong response. Inspection of the graphs in the original report shows lower overall response rates in this experiment than in the previous one (~57% vs ~68%), indicating that it was a more difficult task. The outcome of the statistical analysis presented by Plaisted et al. mirrors the findings of the first experiment, in that the children with ASD were significantly better (in this case, marginally so) than the comparison group on the feature (second) task and not significantly different from them on the configural task. However, inspection of Figure 3 in the original report shows non-overlapping standard error bars on both tasks, suggesting that there was some decrement in performance on the configural task by the children with ASD. The small number of participants in this experiment ($N = 12$ in each group) may not have yielded sufficient statistical power to render this difference significant. A decrement in configural processing would be in line with the findings of impaired gestalt processing identified by Brosnan et al. (2004) and with WCC theory. These findings tell us that enhanced featural or local processing in individuals with ASD is coupled with intact or almost intact processing involving combinations of features resonating with the study by Wang and Mottron (2005) described above, which showed that individuals with ASD were equally accurate at processing information at a featural or a configural level.

Up to this point, the terms 'configuration' and 'combination' have been used to describe the global form of a stimulus that is made up of discriminable smaller elements. But another term used by several of the authors of this work is *gestalt*, referring to the tendency, first explored systematically in the first half of the twentieth century, of the human information processing system to organise sensations into larger configural wholes. A particular feature of these configural wholes or gestalts was that their properties consisted of more than just the sum of the parts comprising them, an observation that led to the aphorism that 'the whole is more than the sum of its parts'. However, as Brosnan et al. (2004) point out, perceiving gestalts and perceiving overall configurations of perceptual elements, although related processes, are not identical. They take the example of the Navon-type figures illustrated in Figure 5.7. The global form of a letter H made up of smaller letter As is unaffected by the substitution of Ts for the As. Brosnan et al. contrast this situation with the Titchener Circles illustrated in Figure 5.2, where the impression of the size of the middle circle depends on its relation to the size of the surrounding ones. It is clear, therefore, that not all of the research described in the preceding paragraphs deals with gestalt processing in ASD, even if this term is often used in that context (see Plaisted et al., 1998a, p. 773; Plaisted et al., 1999, p. 733). We now know from the work of Brosnan et al. (2004) that children with Kanner-type ASD make less use of gestalt processing principles when describing stimuli that are subject to the operation of these principles. Difficulties with forming or perceiving gestalts imply difficulties with integration of local features into a global whole, whereas the reverse is not the case (it is possible to imagine a situation where local configurations can be integrated into a global whole but where an overall gestalt does not emerge). Brosnan et al.'s findings, as well as those by Foxton et al. (2003) on musical contour, tell us that the difficulties experienced by individuals with Kanner-type ASD in integrating local elements into global wholes extend beyond just the summing of the parts. What remains to be demonstrated is whether or not this difficulty is experienced by individuals from other parts of the autism spectrum. However, even if future studies manage to demonstrate a mild impairment in configural or gestalt processing in ASD, as Plaisted et al. (1998a) point out, gestalt-based arguments do not explain why such individuals generally show superior perceptual learning than comparison participants. Plaisted et al. (1998a) argue that this pattern of performance is best explained by positing an enhanced processing of unique features by the participants with ASD. They accept that this pattern of processing needs further explanation and suggest that it may be rooted in a difficulty in shifting attention from common to unique aspects of the display. Problems with shifting attention would limit the extent to which an individual could process all aspects of the stimulus config-uration and consequently diminish generalisation. The topic of attention is dealt with in more detail in Chapter 6.

Given that individuals from the autism spectrum appear to prefer to process at a local rather than a global level, and given that they appear not to have any particular difficulty in apprehending both the local and the global aspects of hierarchical, Navon-type stimuli and both interpretations of ambiguous stimuli, we are left with the question of why they respond to hierarchical stimuli the way they do. Both Plaisted et al. (1999) and Rinehart et al. (2000) invoke the concept of inhibition as a possible explanation of the tendency by individuals with ASD to opt for a local strategy when processing hierarchical stimuli. Plaisted et al. argue that in the absence of instructions to do other-wise, it is argued that the surfeit of global information produced by local pro-cessing mechanisms determines the overall processing strategy because of deficient systems that inhibit that local activity. Rinehart et al. argue that even when the global image has been identified, individuals with ASD cannot inhibit further processing of the image at the local level. Yet as we have seen in Chapter 4, inhibition does not appear to pose problems for people with ASD (Ozonoff & Strayer, 1997). An explanation that would be more in line with the findings on executive dysfunction would be to invoke difficulty in disen-gaging attention, which can be impaired in ASD (see Chapter 6). Because the local level appears to be more salient to individuals with ASD, their attention is captured by it and they subsequently find it hard to disengage and shift attention to the global level (see Mann & Walker, 2003).

IMPAIRED TOP-DOWN PROCESSING

An alternative explanation for the global/local findings in ASD centres on the suggestion that we have already encountered in relation to perception of impossible figures. That is, that they may experience difficulties in top-down processing – the use of prior knowledge to modulate current perception. This explanation is supported by Plaisted et al.'s (1998a) demonstration that for individuals with ASD, discrimination learning is not enhanced by prior expo-sure to configurationally similar material as well as by a series of experiments by Mitchell and colleagues who asked participants to judge or to reproduce images of circles and ellipses. If we imagine looking at a circle or circular object with the plane of the circle at right angles to our line of sight, the image pro-jected on our retinas is circular and we see a circle. But if we rotate the plane of the circle about its diameter, the retinal image becomes more elliptical, until it eventually becomes a vertical line. Throughout this process, we continue to *know* that the object is a circle, and perceive and judge it as such. But when asked to draw a circle that has been rotated so as to appear elliptical, even individuals experienced in drawing tend to exaggerate the circularity of the object. In other words, their knowledge that the ellipse really is a circle tends to make them draw it as being more circular and less elliptical than the retinal image actually is. This tendency to overestimate circularity is also found if participants are asked to select the best match from a range of possibilities (Mitchell & Taylor, 1999). To test whether or not such misjudgements resulted from a failure to use context cues or from a tendency to overuse prior knowledge of the object's circularity, Ropar and Mitchell (2002) carried out a series of studies with adolescents who had ASD and intellectual disability, intellectual disability only, or typical development. They also included a group of adults with typical development. The variables manipulated were the amount of context present that might suggest that what was being looked at was a circle, and the prior knowledge of whether or not what was being looked at actually was a circle. Ropar and Mitchell found that all groups showed a tendency to exaggerate circularity, but that the individuals with ASD were less likely to do so either when perspective cues were absent or when they had no prior knowledge of what the object really was. What is interesting about these findings is that the autistic participants appeared to be less influenced by prior knowledge when perceptual cues were absent. It is as if when there is no reminder to the fact that the ellipse might be a circle, then they seem to forget that it is a circle and draw it more accurately as an ellipse. This greater requirement to have explicit cues in order to recall relevant earlier information seems to be a major feature of the way people with ASD interact with the world and will be discussed in greater detail when we consider the topic of memory in ASD in Chapter 7. What is important for the present purposes is that individuals with ASD can use prior knowledge when making perceptual judgments but that this tends not to occur automatically, but requires prompting in some way.

CONCLUSION

Several themes emerge from the empirical findings discussed here. The first is that individuals from all parts of the autism spectrum are likely to process complex stimuli by focusing on details rather than overall configurations. They also tend to make less use of prior knowledge when making perceptual judgments. The second is that if an individual with ASD is to process information globally, then some cueing, priming or indication of context must be present in the task (Plaisted et al., 1999; Ropar & Mitchell, 2002). If none of these are present, then a more locally oriented option is likely to be triggered. Both these conclusions nuance considerably the WCC account of ASD by firmly placing the emphasis on the notion of *weak* rather than *absent* central coherence (it is perhaps worth noting that no one ever claimed that central coherence was absent in ASD). Diminished 'coherence' or the capacity to see wholes rather than parts, or objects in context rather than in isolation, yields patterns of behaviour that are characteristic of ASD. One of the challenges to investigators raised by this conclusion is to identify circumstances in which typical individuals would engage a local processing strategy for optimal performance but where the structure of the task would trigger an inappropriate global strategy in individuals with ASD.

But whereas the nuanced version of WCC theory just outlined remains useful as an explanation of autistic behaviour that results from activity occurring 'higher up' in the information processing system, the findings so far discussed in this chapter raise a further set of questions relating to why people with ASD are more likely to opt for local or element-based patterns of processing than are people without ASD. We have already mentioned the possibility that task factors that cue a global strategy might be important, but researchers have also investigated other possibilities. The most researched of these is the notion that when an individual is presented with a complex stimulus array, attention becomes directed to one or more of the components of that stimulus. It can be argued that in order to process configural aspects of complex stimuli, attention not only has to be focused on the components making up the configuration, but also has to be disengaged from one component and re-directed at another as well as at a more global, configurational level. This conceptualisation of what is involved in processing complex stimuli implicates a range of attentional processes, impairment in any one of which might result in atypical performance on the kinds of tasks described in this chapter.

6 Attention and Perception

We saw in the last chapter that it is likely that individuals with ASD are aware of and can respond to aspects of their environment that are characterised by configurations of elements. Where they experience difficulty, however, seems to be in their ability to manage shifts of attention from the global form of a complex situation to its component elements. This invocation of attention as an explanation of difficulties in global processing prompts a closer consideration of attentional processes in individuals with ASD. Atypical attentional processes themselves have to be explained, and one major potential determinant of the deployment of attention is perception, which is the set of processes that organises individuals' sensory encounters with their environment and fundamentally structures the way they engage with the world. The relation between perception, attention and adaptive function should not, however, be thought of as a simple, linear process. As we have seen in the last chapter, some aspects of perception are modulated by existing knowledge through the operation of top-down processing, both of which have consequences for adaptive action, which in turn may affect perception. Thus, we continue to move away from accounts of ASD that posit damage to components in linear chains of processes to the reciprocally operating knock-on effects of disruption of elements of a system that in turn depend on and contribute to a larger, complex network of events.

ATTENTION

The experimental study of attention is situated firmly within the information-processing tradition in psychology, and takes as its starting point that successful adaptation to the environment involves selection of appropriate input from the range of stimulation that an organism experiences at any one time. The concept of attention encompasses a wide range of interrelated processes that serve to achieve this input reduction and the resultant behavioural or psychological directedness. Exactly how the component processes of attention are conceptualised varies across investigators, although there is considerable overlap among the constructs used. Burack, Enns, Stauder, Mottron and Randolph (1997) mention orienting, gazing, filtering, searching and expecting, all of which can occur in different sense modalities, and can either be focused or divided. Allen and Courchesne (2001) consider attentional phenomena under the headings of selective, sustained, distribution, shifting and rapid shifting. Authors such as Posner (1988) divide attentional processes into those relating to arousal, vigilance and sustained attention, those that select material in a more or less automatic fashion and those that involve frontal brain processes and resemble the executive functions discussed in Chapter 4. This last subdivision mirrors that between exogenous attentional phenomena, which are automatically triggered by external events, such as redirecting one's gaze in response to some event on the periphery of the field of vision, and endogenous processes, which are those that result from more controlled processing, such as shifting one's gaze in response to the direction cue provided by an arrow. The ability to maintain attentional focus but yet to shift it appropriately in response to changing environmental demands is an important factor in the development of adaptive behaviour and merits consideration in trying to understand the specific ways people with ASD relate to their environment.

Descriptions of the behavioural profiles of people with ASD are replete with examples of abnormalities in the way in which they direct their attention towards aspects of their surroundings. They are often described as being over-focused on certain tasks, with a resultant tendency not to notice other things going on around them. In the social sphere, this can manifest itself in the kinds of difficulties in joint attention that we have discussed in Chapters 1 and 2 in which young children with ASD less often use cues from other people to direct their own attention and are less likely to direct another's attention to objects and events they themselves are interested in. It is this directedness of an individual's own awareness towards a particular aspect of the environment that is the hallmark of attention, at least in its everyday sense. Experimental research on attention takes a more all-encompassing view and such research in individuals with ASD has been carried out into virtually all of the putative component processes described above. It has also attempted to use behavioural attentional phenomena as markers of brain involvement. For reasons of space, and in an attempt to provide more focus, the discussion here will cover examples of behavioural attentional research that relate to the most prominent features of the symptomatology of ASD, namely repetitive behaviours, poor generalisation of learning and social impairments. These characteristics are seen right across the autism spectrum and involve sustained attention and filtering out of extraneous stimuli as well as the switching of attention from one aspect of the environment to another. The issues raised by a consideration of these areas of investigation can be generalised to other areas of attentional research.

AROUSAL AND SUSTAINED ATTENTION

Early attempts to explain the behavioural profile seen in children with Kanner-type autism centred on disturbances in the modulation of arousal (Dawson &

Lewy, 1989; Hutt, Hutt, Lee & Ounsted, 1964; Ornitz & Ritvo, 1968); however, the results of these studies proved inconclusive. For example, Ornitz (1969) argued that children with ASD did not filter incoming information efficiently, with a resultant increase in arousal. This had the behavioural consequence of children trying to shut out external stimulation in order to bring down arousal levels. By contrast, Rimland (1964) argued that ASD was the result of lowered arousal. But as both Burack et al. (1997) and Goldstein, Johnson & Minshew (2001) have observed, the study of arousal has been abandoned by autism researchers in favour of the investigation of more precisely formulated components of the attentional process.

In the context of the behavioural characteristics of ASD, an important component is sustained attention – the capacity to maintain attentional focus on a task over an extended period of time – and among the most frequently used tasks used to measure sustained attention are continuous performance tests (CPT, see Rosvold, Mirsky, Sarason, Bransome et al., 1956). Such tasks typically ask participants to monitor a sequence of visually or auditorily presented stimuli (letters or words) and to press a key either every time the letter P appeared, or only when the letter X appeared after the letter B. Early studies of children with Kanner-type ASD failed to find any impairment on CPT performance. For example, Casey, Gordon, Mannheim and Rumsey (1993) found no difference between a group of high-functioning adult savant calendrical calculators with ASD and a typical comparison group. However, the groups were not matched on IQ and the comparison groups were performing at ceiling, thus raising the possibility that had the task been harder or had the groups been better matched, differences might have been observed. When different versions of the CPT that varied rate of presentation of the stimuli and the kind of rewards given (social vs non-social) were administered to groups of children with ASD and comparison groups matched on verbal and non-verbal mental age, Garretson, Fein and Waterhouse (1990) observed no group differences on CPT performance. These investigators did find, however, that the children with ASD performed worse under the social reward condition, suggesting that motivational factors may play a part in studies of attentional performance. Similarly unimpaired performance on a CPT and a digit cancellation task was reported by Pascualvaca, Fantie, Papageorgiou and Mirsky (1998).

FOCUSING, FILTERING AND SELECTION

In his clinical account of children with ASD, Kanner (1943) remarked on how one of his cases appeared to be overfocused on what he was doing to the extent that it was difficult to disengage his attention in order to get him to do anything else. Such behaviour suggests a number of dysfunctional processes. It may signal a tendency to overselect aspects of the environment on which to focus, or a tendency to filter out too much extraneous noise; or there may be a difficulty in disengaging from one stimulus and switching to another. The theme of overselective attention formed the basis of some of the earliest experimental investigations of attention in children with ASD. Lovaas, Schreibman, Koegel and Rehm (1971) demonstrated that when children with ASD and intellectual disability were trained to respond to a complex stimulus made up of auditory, visual and tactile components, they often tended also to respond when single elements of the complex configuration were presented. This pattern of responding contrasted with that of comparison children with and without retardation, who did not respond to the same extent to partial configurations. Such observations led Lovaas et al. to conclude that children with ASD show 'stimulus overselectivity' due to an overfocusing of attention on a restricted range of stimulus elements (see Lovaas, Koegel & Schreibman, 1979), However, other studies have indicated that overselective responding to complex stimuli is not specific to ASD (e.g. Litrownik, McInnis, Wetzel-Pritchard & Filipelli, 1978; Schover & Newsom, 1976), prompting Burack et al. (1997) to conclude that when proper care is taken to match on developmental level, such overselectivity appears to be more a function of low mental age than of ASD. Moreover, the work of Lovaas and colleagues confounds selectivity of attention with difficulties in integrating input from various sensory modalities.

Despite the considerable caveats that apply to the early work on overselective responding in ASD, the notion that such individuals are overselective persists, although much of the subsequent research has, in fact, explored focusing of attention within a single sensory modality. For example, Courchesne and colleagues (Townsend & Courchesne, 1994; Townsend, Courchesne & Egaas, 1996) found that participants with ASD showed a greater reduction in reaction time when responding to a stimulus that was presented at a location to which they were currently attending than one that appeared elsewhere – they showed a steeper gradient of attention – thus justifying, according to these authors, that they show overfocused attention. Mann and Walker (2003) take issue with this view. Starting from the findings on the processing of hierarchical stimuli and impossible figures by individuals with ASD (see Chapter 5), they argue that the findings of these studies are consistent with a difficulty in broadening a focus of attention that has been fixed by a prior stimulus configuration. Switching to the global form of a Navon-type stimulus (see Figure 5.7) after attending to the local elements requires a broadening of the attentional focus, which Mann and Walker argue poses problems for individuals with ASD. They tested their hypothesis by asking children with ASD and comparison participants with and without intellectual disability to judge sequences of large and small cross-hair stimuli. Cross-hairs consisted of a long and a short line, either of which could be the vertical or the horizontal component. On the presentation of each cross-hair, participants had to press a button to indicate which line (vertical or horizontal) was the longer one. The results showed that for the children with ASD only, accuracy rates declined and response times increased when a large cross-hair followed a small one, but not in any of the other conditions (large–small, small–small, large–large), which is consistent with the hypothesised difficulty in broadening (but not narrowing) and existing focus of attention.

Related to the issue of focusing of attention is the capacity to filter out extraneous material. Burack (1994) assessed the ability of children with ASD and intellectual disability to filter out extraneous stimuli in an attention task. Participants had to identify which of two target stimuli were presented at the centre of a screen in the presence of zero, two or four distractors that were located near to or far from the target. On some trials, a rectangular window was superimposed on the screen. Targets and near distractors lay inside the window; far distractors lay outside it. The children with ASD were found to benefit most from the presence of a window and were most hampered by distractor stimuli, even when these were located far from the target stimulus. Burack (1994) concludes from these findings that, far from being attentionally overfocused, children with ASD had an inefficient 'attentional lens' that could not efficiently narrow its focus in the presence of distractor stimuli. However, in a study exploring the effects on reflexive orienting of the presence of distractors, Iarocci and Burack (2004) found no difference in ability to filter distractors between children with ASD and comparison intellectually disabled children matched on mental age. They argue that the discrepancy with the findings of Burack (1994) may have resulted from the different levels of perceptual similarity between targets and distractors in the two studies, or to the absence of the attentional lens manipulation in their own study (they did not manipulate the distance of the distractors, nor did they use a window manipulation). It is clear that, given these contradictory findings, more research needs to be carried out into how different types of distractor affect the performance of people with ASD, as well as on how manipulations that direct the focus of attention (such as the window manipulation used by Burack, 1994) operate in individuals with and without ASD. Burack's (1994) finding that children with ASD were less affected by distant distractors in the absence of a window is consistent with Mann and Walker's (2003) findings on poor broadening of the focus of attention in ASD. Indeed it may be the case that the inclusion of the window in their study may have focused the attention of the children with ASD in a manner that made it hard for them to 'zoom out' to attend to the distant distractors. What is needed is a study that combines the methods of Burack (1994) and Mann and Walker (2003) in a way that allows the effects of the presence or absence of a frame and the temporal ordering of zoom-in and zoom-out trials to be manipulated systematically. Such a study would allow us to evaluate the separate and combined effects of distraction and zooming in and out on overall attentional efficiency.

ORIENTING, ENGAGEMENT, DISENGAGEMENT AND SWITCHING

Impaired joint attention or the ability to use the directedness of the behaviour of others as a guide to which aspects of the environment to attend to, as well as the capacity to use one's own behavioural directedness to affect that of others, is a hallmark of the developmental trajectory of individuals on the autism spectrum. In addition to the investigations that have described these phenomena (see Chapter 3), a number of laboratory studies have demonstrated that children with ASD develop the ability to use a meaningful cue to shift attention later than typical children. It may also be the case that they have particular difficulty in using social stimuli such as eye gaze and face direction as cues, although the restriction to social stimuli has not been conclusively established (see Leekam, Hunnisett & Moore, 1998; Leekam, Lopez & Moore, 2000; Leekam & Moore, 2001). Cues to look at an object to the left or the right of the child were provided by the experimenter sitting opposite the child and looking to the left or right, where there was either no object, or an object that remained invisible on some trials or became visible when either the adult or both the adult and child looked at it. The results of these studies showed that children with ASD and developmental disability were delayed in gaining a grasp of another person's gaze direction as a cue to the location of an object. This delay was not found in non-developmentally delayed children with ASD or in children with developmental delay but not ASD. A similar deficit was found when the experimenter was replaced by a non-social directional cue (a 'Thomas the Tank Engine'). Leekam and her colleagues argued that this difficulty with gaze following could result from factors such as difficulties in switching attention from one object to another or to disengaging attention from one object and switching it to another.

Disengagement and shifting of attention in individuals with ASD is a topic that has received considerable research attention. A major paradigm employed to explore the ability to redirect attention from one stimulus to another in response to a variety of cues is that developed by Posner (1980), illustrated in Figure 6.1. Participants are asked to fixate a central point on a

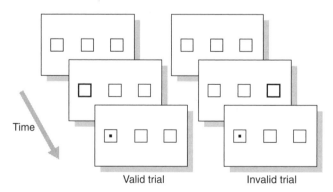

Figure 6.1. Posner Task used in studies of attention. Reproduced from H. Pashler (ed.) (1998). *Attention*, Figure 5.6, p. 211, Hove: Psychology Press, by kind permission of Taylor & Francis.

screen. Once they have fixated, a cue is presented for a fixed period of time and after another delay (short delays are typically 200 ms; long delays are typically 1000 ms), a target is presented on either the right or the left of the screen. Cues can either validly, invalidly or neutrally cue the location of the target and can be either symbolic (an arrow pointing to the right or left of the screen or a line equivalent to the arrow shaft without the head) or non-symbolic (a flash of light to the right, left or in the centre of the screen). In some versions of the task – the 'gap' version – the offset of the cue precedes the onset of the target; in others – 'overlap' versions – the cue stays on when the target is presented. Distractor stimuli can also be presented along with target stimuli. Simpler versions of the task use no cue and just present a fixation stimulus followed by a target presented to one side or the other. In all versions, the experimenter looks for a behavioural index of the participant's awareness of the side of the screen on which the target appeared. This indication is achieved by a number of means; it can be done by getting participants to press appropriate response buttons as quickly as possible, or by measuring the time it takes to shift gaze from one stimulus to another.

Wainwright and Bryson (1996) employed a task in which participants fixated a central asterisk on a screen. Once fixation was established, the asterisk disappeared and a target stimulus was presented to the left, in the centre or to the right of the fixation point. They found that a group of adults with ASD showed faster orientation to central than to lateralised stimuli by comparison with groups matched on verbal mental age and chronological age. Wainwright-Sharp and Bryson (1993) tested a group of high-functioning adolescents and adults with ASD using a cueing task in which a central arrow (symbolic cue) either validly, invalidly or neutrally cued a target location with either brief (100 ms) or extended (800 ms) cue–target delays. They found that the validity effect (the reduction in response time to identify a target consequent on a prior valid cue) was diminished in the ASD group under the brief delay but was similar to that of the comparison group under the longer delay. Using non-symbolic, peripheral flash cues (50 ms flashes to the left or right of the visual field), Townsend, Courchesne and Egaas (1996) found that adults with ASD showed slower orientation but improved performance if the delay between the cue and the target was increased to 1200 ms. The general interpretation of these and other studies (see Allen & Courchesne, 2001; Iarocci & Burack, 2004; Minshew, Johnson & Luna, 2001) is that reflexive or exogenous attentional processes are intact but that controlled or endogenous processes are impaired in individuals from across the autism spectrum. Thus if there is a brief external cue and its location is congruent with that of the target, then individuals with ASD perform similarly to comparison participants. But if the cue requires processing (i.e. is symbolic, such as an arrow) and forms the basis of a decision as to where attention should be directed, then people with ASD experience difficulties. However, as van der Geest, Kemner, Camfferman et al. (2002a) point out, there are a number of possible confounding factors that might have affected performance in the kinds of tasks employed in the studies just described.

The process of redirecting attention in response to a symbolic cue in a Posner Task can be thought of as involving several components. The cue must be recognised and interpreted, attention must be disengaged from the central fixation point, shifted to a new point and then re-engaged at that point. Difficulties on the task may result from impairments of one or more of these different points and numerous studies have attempted to determine where in this chain of events people with ASD experience difficulty. Van der Geest et al. (2002a) used a gap–overlap paradigm to explore attention shifting in children with ASD and to overcome some of the confounding factors outlined earlier. In the gap–overlap task, participants had to fixate a central stimulus. After a short interval (about 1 s) another stimulus was presented for about 800 ms either to the left or to the right of the fixation point. In the gap condition, the fixation point disappeared about 200 ms before the onset of the lateral stimulus. In the overlap condition, it remained on the screen throughout the presentation of the lateral stimulus. The rationale behind the task is that in the gap condition, attention is disengaged from the fixation stimulus, thus facilitating a shift of attention to the lateral stimulus. The time taken for the participant to shift eye gaze (to make a saccade) is measured under both conditions, and the difference in saccade latency between the overlap and the gap conditions is taken as an index of ability to disengage attention. On the basis of clinical observation and the literature on executive functions (see Chapter 4) that show disengagement difficulties in ASD, it can be hypothesised that individuals with ASD would show a greater gap–overlap latency difference than comparison participants. By contrast, if individuals with ASD are less attentionally engaged, then their latency difference should be diminished. Van der Geest et al. (2002a) found a smaller gap–overlap difference in a group of high-functioning children with ASD compared to age- and IQ-matched typical children on a gap–overlap task and concluded that the ASD group had a lower level of attentional engagement. Similar findings are reported for the gap–overlap task by Kawakubo, Maekawa, Itoh et al. (2004) who tested a small group of adults with PDD, but the findings of their study are somewhat marred by small sample size and low power.

The relative contributions of disengagement and shifting to performance on attention tasks was further investigated by Landry and Bryson (2004). They used an apparatus consisting of three computer monitors, one placed in front of the child and one each to the child's right and left. Stimuli were first presented on the central monitor, and when the child fixated that stimulus, a second stimulus was presented on one or other of the two side monitors. On some trials, the central stimulus remained on the screen when the second one was presented (disengage trials); on others the fixation stimulus was switched off 250 ms before the onset of the second stimulus (shift trials). The dependent measure was the time taken for children to shift gaze from the central to the side monitor. They found that for 5 year old children with ASD, verbal mental age-matched typically developing children and children with Down syndrome, all groups took longer to shift gaze in the disengage trials than in the switch trials, but that this difference was much greater for the children with ASD. Landry and Bryson conclude from these findings that children with ASD have a particular difficulty in disengaging attention but not in shifting or switching their attention to another stimulus. They note that this finding contrasts with those of earlier studies (Townsend & Courchesne, 1994; Townsend, Courchesne & Egaas, 1996) who found that under half of their adult participants with ASD had problems disengaging. But as Landry and Bryson observe, the samples in those studies were much older than the participants tested in their own investigation, and measures of covert attention (where participants press buttons corresponding to where the target item occurred) rather than overt measures were taken. But it is also striking that Landry and Bryson's findings also go against those of the two gap–overlap studies described earlier. Those two studies reported *less* engagement with the fixated stimulus on the part of participants with ASD, whereas Landry and Bryson report what they term 'sticky' or 'obligatory' attention, i.e. that their children with ASD found it especially hard to disengage from the fixated stimulus.

Several procedural and methodological differences between these studies might explain their contrasting findings. Van der Geest et al. and Kawakubo et al. tested older children and adults, whereas Landry and Bryson tested 5 year old children. As the last authors point out, the kind of disengagement that they report as deficient in their ASD sample typically develops at about the age of 4 months, which means that the children in their ASD sample were markedly delayed. Nevertheless, it remains possible that they might eventually develop the capacity to disengage, but at such a late stage that it compromises their developmental trajectory. In relation to the point on covert versus overt switching made in the previous paragraph, it is worth noting that both van der Geest et al. and Kawakubo et al. used a covert orienting procedure. But it is possible that the processes that mediate shifting gaze from one part of a single screen to another (as in those two studies) may be different from switching gaze from one screen to another as in Landry and Bryson's study. It may also be the case that the children in Landry and Bryson's study were experiencing difficulties in controlling their gaze switch – i.e. with so-called endogenous control over attention. This does not rule out the possibility that they may still have been able to direct their attention covertly or in response to the exogenous stimulus on the target screen. In this regard it is worth noting the work of Minshew, Luna and Sweeney (1999) who found that adults with Asperger's syndrome continued to show difficulties with slower, controlled attention-switching even though their more reflexive processes were intact.

A final and compelling reason why Landry and Bryson may have obtained different findings relates to the stimuli they used. Whereas van der Geest et al. and Kawakubo et al. both used static, geometric stimuli – white crosses for fixation and white squares for targets stimuli – Landry and Bryson used an animated stimulus of cascading geometric shapes that filled up the screen. This was presumably because young children would not be particularly motivated to engage with the simpler stimuli used in the other studies. Yet it is precisely the attention-grabbing aspects of the animated stimuli that may have rendered them attentionally 'sticky'. But even if this were the case, the phenomenon remains that children with ASD find it harder than typical children or children with Down syndrome to disengage from this type of stimulus, an observation that might help to explain why individuals with ASD often appear to be overfocused on particular aspects of their environment. The question of the naturalistic nature of the stimuli used in attention research is also relevant to the kinds of symbolic cues to target location employed in Posner-type tasks. In most of the studies described here, arrow cues were used, raising the question of whether any impairments reported were the result of difficulties with attention or difficulties in understanding the symbolic function of arrows. There is also the question of ecological validity. Just because someone shows unimpaired attention on tasks employing arrows, crosses and circles does not necessarily mean that such individuals will not have attention-related difficulties in the real world. The discrepancy between the findings of Landry and Bryson (2004) and other studies illustrates this point nicely.

ATTENTION TO GAZE AND TO FACES

One of the most important environmental stimuli that prompt us to shift our attention is the eye gaze of another person. We have already seen at several points in this book how eyes, faces and their directedness are a major issue in research into ASD and that people from all parts of the autism spectrum have particular ways of processing this kind of information. In Chapter 2 we saw how very young children with ASD engage less often in joint-attention behaviours and are less likely to monitor the gaze of another person. In Chapter 2, we saw how older children with ASD are less likely to make use of the gaze of another person in order to direct their attention to an object that that person is talking about. And in the next chapter, we will see how people with ASD have particular ways of looking at faces, tending to concentrate on the lower region of the face. Several investigators have used these observations as the basis of studies of attention shifting. We have already mentioned the work of Leekam, Moore and colleagues (see Leekam & Moore, 2001 for a summary), which reports delayed development of gaze following in children with ASD and developmental delay. This happens even in cases where the adult facing the child looks to the right or the left in the absence of objects in these locations. The same difficulty does not appear to emerge when, instead of an adult, the child sits in front of a box from which a toy train engine emerges. A gap–overlap manipulation was also included in which the central train remained in place or was returned to its box shortly before another train appeared either to the right or the left of the child's visual field. Contrary to some of the work described above, Leekam et al. (2000) did not find any evidence of difficulty in shifting or disengaging attention in their children with ASD, whether with or without developmental delay. Leekam and Moore (2001) highlight two reasons for these discrepant findings. First, the problem may not be with disengagement *per se*, but with prediction of the location of an object from the state of a cue, and second, the differentiation between exogenous (or reflexive) and endogenous (or controlled) attention may not be as clear cut in the case of gaze following, since orienting in response to a gaze in the absence of a peripheral object requires an awareness of the informational content of the face and its orientation, an awareness that is not required in order to respond to the presentation of an object at the periphery in the absence of a central signal. A third possible reason for the discrepancy is that the children in Leekam et al.'s (2000) gap–overlap experiment had just previously taken part in another attention cueing experiment. This additional experience may have served to improve their performance. In relation to their own explanations, Leekam and Moore report findings that children with ASD were less responsive to an experimenter's bids for attention, a tendency that correlated with difficulty in gaze-following leading them to conclude that despite relatively good exogenous orienting to non-social stimuli, children with ASD have difficulty in reflexively orienting to the overtures of another person, thus suggesting '. . . that some very basic dyadic problems could underlie the triadic interaction difficulty between child, other and object in joint attention' (Leekam & Moore, 2001, p. 124).

More recent research on attentional cueing by faces does not always support Leekam and Moore's conclusion. For example, Swettenham, Condie, Campbell et al. (2003) tested high-functioning children with ASD and typical children matched on a non-verbal test with a Posner-type paradigm using pictures of faces gazing to the left or the right as cues to the target location. Participants were told to ignore the face when responding. Yet both groups showed a validity effect, that is, they shifted their gaze more quickly to the target on trials where the gaze of the face was in the direction of the target. In a second experiment, this effect was again demonstrated when inverted faces were used as cues. Similar findings to those of Swettenham et al. were also reported by Kylliäinen and Hietanen (2004). At first sight these findings suggest that the gaze-following and joint attention deficits seen in children with ASD do not stem from a basic attentional difficulty with the signalling function of the eyes. But as Swettenham et al. point out, their participants were 10 years old, and their intact performance may therefore have been the consequence of delayed development. It is also worth noting that the stimuli used in their study were simple crosses and asterisks. In real life, children have to shift and redirect attention to more complex (and often more interesting to them) stimulus configurations. The Swettenham et al. study merits replication with fixation and target stimuli similar to those employed in the study by Landry and Bryson (2004) described above.

Despite contradictory findings, there appears to be an emerging consensus that individuals from all parts of the autism spectrum do have some atypical performance on tests that are thought to measure components of the attentional process. Sustained attention seems to be intact, but there may be difficulties with switching and disengagement, especially when these require more controlled processes such as voluntary switching and zooming out rather than reflexive processes such as orienting to an extraneous cue. But even controlled switching of attention in response to naturalistic cues such as eye gaze eventually seems to develop to levels comparable to those of mental-age-matched typical individuals. Given the importance of attention switching in the unfolding of a typical developmental trajectory, it seems reasonable to speculate that such a delay severely compromises psychosocial development in ASD. This hypothesis can only be tested by longitudinal investigations. Findings that are inconsistent with this picture often come from studies in which issues relating the level of cognitive functioning of the participants to their developmental level may not have been adequately addressed (see Burack et al. 1997). As has been mentioned several times in this book, the issue of the interaction between global cognitive impairment and ASD is one that merits a more systematic research strategy such as that represented by the work of Leekam and Moore described above. Such work emphasises the importance of a developmental approach, the importance of which is corroborated by the small sample of studies covered in earlier paragraphs, which have shown some evidence of delay in the development of attentional processes in individuals with ASD.

A potentially worrying aspect of some of the findings on attention in ASD is the fact that small changes in procedures or stimuli often dramatically affect the conclusions we can draw. This fact should alert us to the possibility that a concept such as attention, despite its considerable intuitive face validity, was developed in the context of typical development and might not transfer easily to an atypical population. The concept of attention assumes that there is an organism that somehow directs its awareness towards particular aspects of its environment and that this directedness is a function of automatic and controlled processes. This formulation conceals a wealth of complexity that can sometimes be obscured by the invocation of a single overarching explanatory concept. The apparently simple notion of 'aspects of its environment' referred to in the last but one sentence must take into account the fact that these aspects are to some extent defined by the structure of the organism and that atypical populations may well define their environment in ways that are sufficiently different from the typical case as to compromise the emergence of higher-level properties such as attention that can prove quite powerful explanations of typical behaviour but can be found wanting in the atypical case.

Moreover, we also need to be wary of the trap, identified by Bowler (2001) in the context of research into theory of mind, of overidentifying explanatory constructs with the tasks used to operationalise them. In fact, although these arguments should be kept in mind in the context of attention research, many of the studies cited above (see for example Landry & Bryson, 2004) do show an awareness that using a term like 'attentional impairment' as an explanatory construct can and should be broken down into components such as engagement and disengagement. Yet even these processes and their operationalisation need to be handled carefully and due consideration given to considering impairment at other levels of functioning.

ACCOUNTING FOR ATTENTIONAL DIFFICULTIES

It is clear from the research on the processing of complex, hierarchical stimuli discussed in Chapter 5, as well as from investigations of attention, that individuals with ASD have a tendency to manage the way they process complex stimuli differently from typical individuals. In certain circumstances this can result in their responding to details that, in similar circumstances, are overlooked by typical individuals. Why this should come about seems to be a function of difficulties in disengaging attention, in zooming out from a focus on detail to one on the bigger picture, all in the context of the individual's prior knowledge operating in a top-down manner. This atypical pattern of processing is iterative in that it results in a knowledge base that may differ from the typical case and which in turn affects future processing because of the effects on behaviour, through the operation of top-down processing, of the atypical knowledge base. Among other things, this atypical knowledge base will affect the way in which the more controlled attentional processes that are known to be impaired in ASD are deployed.

From the standpoint of an individual's development over time, this analysis suggests that the starting point for the emergence of atypical attentional processes may lie in the way perceptual systems initially handle incoming information. This account prompts us to revisit the question of perception, particularly at the very earliest stages of the perceptual process.

LOW-LEVEL PERCEPTION IN ASD

Much of the material covered in Chapter 5 dealt with aspects of perception – the ability of the brain or the mind to organise incoming sensory information and to make sense of that incoming information by processing it in the context of prior knowledge through the operation of top-down processing. We have seen that individuals with ASD are less likely to organise information according to gestalt laws and are less likely to use prior knowledge to modulate the perceptual organisation of incoming sensory information. In this chapter, we have seen that the way in which attentional processes are managed is different in ASD, and it is plausible to speculate that this difference results from altered perceptual or sensory processing.

Sensation and perception are very closely linked aspects of the way organisms deal with incoming information; sensation dealing with the detection of input from the environment and perception structuring it in ways that are determined both by the way the brain and sensory systems are organised and in the context of prior experience. Different forms of energy (vision, sound, motion) from the environment are detected by specialised receptors (retina, cochlea, touch receptors in the skin) and are transformed into nerve impulses that are fed into the brain for further processing. The brain then interprets and organises this information in the context of stored representations of past experiences and plans the actions of the organism accordingly. This complex system is not a one-way street in which sensed information drives action, but rather a complex network of feedback and feedforward systems in which behavioural outcome is a function of the structure of the sense organs (for example, humans cannot see ultraviolet light, whereas bees can), the individual's past experience and the capacity of the central nervous system to plan and organise action in an informational context. Atypical action patterns may result from any part of the system functioning differently, although different functioning of parts of the system may be compensated for, resulting in typical actions or behaviour flowing from a different operation of the system. In the last chapter and the first part of this chapter, we have seen that individuals with ASD sometimes process complex perceptual stimuli and manage the strategic deployment of attention differently from the way typical individuals execute such processes. It is difficult to establish the causes for these differences. They may lie in damage to the substrates of top-down processing or of attention. Or, alternatively, in damage to the systems that are responsible for perceptual organisation of incoming sensory material, or to sensory processes themselves. Subtle differences in the way sensory processes operate can have considerable knock-on effects in terms of how information is organised, stored and used to direct actions (including attentional processes) that modulate the development of adaptive action patterns.

Early clinical descriptions of ASD remarked on behaviours that suggested abnormal or atypical processing of sensory stimuli. Lockyer and Rutter (1969) observed that children with ASD were often thought to be deaf, and writers from Hermelin and O'Connor (1970) to Rosenhall, Nordin, Sandström et al. (1999) have reported abnormalities of auditory perception. First-hand reports by individuals with ASD describe difficulties in the way they experience the world at the level of sensation and perception. Authors such as Temple Grandin (Grandin & Scariano, 1986) and Donna Williams (Williams, 1994; 1996) report abnormal sensory experiences such as being deluged with sound, having blurred or distorted vision, or experiencing unpleasantly strong sensations of smell. Such authors also recount the way in which such sensory experiences can also be a source of pleasure, such as becoming fascinated and absorbed by the sensory experience of a spinning object or the repetitive tapping of a surface. However, in a review of sensory-perceptual abnormalities in ASD, O'Neill and Jones (1997) argue for a sceptical attitude to these first-hand accounts. They generally come from a small number of authors, and the accounts are frequently co-authored. Also, it is not possible to establish the extent to which the informants in these accounts have been made aware of existing theories of ASD (e.g. that of Ornitz, 1969; Ornitz & Ritvo, 1968) that emphasise a role for abnormal sensory processing. More controlled observations have, however, provided some corroborating evidence for the first-hand accounts, with several experimental studies showing differences in the way individuals with ASD process sensory information in different sensory modalities.

AUDITORY PERCEPTION

Experimental investigations of sensory and sensory-perceptual processing in ASD have confirmed and extended the first-hand reports of atypical sensory processing. For example, studies have shown that individuals with ASD are more likely than comparison individuals to have absolute pitch, that is to identify musical notes in terms of the frequency of the sound vibrations rather than in terms of their musical relations to other tones in a sequence. Although some of these studies (Miller, 1999; Mottron, Peretz, Belleville & Rouleau, 1999c) have involved participants with savant syndrome – isolated abilities out of line with their general level of cognitive functioning – some have demonstrated exceptional pitch processing in non-savant individuals with ASD (Heaton, Hermelin & Pring, 1998; Heaton, 2003; Bonnel, Mottron, Peretz et al., 2003). Heaton (2003) taught high-functioning children with ASD and typical comparison children to associate particular tones (pitches) to particular animals and later asked them which animal corresponded to a given tone. Superior performance was found for the children with ASD on this and another task where the child had to identify the animal whose associated note was missing from a chord made up of the notes trained in the first experiment. Again, the children with ASD showed superior performance. In a third experiment, children with and without ASD had to listen to chords followed by sequences of notes some of which were contained in the chord and some not. Children had to identify whether or not each note had been present in the chord. On this task, children with ASD showed no significant advantage over comparison children. Heaton concludes from this finding that superior pitch processing only occurs in tasks that require pitch memory, as in her first two experiments. When no memory is required, then chords are perceived holistically in a manner similar to that seen in typical individuals. Heaton's analysis hinges on whether or not the experimental procedure involved using the tones as labels for objects (each tone corresponded to an animal in the first two experiments), and thus had retrieval cues. She argues that since such labels were available to both groups of participants in these experiments, the better performance of the children with ASD must be due to more stable pitch representations. This argument is consistent with the conjecture that pitch perception is different in this group.

In order to test more directly the proposition that the auditory trace of a given musical note might be different in individuals with ASD, Bonnel et al. (2003) used a signal detection procedure to test the ability of adolescents with high-functioning ASD (HFA) and a typical comparison group to judge whether pairs of sequentially presented tones were the same or different in pitch. The HFA group showed higher sensitivity to pitch difference than did the comparison group. In a subsequent classification task, participants were asked to classify tones as high or low with reference to a standard low reference tone and high reference tones that were 3%, 2% or 1% higher in frequency. The classification skills of the ASD participants were observed to be better than those of the comparison group. Moreover, whereas the classification performance of the typical group was worse than their discrimination performance, this was not the case for the ASD participants. Bonnel et al. argue that this last finding is consistent with the view that whereas the comparison participants used a pitch comparison in context strategy to make classification judgments, the ASD group relied more on the absolute values of the tone pitches. Taken together, the findings of these studies suggest that the processing of pure tones is different in individuals with ASD, and although the studies rely on behavioural measures, which could be argued to tap later processing rather than pure sensation, they are suggestive of abnormal early sensory-perceptual processing of auditory stimuli.

One of the most important auditory stimuli for the development of adaptive functioning in humans is speech, and it is well established that some (although by no means all) individuals with ASD experience difficulties in the development of expressive speech and of speech understanding. An early behavioural study of 5 year old children with ASD by Klin (1991) found that they were less likely than matched children without ASD to pick up loudspeakers that played their mother's voice at low volume, preferring instead to listen to equally complex nonsense sounds. This lack of preference for speech sounds may be a consequence of the kinds of social impairment discussed in Chapters 1 and 2, or it may result from a primary deficit in the auditory processing of complex sounds. Another way to determine abnormalities of sound perception is to use functional brain imaging techniques to test for differences in the way the brain responds to auditory stimuli. Whereas about 95% of the typical population processes speech and language on the left side of the brain, this figure is much lower in individuals with ASD (Dawson, Finley, Phillips & Galpert, 1986; Prior & Bradshaw, 1979). In addition to finding right-hemisphere dominance in response to verbal auditory material, Muller, Behen, Rothermel et al. (1999), using positron emission tomography (PET) scanning, reported reduced activation of the auditory cortex when listening to non-speech sounds in a group of high-functioning individuals with ASD.

More recently, a series of investigations by Belin, Boddaert, Zilbovicius and colleagues (Boddaert, Belin, Chabane et al., 2003; Boddaert, Chabane, Belin et al., 2004; Gervais, Belin, Boddaert et al., 2004) have shown differences in patterns of brain activation to speech between individuals with ASD and matched controls. Adults (Boddaert et al., 2003) and children (Boddaert et al., 2004) with ASD were presented with synthetic speech-like sounds while the blood flow to different regions of the brain was measured using PET scanning. Activation was found in the superior temporal lobe of the temporal cortex (see Figure 8.1) in both adults and children, but the right–left asymmetry of this activation was reversed in the ASD adults and children, with greater activity in the right cortex in these groups. Boddaert and colleagues conclude from these observations that abnormal brain specialisation for speech-like sounds may be responsible for the language and communication deficits seen in this population. In another study, Gervais et al. (2004) observed a failure to activate regions in the superior temporal sulcus of the brains of individuals with ASD in response to speech and speech-like sounds. This region is typically activated by such stimuli. By contrast, the ASD participants showed normal activation of this area to non-speech-like sounds, suggesting that it is the processing of speech that is abnormal in this group.

Most of the studies reviewed so far have tested individuals with ASD and some degree of global cognitive impairment, leading many authors to conclude that failure to process speech may be one of the underlying causes of social impairment in ASD (see Gervais et al., 2004). However, it is possible to argue that the reverse might be the case. Perhaps different strategies for processing visual material might disrupt the perception of faces and render faces aversive and anxiety provoking. Since faces, in the typical ecology of a developing child, are invariably accompanied by voices, voice processing may become disrupted by the aversive consequences of social interaction rather than being the cause of atypical interaction patterns. The fact that Gervais et al. (2004) observed normal activation patterns for non-speech sounds supports this conjecture. However, contrary evidence comes from a study by Bruneau, Bonnet-Brilhault, Gomot et al. (2003) who reported reduced auditory evoked potentials (measures of brain activity recorded by means of scalp electrodes) in response to pure tones in children who had ASD and mental retardation. The patterning of this relation suggested that children who had greater right-hemisphere activation (the reverse of what is typically expected) had less severe symptoms. The authors interpret these findings in terms of a right-hemisphere-oriented reorganisation of brain processing of auditory stimuli in ASD with increased reorganisation resulting in better adaptation. However, their observation of reduced activation to pure tones, although suggestive of a basic impairment in auditory perception, may, as with the findings of Gervais et al. (2004), be a consequence rather than a cause of autistic social impairment.

Although the details of the findings on auditory processing in people with ASD are not entirely clear cut, there is sufficient evidence to suggest that auditory processing in these individuals is atypical, at least in people who have some degree of global cognitive impairment. What is needed are more investigations of higher-functioning individuals as well as developmental studies, in order to determine first the interaction between cognitive impairment, auditory processing and language/communication development and second how these interrelationships evolve over developmental time.

VISION

We have already seen in Chapter 5 that individuals on the autism spectrum were more likely than those without ASD to respond on the basis of the local level of a hierarchically complex stimulus and often to ignore inconsistencies in visual representations of objects. We also saw that they were less likely to use stored information in a top-down manner when making perceptual judgments. All the stimuli used in those studies were static, whereas much of the visual world as experienced in real life is dynamic. Faces in particular are dynamic, moving visual patterns that pose particular difficulties for individuals with ASD (see Chapter 7). If we are to understand the role of perceptual processes in the genesis of autistic symptomatology, we must, therefore, address the question of how dynamic visual stimuli are processed. Moreover, as dynamic visual stimuli comprise a strong temporal component, identification of atypical processing in this domain would inform the question of whether ASD was a disorder of the temporal processing of sensory input in general, rather than a modality-specific set of impairments.

Only a handful of studies have investigated the processing of dynamic visual stimuli in individuals with ASD. Gepner, Mestre, Masson and de Schonen (1995) measured the ability of children with ASD to maintain their posture when looking at a radiating flow field – a visual stimulus that conveys the effect of moving forwards, and often results in the observer shifting posture to counteract the illusory impression of motion. The autistic participants were less affected by the flow field than were matched participants without ASD. Spencer, O'Brien, Riggs et al. (2000) found that children with ASD were unimpaired at detecting static patterns of oriented lines in an array consisting of the pattern lines embedded in an array of randomly oriented lines, but were impaired at detecting the coherent motion of shapes in a field of randomly moving shapes. These investigators concluded that their findings were consistent with an impairment of the dorsal stream, which is a set of brain pathways that processes where objects are located. The unimpaired static pattern perception is argued to reflect an unimpaired ventral stream, which processes object identity. A similar finding was reported by Blake, Turner, Smoski et al. (2003), who reported intact performance on a task requiring perceptual grouping of elements to form a static figure with impaired perception of human activity conveyed by moving points of light on a screen. Children with ASD were also found to have a higher threshold than matched typical children for perceiving coherent motion in patterns of randomly moving dots in which some dots moved in consort (Milne, Swettenham, Hansen et al., 2002). These authors interpreted these findings in terms of dysfunction of the magnocellular system, which forms part of the channels that carry information from the eye to the occipital lobe of the brain, where visual information is further processed. The magnocellular system processes coarse-grained information and movement, and impairment or less efficient processing may cause greater reliance on the parvocellular system, which processes fine detail.

Bertone, Mottron, Jelenic and Faubert (2003) argue that the ability to generate representations of coherent object motion in tasks like that of Spencer et al. may be the result of the integration of patterns of motion at the local level, rather than impairment of the dorsal stream. To test this hypothesis, they assessed the ability of adults with ASD and normal intelligence and matched individuals without ASD to identify the direction of motion conveyed by particular types of visual pattern. Motion in the patterns they used was determined either by luminance variables (first-order motion) or by texture variables (second-order). These types of stimuli were chosen on the basis of psychophysical evidence that shows that the processing of these two classes of stimuli is carried out by different networks in the visual nervous system (see Bertone et al., 2003 for references). Whereas processing of first-order stimuli was unimpaired, the individuals with ASD were worse than comparison participants at identifying second-order stimuli. Bertone et al. interpret this finding as reflecting less efficient integration of second-order visuo-perceptual information by the nervous system of individuals with ASD. This lack of efficiency may have knock-on effects on how the processed information is stored and subsequently used in tasks employing hierarchical stimuli such as those described in Chapter 5. This is precisely the line advocated by Bertone, Mottron, Jelenic and Faubert (2005) who explicitly contrast the position of theorists such as Blake et al. (2003) and Spencer et al. (2000) who, as we have seen, argue that motion-perception deficits are a consequence of dorsal stream dysfunction, and their own position where such deficits are a consequence of lower-level neuro-integrative processing. Bertone et al. argue that the first argument would predict motion-specific deficits regardless of the level of complexity of the motion stimulus, whereas their own position would predict such deficits only where stimuli were complex according to the description given above. Bertone et al. also argue that their own argument also accounts for the bias towards local features seen in the perception by people with ASD of static stimuli described in Chapter 5. To decide between these hypotheses, Bertone et al. (2005) carried out an experiment in which high-functioning individuals with ASD were asked to determine the orientation of gratings that were defined by first-order (simple) or second-order (complex) parameters (see above). The ASD participants were superior to matched controls on the first type of stimulus, but impaired on the second, leading the authors to conclude that the difficulties described for both static and dynamic stimuli can be explained in terms of stimulus complexity, and by extension, the complexity of the neural networks required to process them.

What is clear from the findings on vision and audition just described, as well as from the work of Mottron and colleagues on local and global processing and Plaisted and O'Riordan on discrimination learning described in Chapter 5, is that individuals on the autism spectrum have a range of sensory experiences that are different from those of typical individuals. Although it has not been conclusively established (especially for the case of speech perception) that these impairments are primary rather than secondary to higher-level impairments such as theory of mind or WCC, the case for a primary, low-level perceptual impairment has formed the basis for several speculations. One such account is that of Ceponiené, Lepistö, Shestakova et al. (2003), who suggest that if individuals with ASD find it hard to encode and represent sensory features of complex stimuli, they would be placed at a disadvantage when required to process multifaceted and changing stimulus configurations such as are found in social situations. We can also speculate that impaired sensory/ perceptual processes may be implicated in the attentional difficulties seen in people with ASD. A more elaborately argued account of how altered perceptual functioning fits into a broader explanatory account of autistic symptomatology has been developed by Mottron and Burack (2001) and further developed by Mottron, Dawson, Soulières et al. (2006). These authors argue that the phenomena of WCC and the findings on perceptual processes can be accounted for by the operation of enhanced perceptual functioning, whereby the operation of lower-level perceptual processes persist into later stages in the information processing chain with the result that behavioural outcomes based on functioning at the perceptual level continue to be available on tasks where they are less in evidence for typical individuals. This state of affairs arises because of a hypothetical developmental process in which damage to particular brain areas compromises the early development of higher-level, global processing of information with a resultant functional facilitation (a term Mottron and colleagues borrow from Kapur, 1996) of lower-level systems. Although Mottron and Burack argue that their system does not compromise the development of global processing, there is more work to be done on elucidating the precise nature of the early damage that would cause functional facilitation of low-level processes whilst leaving the development of higher-level processes intact.

CONCLUSION

We started this chapter with the conjecture that the tendency for people with ASD to focus to a greater extent on the parts of complex stimuli than on wholes is at least in part explicable in terms of attention – the set of processes that defines the subset of environmental information an individual uses to guide action. And we have seen that some attentional processes – particularly disengagement and broadening of attentional focus – pose difficulties for people with ASD. We then raised the question of whether attentional processes could be explained by invoking a different level of analysis, namely perception, and showed that a range of perceptual processes operate differently in people with ASD. What has not yet been established is the nature of the causal relation between attention and perception. Indeed, looking for causal relations may be misguided, as attention and perception are processes that mutually influence each other and in turn, exert reciprocal effects on cognition through top-down and bottom-up processing. What is clear is that the relative degree of activity of different pathways of causal influence is different in people with ASD from that of typical individuals. In particular, there appears to be an enhancement of perceptual processing in ASD, which is often but not always at the expense of more conceptual, holistic processing. This shift in the balance of power between processing the whole and processing the parts, between perceptual and conceptual processing, has repercussions for how individuals with ASD deal with the world. In the next chapter, for example, we will see how they sometimes have difficulties remembering incidentally encoded context in memory tasks. Incidental encoding of context contributes to the pheonomena of source and episodic memory and relies on the ability to attend to more than just the material that is immediately relevant to the task in hand. Inherent in the concept of episodic memory – memory for the personally experienced past – is the notion of a self, an 'I' who is the same person that experienced the past and experiences the present. This notion of a self is also inherent in the more controlled aspects of the directedness of attention, which themselves are impaired in people with ASD. However, the invocation – either implicitly or explicitly – of a self that acts as a conscious controller of some attentional processes means that we have to confront the question of the nature of that self and of how it is constituted. These considerations bring us back to the same kinds of questions that were discussed in Chapter 4 about the nature of the 'homunculus' that exerts control over behaviour in executive tasks. And as with executive tasks, we need to address the question of whether an atypical sense of self is the source or the consequence of attentional difficulties in ASD. As with the relation between attention and perception, any attempt to provide a neat chain of cause and effect is probably misguided. It is more likely that increasingly sophisticated levels of conscious and self-conscious awareness emerge over time, each modulating attentional capacities in a manner that contributes to the development of higher levels of awareness (see Zelazo & Frye, 1998).

Apart from potentially playing a role in the development of an atypical sense of self, the consequences of atypical attentional processes can be seen in other psychological functions that have been extensively studied in ASD, three of which – face processing, concept formation and memory – are discussed in the next chapter.

7 Specific Aspects of Understanding: Faces, Concepts and Memory

In moving from Chapter 3 through to this one, we find ourselves on a journey of increasing detail of analysis. Initially, we dealt with broad, well worked-out theories of ASD. We then shifted focus to processes whose theoretical frameworks were developed outside the field of ASD research. In Chapter 5 we saw how an initial theoretical formulation – WCC theory – has given rise to a range of interpretations of why individuals with ASD process information in a more fragmentary way than typical individuals. In that chapter, and also in Chapter 6, we also explored some of the explanations for this apparent fragmentation. We saw that there might be a preference for processing information at a greater degree of detail, which may override, but does not eliminate, any tendency to see the 'bigger picture' of the overall configuration. Such a preference may in turn influence and be influenced by attentional processes with the result that renders adaptation to the environment atypical in this population. To many readers, the material presented in Chapters 5 and 6 may appear rather arcane and far removed from the everyday world of people with ASD and those who interact with them. This is perhaps an inevitable consequence of an approach to science that breaks complex processes down to simpler ones and derives models or analogues of real-life situations that can be studied in a controlled fashion in the laboratory. In this chapter, I hope to illustrate the relevance of some of the earlier material by analysing three domains of functioning – face processing, concept formation and memory – where findings at basic levels such as attention and perception may prove useful in enhancing our understanding of the way individuals with ASD confront the difficulties of everyday life.

FACE PROCESSING

Even if it is not strictly speaking a universal problem in ASD, the notion of avoidance of eye-contact has become part of the ASD folklore and there is certainly some evidence of atypical functioning in this area. O'Connor and Hermelin (1967) observed that people with ASD made briefer and more frequent fixations when inspecting complex visual material, including faces. More recently, the work of, among others, Osterling, Dawson and Munson (2002) has shown that 1 year old infants who were subsequently given a diagnosis of ASD looked less often at the face of another person than did children with mental retardation who did not develop ASD. The ability to process faces is important because faces are complex stimuli, consisting of configurations of elements that can be processed either individually or in terms of their holistic configuration. So an understanding of face processing in terms of the parameters discussed in this chapter would provide an important link between basic psychological processes and social functioning. As we have seen in Chapter 3, faces constitute an important component of bodily expressions of emotion, and an understanding of eye gaze gives important clues to the directedness of an individual's thoughts and actions. Hobson's work has shown that more cognitively impaired individuals have a marked difficulty in matching facial expressions with other indices of emotion, and when facial features are progressively masked off, the attenuation of emotion recognition ability is greater in individuals with ASD than in comparison participants. Although findings like these have been used to bolster accounts of ASD in terms of deficits in the perception of emotions, they also raise the question of whether difficulty in seeing facial expressions of emotion may be a by-product of impaired face processing, which in turn could result from an altered balance of global/local or elemental/configural processing described in the last two chapters. If a child learns about expressions of emotion through an appraisal of facial expressions, then disrupted face perception would compromise this process. If individuals with ASD tackle the processing of complex stimuli differently from typical individuals, the anomalies should be discernible in their processing of faces and should not be limited to the reading of emotion in the face. The work of Hobson and colleagues and the rise of WCC theory has given the study of face processing in ASD a boost in the last decade or so. Some of the more recent research has focused on elucidating those areas of the brain that might be involved in face processing. That research will be dealt with in Chapter 8; this section will focus on behavioural findings in the area.

One of the first systematic investigations of face processing in ASD was that of Langdell (1978). He asked older and younger children with ASD and comparison children with typical development and with intellectual disability to identify photographs of faces of other children from their school. Faces were inverted or had parts masked off (upper or lower half, all except nose or eyes). Whereas the younger children with ASD tended to make fewer errors when only the lower part of faces was shown, this was not true of older children. Moreover, the latter group made fewer errors in identifying inverted faces than did younger children with ASD or children in the comparison groups. This lack of a face inversion effect was also reported by Hobson, Ouston & Lee, 1988b and by Tantam, Monaghan, Nicholson & Stirling, 1989). Hobson et al. asked children with and without ASD to sort upright or inverted faces by either identity or emotion when parts of the face were progressively blanked off. In the inverted condition, the children with ASD significantly outperformed the matched comparison children on both the identity and emotion-sorting task. Tantam et al. asked children with ASD and comparison children matched on non-verbal mental age to pick one of a set of four pictures of upright or inverted faces that differed from the other three on either emotional expression or facial identity. Their results showed that the children with ASD were worse than the comparison children at picking out the odd face, whether on the basis of identity or emotional expression. They also replicated Langdell's (1978) finding of superior recogition of inverted faces.

Other studies have compared face recognition with recognition of other complex, configural stimuli. For example, Boucher and Lewis (1992) compared timed and untimed matching of faces and houses in high- and low-functioning children with ASD. They chose buildings because they argued that these were complex, configural stimuli that compared to faces in that they were familiar to participants, encountered every day and consisted of a global outline made up of a number of canonical details. They report overall impairment in matching of faces, even though the children with ASD were as good as comparison children on a discrimination task. But as Boucher and Lewis observe, the ASD group were faster at discriminating houses than faces, and had the groups been equated on this measure, then the ASD group would probably have shown impaired face discrimination. They also observed that the faster discrimination of houses may have been an artefact of the fact that groups were matched on verbal ability, thus giving a non-verbal (i.e. a visuo-spatial) advantage to the children with ASD.

The general conclusion from these early studies of facial inversion was that individuals with ASD process faces differently from typical individuals. More specifically, the findings suggested that they tended to adopt a feature-based rather than a holistic strategy, the former being less liable to disruption by turning the face upside-down. However, the findings of more recent research have qualified this conclusion considerably, principally because of methodological improvements. Joseph and Tanaka (2003) directly tested the conjectured primacy of a feature-based approach by comparing face recognition in high-functioning children with ASD with that of comparison children matched on IQ and chronological age. Children were shown upright or inverted whole faces or faces that were blanked off to reveal just the eyes, nose and mouth. After each face was presented, the child was shown the original face and the same face with different eyes, nose or mouth, and was asked to identify the original face. The children with ASD showed superior recognition for upright faces only on trials where the mouth had changed. This effect was not found for trials where the eyes had been changed, which was the reverse of the pattern seen in the typical children. Contrary to the findings of earlier studies, these observations suggest that high-functioning children with ASD do engage in holistic face-processing strategies and are subject to the face inversion effect, at least when facial differences centre on the mouth region. Not only does the differential focus on the mouth region echo the findings of Langdell (1978), it also mirrors those of Klin, Jones, Schultz et al. (2002) who used eye-tracking measures to determine what parts of the face high-functioning individuals with ASD looked at when viewing a videotape of a sequence from the film *Who's Afraid of Virginia Woolf?*. Klin et al. observed that the participants with ASD looked more often at the actors' mouths than at their eyes, whereas the reverse was true for comparison participants.

Teunisse and de Gelder (2003) argued that the inversion effects found in earlier studies may have resulted from floor effects – i.e. that the task was too hard for the children with ASD. They tested high-functioning adolescents with ASD and typical comparison participants on a paradigm that involved the presentation of a full-view upright or inverted face followed by two three-quarter view faces (in the same orientation as the first face), one of which was the original. Participants had to identify which member of the pair was the one that had just been presented in full view. The results confirmed the hypothesis that reducing the demands of the task produced an inversion effect in the participants with ASD and suggest that the absence of an inversion effect reported in other studies may have resulted partly from task difficulty rather than from more specific face-processing difficulties. In a second experiment, the same groups of participants were asked to select which of two composite, full-view faces matched a face presented just previously in three-quarter view. Composite faces consisted of the top half of the target face and a distractor face, each paired with the bottom half of another face. Composites were presented either fully aligned or misaligned so that the contours of the two halves did not line up. Trials with upright and inverted faces were included. The results of this study showed that the adult comparison group recognised non-aligned composites faster than aligned ones for upright but not for inverted faces. However, this effect was not in evidence for the comparison children or for the participants with ASD, suggesting that they were not using the same face-processing strategies as the typical adults. Taken together, Teunisse's and de Gelder's findings suggest that although individuals with ASD are capable of holistic face-processing strategies on certain tasks, when the task demands change a more feature-based strategy is adopted. It would be interesting to see if the ASD group would have shown less impairment on composites that kept the eyes rather than the mouth constant. On the basis of Joseph and Tanaka's (2003) findings, we would expect diminished impairment under these conditions.

In a study of face processing in children with high-functioning ASD or Asperger's syndrome, Deruelle, Rondan, Gepner & Tardif (2004) used a two-alternative forced-choice procedure that was designed to minimise the memory demands inherent in the procedures of many earlier studies. Participants were shown a target face with two faces below it and asked to select which of the two lower faces matched the target. In their first experiment, participants had to select faces on the basis of identity, emotional expression, gender, gaze direction or the letter made by the lips of the person in the picture. The children with ASD were impaired on all but the identity recognition task which, the authors conclude, points to a generalised difficulty in face processing. In a second experiment, the authors tested the same participants with the same forced-choice procedure on faces that were either high-pass filtered, which emphasises features, or low-pass filtered, which emphasises global configuration. The results showed better performance in the low-pass (configural) condition for the comparison groups, but the reverse for the ASD group. Deruelle et al. also observed that face recognition performance was correlated with age for the ASD but not for the comparison participants and conclude that facial identity matching in individuals with ASD is likely to be based on a more feature-oriented strategy and that they depend on experience with faces to become proficient at processing them.

Maurer, Le Grand and Mondloch (2002) argue that faces can be analysed in terms of first-order relations (where each part is in relation to the others), second-order relations (the distances between the parts or between each part and the face outline) and holistic processing, in which the processing of the whole takes precedence over the processing of the parts. They further argue that second-order processing is particularly disrupted by face inversion. A corollary of this is that individuals who show reduced inversion effects would be impaired in second-order relational processing. In the Thatcher illusion (Thompson, 1980) participants are asked to recognise upright and inverted faces in which the eyes and mouth have been inverted. The grotesque effect generated by this manipulation disappears when faces are turned upside-down, a fact that is explained by disruption of the ability to process second-order relational features in the face. Rouse, Donnelly, Hadwin and Brown (2004) investigated susceptibility to the Thatcher illusion in children with ASD and retardation and comparison groups of children with retardation or with typical development. The ASD group matched the typical group on non-verbal ability and the group with retardation on verbal ability. Participants were shown upright and inverted 'Thatcherised' faces (those in which the eyes and the mouth had been inverted) and upright and inverted 'Thatcherised' houses and asked them to point to the one that looked odd. Houses were chosen for reasons first put forward by Boucher and Lewis (1992), namely that they resembled faces in that they had an outline with internal component features that were configurally arranged, and were familiar to the children (see Figure 7.1). They found a similar level of enhanced accuracy in spotting facial oddity in upright faces in the children with ASD as in the two comparison groups, suggesting that all three groups were capable of processing second-order relational features in faces. Had the ASD group been using a piecemeal, feature-oriented strategy, they would have been as accurate in spotting inverted features in inverted as in upright faces. To counter the possibility that a deficit in the ASD group had been masked by a ceiling

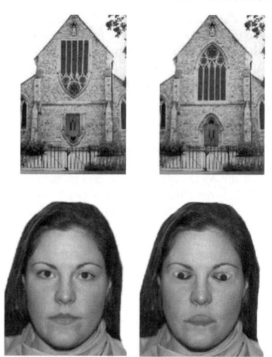

Figure 7.1. Stimuli of the kind used by Donnelly and Hadwin (2003). Reproduced by kind permission of Nick Donnelly, University of Southampton.

effect in the typical comparison group, for whom the task was extremely easy, Rouse et al. repeated the experiment employing high-contrast Mooney-type faces (see Figure 7.2), which make more processing demands on the partici-pants. Their results showed a marginal diminution in the upright face advan-tage in the children with ASD compared to the typical children but not for those with retardation. Rouse et al. argue that although these results could be interpreted as supporting a diminished capacity for second-order processing in ASD, the fact that for all participants, performance on the face task corre-lated with verbal and not with non-verbal mental age, suggests that the appro-priate comparison group should be that matched on verbal mental age, i.e. the group with mental retardation. On this basis, they conclude that there is no impairment in second-order relational processing in ASD that is not related to verbal mental age. This last argument is questionable, since Rouse et al. did not report face task–mental age correlations for the three groups separately. It could be the case that there were different patterns of correlation in the three groups. If, for example, the children with ASD did not show the corre-lation with verbal mental age, but did for non-verbal mental age, then Rouse et al.'s logic would yield quite a different conclusion. Some earlier studies

Figure 7.2. Examples of Mooney figures. Reproduced by kind permission of Aaron Schurger, Princeton University.

report correlations between face-processing measures and both verbal and non-verbal mental age, but the results are contradictory, with some reporting correlations with non-verbal but not verbal measures in typical participants only (e.g. Langdell, 1978) and others showing no correlations in any group (e.g. Robel, Ennouri, Piana et al., 2004). Given the small sample sizes of many studies coupled with differences in mental age measures and the procedures used to measure face processing, it is perhaps not surprising that this should be the case. But we should be careful about drawing premature conclusions regarding which mental age measures to use when matching groups of participants in face processing studies.

The procedures used in the studies described so far have involved asking participants to match pictures of faces, or to recognise pictures that they have seen before, or to identify similarities and differences between different faces. Some of the findings suggest that individuals on the autism spectrum attend to different parts of the face, and that this differential focus of attention may affect the extent to which and the circumstances under which they may respond on the basis of a holistic rather than an elemental processing strategy. However, even when investigations report no differences between groups on methods like these, it remains possible that the processes by which individuals with and without ASD represent faces differ. One way of exploring this possibility is to examine patterns in the way individuals look at faces during an experimental task. Techniques have been developed that enable gaze fixation patterns during face inspection to be measured.

In addition to the particular patterns of face inspection reported by Hermelin and O'Connor (1967), Osterling et al. (2002) and Klin et al. (2002), two other studies have used eye-tracking methods to measure the way people with ASD scan pictures of faces (Pelphrey, Sasson, Reznick et al. 2002; van der Geest, Kemner, Verbaten & van Engeland, 2002b). However, these last two studies gave contradictory results: Pelphrey et al. showed that there were marked differences in the scan paths of the autistic group compared to a control group, whilst van der Geest et al. found no difference in looking behaviour between autistic and typical individuals. The discrepancy in findings is intriguing, since both studies were similar in that participants had to look at pictures of human faces. Both also measured the fixation time (time that a participant looked at a certain region of the face) for faces and their most important regions, such as eyes and mouth. And in a second phase, participants in both experiments also had to name the emotion of the face. However, the two studies differed in a number of respects. Van der Geest et al., who found no differences between groups, tested high-functioning children with ASD who were well matched on chronological age and verbal IQ. By contrast, the study in which Pelphrey et al. reported ASD-linked abnormalities tested five male adults (mean age 25.2 years) with ASD and five controls. All individuals in the ASD group had IQs in the normal range but there was an average difference of about 30 IQ points between verbal IQ and performance IQ for some of these individuals, by contrast with the small difference in the van der Geest et al. study. Moreover, Pelphrey et al. did not report IQ scores for the control group, but did mention that members of the control group had completed a college degree and so were likely to have had a higher than normal IQ. Pelphrey et al. acknowledge that their findings may have been due to this possible difference in IQ. Both investigations also differed in terms of the instructions they gave to participants. Pelphrey et al. asked participants to identify the emotion in the face (a task that is known to be difficult for people with ASD), and found abnormal scan paths, whereas van der Geest et al. asked participants to look at each face carefully, perhaps thus prompting an already-learned search strategy that yielded typical patterns of performance. Thus, there is little we can conclude from eye scanning studies of faces in ASD other than to say that there may be a tendency to focus on the mouth and that some people with ASD may perform differently from typical individuals. Further, better-controlled studies are needed before any firm conclusions can be drawn from this promising method of investigation.

It is worth noting that the behavioural work on face processing in ASD has served to refine the conclusions from earlier findings that show children with ASD attending less to faces in social interaction (see Osterling et al., 2002). As Joseph and Tanaka point out, the differential focusing on the mouth to the detriment of the eyes is consistent with other observations of individuals with ASD, and in Chapter 2 we discussed how children with ASD make less use of a speaker's direction of gaze to determine the meaning of a new word. Several studies also show that children with ASD are delayed in following the gaze of others (see Leekam & Moore, 2001), suggesting that diminished attention to the eye region of the face is a fundamental characteristic of face processing in this population. Yet two recent studies suggest that the picture may not be so straightforward. Swettenham, Condie, Campbell et al. (2003) found that high-functioning children with ASD performed similarly to comparison participants in a task where they had to ignore a briefly presented face in which the eye direction provided a misleading cue to the location of a target. This suggests that they were sensitive to the eye region of the faces. And in a study of perceptual priming and face perception, Lahaie, Mottron, Arguin et al. (2006) explored the priming effects of face parts in adolescents and adults with ASD and Asperger's syndrome. Participants had first to learn to associate letters with members of a set of faces. These faces were then presented one by one in a priming task in which a 500 ms fixation point was followed by a 400 ms prime (either a neutral, generic face or one or more face parts) followed by a 13 ms mask (a face outline filled with a chequerboard pattern) followed by a full face. Participants had to call out the letter corresponding to the face as quickly as possible. Primes consisted either of natural face parts (eyes, nose, mouth) or of arbitrary sections of a face (e.g. corner of eye + side of nose + corner of mouth; part of mouth + chin). For arbitrary face parts, increasing the number of items in the prime decreased naming latencies to a similar extent for both groups of participants. A similar effect was noted in both groups when primes contained two, three or four natural face parts. But when the prime consisted of a single natural face part, response latency decreased only for the ASD group. Lahaie et al. conclude from these observations that the ASD participants are capable of configural processing (because they show a similar reduction in naming latency as comparison participants) but enhanced processing of local elements (because they are more sensitive to a single-element prime in the natural prime condition). This enhanced featural processing in the presence of intact global processing (Lahaie et al.'s first experiment showed typical face inversion effects in their ASD group) resonates with the work on discrimination learning and the processing of hierarchical figures discussed in Chapter 5.

These last two studies demonstrate that low-level perceptual processing of faces appears to be intact, at least in older individuals with ASD, and do not sit easily with the literature that shows impaired inference of emotion from facial expressions, or impairments in the use of eye gaze or many of the other apparent impairments of face processing in ASD. The challenge facing researchers is to reconcile these two conflicting sets of findings. One possibility, suggested by Swettenham et al. (2003), is that intact low-level processing may be seen in older children, adolescents and adults, but may have developed late, and was not available at a time when children typically learn to use and learn from the facial expressions of others. Such a conjecture can only be tested by studies that track the development of the same children over long periods of development.

In some respects, the most recent studies of face processing in ASD have called long-held conceptions into question. It now appears that people with ASD can process faces holistically, but that they do not always, or indeed habitually, do so. It also appears that they have enhanced processing of facial features that may yield a processing style that appears on the surface to suggest impaired configural processing. Taking an historical overview of the findings, we can make some tentative observations. First, in retrospect, many of the early studies had methodological flaws. The tasks used often produced floor or ceiling effects in one or other group (see Jemel, Mottron & Dawson, 2006). But there is another way in which the earlier studies differ from the later ones. Increasingly (see Swettenham et al., 2003 and Lahaie et al., 2006), more sophisticated experimental paradigms are being employed in this area of research. If we compare Langdell's (1978) study with that of Lahaie et al. (2006), the former asked children to identify pictures of faces of schoolmates that had had different areas blanked off. Pictures were placed on a table and the child invited to make a response. By contrast, Lahaie et al. presented very carefully controlled images of unfamiliar faces for very precise times (less than 1 s) followed by a backward mask (a very briefly presented complex visual stimulus designed to attenuate any afterimages) followed by a target face, the duration of which was determined by the participant's response time. Similar procedural precision can be found in Swettenham et al.'s (2003) study. We have thus moved from very gross measures of face processing, where participants have considerable amounts of time to deploy conscious strategies in the context of the experimental task, to situations where the information available – or at least some of it – is tightly constrained, thus bringing into play more automatic processes that are less open to conscious control. It is interesting that these more constrained methods are the ones that are showing unimpaired or superior performance. The challenge to scientists is to explain how such unimpaired or superior performance at a very low level often gets translated into atypical performance on other experimental tasks or in real life.

The most recent studies have considerably refined our understanding of face processing in ASD. It now seems that individuals with ASD can process faces holistically and configurally but appear to show a preference for focusing on particular regions of the face, especially the mouth region. This preference for processing elements rather than configurations means that task demands, if sufficiently high, can create an apparent inability to engage in global or configural processing, which when translated into everyday life, can compromise social interactions that capitalise on an accurate appraisal of facial configurations with considerable downstream consequences for adaptive functioning. This conclusion strongly echoes that of the literature reviewed in Chapter 5 on hierarchical and local/global processing, where it was argued that individuals with ASD, because they are more likely than typical individuals to focus on lower-level aspects of complex stimuli, sometimes interpret the world in a way that is different and which compromises their capacity to develop shared representations in the context of social interactions.

CONCEPT FORMATION

The ability to gloss over minor perceptual differences between individual objects and to group similar items together into classes is of considerable advantage to any organism interacting with its environment. Such a capacity overcomes the need to respond to every event as if it were totally novel and thus enhances adaptive behaviour by enabling responses to classes rather than individual objects or events. Every apple we have ever encountered is slightly different from all other apples; no two are identical. Imagine what life would be like if we were unable to ignore these slight differences and group these 'different' objects under the single heading 'apple'. Each apple encountered would constitute a novel event, and would be less likely to trigger actions that had been directed to other apples. This rather far-fetched example is meant to give some idea of how our behavioural adaptation to our environment would be severely compromised if we did not possess some mechanism to integrate features of complex stimuli and to group stimulus complexes into sets based on the elements they have in common. These sets, or categories, can then become objects of thought in themselves, and new experiences or objects can be thought of as members of a particular set, even if they do not share every single feature held by each of the other members of the set. Thus two apples can be considered as members of the set 'apple' even though one is large and one is small, or one is red and one is green. Usually, no single perceptual feature completely defines membership of a particular set or category.

Theories of how humans form concepts and how their conceptual system is organised and operates abound (see Murphy, 2002 for a detailed exposition). So-called 'classical concept theory' (see Medin & Smith, 1984) argues that all conceptual classes can be defined by combinations of features that are individually necessary and jointly sufficient to define a category member (so a dog has to have four legs, bark, etc.). Prototype theories (Rosch, 1975) posit that concepts are represented by 'prototypes' – representations that are abstracted from encounters with specific examples of such category members, and are characterised by some weighted average of the characteristics present in those examples. Exemplar theorists (e.g. Nosofsky, 1991) argue that individual category instances are represented, and that the decision to admit a novel item to a category depends on the similarity distance between features of the stored exemplars and the new item. Common to the second two accounts is the notion that abstractions are made on the basis of elements of experience in a manner that reduces information and enables the creation of object classes that can themselves be treated like objects. This ability to transcend minor variations in stimulus situations enables, among other things, learning to generalise to similar but not identical situations to those in which it took place (cf. the work of Plaisted et al., 1998b described in Chapter 5).

It is clear that there is at least a *prima facie* case for impaired concept formation in individuals with ASD. The 'insistence on sameness' described by Kanner (1943) is consistent with the idea that novel events are sufficiently different from what the individual already knows as to be distressing. WCC theory implicated impaired conceptual processes when it argued that ASD represented a focus on the parts at the expense of overall meaning. But the findings of the experimental material presented here make a more mixed set of predictions. At worst, conceptual processes should be damaged but not absent; at best they should be unimpaired. But before presenting the empirical findings on concept formation and conceptual processing in ASD, it is worth noting that this is an area that straddles several levels of psychological processing. Concepts can be formed at the perceptual level, where items with similar but not identical clusters of perceptual features are treated as equivalent. Behaviourists call such concepts *equivalence classes*, and have demonstrated their existence in pigeons (Jitsumori, Siemann, Lehr & Delius, 2002), indicating that such a capacity is a fundamental property of the psychological processes of behaving organisms. But humans also possess language, in which words are used to describe concepts, and the branch of linguistics known as semantics attempts to understand the relation between the structures of language, category structures and the actual structure of the world. Although there has to be a high level of congruence between the linguistic and the perceptual conceptual system, they are not identical. For example, although a whale has many of the perceptual attributes of a fish, it is not a fish. And penguins, although birds, cannot fly, and as such lack one of the common (but by no means universal) characteristics of birds. Thus, conceptual processing can be considered at both the perceptual and the linguistic level.

We have already seen that when individuals with ASD have to call on stored information to aid task performance, impairment will be evident. When a task requires less reliance on stored categorical representations, then performance tends to be unimpaired. These observations suggest that the way categorical information is stored is different in some way in ASD. Among the earliest studies of semantic and conceptual processes in ASD are those in the area of memory. Typically, memory for learned material is enhanced if that material can be grouped in some way that aids its organisation. It has long been known that lists of words are better recalled if the words come from a single or a small number of semantic categories (e.g. furniture or fruit). Tager-Flusberg (1985a) and Ungerer and Sigman (1987) found that lower-functioning children with ASD were unimpaired on a categorisation task that included natural kind (e.g. animals, fruit) and artefact (e.g. furniture) categories. And Tager-Flusberg (1985b) also found unimpaired basic and superordinate level categorisation skills in similar children. However, Dunn, Vaughan, Kreuzer and Kurtzberg (1999) found that higher-functioning children with ASD did not show the same electrophysiological event-related potentials (ERP) to higher-order category labels (such as 'animals' or 'plants') as did typical comparison children. And when Dunn, Gomes and Sebastian (1996) asked children with ASD to list examples of category members, they were less likely than comparison participants to list prototypical category members. We saw earlier that, contrary to the predictions of WCC theory, adults with Asperger's syndrome can use categorical relations among items to generate illusory memories (Bowler et al. 2000b), suggesting that they had some awareness of the semantic relatedness among the learned items. Thus at the level of linguistic concepts, it would appear that individuals from across the autism spectrum have some awareness of the fact that individual items are related in some way, and that this relational awareness can influence behaviour. Yet for individuals on higher- and lower-functioning parts of the autism spectrum, category knowledge has been observed to be less likely to improve recall on memory tests (Bowler, Matthews & Gardiner, 1997; Hermelin & O'Connor, 1970; Smith, Gardiner & Bowler, in press; Tager-Flusberg, 1991). These findings show that there is an impairment in the use of categorical knowledge to aid memory. Although Shulman, Yirmiya and Greenbaum (1995) found impaired free sorting into categories of objects and natural kinds as well as impaired class inclusion, where children were presented with sets of geometric shapes of different colours and asked questions designed to test their knowledge of whether all the squares were red or all the triangles blue, etc., the children's sorting of geometric shapes was unimpaired. Shulman et al. conclude from these findings that categorisation impairments are evident in ASD only when symbolic material is involved or when not all the information necessary for the task is present in the stimulus array.

The findings of enhanced processing of elements accompanied by unimpaired or almost unimpaired processing of global configurations of complex visual stimuli lead us to predict that people with ASD should show particular patterns of performance on tasks that required conceptual abstraction from sets of stimuli that overlapped in terms of the amount of detail they share. The prototype theory of conceptual representation posits that when we encounter a series of exemplars of a particular category (e.g. apples or cars), our cognitive system computes an idealised representation – a prototype – of these exemplars, the features of which represent the average of the features of the objects encountered. When a new object is encountered, category membership is evaluated in terms of the similarity of the characteristics of that particular object with those of the stored prototype. The construction of a prototype implies the integration of individual features across a range of exemplars, and both WCC theory and the findings of enhanced local processing and processing of unique features in ASD predict impaired prototype formation in this group.

To date, only three experimental investigations of prototype formation in ASD have been reported in the literature. We have already mentioned the work of Dunn, Gomes and Sebastian (1996) who found that children with ASD listed fewer prototypical items than did the children in the other two groups and were also more likely to list unusual exemplars of a category. Two studies of perceptual prototype formation have been carried out; one with higher-functioning (Molesworth, Bowler & Hampton, 2005) and one with lower-functioning individuals with ASD (Klinger & Dawson, 2001). In the latter study, children with ASD, Down syndrome and typical development were familiarised with drawings of cartoon animals that were highly similar but varied in different features such as leg, neck or beak length or head width. The investigators then tested the children's capacity to recognise members of that category, including a prototype exemplar, which they had not seen during the familiarisation phase. Klinger and Dawson's reasoning was that if the children were able to abstract the features of the prototype from the exemplars seen in the familiarisation phase, then they should mistakenly identify the prototype as a category member. By contrast, if the children were adopting a more detail-focused approach to representing category exemplars, then the prototype should be rejected. Their findings showed that the two clinical groups showed the prototype effect less often than did the typical children, supporting the idea that the children with ASD adopted a more detail-focused approach, and thus supporting the predictions of WCC theory. However, the same finding was also true of the children with Down syndrome, indicating that the lack of a prototype effect may have resulted as much from developmental delay as from ASD (see Figure 7.3).

To test the generality of Klinger and Dawson's findings, Molesworth et al. (2005) investigated prototype formation in high-functioning children with ASD and Asperger's syndrome. Participants were given a set of drawings of birds and insects that varied along similar dimensions to those in Klinger and Dawson's study and were told that they had to memorise them for a later memory test. To encourage attention to the stimuli, children were asked to sort them into the two categories. At test, studied items and lure (non-studied items that were similar to the studied ones) were presented, including the prototype representing the average of the features of the studied items. Participants had to state whether or not each item had been seen in the study phase. It was

Figure 7.3. Exemplar and prototype stimuli used by Klinger and Dawson (2001). Reproduced by kind permission of Cambridge University Press.

hypothesised that participants who integrated the features of the studied items into a prototype should falsely recognise the prototype at test, but those who did not would not show such a false recognition effect. Moreover, because Plaisted's common features theory of impaired generalisation predicts that the less a studied item resembles the prototype (or average) of the items studied (the item's 'family resemblance'), the less likely it is to be remembered, because it has less in common with the majority of studied items. Thus we would expect a steeper drop-off in recognition accuracy with diminishing family resemblance in participants with ASD but not in those with typical development. This is because the former group process unique features more efficiently and should therefore see a greater drop in similarity for a given diminution in family resemblance. However, Molesworth et al.'s findings gave no evidence either for absence of false prototype recognition or a steeper family-resemblance-related response gradient in the ASD group.

Molesworth et al.'s findings contradict the findings of Klinger and Dawson and are also inconsistent with the common features account of stimulus generalisation developed by Plaisted et al. (1998b) described earlier. The first discrepancy suggests that the impairment observed by Klinger and Dawson may have resulted from general cognitive delay rather than ASD. But Molesworth et al. also identify a methodological difference between that study and their own. In Klinger and Dawson's study, children were asked to choose which of two pictures presented was the best example of the category, whereas Molesworth et al. used a false recognition procedure. Children with developmental delay may have had difficulties understanding the word 'best', whereas it is known that high-functioning individuals with ASD are subject to false recognition effects (Bowler et al., 2000b). And Holland (2005) observed that the familiarisation procedure used by the two studies differed: Klinger and Dawson displayed items one by one, whereas Molesworth et al. gave participants all the items and asked them to sort the items into categories. Holland (2005) argues that Molesworth et al.'s procedure may have promoted a more integration- and category-oriented strategy than did that of Klinger and Dawson, thereby increasing the probability of their forming links among the stimuli.

The discrepancy with Plaisted's common features account of generalisation may be the result of the different ways in which stimuli from the two tasks need to be processed for successful task completion to take place. The stimuli used by Plaisted et al. are shown in Figure 5.6 and require participants to recognise configurations and to group them into families. The elements of the configurations remain constant across stimuli and families of stimuli. Molesworth et al., by contrast (see Figure 7.4 for stimuli), required participants to classify sequences of clusters of elements based on small changes in the identity of the elements themselves. Their configuration, however, remained the same. Readers may remember the earlier discussion of Plaisted et al.'s (2003) finding that demonstrated enhanced processing of elements and typical levels of configural processing in children with ASD. Molesworth et al.'s findings may result from enhanced processing of the minutiae of the elements of the stimuli they used, especially as their task did not tax configural processing *per se*.

It is clear that the current state of play in the relatively small amount of research on conceptualisation and categorisation in ASD does not justify hard-and-fast conclusions. But there are some themes that can help to decide the direction of further research. The first question relates to the role of global cognitive delay. It would appear that impairment is more evident in individuals who have some degree of intellectual disability. However, it would be a mistake to assume that such impairment operates similarly in cases where ASD is present and where it is absent. Further research is needed to explore the ways in which ASD, intellectual impairment and categorisation, and concept formation interact. The second issue relates to the first and concerns the kinds of conceptualisation being studied. The investigations described above have explored both language-based and perceptual categorisation. In the case of a developed adult, these two phenomena cannot be easily dissociated, but for the purposes of analysis they can be considered separately. From a developmental point of view, the first task that faces an infant is the perceptual categorisation of experiences. This forms the basis of subsequent adaptive behaviour, but also feeds into language development, where words are

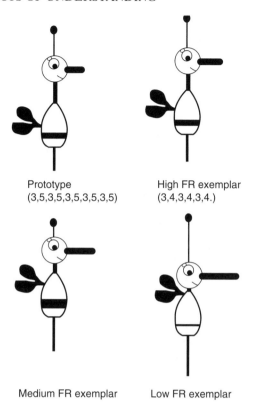

Prototype
(3,5,3,5,3,5,3,5,3,5)

High FR exemplar
(3,4,3,4,3,4.)

Medium FR exemplar

Low FR exemplar

Figure 7.4. Exemplar and prototype stimuli used by Molesworth et al. (2005).

learned, which describe particular perceptual classes. Thus, every red square (of whatever size and whatever the shade of red) can be described as a 'red square'. Category labels can then be organised into hierarchical systems (the category 'shapes' consists of squares, circles, diamonds, etc.; that of 'colours' comprises red, green, blue, etc.). On this analysis, higher-order categories are grounded in lower-order ones and the category labels of language are grounded in the categorical experiences of perception. But as we have seen in the whale and penguin example discussed earlier, linguistic categories and perceptual categories sometimes conflict, and our wider knowledge base has to intervene to decide the matter in a top-down fashion. We have seen that people with ASD can use top-down processing in dealing with perceptual stimuli, at least under certain circumstances (see Mitchell & Ropar, 2004). And we have also seen that what research there is suggests that they (including those with some global cognitive impairment) have little difficulty with linguistic categorisation systems. What remains to be demonstrated is the extent to which linguistically encoded general knowledge can modify perceptual judgments by operating in a top-down fashion. What little evidence there is suggests that this form of influence is attenuated in people with ASD.

There remain some difficulties with categorisation at the level of perceptual organisation. Categorisation of perceptual experience involves the organisation of stimulus complexity. And as we have seen, there is some evidence for slight impairment at this level in individuals with ASD. Although the experiments using hierarchical stimuli have shown unimpaired global processing in this group, the data from Plaisted et al.'s (2003) second experiment suggests that there may be some subtle impairment when successful task performance requires configural processing of stimulus elements. Moreover, Plaisted et al.'s (1998a) demonstration of enhanced processing of non-common features in a generalisation task also suggests that the features common to the stimuli, which were defined configurationally, were less well processed by the participants with ASD. The studies that have shown unimpaired prototype formation have not used stimuli that would generate prototypes on the basis of stimulus element configurations, and as such may not tap into an area of difficulty for individuals with ASD. Thus we need to carry out investigations that test prototype formation on the basis of element configurations rather than the properties of the elements themselves.

If people with ASD categorise experiences differently then it is plausible that the way in which they store and retrieve these experiences will also differ. This observation leads us to a consideration of memory in ASD.

MEMORY

Fundamental to the capacity of any organism that behaves in response to its environment is the notion of memory. In order to profit from experience, the behaving organism must have some mechanism of registering what it encountered previously in a manner that enables appropriate responses when these circumstances occur again. On this account, any change in the organism that results from experience and enables a later adaptive response constitutes memory. So, for example, when we get a cold, our immune system develops antibodies that stay in our bloodstream and when we are next infected with that particular strain of the cold virus, we fight it off rather than succumbing to illness. To many readers, labelling this phenomenon as 'memory' might seem rather far-fetched. Indeed, it represents what Perner (2001) has referred to as the inflationary tendency in the use of the term memory in recent decades. Yet this example, although it seems a long way from everyday notions of remembering where one left one's spectacles or what one had for dinner last Monday, does embody the main features of any memory system, whether biological or psychological.

Current psychological conceptions of memory are cast very firmly within the information-processing metaphor. According to this view, memory involves the encoding, storage and retrieval of information. But behind such an apparently simple statement lies a wealth of complexity, argument and debate. Researchers and theorists disagree profoundly about how information is encoded, how and where it is stored and what form the retrieval processes take. Added to different conceptualisations related to these dimensions are the different procedures used to measure memory, any or all of which are used by theorists of different orientations. This is not the appropriate place to discuss the merits of different conceptualisations of memory. Readers interested in this topic should see an introductory chapter by Gardiner (in press) or textbooks on memory such as Neath and Surprenant (2003). What will be presented here is an overview of research on memory in ASD carried out within these different frameworks.

A major theoretical debate concerns the question of whether memory consists of one unitary 'memory system' or of several systems. Related to this is the question of whether these systems are temporally ordered within the information processing stream. Some theorists argue that we have separate systems for the short-term retention and manipulation of information, some of which becomes deposited in a longer-term store of infinite capacity and unlimited durability. Such multi-store models of memory were developed and refined by theorists such as Atkinson and Shiffrin (1968) and further developed into the 'working memory' model of Baddeley (1986). In these formulations, the short-term store has limited capacity and draws information both from current experience and from long-term storage, and manipulates it in what Baddeley refers to as the central executive. The central executive is not, strictly speaking, a memory system but a set of processes that require a memory system in order to function. The fundamental characteristic of short-term stores is that they have limited capacity and are temporary. Information that taxes the store beyond its capacity or which is not manipulated in some way, either to maintain it in store or to transfer it to a longer-term store, is lost for ever. Studies of working memory, therefore, may investigate the operation of the central executive or the various memory subsystems associated with it. When encountering a claim for a 'working memory deficit' in a clinical group such as ASD, readers need to be aware what aspect of the system is being discussed.

Many theorists reject the idea that there are separate memory systems for the processing of information in the short term and argue for a single memory system that might operate in particular ways over short periods of time. But whichever model one adheres to, the question arises of how this long-term or unitary system is organised. Different theoretical systems can be found in the literature. A major distinction often made is between procedural and declarative memory. *Procedural memory*, as its name implies, refers to memory for motor procedures such as how to play the piano or to drive a car. *Declarative memory* refers to the conscious recall of verbal or imagined material. Some theorists argue that a distinction can be made between so-called *implicit memory*, which does not involve conscious recollection, and *explicit memory*, which does. Further differentiation of the declarative memory system has been made either on the basis of different memory processes (such as familiarity and recollection, Jacoby, 1991) or different systems (Tulving, 1995). In contrast to Jacoby, Tulving argues that there are different memory systems defined by the kinds of conscious awareness associated with them and that we have three main memory systems, the procedural, semantic and episodic, each associated respectively with anoetic, noetic and autonoetic states of conscious awareness. But however the memory system or process is conceptualised, all theorists base their conclusions on the results of studies that share much in common. All involve the learning of material and its subsequent retrieval in a memory test. This has the result that the findings of a given investigation can be considered in terms of the procedures used as well as in the context of the theoretical framework within which the investigation was first conceived.

Traditionally, memory has been investigated using laboratory procedures principally involving the studying or learning of verbal material in the knowledge that memory for that material will be assessed in a subsequent test. The one exception to this explicit memory procedure is the so-called implicit or indirect tests of memory (see Richardson-Klavehn, Lee, Joubran & Bjork, 1994). In implicit tests, participants are exposed to material (such as words, often in the form of another task, such as 'what is the opposite of FRIEND?'). Later, participants are given another task, such as a word-stem completion test ('Complete this part-word with the first thing that comes to mind: E__M_'). Some of these stems are of words that were seen in the initial list and others are of new words. Participants typically correctly complete more of the first group than the second. What is noteworthy is that at no point are participants informed that the two tasks are related. Methods of testing in explicit tests involve either recall or recognition. *Serial recall* requires participants to recall the learned material in the order in which it was presented; *free recall* allows participants to recall the material in whatever order they choose, while *cued recall* provides hints to the remembered material, such as initial letters, rhymes or categories. Recognition memory involves learning of a list of words and later testing either by a yes/no procedure, in which studied and non-studied words are presented one by one with the participant being asked to state whether the word had been seen at study or not, or a forced choice procedure in which a studied and a non-studied word are presented together, the participant being asked to select which one they had seen before.

The early clinical accounts of ASD and Asperger's syndrome commented on memory performance. Kanner (1943) noted that the children he described had good rote memory – memory for material without much reference to its meaning or the context or use to which it is to be put. Wing (1981) noted that individuals with Asperger's syndrome often accumulated vast stores of factual material about very specific topics such as bus timetables or dinosaurs, often with little interest in the phenomena themselves. These and similar observations gave rise to a general conclusion that memory, or at least the capacity of the memory storage system, did not constitute a particular difficulty in individuals with ASD, even if the ways in which memory was used did. These two themes – memory capacity and memory use – are the themes around which the first experimental investigations of memory in ASD were constructed.

Good rote memory implies a memory span – the number of items that can be correctly recalled in the order in which they were presented – within the normal limits. Early studies of memory span were carried out with individuals who had classic Kanner-type autism and some degree of intellectual disability (Boucher, 1978; Hermelin & O'Connor, 1967; see Hermelin & O'Connor 1970 for review). Yet the consensus from these investigations is that this group has unimpaired memory span. But as Poirier, Gaigg and Bowler (2004) have observed, comparison groups in these studies were matched on psychometric digit span, thus casting doubt on the finding of a null effect in experimental measures of span. Poirier et al. argued that simple, single-trial span tasks may not be sufficiently taxing to reveal short-term memory deficits and that a more difficult, multi-trial task might be more appropriate. They tested adults with Asperger's syndrome and typical individuals matched on verbal IQ on a 12-trial, 7-digit span task and found a significant group difference in overall span, thus calling into question the earlier findings of unimpaired span using less demanding measures.

Memory span is generally agreed to be a measure of short-term memory capacity, and is a component of the working memory system referred to earlier on. The working memory system consists of a central executive and two storage systems. Thus impairments of working memory can result from dysfunction of any of these systems. Experimental studies of working memory in ASD have given mixed results. Tower tasks, discussed in Chapter 4, are often thought of as measures of working memory, and are consistently impaired in individuals with ASD. Impairments have also been demonstrated on tasks where participants have to furnish the missing last word of a series of sentences and then recall all the missing words, or to count dots on a series of cards and then recall the numbers of items on each card (Bennetto, Pennington & Rogers, 1996). Russell, Jarrold and Henry (1996) found unimpaired short-term recall of words and recognition of pictures by adolescents with ASD, suggesting that the phonological loop (one of the subsystems in Baddeley's working memory model) is intact in ASD. Similarly, Koshino, Carpenter, Minshew et al. (2005) found no impairment in high-functioning adults with ASD in an n-back working memory task in which participants monitored sequentially presented digits and were asked on some trials whether the digit shown was the same as that presented 1, 2, 3 or n trials previously. But Luna, Minshew, Garver et al. (2002) found ASD-related impairment using an oculomotor delayed response procedure. This task required participants to fixate a cross on a screen on which a dot was projected for 100 ms followed by a delay of between 1 and 8 s, at the end of which participants had to shift gaze to the location of the dot. Shifting of gaze to the remembered location of the dot was less accurate in ASD participants, despite their unimpaired performance on a visually guided saccade task, which required an immediate gaze shift to a peripheral dot location.

The conflicting findings on working memory in ASD stem principally from the fact that working memory is a complex construct that can be operationalised in a variety of different ways. It involves storage of information over the short term as well as strategic manipulation of that information in the context of a particular goal or problem to be solved. In this respect, the concept of working memory poses similar difficulties to other high-level constructs such as theory of mind. Almost any task used to operationalise working memory or its components will inevitably involve other psychological systems, and impairment may equally well result from dysfunction in those systems as from the working memory components themselves. In relation to individuals with ASD, the existing findings on working memory suggest that impairments seem to be more evident on tasks that involve manipulation rather than storage of information, although as the results of Poirier et al. (2004) show, if the storage task is sufficiently demanding, diminished performance can be observed on this dimension also. As such, impairments of working memory in this population seem to be an aspect of executive dysfunction rather than deficient memory.

We have already noted that clinical reports of memory capacities of individuals from different parts of the autism spectrum have remarked on how apparently good memory skills are often not utilised in any meaningful way. Individuals with Kanner-type autism often rote-learn material with little evidence that they understand it, and people with Asperger's syndrome often appear unable to put their encyclopaedic stores of information to use in an occupational context. This theme of the meaning of remembered material was the first to emerge from experimental studies of memory in ASD. Hermelin and O'Connor (1967) compared children with ASD and typical children matched on digit span (the maximum number of auditorily presented digits that can be recalled exactly in order) on their recall of sentences or random strings of words of the same length as the sentences. Whereas the typical children were better able to recall sentences than random strings containing the same number of words, the children with ASD did not. Moreover, when words that were meaningfully related (e.g. from similar categories such as furniture or fruit) were scattered through the random lists, the typical children tended to cluster related words together in their free recall, whereas the children with ASD did not. Findings such as these led Hermelin and O'Connor (1970) to conclude that individuals with ASD fail to encode information meaningfully. But as Ramondo and Milech (1984) point out, it is not clear from these findings whether the problem derives from the semantic (i.e. meaning-related) aspects of the memorised material or the syntactic (i.e. structural or grammatical) structure of the sentences that poses problems for the participants with ASD. They carried out an experiment in which they asked children with

ASD, intellectual disability and typical development to recall strings of words that were either sentences, jumbled sentences or strings of semantically related words (exemplars of three different categories). They replicated the earlier findings on impaired recall of sentences by the children with ASD. But they found no ASD-linked deficit of semantic relatedness on recall, and concluded that the difficulties experienced by the children with ASD were due to difficulties in using structural or grammatical aspects of verbal material. Tager-Flusberg (1991) argued that the syntactic and semantic comparisons in Ramondo and Milech's study were flawed by the fact that the first condition contained content and function words whereas the second contained content words only. She carried out an experiment in which children with and without ASD, matched on verbal mental age and chronological age, were tested on their free recall of two lists of 12 words, one of which contained only animal names, and the other of which contained words from different categories. Whereas both groups recalled similar numbers of words from the second list, the children with ASD were poorer than the comparison children in their recall from the animals list. This finding was replicated in part by Leekam and Lopez (2003), who found a similar effect when Tager-Flusberg's words were used, but when words that were more closely matched for frequency, or when pictorial rather than verbal stimuli were employed, their children with ASD performed similarly to typical comparison children. Further replications on groups of adults with Asperger's syndrome have also been reported (Bowler, Matthews and Gardiner, 1997; Smith, Gardiner & Bowler, in press), and Bowler, Gardiner, Grice and Saavalainen (2000b) found a small but significant impairment in free recall in adults with Asperger's syndrome when they were asked to recall lists of items that were associatively related.

The findings just presented appear to paint a picture of a difficulty (albeit intermittent) in using semantic relatedness to aid recall by people on the autism spectrum, suggesting, as Hermelin and O'Connor (1970) did, that such individuals have problems processing meaningful material. Yet other studies appear to show intact semantic processing. For example, Boucher and Warrington (1976) tested children with and without ASD, matched on verbal ability on a cued recall task, where semantic cues were given ('something to sit on' was used as a cue for 'stool') and found no impairment in the ASD group. A similar finding was reported by Tager-Flusberg (1991) using category labels (e.g. 'fruit' for the studied word 'cherry'). However, in a recent study of high-functioning adults with ASD and matched comparison participants, Mottron, Morasse and Belleville (2001) found that orienting participants to the semantic aspects of words as they were studying them enhanced free recall compared to attending to syllabic aspects or to neither aspect, and that this effect occurred equally in both groups of participants. By contrast, whereas the participants with ASD showed similar performance on a semantic or syllabic cued recall test, semantic cues were more effective for the comparison participants. Similar findings were reported by Toichi and Kamio

(2002), who asked participants with high-functioning ASD and a typical comparison group to learn lists of words written in two types of Japanese characters. At study, questions were asked about the kinds of characters used, the sounds of the words or about their meaning, representing graphic, phonemic and semantic levels of analysis. As in the Mottron et al. (2001) study, overall levels of memory performance were similar for both groups, but whereas recall of the semantically processed words was higher than that of the graphically or phonemically encoded ones for the typical group, no such difference emerged for the participants with Asperger's syndrome. Although both these findings appear to contradict the findings of Boucher and Warrington (1976) and of Tager-Flusberg (1991), it is worth noting that the difference in performance under the semantic and syllabic cue conditions of Mottron et al.'s and Toichi and Kamio's studies did not differ for either of the two groups. This means that although the ASD groups did not show an *advantage* from semantic over syllabic cueing in the way the comparison group did, they nevertheless benefited from it.

The memory illusions literature also provides evidence that individuals with ASD are not completely impaired in their use of meaning to aid memory. The standard procedure used to demonstrate memory illusions is that developed by Deese (1959) and subsequently revived by Roediger and McDermott (1995). In this procedure, participants study a list of words that are strong associates of a non-studied word (e.g. 'bed', 'slumber', 'blanket', 'night' are associates of 'sleep'). Testing uses either a free recall or a yes/no recognition procedure, and a large body of research now shows that participants typically falsely recall or falsely recognise the word 'sleep', even though they did not study it. If participants were not sensitive to the associative relatedness of the studied words, then they would not be subject to this illusory memory effect. Bowler et al. (2000b) used the Deese, Roediger and McDermott (DRM) procedure with a group of adults with Asperger's syndrome and a group of typical individuals matched on verbal IQ. In both free recall and recognition, the Asperger group produced illusory memories, demonstrating susceptibility to the relatedness among the studied items. However, Beversdorf et al. (2000), using a different procedure and data analysis strategy, report increased ability to discriminate non-studied associates of studied words in recognition memory, and infer that associative sensitivity is diminished in Asperger's syndrome. However, as pointed out in Chapter 5, there are methodological differences between the two studies that may have affected the outcome. In particular, Beversdorf et al. asked participants to rate the confidence with which they thought they had heard the target (i.e. the non-studied strong associate) item, whereas Bowler et al. asked for a yes/no judgment. Beversdorf et al.'s procedure may have prompted participants with ASD to focus on each individual item rather than on the relations among items, thus slightly but significantly diminishing their tendency to have an illusory memory.

The research described in the preceding paragraphs suggests that to assert that individuals with ASD do not encode material meaningfully may be an overstatement. Yet, under certain circumstances, they do appear to have semantic-related difficulties. It is possible that some of the processes underlying meaning formation may be dysfunctional in a manner that disrupts but does not obliterate semantic processing in this group. Understanding meaning involves processing relations among studied items, and given the enhanced tendency to process elements rather than configurations of complex stimuli seen in ASD, it could be argued that the memory difficulties seen in this group could result from impaired relational processing, enhanced item-specific processing or a combination of the two. When typical individuals are asked to study lists of words that contain a small number of words (say 2 or 3) from one category and larger numbers of words (say 12 or 16) from another, then tasks encouraging item-specific encoding at study (such as rating each word's pleasantness) will tend to increase memory for items in the larger category, whereas tasks encouraging relational encoding (such as giving a higher-order category label for each word) will enhance recall of items from the smaller categories (Hunt & Seta, 1984). On the basis of the literature discussed in Chapter 5, Gaigg, Bowler and Gardiner (2004) argued that individuals with Asperger's syndrome are impaired on relational but not item-specific processing and that when left to their own devices on a memory task they should show better memory for items from smaller categories. Instruction in relational encoding strategies should improve the memory of Asperger individuals whereas instruction in item-specific encoding strategies should enhance memory in typical individuals. Gaigg et al. (2004) tested these hypotheses with a group of adults with Asperger's syndrome matched on verbal IQ and chronological age who were asked to study words presented on decks of 56 cards. Words came from categories with 2, 4, 8, 12 or 16 exemplars in the study list. Participants were asked either to try to learn as many of the words as they could, or to sort the cards into categories to help them remember them or to rate each word's pleasantness as an aid to memory. The baseline results showed that for smaller categories the Asperger participants recalled fewer items than did the comparison group, suggesting that they were making less use of a relational strategy. Instructions to engage in relational or item-specific encoding produced similar effects in both groups, but the Asperger participants did not benefit as much from the relational strategy as did the comparison participants. This finding may give a clue to why some studies on the effects of semantic manipulations on memory show an ASD-related deficit whereas others do not. If the task does not entail any specific instructions to encode in a relational manner, then participants with ASD will tend not to do so. But if aspects of the task do promote (either by direct instruction or incidentally) relational encoding, then performance changes in a manner that is congruent with relational encoding, even if not always to an extent that matches typical levels of performance.

Difficulties with relational encoding may help to explain another area of memory functioning in which individuals from the autism spectrum have been shown to experience difficulties. Tulving (1995) has argued that the human memory system comprises a number of distinct subsystems, each accompanied by a particular type of conscious awareness. The procedural memory system consists of our capacity to retain well-learned routines such as driving a car or playing a piece of music fluently. Operation of the procedural system is accompanied by *anoetic* conscious awareness. The semantic memory system contains what Tulving refers to as 'timeless facts', such as capital cities, the boiling point of water or the names of trees and plants. Operation of this system is accompanied by *noetic* conscious awareness. Memory for personally experienced events, in which we engage in 'mental time travel' and re-construct a rich image of the past event and our involvement in it is handled by the episodic memory system, which is accompanied by *autonoetic* conscious awareness. There are a-priori reasons for thinking that individuals with ASD might have an impaired episodic memory system or impaired autonoetic awareness. As we have seen, they tend to perform less well than comparison groups on tests of free recall, which Tulving argues makes more demands on the episodic memory system. They also show impairments on some executive function tests, which implies frontal lobe difficulties, and as patients with frontal lobe damage exhibit impaired episodic remembering (Wheeler & Stuss, 2003), it is reasonable to predict a similar impairment in ASD.

Episodic remembering or autonoetic awareness can be measured by first alerting participants to the different experiences they have when they recall a fact such as the capital of France and the way they remember an episode such as when they last went to a restaurant. They are then asked to study a list of words for a later memory test. After a delay of a few minutes, they are shown the studied words one by one, interspersed with non-studied words, and asked to say whether or not they had seen the word before. If they say that they had, they are asked to state whether they remember the episode of having seen the word or whether they just know that it had appeared on the screen without recollecting the precise episode. They then describe the memory. Bowler, Gardiner and Grice (2000a) carried out this procedure with a group of adults with Asperger's syndrome and a typical comparison group matched on verbal IQ and chronological age and found that although overall rates of recognition memory were comparable across the two groups, the Asperger group made fewer 'remember' and more 'know' responses than did the typical group. This observation suggests that they engage in less 'mental time travel' when recalling events that happened to them, experiencing them rather as timeless facts.

It is important to note that episodic remembering appears to be diminished, not absent, in the participants tested by Bowler et al. (2000a), which raises the question of the nature of the episodic remembering that they do report. In Chapter 3 there was some discussion of how more able individuals with ASD might pass even quite advanced 'theory of mind' tests by 'hacking out' solutions (Bowler, 1992; Happé, 1994). A similar possibility occurs here; Asperger participants may have been labelling 'know' experience as 'remember', in which case their impairment was even greater than the results would suggest. Bowler et al. (2000a) addressed this possibility by including common and uncommon words in the study list. It is known that uncommon words are more likely to yield a 'remember' response. If the Asperger participants were mislabelling some of their 'know' responses as 'remember' then they would be unlikely to show this word frequency effect. However, the results showed the same word frequency effect as did the comparison group, suggesting that their reports of remembering were based on similar experiences to those of typical individuals. Bowler, Gardiner and Gaigg (in press) studied four other manipulations that differentially affect rates of remembering and knowing in the typical population, and found that they affected the responses of an Asperger group similarly to that of a typical comparison group. Thus, we can conclude that individuals from the higher-functioning end of the autism spectrum have diminished autonoetic awareness when recalling personally experienced events. However, when they do experience such awareness, it appears to be qualitatively similar to that of typical individuals. The task that now faces investigators is to determine the nature of the autonoetic impairment just described. Having an autonoetic experience involves the self travelling back in time and re-experiencing an episode in its spatio-temporal context. If we assume that these three components are relatively independent, then impairment can be in any one of them – the self, the ability to order events temporally in memory or to recall context.

The idea that individuals with ASD have impaired recall of self-related information is supported by a number of strands of empirical evidence. Russell and Jarrold (1999) asked children with ASD and intellectual disability to take part in a game in which either the child or a doll partner had to place pictures of objects on a grid. Children then had to return the cards to the person who had placed them (either themselves or the doll). Not only was overall performance more accurate for children with ASD, but they were less accurate at recalling which cards they themselves had placed. The reverse pattern was found in children without ASD. Millward, Powell, Messer and Jordan (2000) took children with ASD on a walk in which they engaged in specific activities and watched other people engage in activities. Their recall of these events was later tested and it was found that the children with ASD recalled fewer of the activities they themselves performed, a pattern that contrasted with that of the comparison group which was matched on verbal mental age. Both these studies show that individuals with ASD experience difficulties in recalling actions that involve the self.

Impaired self-awareness is also supported by findings from areas outside memory. Hurlburt, Happé and Frith (1994) asked three high-functioning men with ASD to carry a device that sounded a bleeper at random intervals throughout the day. When the bleeper sounded, they were asked to record what they were thinking about at the time, and these records formed the basis of a later interview about the contents of their consciousness. In contrast to typical individuals, the participants in Hurlburt's study reported visual, static images of what was in their minds at the time, and at no point did they show any interest in how their own reports compared with those of other people. In a case study of RJ, a 21 year old man with ASD, Klein, Chan and Loftus (1999) found that although RJ could give an accurate description of his own personality in terms of appropriate personality traits, he experienced great difficulty, even compared with typical individuals matched on verbal mental age, in recalling episodes that illustrated those traits. For example, although he could describe himself as a shy person (a fact that was corroborated by people who knew him well), he found it hard to come up with specific examples of when he was shy around other people.

The thrust of the findings just described suggest that individuals with ASD experience particular difficulty in recalling self-related aspects of the past, suggesting that their conception of themselves as being involved in events that they experienced is diminished (see Chapter 10 for further discussion). However, diminished self-awareness may not be the only factor involved in impaired episodic memory in ASD. Episodic awareness, in addition to involving the self, also entails an understanding that events occur at different times and that these times occur in a fixed, temporal order. Boucher (2001), in an essay on time processing and ASD, cites several clinical reports such as Wing (1996) and Peeters (1997) of an impaired sense of time in individuals from the ASD spectrum. And self-reports of people with ASD also report temporal information in ways that appear odd or idiosyncratic to individuals without ASD. There have not been very many controlled observations of time processing in ASD. O'Connor and Hermelin (1973) presented digits one by one in a three-window array in a manner in which the temporal and left–right spatial order conflicted (e.g. 1 in the middle, 2 on the left and 3 on the right, giving a spatial order of 213 and a temporal order of 123) and found that children with ASD tended to recall the digits in their spatial order, whereas typical children used the temporal order. Bennetto, Pennington and Rogers (1996) employed the Corsi memory test (Milner, Corsi & Leonard, 1991) to test the temporal order memory of a group of high-functioning adolescents with ASD and a typical comparison group matched on IQ. The task involved presenting participants with a sequence of cards containing pairs of pictures or words. From time to time, a test card was presented on which either a previously seen and a new item (recognition trials) or two previously seen items (temporal order trials) were presented. Participants had to point either to the item they had seen before or to the one that they had seen most recently. The ASD group was found to show impaired memory for temporal order relative to recognition memory in the ASD group for words but not for pictures. This observation shows that individuals with ASD have difficulty in organising events in time, especially when those events are verbally encoded. The reason why the phenomenon is not evidenced for non-verbal material is interesting and merits further exploration.

Difficulty in differentiating events that are separated in time may result from difficulties in encoding the contexts that characterise each of those events. Memory for context – often referred to as *source memory* – appears to show some impairment in ASD. Benetto et al. (1996) tested high-functioning children and adolescents with ASD on part of the California Verbal Learning Test (CVLT, Delis, Kramer, Kaplan & Ober, 1986) in which participants had first to free recall one supra-span list of words on five trials, and then to learn and free recall another list. Intrusions of words from the first list in the recall of the second were classed as source errors and were produced significantly more often in the ASD group. However, Farrant, Blades and Boucher (1998) found no evidence of source memory impairment in a group of children with ASD and retardation when compared to children without ASD matched on verbal mental age. But their procedure involved the child's learning a list of words spoken by two experimenters, one of whom held a blue block and the other a red block. At test, children were presented with the studied words one by one, interspersed with non-studied words, and asked if they had heard the word at study. If they said that they had, they were asked to point to which of the two blocks the person who spoke the word had been holding.

There are two major points of contrast between Bennetto et al.'s and Boucher et al.'s studies. The first relates to the ability level of the participants. The participants in the former were from the higher-functioning end of the autism spectrum, whereas the latter study tested lower-functioning individuals. This is unlikely to be the reason for the difference, however, as the better performance was observed in the lower-functioning group. The two investigations also differed in the way source memory was assessed. Bennetto et al. used a method based on free recall, which as we have seen poses problems for people with ASD. By contrast, the recognition method used by Farrant et al. is a procedure on which people with ASD experience less difficulty. To test the hypothesis that individuals with ASD were impaired on source recall but not source recognition, Bowler, Gardiner and Berthollier (2004) carried out an experiment in which high-functioning adolescents and adults with Asperger's syndrome studied words in a variety of contexts and in a subsequent recognition test for the studied words were asked either to recall or to recognise the context in which the word was studied. They found that whereas the Asperger and comparison groups showed similar levels of context recognition, the Asperger participants' recall of context was significantly less than that of the comparison group. These observations show that even when individuals from the autism spectrum correctly recognise something that happened in the past, the context of that event does not readily come to mind unless some prompts or clues are provided. Thus, when asked where they last went out to eat, they can tell you, but are less likely spontaneously to say what they had to eat or with whom they went to the restaurant. Boucher (1981) and Boucher and Lewis (1989) made similar observations. Working with children who had Kanner-type ASD, they found their participants to be worse than comparison children matched on non-verbal mental age on open-ended questions such as 'what did you do in class this morning?' than on more specific questions such as 'what picture did you draw this morning?'

The contrast between performance on tasks such as cued recall on which individuals with ASD usually show unimpaired performance and free recall, on which they are often impaired was first noted by Boucher and Warrington (1976) and developed by Bowler and colleagues (Bowler et al. 1997; 2004) into what they call a *task support hypothesis*, which states that individuals with ASD will perform well on any task where support is provided at test. Where support is absent, performance will tend to be impaired. Cued recall is the best example of a supported task, since participants are presented with a clue to a studied word and asked to make a yes/no judgment on whether they had seen or heard it at study. Free recall, by contrast, requires the participant to generate candidate words and decide whether or not they were present during the study phase. Moreover, free recall under conditions where performance can be improved by attending to relations among the studied items (as in the recall of categorised lists) is especially difficult for people from all parts of the autism spectrum and suggests that they require particular support in the domain of relations among items. Recognition memory, although apparently a supported test procedure, has produced mixed results in studies of individuals with ASD. Recognition memory tests involve studying a list of words and testing after a short delay by means of either a yes/no test, in which studied and non-studied words are presented one by one with a request for a yes/no decision on whether they were on the study list. Alternatively, a forced-choice procedure can be used, in which pairs of words consisting of a studied and a non-studied word are presented, the participant having to select which was the studied word. Recognition memory performance in individuals with ASD tends to be impaired on tasks using forced-choice methods (Ameli, Courchesne, Lincoln, Kaufman & Grillon 1988; Boucher & Warrington, 1976; Summers & Craik, 1994), but not when yes/no procedures are used (Benetto et al., 1996; Bowler et al., 2000a; Minshew, Goldstein, Muenz & Payton, 1992; but see Bowler, Gardiner & Berthollier, 2004). Thus, when the support provided at test gives indices to material that was not studied, performance may be compromised.

The phenomena that led Bowler and colleagues to develop the task support hypothesis can also be observed in the literature on memory impairment that accompanies the normal ageing process. Craik and colleagues (Craik & Anderson, 1999; Craik, Morris, Morris & Loewen, 1990) observed that normal ageing, especially when accompanied by decreased performance on frontal lobe tasks, shows decrements on memory tasks such as free recall, whereas supported tasks such as cued recall and recognition remained relatively intact.

This analogy with ageing provides a useful framework for generating hypotheses about the patterning of memory performance in ASD. For example, older people when remembering complex events (such as sets of objects presented in different colours in a range of locations) are better at recalling the objects, colours and locations but are less good at recalling which object was in which colour in which location (Dumas & Hartman, 2003). If this were to be the case for individuals with ASD (and there are strong reasons for arguing that it might be), we would have an explanation of why recall of temporal aspects of events is sometimes difficult for this population, since temporal differentiation of events in memory entails accurate recall of combinations of features that are specific to the partiular point in time at which they were experienced. If the ageing analogy holds for memory of complex stimuli, then it would seem that people from the autism spectrum experience difficulty in ordering events in time because they cannot retrieve material in a way that reactivates the specific pattern of elements defined by a particular episode, thus rendering a narrative sense of the past difficult. It is possible to speculate that such difficulties would render conversations about the past difficult.

In the context of children's development, conversations about the past have been found to bear an important relation to the development of theory of mind. Welch-Ross (1997) found that in typical 3.5–4.5 year old children, mother–child conversations about past events were predictive of later performance on unexpected change (Baron-Cohen et al., 1985) and representational change (Perner, Leekam & Wimmer, 1987) false-belief tasks. It is possible to speculate that if children experience difficulties in constructing a coherent sense of the personally experienced past, then such conversations will be difficult and will not lead to the kinds of understanding of other people's mental states that enables children to pass tests that are thought to measure their theory of mind. This argument links impaired understanding of mental states to difficulties in processing episodically determined links among elements of complex stimuli and, although as yet speculative, resonates with existing research. The role of complexity in understanding mental states in others has been discussed in Chapter 2. Difficulties with complexity may well depend on problems in directing attention to specific aspects of situations or in shifting attention from one aspect of a situation to another, a conjecture that leads us back to where we left off at the end of Chapter 6.

CONCLUSION

In a chapter such as this that deals with different but related aspects of psychological functions, it is difficult to provide a neat summary of the state of our understanding. Yet a number of themes emerge. It is clear that we should be cautious when attributing impaired higher-level processing to individuals with ASD in whatever domain. Whether we are dealing with the topics discussed here, or those discussed in earlier chapters, the picture seems to be that higher-level processing (responding to complex configurations, understanding mental states in others or recalling personally experienced episodes) is not entirely obliterated in ASD. Indeed, it is difficult to see how any adaptation to the environment could occur if this were to be the case. But what seems to happen in ASD is a tendency to remain aware of simple or more elemental components of experience. This is a tendency that sometimes interferes with processing at a higher level and as a consequence may alter the way in which these processes are deployed in day-to-day activity. Although it is tempting to argue that this patterning of behaviour is the result of a single dysfunctional element such as perception, it is clear that such an approach may be too simplistic. It is true that perceptual processes sometimes work differently in people with ASD, but as the work of Mitchell and his colleagues discussed in Chapter 5 shows, altered perception is sometimes the result of impaired top-down processing, in which prior knowledge influences the perceptual process. Whether such impaired top-down processing results from impaired perception having generated altered long-term representations that operate differently on perception, or whether it results from some other aspect of the process is not clear. What does emerge, though, is that we must move away from looking at the psychological system as a linear process whereby the environment 'writes' on the organism. It is a dynamic process whereby the organism interacts with its environment, both changing and being changed by it. Differences and perturbations can occur in any part of the system. The challenge is to try to identify precisely how and where this happens in ASD.

8 Psychology, Autism and the Brain

One of the most spectacular developments in recent decades has been the exponential growth in the study of those brain and neural systems that are thought to underlie the behavioural manifestations of ASD. Initial speculations about the role of particular brain structures in autistic symptomatology came from inferences from the behavioural consequences of experimental brain lesions in non-human animals as well as from observations of brain-injured children and adults. Early investigations of brain structure relied on standard post-mortem procedures that examined the gross and fine anatomy of the brain. The development of techniques such as computed tomography (CT) and structural magnetic resonance imaging (MRI) have permitted the non-invasive study of the brains of living individuals and the study of brain function has been enhanced by the development of procedures such as those that measure event-related potentials (ERP) as well as by means of imaging techniques such as positron emission tomography (PET), single-photon emission computed tomography (SPECT) and functional magnetic resonance imaging (fMRI). In a book that is primarily about psychology, it is legitimate to question the need for devoting a whole chapter to the study of the brain. The brain is the organ that is most closely involved in the organisation and control of behaviour, and understanding its organisation can give some clues to understanding pathological behaviour. But more importantly, as inferences about brain dysfunction are often made on the basis of performance on behavioural and psychological tasks, our speculations about brain dysfunction crucially depend on how we conceptualise the psychological functions thought to be measured by these tasks. As we have seen in earlier chapters, this last task is not as straightforward as it might initially seem.

STUDIES OF BRAIN SIZE AND STRUCTURE

Perhaps the most obvious way to determine brain involvement in ASD is to examine the brains of people with this diagnosis. Traditionally, such an approach has employed post-mortem techniques in which the brains of deceased individuals are examined for abnormalities both of gross anatomy and of fine structure. The first comprehensive accounts of brain anatomy in individuals with ASD were reported in a case study by Bauman and Kemper

(1985) and a further eight cases by Kemper and Bauman (1998). These initial studies detected abnormalities in the limbic system and the cerebellum (see Figures 8.1 and 8.3). The limbic system is a cluster of brain structures including the hypothalamus, the hippocampus and the amygdala, which play important roles in homeostasis, memory and emotional processing. The most notable abnormality noted by Bauman and Kemper was that the cells in parts of the limbic system were packed more densely and were decreased in size compared to those of the comparison, typical individuals. In the cerebellum, there was a decrease in the number of Purkinje cells, a finding that was replicated by a number of other researchers (Bailey, Luthert, Dean et al., 1998; Ritvo, Freeman, Scheibel et al., 1986).

The studies by Bauman and Kemper did not report any abnormalities of the cerebral cortex, which is surprising given that this is the part of the brain devoted to what have been called the 'higher mental processes', such as thinking and language (and arguably the capacity for social interaction) and is thus an area where we would expect to find evidence of damage. However, a more recent study of the neuropathology of the brains of six individuals with intellectual disabilities and ASD carried out by Bailey and colleagues (Bailey et al., 1998) did identify cortical abnormalities in four cases, and the authors claim that these observations support the case for cortical involvement in the symptomatology of ASD. A recent post-mortem study of the brains of nine individuals with ASD and four comparison participants has concentrated on the columnar structure of the cell assemblies in the prefrontal and temporal lobes of the cerebral cortex (Casanova, Buxhoeveden, Switala & Roy, 2002). They report that the structure of these areas was abnormal in the ASD group, with evidence of smaller, more numerous and more widely spaced columns. Taken together with the anatomical studies showing increased cell packing, these findings suggests that the brains of individuals with ASD are thought to remain in a state of overconnectivity, which alters the way information is processed and has implications for connectionist and other neural modelling approaches that will be discussed later on in this chapter. An important point to note in connection with post-mortem studies is that often not all cases show cortical abnormalities, a fact that highlights an important caveat that hangs over all research into brain abnormalities in ASD, namely that absence of evidence for an abnormality, whether of structure or function, is not evidence that no abnormality exists. Methods for investigating brains are still relatively crude (although the neuroanatomical methods used in these studies are among the most advanced in this field) and may be insufficiently sensitive to detect subtle abnormalities.

One aspect of brain structure that has proved to be highly replicable across studies is that of brain size. A crude index of brain size is head circumference, and Kanner (1943) noted large heads in some of the children he described. Many studies since then have also reported a higher incidence of macrocephaly in individuals with ASD (see Palmen & van Engeland, 2004 for a

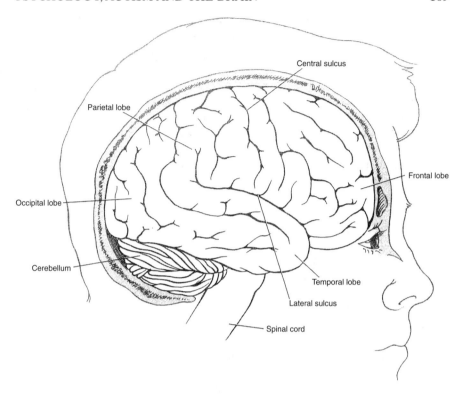

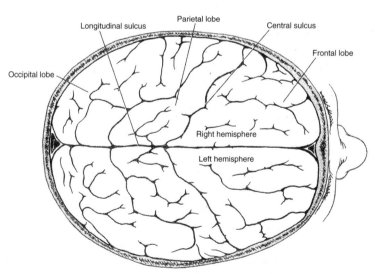

Figure 8.1. Structure of the human brain. Reproduced from Plotnick, R. and Mollenauer, S. (1978). *Brain and behavior: an introduction to physiological psychology.* Adapted by permission of Pearson Education Inc., Upper Saddle River, NJ.

review). Deutsch, Folstein, Gordon-Vaughn et al. (cited in Deutsch & Joseph, 2003) found that enlarged head circumference was a function of cranial width but not cranial length and that it was also prevalent in the relatives of individuals with ASD. Although many investigators have attempted to identify psychological correlates of increased head and brain size in ASD, the only positive findings have come from a study by Deutsch and Joseph (2003). They found that although head circumference was not correlated with measures of language or executive functioning, or with verbal or non-verbal IQ, it was inversely correlated with the difference between verbal and non-verbal IQ, suggesting that possession of a discrepantly high non-verbal IQ was associated with atypically large head circumference. Courchesne, Karns, Davis et al. (2001), in a study of brain growth in boys with autistic disorder, observed that brain volume was increased in 90% of the sample by the ages of 2–4 years, despite having been normal at birth (this was inferred from clinical records of head circumference). However, this increase in volume was not in evidence in older children, suggesting that brain enlargement may develop in the first year and may then attenuate, although the latter possibility is qualified by the considerable number of studies that show enlarged heads and brain volume in older individuals with ASD (see Polleux & Lauder, 2004 for review).

The development of structural neuroimaging techniques, although holding great promise for the detection of structural abnormalities in the living brains of individuals with ASD, has not yet added as much new information as might initially have been hoped. Despite a growing number of studies, three comprehensive reviews carried out in the past few years are unanimous in their conclusion that many of the existing findings are conflicting, a state of affairs that probably results from methodological difficulties, poorly matched comparison groups and rapidly evolving technology, with new and more powerful scanning techniques coming on line every few years (Cody, Pelphrey & Piven, 2002; Filipek, 1999; Palmen & van Engeland, 2004). Yet these three reviews are equally unanimous in concluding that increased brain size is a robust, well-replicated finding in the imaging literature. Some researchers speculate about the meaning of such enlargement and relate it to the increased cell packing and cell immaturity identified in the neuroanatomical studies described above, arguing for the possibility that there is a failure of the normal processes of dendritic pruning in the brains of individuals with ASD. Dendrites are tree-like branches from nerve cells (see Figure 8.2) that enable communication between cells and it is now widely believed that typical development consists of the pruning of these dendritic connections with a consequent reduction in brain volume (see Segalowitz & Schmidt, 2003 for further discussion).

Two other specific brain structures – the amygdala and the cerebellum – have also been examined with a view to identifying structural abnormalities. In contrast to many brain structures, which can prove difficult to delineate accurately, the cerebellum is a clearly separate brain structure (see Figure 8.1) yet despite its less ambiguous anatomical boundaries, anatomical and neu-

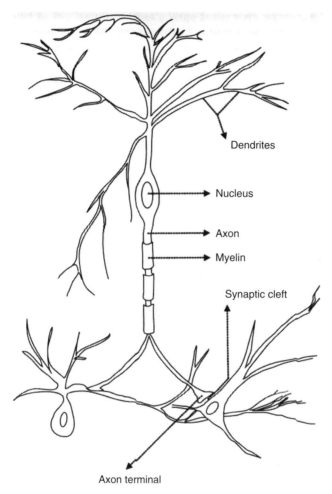

Dendrites

Nucleus

Axon

Myelin

Synaptic cleft

Axon terminal

Figure 8.2. Simplified diagram of a neuron. Reproduced from Hines (2004) by permission of Oxford University Press.

ropathological studies tend to present a rather inconsistent picture. Although Courchesne, Yeung-Courchesne, Press et al. (1988) reported a reduction of the cerebellar vermis in individuals with ASD, Cody, Pelphrey and Piven (2002) in a review of subsequent studies conclude that no subsequent independent attempts to determine differences in cerebellar size have replicated these findings. Piven, Saliba, Bailey and Arndt (1997) found increased cerebellar volume in a structural MRI study of adults with HFA, but this difference was proportional to the overall larger brain size in this group. Yet Hardan, Minshew, Mallikarjuhn and Keshavan (2001) report cerebellar enlargement in a group of adults with ASD even when overall brain enlargement was taken into account. We have already seen that the early neuropathological studies of the cerebellum (see Palmen and van Engeland, 2004 for review) have tended to show decreased numbers of Purkinje cells in the cerebellar vermis, and in a recent study, Fatemi, Halt, Realmuto et al. (2002) report decreased Purkinje cell size in adult males with ASD. Thus, as with studies of other brain regions, there is still no consistent picture emerging of ASD-related cerebellar pathology.

The amygdala is a structure located in the medial temporal lobe, near the hippocampus (see Figure 8.3). It receives input from a range of other brain areas including the hippocampus, sensory cortex, and prefrontal cortex. Although anatomically distinct, is difficult to delineate accurately on MRI images (see C. Frith, 2003), a factor that may contribute to some of the conflicting findings on abnormalities of its size and structure in ASD. Howard, Cowell, Boucher et al. (2000) took structural MRI measures of amygdala size in a group of adults with ASD and found evidence of bilateral amygdala enlargement, a finding that is in line with the post-mortem studies of Bauman and Kemper described earlier. Haznedar, Buchsbaum, Wei et al. (2000) found no evidence of abnormal amygdala volume. Differences in sample size, comparison group selection and imaging procedures may well account for some of the discrepant observations, but the findings of a study by Sparks, Friedman, Shaw et al. (2002) may provide some other reasons for the difference. Sparks et al. tested a large sample of young children with ASD and found that although increased amygdala volume was proportional to overall brain

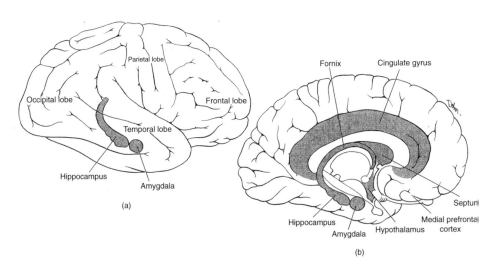

Figure 8.3. Lateral view and sagittal section through a human brain showing components of the limbic system. Reproduced from Plotnick, R. and Mollenauer, S. (1978). *Brain and behavior: an introduction to physiological psychology.* Adapted by permission of Pearson Education Inc., Upper Saddle River, NJ.

volume, the amygdalae of children with more severe autistic features were disproportionately larger, which suggests that increased volume may be associated with more severe autistic symptomatology. Yet this observation does not fit easily with the findings of Howard et al. (2000) described above nor with those of Pierce, Müller, Ambrose et al. (2001) who found decreased amygdala volume in a group of individuals with autistic disorder, and who argued that those studies that reported increased amygdalae volume tested mixed groups of individuals with autistic disorder and Asperger's syndrome. Sparks et al.'s (2002) findings also do not sit well with studies that have reported decreased amygdala volume in ASD samples (Aylward, Minshew, Goldstein et al., 1999; Herbert, Ziegler, Deutsch et al., 2003; Pierce et al., 2001). In short, although on the basis of current research, the balance of probabilities points to some structural amygdala abnormalities in ASD, the picture is far from clear as to why in some cases this manifests itself as enlargement and in others as reduction.

Despite the inconclusive nature of existing studies of brain structure in ASD, it is clear that there are some structural abnormalities in these conditions, an observation that finally lays to rest any notion that ASD might be psychogenic in origin. However, such a conclusion does not rule out a potential role for psychological processes in the development of autistic symptomatology. It can be argued that the presence of impaired dendritic pruning and the persistence of an immature cortical structure into adulthood sets the scene for atypical processing strategies that utilise other, typically structured parts of the brain in an atypical fashion to produce behavioural outcomes that may or may not resemble those seen in typically developed individuals. Such an analysis posits widespread functional abnormalities as a consequence of possibly highly circumscribed structural damage and acknowledges the fact that the later development of initially undamaged brain regions may be compromised by abnormal input from damage elsewhere.

LESION-BASED MODELS OF AUTISTIC BEHAVIOUR

Another approach to determining the brain structures implicated in ASD is to examine the effects of selective damage to parts of the brain on subsequent behaviour. This has been done in several different ways: either by lesioning the brains of non-human animals and observing the behavioural consequences, or by observing the consequences of accidental brain damage in humans. One of the earliest examples of the first kind of investigation was carried out some years before Kanner published his seminal description of autistic children, by Klüver and Bucy (1938; 1939) who described the behavioural consequences of the removal of both temporal lobes from the brains of adult monkeys. The behavioural syndrome – known as the Klüver–Bucy syndrome – comprises an inability to recognise objects (visual agnosia), increased sex drive, decreased emotional responsiveness, in particular a lack of fear responses, impaired social behaviour and a tendency to mouth objects. Apart from increased sex drive, this behavioural pattern is similar in many respects to that seen in severely autistic individuals of the kind described by Kanner and makes the components of the medial temporal lobe candidate structures for further investigation in relation to autistic symptomatology. The medial temporal lobe consists of part of the temporal cortex, the hippocampus and the amygdala (see Figure 8.1), damage to one or more of which are responsible for the behavioural pattern seen in the Klüver–Bucy syndrome. Damage to these structures in adult humans does not typically produce the kinds of behaviour patterns seen in ASD. By contrast, damage occurring in childhood does result in symptoms characteristic of severe ASD (DeLong, Bean & Brown, 1981; DeLong & Heinz, 1997), suggesting that the timing of the lesions is as important as their location.

A major problem with human studies is that lesions can be caused by a range of factors including infections, tuberous sclerosis (a condition that causes calcified tubers to grow in parts of the brain) or tumours. Such conditions tend to spread their damage widely, making it difficult to attribute behavioural consequences to a specific brain structure. The only acceptable way to address the question of the effects of lesion precision and timing is to carry out investigations on non-human animals. The work of Bachevalier (see Bachevalier, 1994 and Machado & Bachevalier, 2003 for reviews) has explored the effects on behaviour and development of selective hippocampal and amygdala lesions to the brains of infant macaque monkeys. Bachevalier and her colleagues bilaterally removed the amygdalae and hippocampi along with some adjacent cortical areas from newborn rhesus monkeys (referred to here as the operated monkeys) and observed the behavioural consequences at 2 and 6 months of age. When placed in a play cage with a familiar, non-operated age mate, at 2 months of age the operated monkeys were more passive, manipulated objects less and made fewer social initiations. By 6 months of age, the operated monkeys were more socially withdrawn, appeared to be uninterested in social interactions, and had blank, unexpressive faces and unexpressive body postures. Their behaviour was also characterised by what Bachevalier (1994) describes as locomotor stereotypies and self-directed activities. Yet at 9 months of age, they did not mouth objects any more than control monkeys and showed the same preference for familiar over unfamiliar objects, as did both unoperated control monkeys and controls who had received a different operation. Bachevalier notes that this pattern of behaviour differs from that seen in monkeys who had their temporal lobes removed when older and who displayed the Klüver–Bucy syndrome, with its characteristic mouthing of objects and lack of fear of novel stimuli. When the operated monkeys were observed in adulthood, they were found to retain all the socio-emotional disturbances observed when they were younger. Bachevalier (1994) concludes from these observations that early damage to the medial temporal lobes produces lasting socio-emotional damage in rhesus monkeys but does not yield the

Klüver–Bucy syndrome seen in late-lesioned animals, thus highlighting the differential effects of timing of lesions on behaviour.

In a further series of experiments Bachevalier explored the effects of selective lesions to components of the medial temporal lobes, especially the hippocampus and the amygdala. The behaviour of hippocampectomised and amygdalectomised monkeys was compared with that of non-operated monkeys and with that of monkeys who had undergone complete removal of the medial temporal lobe. Lesions of the amygdala in infancy produced similar patterns of socio-emotional impairment to those described above for total medial temporal lobe removal, although the intensity of the impairment was diminished. In addition, amygdalectomised monkeys at 6 months of age were more accepting of approaches from other monkeys and did not show the stereotypic behaviours or loss of emotional expressiveness seen in the group with larger lesions. They were also less impaired in recognition memory. Removal of the hippocampus in infancy produced some early diminution in the initiation of social contacts and increased levels of inactivity, but these impairments had disappeared by 6 months of age. Bachevalier (1994) concludes from these findings that the early emergence of autistic-like behaviour patterns in rhesus monkeys is more likely to be a result of early damage to the amygdala than to the hippocampus, but that more severe autistic-like symptoms are found when damage to both these structures occurs. Although DeLong (1992) has argued that hippocampal dysfunction may be primary in the neuropathology of ASD, Bachevalier's conclusions were further supported by the work of Vargha-Khadem, Gadian, Watkins et al. (1997) who demonstrated that early damage to the hippocampus, although it had profound effects on episodic memory, did not produce symptoms of ASD. Such observations suggest that the amygdala is a more likely candidate as the locus of autistic symptomatology.

Our discussion so far has centred on the elucidation of ASD-specific damage to particular brain regions or structures. Underlying these approaches is the idea that specific functions tend to be localised in particular regions of the brain. There is, however, another way of thinking about brain function, which is to consider the brain as a coordinated system that can operate in different ways, some of which produce atypical or dysfunctional behaviour. Several attempts have been made to analyse ASD in terms of systemic changes in brain functions, and it is to these that we now direct our attention.

THEORIES OF GLOBAL BRAIN DYSFUNCTION

THE 'EXTREME MALE BRAIN'

A recent attempt to characterise the way that different brain organisation might mediate the symptomatology of ASD is the 'extreme male brain' hypothesis developed by Baron-Cohen (2002a, b, c). The starting point for this account is a consideration of the substantial body of research that shows that on a range of psychological measures men perform differently from women (see Hines, 2004 for a review). For example, girls are less likely than boys to be competitive in interactions with others, preferring to allow others their turn and to ensure everyone gets a fair deal (Charlesworth & Dzur, 1987). By contrast, boys prefer to engage in rough-and-tumble play (DiPietro, 1981) and to establish dominance hierarchies (Strayer, 1980). On the basis of a catalogue of these and other gender differences in behaviour, Baron-Cohen draws up a framework within which such differences can be understood. He argues that the tasks on which females excel are examples of situations that require a strong capacity for what he terms *empathising* and those on which males excel require a strong capacity for a process he refers to as *systemising*. Empathising in this context is defined as the ability to take on board the thoughts and feelings of others and to use the information thus gained as a basis for decision-making. Baron-Cohen (2002b) points out that the term resonates with the ordinary meaning of the words 'empathy' and 'sympathy' and that it entails but is not limited to the notion of 'theory of mind' or 'mentalising' (see Chapters 2 and 3 of this book). Empathising involves '. . . the attribution of mental states to others, and an appropriate affective response to the other's affective state' (Baron-Cohen, 2002b, p. 248). Systemising, by contrast refers to the set of capacities that enables an individual to take available information and organise it into a system. Baron-Cohen defines a system as '. . . anything that takes inputs and deliver (*sic*) outputs' (Baron-Cohen, 2002b, p. 248). Systemising involves an eye for detail and the capacity to observe changes in variables and map these on to changes in another variable with a view to determining correlations and thus inferring systematic relations between the two. A person who systemises aims for precise prediction of relations between two variables, whereas an empathiser is content with looser, more probabilistic explanations. Baron-Cohen (2002b) asserts that the kinds of explanations that result from a systemising analysis of a problem are by nature defeasible. For example, the statement 'when the key is turned, the engine will turn over' implies the existence of a mechanistic system linking the key and the engine, which can be tested by intervening in the system in various ways. Explaining why someone did not turn up for an engagement by referring to possible hurt feelings because of an earlier disagreement (an explanation based on empathising) is much harder to test out in this way. Baron-Cohen is at pains to point out that empathising and systemising are two processing styles and that they can coexist in the same individual. Different individuals will tend to use more of one than the other, but even those who habitually opt for one or other strategy will be capable at times of adopting the other to some extent. Baron-Cohen develops his argument by asserting that the two processing styles are likely to be independent and to reflect the operation of independent brain systems. Out of this he develops a taxonomy of brain types (set

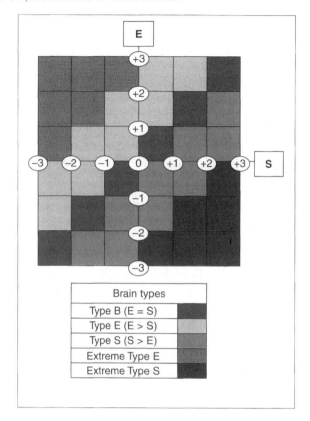

Figure 8.4. Schematic diagram of empathising and systemising. Reproduced and adapted from Baron-Cohen (2002a) by kind permission of Penguin Books.

out in Figure 8.4) in which individuals can be classified along the two axes of systemising and empathising. Extreme values on either of these dimensions are rare, with the result that most people, although they might show a bias in favour of one or other style, have what he terms a 'balanced brain'. The combination of extremely high systemising and extremely low empathising is rare, and is argued to characterise individuals on the autism spectrum. Baron-Cohen also argues that our increasing understanding of the way in which brain specialisation and development is influenced by sex-related hormonal changes throughout development (see Hines, 2004 for review) may provide pointers to the precise nature of the brain basis for ASD.

Three strands of evidence are needed to root this account in reality. The first is to establish the existence of the two styles of processing, the second is to locate their functioning as independent aspects of brain processing and the third is to establish that ASD is characterised by low empathising and high systemising. The first task is more difficult than it might at first appear. It involves developing operational definitions of the two processing styles and then developing tasks that reflect these operational definitions. One way in which Baron-Cohen (2002b) has done this is to take examples from the literature on gender differences in cognitive tasks and analyse those that show a male superiority or a female superiority in terms of his definitions of systemising and empathising respectively. For example, Lawson, Baron-Cohen and Wheelwright (2004) use the findings of Baron-Cohen, Jolliffe, Mortimore et al. (1997b) on the Reading the Mind in the Eyes Test, in which females were better than males at judging a person's mental state from a photograph of the eye region of the face. Since empathising requires an ability to detect what others are feeling, there is a *prima facie* case for accepting performance on this test as a measure of empathising. Lawson et al. also cite the work of Cutting and Dunn (1999) on typical children's performance on false belief and emotion understanding. These authors report a female superiority in false belief but interestingly, not in emotional understanding, somewhat undermining the notion that males are worse at this kind of task. Tasks on which females typically perform less well than males include mental rotation tasks (Collins & Kimura, 1997) and tasks involving the effects of context on judgments of line orientation (see Linn & Petersen, 1985), both of which are illustrated in Figure 8.5. Baron-Cohen (2002b) argues that these and other tasks require an ability to attend to detail and to engage in the kind of 'if–then' reasoning that is supposed to characterise systemising and, as a consequence, are easier for men than for women. Baron-Cohen and colleagues draw on this sex-difference literature to develop tests that measure a Systemising Quotient (SQ, Baron-Cohen, Richler, Bisarya et al., 2003) and a Social Stories Questionnaire (SSQ, Lawson, Baron-Cohen & Wheelwright, 2004) that is thought to measure empathising ability. In addition, Lawson et al. employed a Physical Prediction Questionnaire (PPQ) to measure the understanding of mechanical systems, which, they argue, draw differentially on systemising ability. Typical individuals show the expected sex differences on these measures, thus establishing the validity of the measures as a test of gender-typical processing styles.

The second strand of evidence mentioned in the previous paragraph is harder to come by. It is certainly the case that different psychological tasks differentially engage particular brain regions and systems, and that there is an emerging picture of those brain regions that are involved in some mentalising tasks (see later section on 'theory of mind', p. 219). But the current state of play in relation to brain regions involved in tasks that are thought to mediate systemising tasks is less clear-cut and has yet to be comprehensively reviewed. However, on mental rotation – a task that shows one of the largest effect size differences between males and females (see Hines, 2004) – several investigators have demonstrated right parietal lobe involvement (Parsons, 2003; Yoshino, Inoue & Suzuki, 2000). What is needed to validate the extreme male brain theory is a catalogue of brain regions or systems involved in empathis-

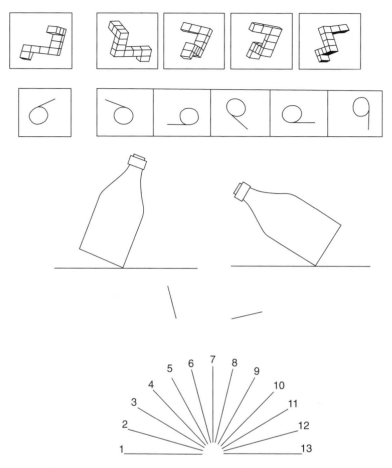

Figure 8.5. Mental rotation, water level and line orientation tasks. Reproduced by kind permission of Elsevier and of Lynn Liben. Bottom figure is a sample item from the Judgment of Line Angle and Position Task (JALP-15), courtesy of Marcia Collaer, task adapted from A. Benton et al's, Judgment of Line Orientation Test.

ing and a similar catalogue for systemising so that presence or absence of substantial overlap can be determined.

The proposition that ASD is characterised by low empathising and high systemising is supported by a number of pieces of evidence. It is hardly controversial to state that individuals with ASD experience difficulties with social understanding and affective relatedness; these are defining characteristics of the conditions. But as we have seen in Chapters 1 and 2, whether this is because of damage to mechanisms specific to these behaviours or particular aspects of more general impairment remains an open question. We have also seen in Chapters 5 and 6 that people with ASD also show a tendency to focus on details rather than global configurations as well as having difficulties in processing contextual information. Baron-Cohen (2002b) argues that these aspects of cognitive processing in ASD contribute to a tendency to systemise and to enhanced performance on tasks such as the Embedded Figures Test, which, as we have seen in Chapter 5, can often be observed in individuals with ASD. A further strand of evidence adduced by Baron-Cohen in support of his theory is the tendency seen in the fathers of children with ASD to have chosen careers in professions, such as engineering, that can be argued to require a high degree of systemising (Baron-Cohen, 1997 but see also Jarrold & Routh, 1998 and Wheelwright & Baron-Cohen, 1998). This analysis also predicts enhanced performance on tests such as mental rotation and the rod and frame test. But as yet there are no published data on the performance of individuals with ASD on these measures. Using the SSQ, PPQ and SQ described above, Baron-Cohen et al. (2003) and Lawson et al. (2004) found that individuals from the autism spectrum tend to perform better than typical males on the SQ and PPQ and worse than typical males on the SSQ. These authors claim that such findings confirm that individuals with ASD have a cognitive style that emphasises systemising and that they do this to a greater extent than typical males, thus confirming the extreme male brain theory.

A cornerstone principle of the theory is the distinction between the two styles of empathising and systemising. Systemising, as we have seen, requires an eye for detail as well as a capacity for precise mapping of inputs to outputs in a way that allows predictions to be made on the basis of 'if-then' reasoning. It is evident that tasks such as the Embedded Figures Test or mental rotation tasks (see Figures 5.1 and 8.5) require a certain eye for detail. But it is less evident that the former entails 'if–then' reasoning. Empathising requires an ability to detect the emotional state of another person and to make inferences about how that person is likely to act on the basis of their knowledge and feelings. But it could be argued that detecting the subtleties of the eye region of the face, as in the Reading the Mind in the Eyes Test, requires an attention to detail far in excess of that required by the Embedded Figures Test. Against this, it could be argued that it is not the perception of detail *per se* that is important but the way this subsequent detail is processed. In the case of the eyes test, it may be processed configurally in a manner that yields a complete gestalt, whereas in the Embedded Figures Test, it is dealt with piecemeal, in a manner that better feeds into an analytical reasoning process. The problem with employing test procedures that already exist is that any attempt to classify them along a systemising–empathising dimension is inevitably post hoc. What is needed is a set of tests that represent operationalisations of the definitions of systemising and empathising that are established on an a-priori basis. Such tests could then be validated in terms of the theory by administering them to large samples of males and females in order to ascertain which showed a gender bias and which did not. Such a process would help to provide constraints on the systemising–empathising dichotomy.

It is also possible that the way a task is classified in terms of sympathising and empathising depends on the perspective from which it is viewed. The Sally–Anne task of false-belief understanding, if thought of as a 'theory of mind' task, would be classified as a measure of empathising. And the findings of a female superiority on the task (Cutting & Dunn, 1999) would appear to bear this out. But in Chapter 2 we discussed a re-analysis of the task in terms of signals, goals and actions (see Bowler et al., 2005), which could arguably place the task under the heading of systemising, thus rendering it easier for individuals with ASD. Yet the mechanical analogue that derives from Bowler et al.'s analysis of the task proved to be just as difficult for children with ASD as did the false-belief version embodying persons and beliefs. Such findings can be taken as counter-evidence to the characterisation of ASD as over-developed systemising. Alternatively, they can be interpreted as supporting the notion that not all tasks that involve the systemic manipulations of 'if–then' rules are easy for individuals from the autism spectrum. Another task that could be thought of as involving the kind of attention to detail that Baron-Cohen argues is crucial to the process of systemising is the number/digit cancellation task (Ekstrom, French & Harman, 1976). In this task, participants are presented with columns of multi-digit numbers and have to check that the digits in each number are exactly the same. For example:

4549492041345   4549492041345

9275145138583   9275146138583

This task produces one of the largest effect sizes for a female advantage in the literature, with females out-performing males both in accuracy and number of items completed in a given time period. Thus, performance on a task that meets one of the criteria for systemising shows a bias in favour of females in the general population. Moreover, data from our own laboratory (Bowler, Gaigg & Hines, in preparation) replicates the female superiority in accuracy on this task (mean accuracy for males = 22.0, mean accuracy for females = 26.0), yet male participants with ASD performed similarly to typical males (mean accuracy = 22.5) whereas females with ASD were significantly worse than all the other groups (mean accuracy = 17.4). The extreme male brain theory would predict that males with ASD would perform worse than typical males, and that females with ASD would perform somewhere between the two. But this is not the pattern of results observed in our study.

Clearly, both in terms of the analysis of the task and on the basis of the results from individuals with ASD, this example suggests that the extreme male brain theory of ASD needs to be re-thought, if not in its entirety, at least in part. A particular problem seems to stem from the initial conceptualisation of tasks and their associated processing styles in terms of a simple systemising–empathising dichotomy. The assumption is made that these are mutually exclusive processes on to which any task can be mapped. But, as Bowler et al.'s (2005) Train Task shows, a supposedly empathising task can be conceptualised in terms of systemising processes. This analysis alone gives us a clue that empathising and systemising might not be mutually exclusive processes, but facets of the operation of a larger number of underlying operations that contribute in different ways to a given behavioural outcome. Paradoxically, such an analysis illustrates one of the potential strengths of the extreme male brain account, which prompts us to think in terms of types of brain process that contribute to a range of tasks rather than each task being considered as specific to a particular brain region.

The extreme male brain theory of ASD claims that we can work out which brain systems might be responsible for the symptoms of ASD and, by invoking the mechanisms that give rise to gender differences in behaviour, may provide clues to possible mechanisms that cause ASD. However, in order for the logic of the theory to work, particularly in this last respect, it must be demonstrated that ASD is an extreme manifestation of all psychological aspects of maleness and not just of some of them. As it stands, the theory rests on a male pattern of performance on a selected set of tasks that show sex differences in the general population. But, as the digit-cancelling example outlined earlier shows, matters may be somewhat more complex. For example, a task that shows one of the largest sex-differences in the general population is target throwing (Watson & Kimura, 1991), on which males show superior performance. Yet individuals with ASD, especially those from the higher-functioning end of the spectrum, are often characterised as being clumsy and would be expected to perform poorly on such a task. The extreme male brain theory would predict the opposite. Although a fruitful heuristic generator of hypotheses, a complete theory of ASD that is based on the idea of extreme maleness must accommodate such contrary evidence in a systematic way.

CONNECTIVITY AND CONNECTIONISM

Our discussion of the extreme male brain account of ASD has introduced the idea that the behavioural symptomatology associated with these disorders is a result of dysfunction of the coordinated activity of the brain. This approach is also evident in interpretations of the brain basis of mentalising and face processing, which increasingly invoke the coordinated activation of a set of different brain regions, each specialised for a subcomponent of the higher-level process. This shift in perspective places as much emphasis on region-specific damage as on disruption of the connectivity between different brain regions or structures. An important theoretical account of reduced connectivity comes from Brock, Brown, Boucher and Rippon (2002) who take Frith's (Frith & Happé, 1994) notion of weak central coherence (WCC, see Chapter 5) and argue that the phenomena of WCC may result from reduced integration of specialised neural networks. The starting point of Brock et al.'s analysis is the *binding problem*, which relates to how the brain constructs a unified experience from activations of disparate and often anatomically remote brain regions. A key concept in Brock et al.'s analysis is that of *temporal binding*, which is the process by which integration occurs by means of the activation in synchrony of brain systems responsible for the processing of different aspects of a complex stimulus. Such synchronous activity is evidenced by EEG activity in the gamma band. Drawing both on the literature on WCC in ASD and on studies of temporal binding in response to complex visual and verbal stimuli, Brock et al. make a number of speculations, for example that the effect reported in typical individuals by Rodriguez, George, Lachaux et al. (1999) would be less in evidence in individuals with ASD. Rodriguez et al. noted that when a Mooney figure such as that shown in Figure 7.2 is rotated through 180° it is perceived as a face in shadow and that this is accompanied by increased EEG gamma synchronisation between the frontal and parietal lobes. Brock also predict similar diminution in synchronisation in ASD on a task in which Braeutigam, Bailey and Swithenby (2001) report synchronised EEG gamma activity when typical participants had to judge the congruity or otherwise of the final word of a sentence of the type '*To keep warm, Mark wore a scarf and a furry hat/glass*'.

The study of coordinated activity among brain regions has been facilitated by a number of technical advances. Most recently, the development of diffusion tensor imaging in the context of fMRI has enabled the tracking and evaluation of coordinated cerebral activity. All these developments have led to speculations that ASD is a disorder of connectivity. We have already come across some work that constitutes an empirical test of underconnectivity theory. Later on, in the context of face perception, we will see how gamma EEG patterns indicate poor integration of facial features in individuals with ASD (Grice et al., 2001) and in our later discussion of brain areas thought to be involved in mentalising, we will encounter the work of Castelli, Frith, Happé and Frith (2002), who found diminished functional connectivity between extrastriate cortex and the superior temporal sulcus in individuals with ASD when viewing mentalistic animations, suggesting that coordination between these two areas is necessary in order to perceive the animations in mentalistic terms. Lack of inter-region connectivity was also reported by Just, Cherkassky, Keller and Minshew (2004) in a study of sentence comprehension in a group of high-functioning adults with ASD and a typical comparison group. Participants had to decide who was the agent or the recipient in active and passive sentences such as '*The cook thanked the father*' or '*The editor was thanked by the secretary*'. In addition to showing stronger activation in different areas (Wernicke's area in the ASD group; Broca's area in the typical group), the correlation of activation between the two areas was lower in the ASD group, leading Just et al. to conclude that language processing in ASD does not activate the same large-scale neural network as is activated in typical

individuals, thus supporting the notion that ASD is a set of disorders characterised by underconnectivity. These authors also argue that their underconnectivity theory is consistent with the pattern of increased followed by
decreased brain size seen during the early years of development of individuals with ASD as well as the neuropathological findings on increased cell
density and the observations of Casanova et al. (2002) of increased cortical
minicolumn density discussed earlier.

The approaches just described represent a conceptual shift away from interpretations derived from observations of the effects of lesions to particular areas
of the brain. Although such lesions can sometimes result in quite specific behavioural effects and although there are quite distinct anatomical components of
the brain, such as the brain stem, the hypothalamus, the cerebellum and the
cerebral cortex, many investigators, from Luria (1966) onwards, have observed
that focal lesions sometimes produced quite global effects. Just because
damage to a specific area can impair some psychological functions and leave
others spared does not mean that the damaged area is the sole locus of the
impaired psychological function; it may be simply that the functioning of an
important component of a system that handles the impaired function has been
disrupted, thus compromising the operation of other components of the
system. This latter conceptualisation takes us beyond a rather naive (and, it
must be said, not very widely held) conception of the relation between the brain
and behaviour to one that sees functions as the result of the operation of the
systemic operation of specialised brain centres. Examples of such reasoning
have been presented in the sections on mentalising and face processing discussed earlier in this chapter, an example of which is presented in Figure 8.6.
Yet analyses like these borrow heavily from the information-processing
metaphor and attempt to map analyses of psychological processes in terms
of the way in which processed information is mapped onto brain structures. Such models are heavily reliant on concepts derived from computer
science and ultimately are based on the properties of what are known as
Von Neumann architectures. These architectures entail the storage of information at precise locations in the system and its transfer along communication channels. These channels are the weak point of the operation of such
systems because they can easily become overloaded, a phenomenon known as
the *Von Neumann bottleneck*. Such bottlenecks severely limit the capacity of
Von Neumann machines to process large quantities of information quickly and
they heavily constrain the utility of Von Neumann machines as models of brain
function.

An alternative conceptualisation of the way the brain (or at least the
cortex) operates is to regard it as an initially non-specialised system that differentiates and specialises in response to experience. According to this view,
what we see in the adult brain as regions or systems that appear to be specialised for particular functions or processes did not in fact start out that way,
but evolved in response to the individual's experiences in the world. These

approaches to explaining brain function share with those just described the view that psychological processes are a result of activity distributed across the brain. But they differ in the way they argue that information is represented in the brain. Rather than seeing a given object, event or piece of knowledge as represented in a specific location, they propose that it is widely distributed in a network of nerve cells, the interconnections of which reflect the knowledge state of the organism. Such accounts are often grouped under the heading of *connectionist systems* or *parallel distributed processing* (PDP). Within the broad framework of connectionist theory there are several different conceptualisations of how a system can evolve (see Clark, 1997; Edelman, 1987; Elman, Bates, Johnson et al. 1996; Hendricks-Jansen, 1996 for more detail).

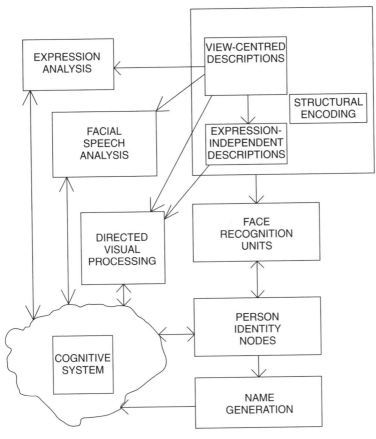

Figure 8.6. A functional model of face perception that illustrates information flows along pathways between hypothetical processing units. Reproduced with permission of the British Psychological Society.

But all accounts share the idea that incoming information alters the strengths of the connections between nerve cells in a manner that causes some connections to become strong and others to wither and eventually die. The patterning of this pruning and growth is dependent on the adaptive value of the organism's response to incoming information and eventually leads to the development of *cortical feature maps*, which embody in their neural organisation the patterning of organism–environment interaction. The connectionist approach borrows heavily on what we already know about the way nerve cells are organised in the cerebral cortex, and has the advantage that it can be readily modelled on computers (see Plunkett & Elman, 2000 for examples of how to do this).

One advantage of the connectionist approach is that it can give a flavour of how the system evolves over time in its processing of information. This pattern of evolution can be compared with the way those processes evolve in the typically (or atypically) developing child, a well-known example of which is Rumelhart and McClelland's (1986) development of a neural network to model the acquisition of the past tense of verbs in English. English has two classes of verb: regular and irregular. The past tense of regular verbs, such as *walk* is rendered by adding -*ed*; the past tense of irregular verbs differs from verb to verb – *run* becomes *ran*, *eat* becomes *ate*, etc. Typically developing children initially imitate what they hear and thereby get the past tenses of the verbs they know right. But they then develop an awareness of the regular rule and overapply it to every case, producing errors such as *runned* or *eated*. It is only later that they come to understand that there are two classes of verb that have to be treated differently. This pattern of improved followed by diminished followed by renewed performance is often referred to as a U-shaped or J-shaped developmental trajectory, and has been demonstrated in other areas such as block-balancing (Karmiloff-Smith, 1992). Rumelhart and McClelland's connectionist network learned the formation of the past tense of English verbs, and demonstrated similar U-shaped curves as are observed in typical children. This example provides some evidence that neural networks, at least in some respects, model the activity of the human cerebral cortex.

A second attribute of neural networks is the way they respond to damage. Whereas damage to components or pathways in a typical Von Neumann machine often results in total shut-down of the system (imagine snipping one or two wires or printed circuit paths inside your computer), damage to neural nets rarely results in such a dramatic curtailment of the capacity of the system. Rather than completely ceasing to function, the system shows patchy performance and what has been termed 'graceful degradation' (Cohen, 1998, p. 8), with considerable levels of residual functioning. This more gradual and subtle impairment of processing mirrors what actually happens when people suffer brain damage (as Damasio, 1994 observes, such individuals continue to experience the world in ways that are not greatly different from the way they did before the damage). It also calls into question the notion that specific processes or pieces of knowledge necessary for the operation of these processes are stored in precise locations in the brain, but rather are distributed across the system, thus making them robust to the effects of damage.

Although connectionist accounts have been around for some time (see Hebb, 1949), it was not until the advent of computers powerful enough to model networks of sufficient complexity that serious testing of their use as models for the brain implementation of complex psychological processes has been possible. As a consequence, there are few examples of their application to ASD, although there has been considerable theoretical speculation (see Belmonte, Allen, Beckel-Mitchener et al., 2004; McClelland, 2000; Thomas & Karmiloff-Smith, 2002). Most commentators highlight the parallels between the abnormal cell densities reported in neuropathological and neuroanatomical studies of ASD and the effects of varying the number of elements and connections in neural networks on their handling of specific tasks. For example, Cohen (1998) tested the effects of a neural network that he argued mirrored the neuropathological findings in ASD in that the number of connections could be either too few or too many. Networks with different numbers of connections were trained to discriminate the symptomatological profiles of children with or without ASD, and the results showed poor classification when the number of connections was either less than or greater than a particular optimal value. In another study, Gustafsson and Paplinski (2004) carried out a series of simulations to test the capacity of cortical feature maps to form abstract representations of clusters of features in inputs provided by the experimenter. They started from Hermelin's (1978) conclusion that children with ASD have difficulty in re-coding input into a more abstract form that allows them to see similarities across situations that transcend the subtle differences among them and further drew on the literature on attentional impairments in ASD (see Chapter 6 for a summary) and on observations that children with ASD prefer familiar over novel stimuli. A self-organising neural network was set up to respond in four different ways to multidimensional stimuli presented from two different sources. The first simulation entailed novelty seeking and was considered to be the normal mode of processing, whereby when information came from the source other than the one currently being processed, that information was chosen for processing. In the second mode – attention shift impairment – the system was engineered to shift to an alternative source with a very low probability, resulting in a tendency to stay focused on one source of information. The third mode entailed choosing a source according to the amount of time the network had previously engaged with that source, i.e. to seek out familiar sources of information. The final mode involved a combination of the attention-shift and familiarity preference. Gustafsson and Paplinski found that novelty seeking and attention shift impairment produced similar patterns of learning but that familiarity preference resulted in maps that reflected the preferred source but not that of the non-preferred source, a pattern that they argued resembled the kinds of islets of ability found in individuals with ASD.

It is important to remember that connectionist accounts of ASD are still in their infancy and that at present the only data come from models of systems that appear to mimic highly circumscribed aspects of the symptomatology of these conditions. Despite the persuasive similarity between neural networks and brain structure, there is no guarantee that the way brains work is anything like the way neural networks operate. It is important to bear in mind that these systems are designed by scientists and that the way that they operate is in part determined by the way they have been designed. Yet one way to understand how something works is to build a machine that does the same thing. Neural networks and connectionist theory at least provide us with a way of building a machine that operates like the human brain (or at least, the cerebral cortex) and of testing out how it might go wrong.

'SOCIAL INTELLIGENCE', THE SOCIAL BRAIN AND THE AMYGDALA THEORY OF ASD

Several writers have made reference to a body of literature in which the idea is developed that the human brain has evolved in ways that enable individuals to engage in complex social interactions (see Dunbar, 1998, and chapters in Brüne, Ribbert & Schiefenhövel, 2003 for further discussion). Much of the evidence that informs this particular debate comes from structural anthropology and evolutionary biology. Its relevance to ASD is indirect, in that arguments are made that evolution has resulted in highly specialised brain systems that have conferred evolutionary advantage to humans, and that because such systems exist, damage can produce specific behavioural consequences, one of which is the kind of symptomatology seen in ASD. Given that ASD appears to be a specific dysfunction of the ability to engage in reciprocal social relations (although the specificity is an arguable point, as we have seen), ASD provides another strand of evidence in support of the social brain theory. However, if we adopt this second stance, we run the risk of generating a circular argument in that we use evolutionary theory to explain intact social function, impairment of which is disadvantageous. This disadvantage is then used to justify the initial invocation of evolution to account for the emergence of human social function. In this respect, a more fruitful starting point might be to argue that it is not the theory of the social brain that helps to inform our understanding of ASD, but rather the reverse. On this argument, we should look for neural correlates of social functioning in people with ASD.

Accounts of the Klüver–Bucy syndrome coupled with reports of the behavioural consequences of amygdala damage in adult humans (Adolphs, Baron-Cohen & Tranel, 2002; Adolphs, Sears & Piven, 2001; Adolphs & Tranel, 2000) and the findings of Bachevalier's lesion studies led to the development of an amygdala theory of ASD, put forward principally by Baron-Cohen and colleagues (Baron-Cohen, Ring, Bullimore et al., 2000). In addition to the evidence just outlined, these authors also draw on the notion of the 'social brain' developed by Brothers (1990). Brothers argued that 'social intelligence' – the ability to '. . . interpret others' behaviour in terms of mental states (thoughts, intentions, desires and beliefs), to interact both in complex social groups and in close relationships, to empathize with others' states of mind and to predict how others will feel, think and behave' (Baron-Cohen, Ring, Wheelwright et al., 1999b, p. 1891) – was mediated by three principal brain areas: the orbitofrontal cortex, the superior temporal sulcus and gyrus, and the amygdala. Baron-Cohen et al.'s approach is based on the analysis that the first two of these structures deal with aspects of mental state understanding of the kind that was discussed in Chapters 2 and 3 of this book but that the amygdala was implicated in aspects of social behaviour such as initiating and responding in social interactions as well as the emotional modulation of approach behaviours. Other evidence cited by Baron-Cohen to support hypothesised amygdala involvement in ASD comes from the post-mortem studies of Bauman and Kemper and the animal lesion studies of Bachevalier described above, structural (Abell, Krams, Ashburner et al. 1999) and functional (Gillberg, Bjure, Uvebrant et al., 1993) imaging studies of abnormal amygdala size and function in individuals with ASD as well as a study that showed diminished activation of the amygdala when performing the Reading the Mind in the Eyes Test (Baron-Cohen, Ring, Wheelwright et al., 1999b). In this last study, participants were shown sequences of pictures of the eye region of faces and asked either to judge the gender of the person in the picture or to choose which of two mental state or emotional terms provided was being expressed in the picture. Whereas the amygdalae of comparison participants without ASD were more activated during the latter task, this was not the case for the participants with higher-functioning ASD. (Other brain regions were activated as well, but these will be discussed in the section on theory of mind and the brain.)

Other evidence of amygdala involvement in ASD comes from a study by Howard et al. (2000) who compared a group of 10 high-functioning men with ASD with 10 matched typical men on tests of facial recognition of emotions, direction of eye gaze and recognition memory for faces and words. Their results showed impairment in the ASD group in the recognition of fearful facial expressions, in the accurate judgment of eye direction and in recognition memory for faces, leading the authors to conclude that the amygdala plays an important role in the social impairment characteristic of people with ASD. Support for this interpretation comes from assessments of patients with amygdala lesions who, similar to individuals with ASD, are impaired in their ability to recognise facial expressions of fear (Adolphs, Tranel, Damasio & Damasio, 1994; Pelphrey, Sasson, Reznick et al., 2002). Similar parallels between amygdalectomised patients and individuals with ASD have been noted on tasks in which photographs of faces are judged for trustworthiness (Adolphs, Tranel & Damasio, 1998; Adolphs, Sears & Piven, 2001). Imaging studies support these findings in both typical (Winston, Strange, O'Doherty & Dolan 2002) and ASD individuals (Wang, Dapretto, Hariri et al., 2004).

The findings just described certainly provide compelling evidence for some form of amygdala involvement in ASD. But quite how we should conceptualise this involvement is far from clear. There are a number of reasons to be cautious when asserting a key role for the amygdala in ASD. First, there is the question of the presence of structural abnormality, which as we have seen is not a reliable finding. A second reason relates to the behavioural measures that have been reported as being associated with activation of the amygdala. As we have seen, Howard et al. (2000) used the Reading the Mind in the Eyes Test to infer the amygdala's role in social intelligence. Similarly, Howard et al. (2000) found amygdala activity related to recognition of facial expressions of fear and to assessments of gaze direction. All these measures can be grouped together under the heading 'social stimuli', with the resultant argument that the amygdala is involved in the processing of social information, and thus is involved in social impairment. But a similar problem arises in this context as arose in the area of 'theory of mind' discussed in Chapter 2. It may be the case that the kinds of processes required in reading the mind in the eyes, or accurately judging gaze direction or whatever, are simply specific aspects of some more general capacity that is handled by the amygdala and by regions that feed it with information. For example, although Schultz, Grelotti, Klin et al. (2003) report activation of the amygdala when typical participants asked to describe animated shapes engaging in actions that resemble social interactions in a film modelled on that of Heider and Simmel (1944), work by Bowler and Thommen (2000) has shown that individuals with ASD appear unable to see patterns of activity that involve action at a distance between two animate objects. So what appears to be an inability to make social attributions may be an emergent property of the ability to link together spatially separate but temporally contingent actions. In relation to the role of the amygdala in recognising gaze direction or facial expressions of fear or in inferring mental states from pictures of the eyes, Amaral, Bauman and Schumann (2003) and Davidson and Slagter (2000) argue that these difficulties may be a by-product of abnormal face processing in ASD (see Chapter 7), a point that is also supported by the findings of Hobson, Ouston and Lee (1988b). They found that when they had to sort faces by identity or emotional expression, children with ASD showed a steeper decline in facial recognition when parts of the face were progressively blanked off than did typical children. This suggests that children with ASD extract information from faces in a different manner from that used by typical individuals. Similar points can also be made in relation to the findings on trustworthiness described earlier on.

A final point of scepticism about the role of the amygdala in social impairment is raised by Amaral et al. (2003) in relation to the studies on monkeys of early removal of the amygdala (Bachevalier, 1994). Amaral et al. point out that the monkeys in the early studies were deprived of normal maternal rearing; they were typically reared in conjunction with age peers but not with their mothers. Amaral et al. point to a large body of research that shows abnormal behavioural consequences of maternal deprivation in macaque monkeys (e.g. Novak & Sackett, 1997) and go on to cite some of their own work (Emery, Capitanio, Mason et al., 2001) in which amygdalectomised adult monkeys who lived in a field cage environment, designed to resemble their naturalistic environment closely, engaged in greater amounts of social interaction than did control monkeys, whether lesioned or not. Emery et al. concluded that the amygdala lesions did not disrupt the basic components of the capacity for social interaction but influenced social behaviour indirectly by rendering the lesioned animals less fearful of certain social situations. In a further series of studies (Bauman, Lavenex, Mason et al., 2003, cited in Amaral et al., 2003; Prather, Lavenex, Mauldin-Jourdain et al., 2001), the researchers lesioned the amygdalae of infant macaque monkeys and reared them with their mothers and with exposure to other mother–infant pairs. These infants showed none of the impairments documented in earlier studies of amygdalectomised monkeys, calling into question the fundamental role of the amygdala in the development of certain aspects of social behaviour, which forms the basis of the amygdala theory of ASD. Yet the question remains as to why the lesioned comparison group in Bachevalier's (1994) report (i.e. monkeys who had lesions to areas other than the medial temporal lobe) did not show the same symptoms of social impairment seen in the experimental group, despite having been maternally deprived. The fact that they were not socially impaired leads us to conclude that the amygdala is involved in some way in the developmental modulation of species-specific social behaviours. The extent to which this involvement is limited specifically to social behaviours or covers a wider range of adaptive functioning, and the extent to which the amygdala is a crucial locus of social understanding or a part of a larger system, remains an open question.

The implication of the amygdala in the symptomatology of ASD on the basis of behavioural similarity resulting from lesions as well as on functional involvement in response to particular task demands provides one illustration of another approach to investigating those regions of the brain that might be implicated in ASD. Rather than starting from the findings of abnormal neuroanatomy or the behavioural consequences of lesions, this approach takes patterns of behaviour and cognition as its starting point and uses functional imaging techniques to try to establish brain structures and brain systems that mediate these patterns.

IMPAIRED UNDERSTANDING OF OTHER MINDS

Following on from the discussion in the previous paragraphs, perhaps the most obvious set of psychological functions to investigate from the perspective of brain involvement is that relating to the understanding of others' minds. As we have seen in Chapters 2 and 3, this area has been a major focus of the behavioural research into ASD over the last two decades. It is not surprising, therefore, that an initial focus of neuroimaging studies should target these deficits. Research in this area has grown at an exponential rate and all that can be done here is to outline the broad findings fleshed out by descriptions of selected studies in order to give a flavour of the kind of research that is under way. Readers interested in greater detail can consult some of the excellent reviews in the area such as Blakemore, Winston and Frith (2004), Frith (2001), and a particularly thoughtful review by C. Frith (2003).

The very first study to report brain imaging findings in the context of ASD was by Baron-Cohen, Ring, Moriarty et al. (1994) in which they asked a group of individuals with ASD and a comparison group of individuals with mental handicap to recognise mental state terms. Fewer correct recognitions were made by the former group, a finding that was taken as evidence that mental state terms were a good analogue for theory of mind, since the ASD group was characterised by impairments in that domain. In a second study, typical participants (but not those with ASDs) were tested for their recognition of mental state terms while undergoing SPECT scanning. Participants were read out lists of words, some of which were mental state words ('. . . describe what goes on in the mind or what the mind can do', p. 643) in the experimental condition, or body-related words ('. . . things in the body or that the body can do', p. 643) in the control condition. Participants had to raise their index fingers when they heard a mental state or a body-related word. In line with the investigators' hypotheses, the mental state term task caused increased blood flow in the right orbitofrontal cortex (part of the right frontal cortex above and behind the eyeball), thus implicating this area in theory of mind and by extension its dysfunction in individuals with ASD. The first investigation to use scanning procedures to determine mental-state-related brain areas in individuals with ASD was carried out by Happé, Ehlers, Fletcher et al. (1996). These authors asked five men with a diagnosis of Asperger's syndrome and a comparison group of volunteers, on whom no information was given, to undergo PET scanning while reading stories of the kind described in Chapter 2. Three types of story were used (see Box 8.1): mental state stories, in which a protagonist's behaviour had to be explained by reference to thoughts or beliefs, non-mental state stories, where a situational explanation was required, and unconnected sentences, which consisted of a series of statements that were not linked to form a narrative. A standard subtraction procedure was used in which the patterns of blood flow in the brain were determined for each of the three story types. These different activation patterns were then subtracted from each other in order to determine areas of activation (or increased blood flow) that were unique to a particular task. This subtraction procedure can also be used to compare patterns of activation across groups on a particular task. In Happé et al.'s study, with one exception, the different story types activated the same regions in both participant groups. The exception was the medial

Box 8.1. Examples of strange stories

Story involving mental state attribution

Helen waited all year for Christmas, because she knew at Christmas she could ask her parents for a rabbit. Helen wanted a rabbit more than anything in the world. At last Christmas Day arrived, and Helen ran to unwrap the big box her parents had given her. She felt sure it would contain a little rabbit in a cage. But when she opened it, with all the family standing round, she found her present was just a boring old set of encyclopedias, which Helen did not want at all! Still, when Helen's parents asked her how she liked her Christmas present, she said, 'It's lovely, thank you. It's just what I wanted.'

(The question afterwards was: *Why did she say this?*)

Story not involving mental state attribution

Mrs Simpson, the librarian, receives a special book which she has to catalogue and find an appropriate place for. She has to decide which section to file it under. The library is very big, and has different sections on many different subjects. The new book is about plants and their medical uses, and is heavily illustrated. However, Mrs Simpson does not put it on the shelf with the rest of the books on botany. Neither does she put it with the books on medicine. Instead, she carefully takes it into a separate room. In this room all the books are kept in special cases, and the temperature is kept constant.

(The question afterwards was: *Why did she do this?*)

Unlinked sentences

She is always saying that someone will eventually find the treasure. Everyone is allowed two visits and no more. At the psychiatry department they were interviewing the new nurses. Jim will win the first race of the meeting. She has taken all the children to visit the zoo today. Simon's uncle is wearing a new suit. The same phrase of twenty-three notes recurred throughout.

(The question afterwards was: *Will Jim lose the first race?*)

From Happé (1994).

prefrontal cortex (the inner part of the frontal lobe in the groove between the two hemispheres, see Figure 8.3), which was activated by the mental state stories in the comparison participants but not in those with Asperger's syndrome, who activated a more ventral area of medial prefrontal cortex to process these stories. When compared with an earlier study using the same materials and procedures with a group of typical individuals (Fletcher, Happé, Frith et al., 1995), Happé et al. noted that although the Asperger participants activated similar areas to those activated in comparison participants when processing narrative stories compared to unconnected sentences, the levels of activation were significantly lower in the latter group, suggesting that they tended to process sequences of sentences that constituted a story similarly to sentence sequences that were not narratively linked. Happé et al. (1996) also noted that the Asperger participants, when processing mental state stories, tended to activate a region of the medial prefrontal cortex that is typically used for general purpose reasoning, suggesting that they may be 'hacking out' an understanding of the stories without employing mental state reasoning (see Chapter 2 for a further discussion of hacking out).

Although 10 years old and using PET scanning, which has now been largely superseded by fMRI, the Happé et al. (1996) study has been presented in some detail because it encompasses all the important elements of virtually all functional imaging studies of ASD that have been carried out subsequently. Since its publication, a small but growing number of studies have appeared that were designed to determine those brain regions that might be implicated in impaired 'theory of mind' in ASD. In addition to the stories developed by Happé, investigators have employed stimuli such as the Reading the Mind in the Eyes Test (Baron-Cohen et al., 1999a) and a series of animated cartoon films in which geometric shapes engage in physical and 'mentalistic' interactions (Castelli et al., 2002; Castelli, Happé, Frith & Frith, 2000). Summarising these findings, U. Frith (2001, 2003) identifies three regions that have been consistently associated with performance on 'mentalising' tasks – the medial prefrontal cortex, the posterior superior temporal sulcus and the periamygdaloyd cortex at the temporal pole (the part of the temporal lobe around the amygdala, see Figure 8.1). U. Frith (2003) speculates that these three regions do not in themselves tell us a great deal about how the mentalising system works, but that we can gain some clues from studies that have shown activation of these areas in response to the performance of other tasks. For example, we have already seen that the amygdala is involved in the appraisal of facial expressions of fear as well as assessments of the direction of eye gaze (Howard et al., 2000). Medial prefrontal cortical activity has been found to be associated with self-referential mental activity (Gusnard, Akbudak, Shulman & Raichle, 2001) and activity in the posterior superior temporal sulcus appears to be sensitive to eye gaze (Hoffman & Haxby, 2000 cited in Frith, 2001) and to biological motion (Grezes, Costes & Decety, 1999 cited in Frith 2001). Both U. Frith (2001, 2003) and C. Frith (2003) are at pains to emphasise that the evidence on the neural substrate for a mentalising system is as yet slim, and that we should be careful when making speculations about exactly how these three areas might cooperate to yield the complex set of abilities that are collectively labelled 'mentalising' or 'theory of mind'.

One speculation, developed by both U. Frith (2003) and C. Frith (2003), is based on some observations by Castelli et al. (2000; 2002) in their study of brain activation in response to mentalistic and non-mentalistic interactions among geometric shapes. A group of adults with Asperger's syndrome or high-functioning ASD were asked to watch these different types of animations while undergoing PET scanning and were then asked to describe what was happening in the animation. The ASD participants were found to give less accurate descriptions of the interactions labelled 'theory of mind' than the non-theory-of-mind animations. They also showed less activation of the three brain areas described above than did comparison participants. But Castelli et al. also noted that an area of the striate cortex was activated in response to the theory-of-mind animations to the same extent for both participant groups and that this activation was poorly correlated with activity in the superior temporal sulcus in the ASD group only. The conclusion drawn from these findings was that as the activated striate forms part of the occipital lobes that process form and object perception, the ASD group were similar to controls at registering the complex nature of the theory of mind animations at this level. But the poor correlation with activity in the superior temporal sulcus in the ASD group only suggests some kind of impaired connectivity between the areas responsible for early (in information processing terms) treatment of the incoming visual information and its treatment later on in the system. Castelli et al.'s preferred explanation for this cluster of observations is to invoke the notion of top-down processing whereby the processing of incoming information is modulated by representations already present in the system. C. Frith (2003) cites some findings from monkeys (Sugase et al. 1999 cited in C. Frith, 2003) that demonstrate the modulatory effects of temporal lobe activity on visual area responses in a face expression-learning task. And Friston & Buchel (2000 cited in C. Frith, 2003) observed how information from the parietal and prefrontal cortex served to modulate connectivity between two visual areas when typically developed participants had to selectively attend to a moving visual stimulus. The invocation of top-down processing and the suggestion that its impairment in ASD may lie at the root of the observed impairments in the Castelli et al. study is reminiscent of the work of Mitchell and colleagues discussed in Chapter 5 (Mitchell & Ropar, 2004). That work showed that the phenomena of weak central coherence in ASD can, at least partly, be explained by a failure to apply prior knowledge to a current problem. It can be argued that the application of prior knowledge entails the recruitment of information stored at different sites in the brain and thus relies on inter-region connectivity. A prediction that can be made from such an analysis is that if top-down processing is a factor that is common to both mental state understanding and central coherence, then we would expect both these measures to correlate, a prediction that was supported by the findings of a study by Jarrold, Butler, Cottington and Jimenez (2000). These authors report correlations between measures of mental state understanding and weak central coherence both in typical children and children with ASD.

It is important to keep in mind that the interpretations of Castelli et al.'s (2002) findings are entirely speculative, a point that is made very clear by the authors of these speculations (see C. Frith, 2003, pp. 161–163 and U. Frith, 2003, pp. 198–201). There is as yet no evidence for the mechanisms proposed, but in the light of existing findings the speculations form the basis for plausible hypotheses on which to base further research.

There are a number of other observations that can be made about the current state of the science on mentalising and the brain. The first of these relates to the logic of the imaging studies themselves. Most of the studies described in the preceding paragraphs have used either PET or fMRI scanning in which images relating to a control task were subtracted from those relating to a task thought to measure mentalising ability – the so-called subtraction method. However, Bates (1993) has argued that the underlying logic of the subtraction method may be flawed. She likened the process to mapping the patterns of muscle tension in a weightlifter holding a heavy barbell over his head. If we imagine adding one extra kilogram to one side of the barbell, then the weightlifter will have to adjust his stance, resulting in a changed pattern of muscle activation. If we subtract the first pattern from the second, then we will have a difference map that will show the muscles that have changed their degree of tension in response to the extra weight and the imbalance it causes. However, Bates argues, it is fallacious to conclude that these are the areas that support the extra kilogram. In fact, the extra weight is supported by the whole of the weightlifter's musculoskeletal system. What differs in the second circumstance is that the system is configured differently, but the whole system is, nonetheless, involved. Bates' critique reflects the fundamental difference of opinion in the neuropsychological literature that we have already encountered in our discussion of connectionist accounts – that between the proponents of there being specific structures or clusters of structures dedicated to specific functions and those who see the brain as operating as an integrated system that may alter its configuration when performing different tasks.

A second observation that can be made relates to the choice of mentalising tasks used in the subtraction studies. To date, none of the scanning studies of individuals with ASD have used versions of the Sally–Anne task (Baron-Cohen et al., 1985) but have tended to use 'more advanced' tests of mentalising such as Happé's Strange Stories, Baron-Cohen's Reading the Mind in the Eyes (see Chapter 2) or the animations developed by Castelli et al. (2000). The reasoning behind the choice of these tasks is not always made explicit, and even where it is (e.g. Happé et al., 1996) it is not followed through. Happé et al. argue that it is meaningless (sic) to scan individuals on a task that they cannot perform, presumably because any differential activations might reflect task failure rather than specifically task-related areas. Yet Happé et al. go on to employ a task that had previously proved to be difficult for high-functioning individuals with ASD and which, from their own data, proved to be harder for the ASD sample they scanned. Presumably, a simpler task (such as the Sally–Anne task, Baron-Cohen et al., 1985) was not chosen because the kinds of individuals typically employed in scanning studies (people with higher-functioning ASD), although they may have experienced some delay in passing such tasks (see Happé, 1995), would nevertheless perform on them at an appropriate level. But this argument hinges on how we conceptualise delay in passing mentalising tasks and on what we imagine is happening when an individual eventually succeeds on them. If we argue that delay and subsequent catching up is a reflection of the late development of typical processing, then indeed it would make little sense to use such measures in scanning studies, since they would probably not show any differences in activation. But if we see delayed development and eventual catching up as the result of some kind of hacking out (Happé, 1995, see Chapter 2), then it makes perfect sense to employ such measures, since any observed differences in brain activity could only be the result of atypical processing. However, to choose a task on which individuals with ASD perform worse than typical comparison individuals seems to muddy the waters by making it uncertain whether the observed activation differences in the ASD group are a result of task failure or a difficulty in understanding the minds of others.

The third observation concerns the choice of tasks used in scanning studies. Two of the studies mentioned above (Baron-Cohen et al., 1999b and Happé et al., 1996) employed so-called 'advanced' measures of theory of mind, for reasons outlined in the previous paragraph. However, as we have seen in Chapter 2, the links between these measures and the underlying theory that proposes impaired mental state understanding in ASD are not entirely clear. Nor is there much in the way of empirical evidence demonstrating correlations among these different measures, which are asserted to assess the same underlying constructs (see Brent, Rios, Happé & Charman, 2004).

A final observation centres on the nature of the control tasks used in the subtraction studies. In Chapter 2 we saw that the widely held view that in the context of Sally–Anne type false-belief tasks, false-photograph tasks of the kind developed by Zaitchik (1990) were considered adequate, non-mentalistic controls and that a more complex task was needed (Bowler et al., 2005). A similar analysis could be applied to the mentalising and control measures employed in the scanning studies under discussion here. Happé et al. (1996) used two control procedures (see Box 8.1), one a 'non-mentalistic' story and the other a series of unconnected yet information-bearing sentences. Comparing mentalising performance with the second control measures narrative comprehension against comprehension of individual sentences. More important is the comparison between the mentalistic and non-mentalistic stories. In both cases there is a protagonist who acts towards an object or speaks to a person in a way that is unusual given the context set up by the previous sentences. The participant's task is to explain why the action or the utterance is unusual. Although this control task answers many of the criticisms made by Bowler et al. (2005) of the false-photograph task, there remain some potential sources of confound. For example, in the mentalistic story, the participant is asked to explain an utterance whereas in the non-mentalistic story an explanation for an action is called for. Slight changes to the plot of the two stories in Box 8.1 (for example by having Helen's auntie present at the scene who then asks Helen what she is going to say to her parents regarding the present, and by having a library assistant present to whom the librarian says where she is going to put the book) could clear up this potential confound and further inform our understanding of mentalising and the brain. The control task in the Reading the Mind in the Eyes Test employed by Baron-Cohen et al. (1999b) required participants to judge the gender of the people whose eyes were depicted in the photograph. A problem with that task is that it asks for a judgment about an unchanging aspect of the person in the photograph, whereas the experimental task requires the identification of one of a number of transient states. Thus, quite apart from their supposed difference on the dimension of mentalising, the two tasks make quite different additional demands on the participant, demands that are likely to influence any performance or brain activation difference that might be observed. In Castelli et al.'s (2002) animation study, the control task was the film that depicted non-mentalistic interactions between agents. As was noted in the last but one paragraph, Castelli et al.'s stimuli are intuitively compelling, and the findings from the comparison participants in their study suggested a high degree of congruity between those individuals' interpretations of the animations and what the experimenters had in mind when developing them, a congruity that was much less in evidence in the ASD group. From the point of view of a control task, ideally we would need some kind of metric of movement and interactional complexity on which to match the different animations independent of any putative mental state content. An analysis in terms of agents and actions such as that developed by Thommen (1992) and employed by Bowler and Thommen (2000) might be appropriate. At present, all Castelli et al.'s findings tell us is that when confronted with ambiguous stimuli, typical individuals tend to converge on a particular kind of interpretation (which in this case happens to be mentalistic for their mentalistic films), whereas individuals with ASD tend to be more idiosyncratic in their approach.

The foregoing analysis suggests that, on methodological and conceptual grounds, we have good reason to be cautious when speculating about the nature of the brain basis for supposed mental state reasoning in individuals with ASD. But the analyses that have resulted from this body of research provide the basis for moving the issue forward. For example, it would appear to make sense to test individuals with ASD on tasks that ostensibly measure mental state reasoning but that are well within their competence, and to compare their performance on control tasks that were similar in all respects except for the mental state component and on which they performed equally well. Two such candidate tasks are the Sally–Anne task (Baron-Cohen et al., 1985) and the Train task (Bowler et al., 2005). Children with ASD and children with typical development perform at a similar level on these two tasks, and it should be relatively easy to recruit samples of children from both groups, all of whom would pass both. The scenarios could be presented in video format while the participants were being scanned. Any differences observed between the participants with ASD and the comparison group could safely be attributed to the mental state content of the Sally–Anne task. Until such studies are carried out, however, we must interpret existing findings with some caution.

FACE PROCESSING

Another important aspect of social functioning is the ability to process faces. We have already seen in Chapter 3 that individuals on the autism spectrum experience difficulties in appraising facial expressions of emotion, and in Chapter 7 we discussed the literature that shows that they are likely to process faces in a manner that is different from that of typically developed individuals, in particular by showing a preference for processing parts – especially the mouth – over the whole configuration. The cerebral and neural correlates of face perception have also received some research attention in recent years although as with imaging studies of mentalising, the results are not entirely clear cut.

Considerable excitement was generated by the observation by Schultz, Gauthier, Klin et al. (2000) that when individuals with high-functioning ASD or with Asperger's syndrome were asked to judge pairs of photographs of faces or of everyday objects as the same or different, the ASD group showed hypoactivation of the middle of the right fusiform gyrus, which is often referred to as the *fusiform face area* (FFA, see Figure 8.7). Numerous studies with typical individuals have shown that this area is differentially activated in tasks involving face processing (see Kanwisher, 2000 for review), and lesion studies have shown that damage to this area produces a condition known as prosopagnosia in which individuals have difficulty recognising faces (Tranel, Damasio & Damasio, 1995), thus lending support to the idea that this area may be specific to the processing of faces.

Schultz et al.'s (2000) initial report of diminished FFA activity in ASD gave rise to considerable speculation that the FFA might be a key component in the neural substrate of these conditions. But since then, the picture has

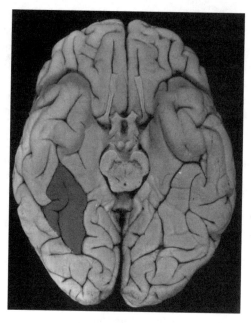

Figure 8.7. Ventral view of the human brain showing the fusiform face area (FFA). Reproduced by kind permission of Robert Schultz, Yale University Child Study Center.

become considerably more complex. Not all investigators subscribe to the notion that the FFA is specifically dedicated to the processing of faces (see e.g. Kanwisher, McDermott & Chun, 1997). For example, Gauthier, Tarr, Anderson et al. (1999) and Gauthier, Skudlarski, Gore and Anderson (2000) have observed FFA activation to non-face stimuli such as cars or birds, but only in individuals, such as car collectors or birdwatchers, who have some expertise in these areas. Furthermore, Gauthier et al. (2000) showed that activation of the FFA could be achieved in response to 'greebles' (small plasticine figures with face-like features) by training participants to recognise different types of greeble. Not only does this last finding confirm the role of the FFA in the expert discrimination of complex visual stimuli, but it also shows that the area remains plastic at least until early adulthood. Gauthier et al.'s findings on the role of the FFA in expertise have led commentators such as Schultz (2005) to argue that the FFA hypoactivation in response to faces seen in ASD is a consequence of a failure to learn about faces because of the different processing strategies for faces used by individuals with ASD. However, not all investigations of FFA activity in ASD have shown hypoactivation in response to faces. Pierce, Haist, Sedaghat and Courchesne (2004) asked high-functioning men with ASD and matched typical comparison participants to respond to female faces in a rapidly presented sequence of familiar and unfamiliar faces. FFA activity was observed in both participant groups, in contrast to the findings of earlier studies, but as Schultz (2005) observes, the level of FFA activity in the ASD group was lower (although not significantly so) than in the comparison group and that low statistical power (there were only eight participants in each group) may have obscured potential differences. Hadjikhani, Joseph, Snyder et al. (2004) asked a mixed group of high functioning adults with ASD, Asperger's syndrome and PDD-NOS and a (significantly younger) typical comparison group matched on verbal and performance IQ to view sequences of faces and objects as well as pictures of the same faces and objects scrambled according to a Fourier mathematical algorithm. Passive viewing was required by presenting a red cross at the centre of the stimulus to be viewed and asking participants to concentrate their fixation on the cross. (Most other studies allowed participants to scan faces, usually in the context of having to make a judgment about the face, e.g. whether it was the same as the previous one, or the gender of the person.) Hadjikhani et al.'s results showed comparable levels of FFA activation to faces as to objects, contradicting earlier observations of specialisation of the FFA for the processing of faces.

There are a number of possible reasons why some studies have shown diminished FFA activation in ASD and others have not. For example, in both studies that showed no significant difference (Hadjikhani et al., 2004; Pierce et al., 2004) participants were shown stimuli one by one, whereas in the Schultz et al. (2000) study, participants had to judge pairs of items. As Hadjikhani et al. (2004) point out, the requirement to scan the pictures may well have led the participants with ASD to process faces differently, thus resulting in a deactivated FFA. Schultz (2005) also argues that in addition to low statistical power and differing experimental tasks, the studies that report FFA activations rather than no activations have employed different scanning techniques and facial stimuli that subtend larger visual angles, both factors that may have contributed to the different findings. Moreover, Schultz argues, the participants in the Hadjikhani et al. study were from the less socially impaired end of the autism spectrum, and he cites some unpublished findings that show a link between degree of social impairment and diminution of FFA activity in response to faces to argue that Hadjikhani et al.'s findings may be an artefact of having chosen a mildly socially impaired participant group. The final argument put forward by Schultz (2005) in support of there being an ASD-related attenuation of FFA activity when processing faces is a probabilistic one, based on the fact that there were 15 studies that report the effect whereas only 2 do not. The problem with this last argument is that science generally works by means of a process of falsification, so that no matter how many white swans we may observe, the sighting of a single black swan invalidates the proposition 'all swans are white' (Popper, 1965). In practice, scientists require more than one black swan (or they make several attempts at scrubbing it clean) before revising their theories.

Yet the existence of contrary evidence on impaired FFA functioning in ASD needs to be taken seriously, especially in the context of perhaps the most important difference between the Hadjikhani et al. and the Schultz et al. studies, namely that the former used a more powerful magnet in their fMRI apparatus, thereby lessening the chances of missing activation that is actually present.

Despite the conflicting evidence, there is one way in which the findings on FFA activation may actually inform our understanding of the cerebral correlates of face processing in ASD. We have already seen that the activations reported by Hadjikhani et al. may have resulted from the relatively low level of social impairment in their participants. We have also seen how the FFA can become activated by non-facial stimuli if sufficient training is provided. This phenomenon has also been demonstrated in DD, an 11 year old boy with ASD and mild intellectual disability who was interested in Digimon cartoon characters. DD showed FFA activation to Digimon characters but not to familiar faces, whereas matched typical children who had an interest in Pokémon characters (similar to Digimon) showed the reverse pattern. This observation supports an expertise model of FFA activation in response to faces developed by Schultz (2005). According to this model, typical individuals are primed early in development to orient to faces and as a consequence spend time looking at them. The experience and training thus provided develops FFA activity. Individuals with ASD, by contrast, because of dysfunction of areas such as the amygdala that are also important in face processing, rarely develop sufficient expertise to affect their FFA in a manner that yields high levels of activation when performing face processing tasks. Such an account sees the FFA as part of a network of brain areas that are involved in face processing. Hypoactivation of the FFA is seen not as a cause of face processing difficulties but as a consequence of problems located elsewhere in the system, such as in the amygdala. The fact that experience with certain kinds of materials can enhance FFA activations in at least one individual with ASD (Grelotti, Klin, Gauthier et al., 2005) holds out some hope that interventions may be feasible in this domain. However, the question remains as to whether training-induced FFA activation for faces will eventually compensate for the consequences of damage that gave rise for the need for training in the first place.

We have already seen in Chapter 7 that the behavioural literature on face processing suggests that individuals with HFA, although not incapable of holistic face processing, have a greater tendency to process faces in a piecemeal fashion, with greater concentration on the mouth rather than the eyes, The neuroimaging literature reviewed above suggests that these difficulties are mediated fairly early on in the processing system, with knock-on effects on specialisation of areas such as the FFA. Further neurophysiological evidence of early face-processing difficulties in HFA comes from a study by Grice, Spratling, Karmiloff-Smith et al. (2001), who examined gamma EEG bursts when typical adults and those with ASD or Williams syndrome viewed upright and inverted faces. Gamma activity is generally agreed to be a measure of perceptual binding of features of a complex stimulus in order to produce a configural whole. Grice et al. observed that although the ASD group showed normal gamma bursts, these did not differ for upright and inverted faces in the way that they did for the typical participants. This suggests that the ASD group engage in atypical processing of features as early as 200 ms after seeing a face. Whether such difficulties are amenable to remediation through training in face-processing strategies, and whether such remediation would yield knock-on beneficial effects on the other components of the face processing system discussed above remains an open question.

BRAIN IMPAIRMENTS INFERRED FROM MORE BASIC PSYCHOLOGICAL PROCESSES

Apart from research into the brain basis of those psychological functions associated with social impairment, some work has also been carried out on processes that are not specifically involved in dealing with the social world. It is to these that we now turn.

ATTENTION

In Chapter 6, we explored the behavioural findings that showed some abnormalities of attention in individuals with ASD, most notably a tendency to overfocus on single aspects of complex stimuli and in managing the focus of attention. Research has also demonstrated difficulties in disengaging and switching attention. We also saw that the phenomena that come under the heading of 'attention' comprise a range of automatic and voluntary processes, many of which are known to be associated with particular brain regions and structures, including frontal, parietal and occipital cortex, as well as the cerebellum (see Haist, Adamo, Westerfield et al., 2005 for review). Courchesne and colleagues have also reported some findings that show that cerebellar hypoplasia in individuals with ASD is accompanied by hyperplasia of the frontal lobes (Carper & Courchesne, 2000) and have used such observations to implicate fronto-cerebellar abnormality in the attentional dysfunctions seen in individuals with ASD. Haist et al. (2005) employed fMRI to assess spatial attention in participants with ASD and typical comparison participants. The task involved discrimination of stimuli following spatial cues that preceded target presentation by short or long delays. Behavioural performance in the ASD group was impaired and activity in frontal, parietal and occipital regions was reduced on the short but not the long interval. Activation in the long interval was less impaired, leading Heist et al. to conclude that the basic neural substrate for attention was functional in their ASD participants. But noteworthy in their findings was that no cerebellar vermis activity was observed in either task condition, nor was any frontal activity observable during the short delay. Frontal activity during the long delay was severely reduced. The conclusion drawn from these observations is that ASD is characterised by a dysfunctional fronto-cerebellar attention system. However, these conclusions must be interpreted in the light of the inconclusive findings on structural abnormalities both of the frontal cortex and of the cerebellum. It may be the case that normal structure may still function abnormally, or that existing methods for assessing structural abnormalities are not sufficiently sensitive to pick up subtle structural problems.

Townsend, Westerfield, Leaver et al. (2001) investigated the late positive component (LPC) of event-related potentials (ERP) during a task in which participants with and without ASD watched a row of five squares on a computer screen, one of which was highlighted briefly. A target consisting of a circle within one of the boxes was presented between 227 and 1000 ms after the square was highlighted, its location being either in the highlighted square (valid trials) or in one of the other squares (invalid trials). Participants were instructed to press a button when the circle appeared in the square that had been highlighted. Other presentations of the circle were to be ignored. The participants with ASD were slower and less accurate than the comparison group and were also less accurate on trials where the target occurred in the peripheral squares. The ASD participants also showed a delayed LPC latency over frontal but not parietal scalp regions and an attenuated parietal LPC. Townsend et al. (2001) argue that such findings implicate cerebellar abnormality because individuals with cerebellar lesions show similar frontal and parietal LPC effects to those documented in their study.

It is clear that impaired performance on attentional tasks is accompanied by evidence of dysfunction of the frontal and parietal lobes, as well as the occipital cortex, and that the problem may be one of coordination of activity among these different regions. What is less clear is the role of the cerebellum. The evidence comes partly from inconclusive findings on cerebellar structure as well as the fact that the evidence for specific cerebellar involvement in ASD is relatively indirect. It does not follow that just because cerebellar damage in patients without ASD is accompanied by similar impairments in attention (and its ERP and fMRI correlates) to those seen in ASD that the directly measured frontal, occipital and parietal impairments observed in the latter group are a result of cerebellar pathology. Only direct observations of such pathology in the context of attentional tasks can settle this question.

EXECUTIVE FUNCTIONS

The fact that the concept of executive dysfunction emerged from the study of individuals with brain damage, especially damage to the frontal lobes, gives strong grounds for believing that the executive dysfunctions seen in individuals with ASD (see Chapter 4) are likely to be associated with functionally abnormal frontal lobes. We have already seen that structural abnormalities of the frontal cortex in individuals with ASD have not been reliably reported. Yet abnormalities of function of intact frontal cortex remain a possibility, especially given the substantial connections that exist between the frontal lobes and other brain structures such as the cerebellum, the amygdala and the limbic system (Damasio & Van Hoesen, 1983).

Almost no direct studies of brain correlates of executive function tasks have been carried out with individuals from the autism spectrum. In one study by Luna et al. (2002), high-functioning adults with ASD were asked to perform a spatial working memory task and an oculomotor delayed saccade task. In the first task, participants had to fixate a central cross whilst a peripheral stimulus was presented. After delays of between 1 and 8 s, participants had to shift their gaze to where the stimulus had been located. In the second task, participants had to fixate a central cross and then shift their gaze to peripheral targets presented unpredictably with regard to timing and location. Functional MRI indicated reduced dorsolateral prefrontal cortical activation in the ASD group when performing the spatial working memory task. By contrast, no between-group activation differences were observed for the delayed saccade task. Luna et al. conclude that because no differences in activation were observed in regions that other work had shown were impaired in spatial working memory, the reduced dorsolateral prefrontal activation they observed must be a reflection of impaired executive processes. However, this is indirect evidence at best. What are needed are studies that either independently manipulate the memory and executive components of working memory tasks, or use 'purer' executive dysfunction tasks. The problem with the latter suggestion is, as we saw in Chapter 4, that 'executive function' is a broad term that covers a heterogeneous set of activities, so we should not expect to find a neat brain locus to underlie them all.

MEMORY

Just as the concept of executive functions covers a range of disparate processes related to the on-line monitoring and control of behaviour, memory comprises an equally diverse range of processes and systems (see Gardiner, in press for review). In Chapter 7 we saw that memory impairments seen in ASD lie particularly in the area of free recall, source memory and episodic memory. Recognition memory appears to be more impaired in people with severe ASD (although see Bowler, Gardiner & Berthollier, 2004). ASD also resembles typical ageing in that memory is less impaired when test procedures that provide support at test, such as cued recall, are employed. Although there have as yet been no direct studies of the brain correlates of memory in ASD, researchers in the field have used the patterns of memory performance in this population to speculate about potential areas of impairment. The first speculations of this kind come from the early work of Boucher and colleagues, in which Kanner-type autism was compared with the amnesic syndrome (Boucher, 1981; Boucher & Warrington, 1976). Amnesia results from damage to the temporal lobe (including the hippocampus and amygdala) and is characterised by poor performance on tests of free recall, and recognition with relatively unimpaired cued recall. As we saw in Chapter 7, and as Boucher and Warrington (1976) demonstrated, ASD is characterised by poor performance on free recall tasks and good cued recall. Impairment of recognition memory is less consistently documented. It tends to be more likely if ASD is accompanied by global cognitive impairment or when testing involves a forced choice rather than a yes/no procedure (Bowler et al., 2004). Boucher (1981) argues that the behavioural parallel between amnesia and ASD is a useful heuristic framework within which to understand the brain correlates of autistic symptomatology (much in the same way as is Bowler et al.'s (1997) ageing analogy). That the pattern of memory performance should signal possible medial temporal lobe involvement is in line with much of the evidence on the role of the amygdala, the hippocampus and surrounding structures reviewed in earlier sections of this chapter. Yet there are reasons to be cautious. First, not all the behavioural evidence is consistent with the amnesia parallel. The fact that recognition memory is not always impaired in ASD marks one point of difference (see Bowler et al., 2000a, b). Also, Bowler et al. (1997) report that free recall impairment in high-functioning individuals with ASD appears to occur only when such recall can be enhanced by capitalising on semantic relations among the studied words. When no such relatedness is present, recall is often similar to that of typical individuals. Yet, as Boucher and Warrington (1976) and Boucher (1981) observe, the amnesia parallel is just a heuristic. People generally develop medial temporal amnesia later in life, whereas ASD is present from birth. This factor alone will affect performance on memory tests. What the autism–amnesia parallel does do, however, is to highlight brain regions and systems that might be implicated in the memory deficits of individuals with ASD and by extension help to identify those regions that might underlie other aspects of autistic symptomatology. DeLong (1992) has written a speculative account of how hippocampal dysfunction (which, when it occurs later in life, leads to amnesia) can also be linked to the symptomatology of ASD. However the only direct test of the behavioural consequences of early hippocampal damage has shown memory impairment but not ASD-like social impairment (Vargha-Khadem et al., 1997), suggesting that the amnesia-like memory impairments seen in ASD are an accidental consequence of wider damage that yields both symptoms of ASD and memory impairment.

The pattern of memory impairments seen in ASD also suggests a role for the prefrontal cortex. People with frontal lobe impairment show a similar memory profile to those with ASD (Gershberg, 1997; Shimamura, 1996), and ERP studies of source and context memory consistently show increased frontal lobe activity when source is correctly recalled (Cycowicz, Friedman & Snodgrass, 2001). There is also a considerable literature on the role of the prefrontal cortex in episodic encoding and retrieval processes (Nyberg, Cabeza & Tulving, 1996). As Bowler et al. (2000a) have demonstrated impaired episodic remembering in high-functioning individuals with ASD, then either episodic encoding or episodic retrieval must be impaired, thus implicating dysfunction of the frontal lobes. In the absence of any specific findings, it is possible only to speculate about brain involvement in memory in ASD. It seems likely that the involvement of medial temporal structures may be functional rather than structural, reflecting difficulties with their reciprocal relations with other areas, most notably the frontal cortex. It is tempting to follow the lead of writers such as DeLong (1992) and Waterhouse, Fein and Modahl (1996) who argue that symptomatology that can be described in terms of memory impairment or impaired theory of mind or whatever, is best seen as an emergent property of the operation of different, more basic systems that interconnect in different ways to produce abnormal behaviour patterns in different domains. Thus we would expect the same areas to appear to be involved in different symptom clusters, such as the frontal lobes in executive functions, and theory of mind and the hippocampus and amygdala in development of social relations and in declarative memory.

CONCLUSION

Of all the chapters in this book, this one is perhaps the most inconclusive. Given the rate of new publication in the area, it is certainly the one most likely to become rapidly obsolete. As befits an area that is both new and in the grip of rapid technological change, these two observations are perhaps not surprising. However, if one were forced to attempt a quick summary of how the brain was involved in the symptomatology of ASD, two consistent themes emerge. There are abnormalities of brain structure, primarily reflected in the developmental trajectory of brain size and the organisation of cell assemblies. And there appears to be some disorganisation of the kinds of synchronised connectivity between different brain regions that are thought to be necessary for the efficient processing of complex stimuli. It is possible to be more specific than this, but the available evidence is much murkier, being compromised by poor sampling, small sample sizes, methodological weaknesses and failures to replicate findings. Added to these difficulties is the fact that there is as yet no generally agreed-upon theory of how brain–behaviour relations actually operate. Some theorists argue that many psychological processes operate in a modular fashion and that this modularity is reflected in dedicated neural architectures. Others adopt a looser version of this approach, seeing higher-level psychological functioning (such as understanding facial expressions of emotion or inferring mental states from behaviour patterns) as reflecting the operation of systems of coordinated activity in different brain regions, the individual components of which might contribute to a range of other higher-level processes. By contrast, connectionist accounts argue strongly against strict localisation of function and that every psychological process is distributed across the brain. And all these perspectives in turn assume that we can agree on how exactly 'psychological processes' should be construed. Readers who have ploughed their way through earlier chapters should be aware that this is by no means a settled question. What has emerged with some clarity is the fact that the brains of individuals with ASD are larger and more immature than those of typical individuals, at least for a period in their development. These observations suggest that much functional abnormality may be a developmental consequence of abnormal early cerebral organisation, and serve to remind us of an aspect of ASD that is often overlooked, namely that it is a set of developmental disorders.

9 Development

Although long considered to be developmental disorders (the principal scientific journal in the field changed its name in 1979 from the *Journal of Autism and Childhood Schizophrenia* to the *Journal of Autism and Developmental Disorders*), the question of the developmental nature of the conditions comprising ASD has received surprisingly little attention. Much of the material in the preceding chapters has concentrated on the characterisation of ASD as a set of behavioural and cognitive deficits, which can to a greater or lesser extent be associated with particular brain atypicalities or dysfunction. However, increasingly, investigators have had to take developmental issues on board. Diagnosticians have had to consider specifically how early developmental trajectories in ASD differ from the typical case. People studying the structure of the brain have had to consider the different patterning of brain development seen in ASD. And, increasingly, cognitive psychologists have seen that complex higher-level processes such as face perception and mental state understanding emerge over time from the coordinated activity of lower-level systems, necessitating a developmental understanding of how this coordination takes place as well as of why it should happen in a way that yields an autistic rather than a non-autistic outcome. Adopting a developmental orientation towards the study of ASD involves not just the charting of developmental trajectories nor the modelling of hypothetical developmental processes, it also necessitates a profound reflection on the kinds of comparisons we should make when deciding whether or not to label a particular developmental trajectory as atypical.

ASSUMPTIONS ABOUT DEVELOPMENT IN ASD: PSYCHOMETRICS, MATCHING AND DEVELOPMENTAL DELAY

Over the six decades since Kanner first described his 11 cases, our conception of the syndrome has evolved from that of a specific, isolated entity to a spectrum of related conditions that can sometimes be accompanied by global developmental delay and sometimes not. Early investigations of people with the syndrome described by Kanner showed that about three-quarters of them had some global cognitive impairment (DeMeyer et al., 1974). The presence of such impairment poses a number of conceptual and practical problems for investigators. First, are we to assume that 'autism' (that is to say, the cluster of symptoms that give rise to a diagnosis of ASD) is independent of an individual's general level of intellectual development? And if we do not make such an assumption, how should the dependence be characterised?

In much of the research presented in earlier chapters, the assumption has been made that no particular dependence between ASD and global cognitive delay need be assumed. As a consequence, investigators have tended to match individuals with a diagnosis of autism or autistic disorder with a group of individuals without such a diagnosis but who are matched either on global, verbal or non-verbal intellectual level. But this strategy immediately poses a problem. Tests of global cognitive development vary considerably. Some such as the British Picture Vocabulary Scale (BPVS, Dunn et al., 1997; in North America, the Peabody Picture Vocabulary Test, PPVT) measure receptive vocabulary. Others, such as the Raven's Progressive Matrices (RCPM,Raven, 1996), evaluate visuo-perceptual matching skills. And others, such as the Wechsler scales (see Chapter 1) employ a battery of verbal and non-verbal tests, take the average performance on these and compare it with that of a comparable sample of the general population. A number of issues face an investigator who wishes to use such tests to match groups with and without ASD on global intellectual development.

The first issue concerns IQ. If we take a group of children with ASD who have a chronological age of 10 years and a verbal mental age measured by the BPVS of 5 years, then we can match them with a group of typical children with a BPVS age of 5 years (and whose chronological ages will, by definition, be in or around 5 years as well). Although matched on verbal mental age (or, strictly, receptive vocabulary age), these two groups will differ markedly on IQ – which in this case is 50 for the children with ASD and 100 for the typical children, and any differences in experimental task performance could be the result either of IQ or of ASD. To overcome this confound, researchers have tried to match on both chronological and mental age, so our hypothetical 10 year old child with ASD and a verbal mental age of 5 years would be matched with a 10 year old child without ASD and with a verbal mental age of 5 years. But even this approach, although removing the confound of low IQ, raises several other difficulties. What kinds of children 'without ASD' do we choose? Those with Down syndrome or some other well-defined condition? Or do we take a mixed group of children with developmental delay? There is now a considerable literature on the specific cognitive and behavioural characteristics of different conditions that give rise to intellectual disabilities (see Hodapp, 2004 for review), and choosing which group to act as a comparison in studies of ASD requires considerable thought in relation to this literature. However, we must be careful not to avoid falling into the trap of designing studies that merely allow us to state something like 'On experimental task X, individuals with ASD perform less well than those with syndrome Y, when matched on verbal mental age and chronological age'. As Burack et al. (2004) argue, we need to exercise pragmatism while maintaining some degree of conceptual rigour; our choices of matching measures must be practically feasible and also relate in some way to the question we are addressing. Thus, we should not aim for individual matching on a battery of lengthy-to-administer measures on a comparison group with an extremely rare psychopathological condition. And we should consider the appropriateness of the matching measures to the dependent variables of interest – using, for example, verbal measures for questions relating to mental state understanding and non-verbal tasks for investigations of visuo-spatial processing.

One possible way around the problem of controlling for global develop-mental delay is to restrict investigations to individuals from the higher-functioning end of the autism spectrum. Researchers adopting this strategy usually compare performance of the ASD group against that of typical indi-viduals matched on chronological age and IQ. Sometimes other variables known to affect the behaviours being studied, such as years of formal educa-tion or socioeconomic status, may also be employed as matching variables. Yet even this strategy does not entirely eliminate the problems associated with considering the ASD group and the comparison group as being equiva-lent in all respects except the measure under investigation. These problems arise whether single-test measures such as the BPVS or RCPM or multi-test measures such as the Wechsler scales are employed. In Chapter 1 we saw that one of the characteristics of ASD is an uneven profile both between verbal and non-verbal measures of ability and also within batteries of verbal and non-verbal tests (see Mottron, 2004), thus confronting us with the ques-tion of which measure to select for matching (see Burack et al., 2004 for further discussion).

Quite apart from the problem of matching itself, matching on overall devel-opmental level makes certain assumptions about how a particular level of test performance comes about and about whether or not this level of performance results from the operation of similar processes in atypical as in typical indi-viduals. These assumptions operate differently when ASD is accompanied by developmental delay than when it is not. But in both cases, when we assert that by reaching the level of a typical 5 year old on the BPVS, a child with ASD has developed receptive vocabulary in a manner similar to typical chil-dren of that age, we make certain assumptions about developmental processes in ASD and their equivalence to typical development. In the case of develop-mental delay, we need to think about the developmental relationship between psychometric test performance and the processes that might give rise to ASD. In other words, how do ASD and global cognitive delay interact, and how does such interaction unfold over time? In other words, are we justified in psycho-logical terms, in assuming that equivalent (delayed) developmental levels on a particular test in a child with and a child without ASD implies equivalently dysfunctional underlying psychological processes? Might it not be the case that the possession of ASD may, for entirely different reasons, yield a behavioural outcome that operationally yields a given normative level of performance on a particular psychometric test? In the case of those whose psychometric test performance falls within the normal range, similar arguments apply. Investigators (the present author included) have tended to assume that normal psychometric test performance betokens a typical developmental trajectory, at least for those functions tapped by that particular measure. But such an assumption is questionable. And questioning this assumption raises the issue of development in ASD. Addressing the issue of development entails a number of research strategies, some of which are emerging in the literature and others of which have yet to be tackled. We need to establish the way different psychological functions evolve over time in ASD and compare this to the corresponding patterns of evolution in typical individuals as well as in those with other types of developmental psychopathology. We also need to establish longitudinal and cross-sectional patterns of correlations among measures. And finally, we need to develop a theoretical framework that will enable us to make sense of our observations.

DEVELOPMENTAL TRAJECTORIES IN ASD

One perspective on the issue of developmental trajectories – the course of behavioural change over time – concerns the question of outcome. Does the symptom pattern of individuals with ASD improve, and if it does, in what domains do we see change? A related question is that of the early factors that are good predictors of later improvement. Patterns of development over time will depend on the developmental level of the participants being studied. For example, we might expect low initial levels and a more abnormal trajectory for language and communication in individuals who have significant global intellectual impairment compared to those who are of normal intelligence.

In terms of overall social adjustment, one of the first large-scale reports of outcome was carried out by Kanner (1973) who followed up 96 people with ASD who were then in their third or fourth decade. Most remained highly dependent, although 11 were in employment and 1 was married. Kanner noted that better outcome was associated with more developed communicative language. In the 1960s and 1970s, Rutter and colleagues carried out a 10 year follow-up of people with Kanner-type ASD and found what they called 'good' social adjustment in 14% of a sample of 38 individuals (Lockyer & Rutter, 1969, 1970; Rutter, Greenfield & Lockyer, 1967; Rutter & Lockyer, 1967). More recent studies, such as those of Rumsey, Rapoport and Sceery (1985) and Venter, Lord and Schopler (1992), both of which examined individuals with IQs above 60, report that around 60% were highly dependent on others for care and were in sheltered occupations or still in some form of special training programmes. More recent studies with higher-functioning individuals with ASD (Howlin, Mawhood & Rutter, 2000; Mawhood, Howlin & Rutter, 2000; Szatmari, Bartolucci, Bremner et al., 1989) have shown higher levels of social adaptation and relationship formation, but reported that the majority (up to 74%) continued to have social and relationship difficulties and problems with ritualistic and repetitive behaviours. The study by Howlin et al. (2000) represented a follow-up in early adulthood (23–24 years) of two groups of men, one of which had received a diagnosis of ASD in childhood and the other had received a diagnosis of dysphasia (developmental language delay). These groups had originally been investigated by Bartak, Rutter and Cox (1975) with a view to establishing whether or not ASD was an extreme manifestation of developmental language disorder. Howlin et al. found that on a measure of social competence derived from the Autism Diagnostic Interview (ADI; LeCouteur, Rutter, Lord et al., 1989), the Vineland Adaptive Behaviour Scales (VABS; Sparrow, Balla & Cicchetti, 1984), the Autism Diagnostic Observation Schedule (ADOS; Lord et al. 1989) and the Socio-Emotional Functioning Interview (SEF; Rutter, Mawhood & Goode, 1998 cited in Howlin, Mawhood & Rutter, 2000), severe difficulties were found in only 10% of the language delay group as opposed to 74% of the ASD group. Using regression analysis, receptive vocabulary measured by the PPVT in the original Bartak et al. (1975) study contributed 32% of the variance in the composite measure, with non-verbal IQ and friendship ratings contributing less than 7%. For the language delay group, none of these three variables contributed more than 2% of the variance in the composite measure.

The conclusion that can be drawn from studies such as these is that individuals with a diagnosis of ASD, even when this is not accompanied by significant global developmental delay, continue to experience adaptive difficulties as they get older, indicating that whatever factors give rise to autistic symptomatology continue to operate later on into the lifespan.

In the area of language and communication, the studies by Rutter and colleagues cited above found improved skills in 50% of their sample although characteristically autistic patterns of speech such as echolalia and flat intonation were present in up to 75% of their follow-up sample. More recently, Mawhood, Howlin and Rutter (2000) report language follow-up data on the Bartak et al. (1975) samples described above. Bartak et al. found lower verbal IQs in the ASD group, with poorer comprehension and more frequent echolalia and pronominal reversal, and because the two groups were matched on expressive language level the authors concluded that these differences were unlikely to be due to language delay. Subsequent discriminant function analysis by Bartak, Rutter and Cox (1977) found that the two groups could be statistically separated, although there were a small number of children who could not be reliably classified into either group. The original samples of children were first followed up by Cantwell, Baker, Rutter and Mawhood (1989), who reported greater improvement in the language skills of the boys with developmental language delay compared to those with ASD. But whereas the level of social impairment seen in the ASD group tended to remain unchanged, that exhibited by the language delay group tended to get worse. In the second follow-up study of these two groups at age 23–24 years (Howlin et al., 2000; Mawhood et al., 2000), the ASD group's verbal IQ and receptive language scores had improved significantly more than those of the language delay group but the social use of language in the latter group, although better than that of the ASD group, had deteriorated with a consequent greater overlap between the two groups revealed by a discriminant function analysis. Mawhood et al. also carried out a regression analysis to determine which factors in the children's early development contributed to later communication skills. In the ASD group, adult linguistic ability was best predicted by childhood receptive vocabulary as measured by the PPVT. Neither non-verbal IQ nor ratings of friendship contributed more than 7% of the variance in the outcome measure. For the language delay group, none of these measures contributed more than 6.1% of the variance in the outcome measure.

Because many of the earlier follow-up studies included individuals with IQs of less than 50, who would almost by definition be expected to have a poor outcome, Howlin, Goode, Hutton and Rutter (2004) carried out a study of individuals who as children had a performance IQ of at least 50. The aim was to examine long-term behavioural, social, cognitive and linguistic outcome, to assess the stability of IQ over time and to establish what childhood measures were predictive of later outcome. At initial diagnosis, the 61 children had an average age of 7.24 years, an average non-verbal IQ of 80 and an average verbal IQ of 61.5. Average age at follow-up was 29 years and the average time between initial and follow-up assessments was 22.1 years.

At follow-up just over half the sample left school without any formal qualifications and about one-third were in some form of employment and 56% had no friends or acquaintances. Approximately 5% lived independently, with the remainder living in sheltered accommodation or with parents. Assessments of cognitive level were complicated by the fact that the same measure could not be administered to all participants, necessitating the use of several tests, more than one of which were given to some participants. Taking the highest score of participants who had been tested on several instruments, the average non-verbal IQ was 75, and the average verbal IQ was 79.8. Using the British Picture Vocabulary Scale (BPVS, Dunn et al., 1997), only 16% of the sample scored above the level of a typical 15 year old. Overall, performance on both verbal and non-verbal IQ measures proved reasonably stable, with correlations between the initial and follow-up measures being .54 for non-verbal and .67 for the verbal measures. But these global estimates were found to hide some variability with children with either verbal or non-verbal IQs below 70 likely to show less stability at follow-up.

Howlin et al. (2004) also investigated the degree to which childhood levels of performance predicted later adaptive outcome. Dividing the sample into normal (IQ 70+) and mildly intellectually impaired (IQ 50–69) groups on the basis of non-verbal measures, the first group had significantly higher parental ratings of social use of language, language comprehension and spelling ages at follow-up. Those in the higher IQ group were also more likely to have friends, to live independently or semi-independently and to be engaged in some kind of employment. No significant differences between the groups were found on abnormal language use or on ritualistic and stereotyped behaviours, although it should be pointed out that the mean values on these measures showed trends in the direction of poorer performance for the lower-IQ group. Overall, even those with a non-verbal IQ >70 in childhood had a variable social outcome at follow-up, indicating that although higher IQ was associated with better outcome, it was no guarantee of it.

The same split was carried out on the smaller group of children on whom verbal IQ measures had been taken in childhood, but no significant differences were observed on any of the outcome measures apart from use of language in adulthood. Contrary to earlier speculations (e.g. Lord & Bailey, 2002), Howlin et al. found that the presence of useful speech before the age of 5 was not a reliable predictor of later language use. Useful language in adulthood emerged in almost half of their children who had little or no useful speech at initial assessment. Prediction of outcome was not greatly improved by combining measures of verbal and non-verbal IQ, and Howlin et al. conclude that their data indicate that it is easier to state what predicts poor outcome (NVIQ < 70 and VIQ < 30) than which measures predict good outcome. In this last respect, Howlin et al.'s findings serve to remind us that the predictive role for early language in later adaptive development is not bidirectional, that is to say that just because poor early language and communication development implies poor later development, good early language development does not neces-sarily guarantee a good outcome,

Sigman and Ruskin (1999) criticise many existing follow-up studies on two principal grounds. The first is that these investigations often rely on clinic samples that have been initially assessed by clinicians or investigators other than those who carried out the follow-up, with the consequence that the mea-sures used and dimensions of behaviour investigated are determined on a rather ad-hoc and opportunistic basis. Second, they argue that this state of affairs can result in the lack of a sound theoretical basis for the investigations. In their own major follow-up study of children with ASD, Down syndrome and general developmental delay, Sigman and Ruskin adopt a theoretical framework derived from several different research traditions including authors such as Bruner (1975) and Vygotsky (1978). Both Bruner and

Vygotsky acknowledge the importance of interpersonal communication and the wider social context for the child's development, and share with Piaget (1952) the importance of the capacity for symbolic representation. Sigman and Ruskin also acknowledge the contribution of Bates and her colleagues (Bates 1979), who emphasise the importance of an understanding of communicative intentions. This theoretical framework forms the background to much of the material presented in Chapters 2 and 3 on the development of interpersonal understanding, in particular, emphasising the parallel emergence in typical development of symbolisation and the shift at age 6–10 months from dyadic interaction, in which the child interacts with a caregiver, to triadic interaction, where the dyadic situation also includes objects to which both participants of the dyad can direct their own and each other's attention. This theoretical background formed the basis of the hypotheses and the measures used in Sigman and Ruskin's study.

Sigman and Ruskin first examined the stability of IQ and diagnosis over the follow-up period. Initial measures were taken when children were aged on average 3 years 11 months and follow-up measures were taken at an average age of 12 years 10 months with an average follow-up period of 8 years 11 months. Initial diagnoses were made either by experienced clinicians or using instruments such as the Childhood Autism Rating Scale (CARS; Schopler, Reichler & Renner, 1986) or the Autism Behavior Checklist (ABC; Krug, Arick & Almond, 1980) and initial intellectual development and mental ages were assessed by means of the Cattell Scales of Development. Follow-up diagnosis was carried out using the ADI-R (LeCouteur, Rutter, Lord et al., 1989; Lord, Rutter & LeCouteur, 1994) and follow-up measures of intellectual development and IQ employed the revised Stanford–Binet test or, for those who were unable to take this test, the Bayley Scales of infant development (Bayley, 1993). Of the 50 children in the ASD follow-up group, 45 continued to meet criteria for autistic disorder at follow-up. Using an IQ level of 70 as a cut-off for mental retardation, 9% of the ASD group were found to be above the cut-off at initial assessment, whereas 33% fell into this category at follow-up. Long-term stability of intellectual level was also examined by looking at changes in mean developmental quotients (DQs) and IQs over time, which revealed a significant increase in mental age (25.4 months vs 60.9 months) but not of DQ/IQ (51.3 vs 48.5 points). Moreover, IQ/DQ at initial assessment correlated ($r = .44$) with IQ/DQ at follow-up, indicating a high degree of stability of intellectual level over time. The stability of these measures over time led Sigman and Ruskin to conclude (as did Howlin et al., 2004 above) that despite the considerable improvements in educational provision and other forms of intervention for children with ASD, they continue to have the disorder and to remain intellectually retarded.

To explore changes in non-verbal communication, play and language skills, Sigman and Ruskin carried out observational measures of the children in structured and semi-structured situations that provided the opportunity for social interaction and for object play. Both initial and follow-up assessments of non-verbal communication employed the standard and a modified version of the Early Social Communication Scales (ESCS; Siebert, Hogan & Mundy, 1982). Verbal communication was variously assessed either by a clinical linguist or by the Receptive and Expressive Emergent Language Scale (REEL; Bzoch & League, 1971) or the Reynell Scales of Language Development (Reynell, 1977), depending on the child's developmental and language level. Levels of symbolic and functional play were found to correlate significantly with concurrent language levels ($r = .60$ and $.34$ respectively), and both these kinds of play were found to correlate significantly with initiation of, and responding to, joint attention bids in social interaction. Hierarchical regression analysis demonstrated that both non-verbal communication and play contribute to the level of language development in children with ASD, by contrast with typical children, for whom only non-verbal communication was associated with language.

Comparison of rates of initiating and responding to joint attention bids from initial measure to follow-up showed that the children with ASD continued to be impaired by comparison with typical and with other developmentally delayed children. Their performance on these measures at the two time points was also highly correlated, indicating strong individual continuity over time on these measures. Similar comparisons on measures of verbal communication showed average increases in language age of 28 months over 8–9 years, which, although comparable to developmentally delayed children without ASD, is lower than would be expected for typical children. Initial and follow-up language ages were also significantly correlated ($r = .56$). Investigation of the relation between play and language gain showed that for the children with ASD, functional play was a better predictor than symbolic play, and that early measures of responses to bids for joint attention also made an independent contribution to language gain. In addition, the investigators found that improvements in mental retardation (moving from an IQ of below 70 to one above 70 at follow-up) were associated with greater response to bids for joint attention, requesting objects and a wider range of functional play actions.

Sigman and Ruskin also examined the predictors of individual differences and change over time in social competence in groups of children with ASD, Down syndrome and developmental delay. For the ASD children, social play was correlated with mental age, language age, child's own initiation of social interactions and the duration of maintenance of interactions. There was also a significant negative correlation between social play and the extent to which children rejected the advances of peers. The authors conclude that the extent to which children with ASD are socially engaged depends more on whether they choose to be engaged rather than on rejection by their peers. Interaction with peers in later childhood was found to correlate with early childhood initiation of joint attention and response to social interaction. But although measures of functional play and symbolic play taken in early childhood correlated with later childhood measures of social play, neither was associated with later initiations of social interaction.

The investigations reported by Sigman and Ruskin (1999) are important not only because they chart the developmental progression of children with ASD over time but also because they attempt to elucidate some of the determining processes of developmental change in a manner that is theoretically driven. A further aspect of their work (which I have not gone into in any detail here) is their attempt to compare developmental trajectories of children with ASD to those with other forms of developmental delay; specifically, children with Down syndrome and a group of children with developmental delay of mixed aetiology. Taken together with the studies of Rutter, Howlin and colleagues described earlier, this group of studies provides much-needed empirical descriptive information on the natural history of ASD, and gives us an image of how these conditions evolve over time. However, the measures they report represent variables and attributes at quite a gross or molar level. This is an important observation in the light of the comments made by both Sigman and Ruskin (1999) and by Howlin et al. (2004), that despite considerable improvements in educational intervention strategies, children with ASD still remain quite impaired as they grow older. It is likely that interventions are aimed at the kinds of variables measured in the studies just reported, and the relative lack of success of such interventions would suggest that the targeting of intervention should be directed elsewhere.

Measures such as 'social adaptation', or even the finer-grained measures derived from the ESCS (Siebert, Hogan & Mundy, 1982) employed by Sigman and Ruskin, although important, represent concepts that can be accounted for in more basic neuropsychological terms. Much of what has been covered in the earlier chapters in this book represents attempts to redescribe these outcome measures in terms of more basic psychological processes. One of the major themes that has run through these accounts is that phenomena at one level of analysis can be analysed into combinations of phenomena at another level. In Chapter 2, we explored the potential role of complex, three-term reasoning in understanding false-belief tasks. In Chapter 6 we considered the role of configural perceptual processing in the processing of faces (something, incidentally, Sigman & Ruskin observed that children with ASD were less likely to do). We know, for example that rate of success on false-belief tasks bears some relation to everyday social adaptation (Frith, Happé & Siddons, 1994), and thus it can be argued that ability to engage in complex three-term reasoning may in some way determine how well a person adapts to their social environment. So what is needed are studies that examine the interrelationships of these kinds of measures at different points of time, but how these interrelationships evolve over time in the same individuals and how earlier measures on one measure predict later performance on others, much as Sigman and Ruskin and Howlin and Rutter and their colleagues did for language, communication, play and general social development.

DEVELOPMENTAL CHANGE IN TWO PSYCHOLOGICAL DOMAINS: THEORY OF MIND AND EXECUTIVE FUNCTIONS

THEORY OF MIND

Some studies of developmental change in the kinds of psychological processes that were discussed in earlier chapters of this book have been carried out. In the domain of theory of mind, two meta-analyses (Happé, 1995; Yirmiya et al., 1998) report that the average verbal mental age at which children with ASD pass false-belief tasks is about 6 years higher than in typical children. Other investigators have looked specifically at change over time in performance on tasks thought to measure theory of mind abilities. Holroyd and Baron-Cohen (1993) carried out a 7 year follow-up of 17 of the 20 children who took part in the original Baron-Cohen et al. (1985) study that demonstrated impaired understanding of false belief in children with Kanner-type autism. Only one participant showed improved performance, with two others moving from passing to failing the test. In a 3 year follow-up of 17 adolescents with ASD, Ozonoff and McEvoy (1994) employed a battery of tasks, including the deceptive box task (Perner, Leekam & Wimmer, 1987), two second-order false-belief tasks (Bowler, 1992; Wimmer & Perner, 1983) and a double-bluff story developed by Happé (1994). They found that only 1 child improved on a first-order false-belief task, with 3 improving on higher-order tasks. A larger scale study of 57 children with an ADI-R and ADOS diagnosis of ASD aged between 4 and 14 years was carried out by Steele, Joseph and Tager-Flusberg (2003). They administered a battery of 10 tests they labelled theory of mind tests, which were divided into groups of early, basic and advanced level of difficulty. Measures of verbal and non-verbal IQ and receptive and expressive vocabulary were also taken. Overall, Steele et al. report a significant improvement in composite theory of mind score as well as in expressive and receptive vocabulary. Both initial and follow-up theory of mind composite correlated significantly with IQ and vocabulary measures and multiple regression indicated that the vocabulary measures (which were taken at the start of the study) predicted a significant but small proportion (3%) of the variance in follow-up theory of mind scores after the effect of initial theory of mind scores had been removed. The authors contrast these findings with what they describe as 'the current pessimistic view portrayed in the literature' (p. 465), arguing that they have supported a developmental view of theory of mind in ASD by showing that with appropriate measures and age ranges of participants (they argue that the samples tested by Holroyd & Baron-Cohen, 1993 and by Ozonoff & McEvoy, 1994 may already have reached ceiling), it is possible to demonstrate improvement in theory of mind skills and to identify determinants of improvement. However, a number of comments are in order.

In Chapters 2 and 3, we discussed the logic of combining measures that intuitively seem to measure mental state understanding into a single index of theory of mind ability, and argued that different tasks could not be assumed to measure the same underlying ability, especially in an atypical population. If we look more closely at the detail of Steele et al.'s data, we can see that the pass rates at initial assessment and at follow-up for the location-change false-belief task were 25% and 26% respectively. And for a second-order false-belief task, corresponding pass rates were 12% and 14%. These are both measures that assess representational theory of mind very well. Most of the overall improvement in this study was carried by measures of pretence and unexpected contents false-belief tasks. Although there are theoretical grounds for arguing that pretence is a precursor of theory of mind, this theory was developed in the context of typical development and cannot be transposed to the atypical case without some reservation. Moreover, given that the knowledge that ASD is characterised by impaired pretence is now widespread among carers and educators, it is quite possible that the children in these studies may have been taught pretence behaviours during the follow-up period. Indeed, if this were the case, then it reinforces the notion that we should not rush to assume that measures that are thought to be conceptually related in typical development are equally related in an atypical population such as ASD. If this were the case, then we would expect improvements in play to be accompanied by improvements in tests of representational theory of mind. Against this point, it can be argued that the children's performance did improve significantly on an unexpected contents false-belief task (pass rates moved from 19% to 32%) and that the benefits of improved pretence behaviour did not have time to transfer to location-change false-belief measures. However, only a study with a longer follow-up period can settle this question.

The issue of assumed interrelation among measures thought to tap a common theory of mind capability was addressed in a study by Peterson, Wellman & Liu (2005). These investigators administered a battery of theory of mind tests to groups of children with ASD, typical development and deafness. The deaf children fell into two subgroups; one group of native signers, i.e. for whom sign language was their first language. The other group was of late signers – children born to hearing parents and who did not acquire sign language until later in development. This last group is characterised by delay in passing false-belief tasks, which is often explained by their delayed language skills (see Peterson & Siegal, 2000). The logic of Peterson et al.'s study was that if individuals with ASD are delayed in their acquisition of theory of mind, then they should show a similar order of acquisition of items in a battery of tests that are thought to measure this capacity. Any difference in the timing of acquisition of the tests would signify developmental difference rather than delay.

To test this proposition, Peterson et al. administered a battery of five tasks that had been shown by Wellman and Liu (2004) to give a good Guttman scale

(Green, 1956) for typical children. For a battery of items to yield a good Guttman scale, they must be acquired in the same order across individual children, so if one child always masters test 1 before test 2, and masters both of these before test 3, then a similar order should be observed in all or most children. The measures used were Diverse Desires, which tested the child's understanding that another person might dislike something the child likes; Diverse Beliefs, where the child must be aware that another person can think something different from their own belief; Knowledge Access, which tests the child's understanding of the fact that someone who has never looked into a container will not know what is inside it; False Belief, where a child needs to understand that a person's knowledge of a state of affairs (the typical contents of a box of well-known sweets) does not change when the state of affairs changes; and Hidden Emotion, where a protagonist turns their back to hide an expression of emotion that would result in teasing. The child must show an understanding of both the real emotion warranted by the situation and the emotion feigned by the protagonist to avoid teasing. It is worth noting that no location-change (Sally–Anne type) false-belief task was included. When the data were subjected to Guttman scalogram analysis, the typical group showed a similarly scaled order of acquisition to that obtained by Wellman and Liu (2004), as did the early and late signing deaf children. By contrast, the children with ASD, although ordering the tests according to a scale, did so in a different way from the other two groups, reversing the order of the last-acquired two items. For these children false belief (as measured by the unexpected contents task) is harder than hidden emotion, whereas the reverse is the case for children in the other groups.

The fact that late signers and children with ASD show delayed acquisition of theory of mind capacities and also show similar patterns of acquisition of the earlier-acquired tasks lead Peterson et al. to suggest that such acquisition depends on socioconversational experience that is lacking (albeit for different reasons) in the two groups. In addition, Peterson et al. argue that the reversal of acquisition of the hardest two tasks in the group with ASD suggests that there is an ASD-specific deficit in the processes needed to handle the kinds of mental state information tapped by this task compared with other mental state tasks. In view of the discussion of commensurability among different theory of mind tasks (see Chapters 2 and 3), it would have been interesting to see where in the order of acquisition a location-change or Sally–Anne type task would have come, and whether it would show the same position of acquisition for all groups.

Another way of exploring the development of mental state understanding in ASD is to examine the effects of training in theory of mind tasks on everyday social functioning. Several questions can be addressed by such investigations. First, we can see whether or not individuals can be taught to pass different kinds of test. We can then see if improvements can be brought about by a variety of means, and finally, we can test to see if any improvements brought about by training yield improvements in social functioning outside the training situation. In general, attempts to train individuals with ASD have met with some success. For example, Swettenham (1996) used a computer-based task in which children were exposed to a series of eight Sally–Anne type false-belief tasks (Baron-Cohen et al., 1985) on which they were given feedback for correct or incorrect performance. Later, transfer of learning was assessed using similar tasks or more 'distant' tasks such as the Smarties deceptive box task (Perner, Leekam & Wimmer, 1987). Although children with ASD, Down syndrome and typical development all improved their performance on the Sally–Anne task, the children with ASD did not transfer their understanding to the distant task, prompting Swettenham to conclude that they might have mastered the first task using different mechanisms from those used by the other children. Ozonoff and Miller (1995) were able to teach high-functioning adolescents with ASD to pass false a similar battery of belief tasks to those used by Ozonoff and McEvoy (1994) described above, but the improvement (in comparison to a no-treatment comparison group) did not affect parent and teacher ratings of social competence, suggesting poor generalisation. It should be noted, however, that the sample sizes in Ozonoff and Miller's study were small (treatment group $N = 5$; no-treatment group $N = 4$) and there was no comparison group without ASD.

Using a technique originally developed by Mitchell and Lacohée (1991) in the context of typical children, McGregor, Whiten and Blackburn (1998) successfully improved the performance of children with ASD on a Sally–Anne type false-belief task. The technique developed by Mitchell and Lacohée was based around the unexpected contents or Smarties false-belief task in which children are shown a box with canonical contents (such as a box of breakfast cereal). After being asked what they thought was inside, the contents are revealed and shown to be not what was expected (e.g. a duster). Children are then asked what they originally thought was in the box. Typical children do not give the correct answer until they are between 4 and 5 years of age, and success by children with ASD is delayed. However, if at the time of answering the first question, children are asked to select a picture of the predicted contents and post it in a box, then their answer to the later, test question is significantly more likely to be correct. McGregor et al. (1998) adapted this procedure to the Sally–Anne test by asking children to post a picture of where Sally left her marble into a slot in Sally's head. The performance of both children with ASD and typical development improved using this procedure. A similar 'picture-in-the-head' procedure was used successfully by Swettenham, Baron-Cohen, Gomez and Walsh (1996) to improve the capacity of children with ASD to predict the behaviour of a protagonist on the basis of a false belief.

Manipulations of the amount of information provided by the 'Sally' character in a Sally–Anne task were carried out by Bowler and Strom (1998). Children with and without ASD took part in scenarios where a confederate of the experimenter hid an object and left the room. During the confederate's absence, the experimenter helped the child to move the object and when the confederate returned and stood by the door, the child was asked where the confederate would look for the object. Progressively higher success rates were obtained in conditions where the confederate went and stood beside the original hiding place or looked in the hiding place and expressed surprise on not finding the object there. However, neither McGregor et al. nor Swettenham nor Ozonoff and Miller found that the improvements in theory of mind task performance brought about by their interventions could generalise either to other theory of mind tasks or to behaviours that are generally thought to depend on a capacity to employ theory-of-mind-type reasoning.

One interpretation of the lack of generalisation typically found in studies that attempt to teach theory of mind skills to individuals with ASD is that the means by which such individuals come to be able to acquire such skills (whether spontaneously or as a result of specific instruction) are different from those that operate in the typical population. As Parsons and Mitchell (2002) observe, we may not understand other minds by applying rules but by imagining other points of view, as theorists such as Harris (2000) or Gordon (1995) argue. On this view, understanding other minds involves envisaging or imagining a counterfactual state of affairs corresponding to the world view of another person holding a false belief.

There is another way in which the findings from attempts to teach theory of mind skills to individuals with ASD can be used to inform our understanding of the development of this domain in such individuals. Not all studies have been as successful as those described above. For example, Bowler and Briskman (2000), contrary to the work of McGregor and colleagues described above, obtained no improvement on a Sally–Anne type task when children (either with or without ASD) either left a visible clue at the location where the target object was first hidden or took a photograph of the hiding place. The same children did benefit from a photographic cue on an unexpected contents task. And in an unpublished study, Bowler and Tessler (in preparation) found that a 'naughty Snakey'* manipulation did not improve the performance of children with ASD on a Sally–Anne task, despite having been shown to be effective with typical children (Bowler, Briskman and Grice, 1999). The

---

*This intervention was based on a study of conservation in children by McGarrigle and Donaldson (1975). In a typical conservation task, a child is shown, for example, two identical rows of counters. Once the child agrees that there is the same number of counters in the two rows, the experimenter then spreads out one of the rows and asks the child whether the two rows are still the same. Children under about 7 years of age generally say that there are more counters in the longer row, but if the transformation is carried out 'accidentally' by a 'naughty Teddy', even young children are likely to give the correct response. In Bowler et al.'s (1999) intervention, a 'naughty Snakey' was made to transfer the marble from the basket to the box in the Sally–Anne scenario.

standard explanation for improvements using this manipulation is that the accidental ('naughty Snakey') manipulation makes more 'human sense' to the child (Donaldson, 1984), that is to say, that even quite young children understand the notion of accident, and that accidental changes (as opposed to purposeful ones) rarely have consequences for certain aspects of the task in hand. On this argument, it is this element of human sense that is opaque to the children with ASD. In other words, they appear to fail to understand the different implications between intentional and unintentional actions. Somewhat ironically, this returns to the core question of what a 'theory of mind' is about, namely knowing about the intentions of others, and neatly illustrates that it is this understanding that is impaired in ASD. It also shows that there is more to this capacity than simply passing false-belief tasks.

From the perspective of understanding development in ASD, it is clear that mental state understanding develops differently in this population. The success on tasks is ordered differently and not all interventions operate in the same way as with individuals who do not have ASD. Moreover, even when interventions are successful at promoting improved performance, this does not generalise to other tasks that are thought to be conceptually related to those used in the training nor does performance improve on tasks that are thought to depend on a higher level of mental state understanding.

EXECUTIVE FUNCTIONS

Given that the term executive functions includes a rather heterogeneous group of psychological processes that are poorly intercorrelated and that are not all impaired in ASD, we should not be surprised if the data on their development in ASD are not all that clear cut. Yet recently there have been some indications that aspects of executive functioning develop in ASD in particular ways. In Chapter 8 we discussed the developmental trajectory of the cerebral cortex in ASD and noted that there appears to be a period of excessive growth followed by a period of abnormally slowed growth (see Akshoomoff, Pierce & Courchesne, 2002; Courchesne, Karns, Davis et al., 2001). This early enlargement also appears to show a gradient from the rear to the frontal regions (Carper, Moses, Tigue & Courchesne, 2002). This observation of a more abnormal growth trajectory in the frontal regions is in line with the findings of Zilbovicius, Garreau, Samson et al. (1995), who measured regional cerebral blood flow (RCBF, a measure of brain activity) in children with ASD at 3–4 years of age and again 3 years later. They observed reduced RCBF when the children were younger but not when they were older, and concluded that maturation of the frontal lobes was delayed in children with ASD. Most recently, Carper and Courchesne (2005) have reported reduced growth of dorsolateral prefrontal cortex in children with ASD between the ages of 2 and 9 years compared to typical comparison children. They also observed enlarged dorsolateral and medial frontal regions in the ASD children between 2 and

5 years. These patterns of abnormal trajectories in brain development and delayed frontal maturation are consistent with the findings on executive dysfunction reviewed in Chapter 4.

Most of the tests employed to assess adult executive functioning are unsuitable for use with children at the age when significant structural changes to the frontal lobes are taking place. However, various researchers have employed tests that are known from lesion studies with non-human primates to involve specific regions of the frontal cortex. For example, the Delayed Non-Matching to Sample (DNMS) test involves presenting the child with a single object which, when retrieved by the child, revealed a food reward. After a short delay, the same object is presented along with a different one, and the child is rewarded for selecting the new item. Animal studies have shown that this task involves the hippocampus and amygdala as well as the entorhinal and orbital prefrontal cortex (see Dawson, Meltzoff, Osterling & Rinaldi, 1998 for references). The Delayed Response (DR) task involves the experimenter's hiding a toy in a container at the child's midline and then displacing the container to the right or left. A screen is then lowered for 5 s, during which time the experimenter places an identical container at the other side. The screen is then raised and the child is allowed to reach for one of the containers. Human and non-human lesion studies have linked this task to dorsolateral prefrontal cortical functioning. Dawson et al. tested children with ASD, typical development and Down syndrome on both these measures. Children in the ASD and Down syndrome groups had an average chronological age of 5.5 years and a language age of between 2 and 2.5 years; the typical children's chronological age was close to their language age. Compared to both the group with Down syndrome and the typical group, the children with ASD performed significantly worse on the DNMS and the DR task, but only the former correlated significantly with measures of severity of autistic symptomatology such as social orientation, immediate and delayed imitation, shared attention, response to distress in others and symbolic play. Dawson et al. concluded from these findings that the core symptomatology of ASD was likely to be the result of dysfunction of the medial temporal lobe and associated orbitofrontal cortex, which is tapped by the DNMS task, rather than to dysfunction of the dorsolateral prefrontal cortex, which is tapped by the DR task. This study was extended by Dawson, Munson, Estes et al. (2002), who tested larger groups of younger children with ASD, developmental delay and typical development. The atypical groups were aged between 3 and 4 years and were matched on mental age with the typical children who were aged on average 27 months. Dawson et al. (2002) also employed a larger number of neuropsychological tests that tap functioning of the dorsolateral and the ventromedial prefrontal cortices. Severity of autistic symptomatology was assessed by measures of initiation and response to joint attention.

The first and perhaps the most surprising aspect of the results of Dawson et al.'s (2002) study is that it revealed few between-group differences in executive functioning, suggesting that younger children with ASD are not as executively impaired as are older individuals. Yet despite this lack of difference, structural equation modelling showed that measures of ventromedial prefrontal functioning significantly predicted differences in joint attention ability whereas measures of dorsolateral prefrontal functioning did not. This association held (albeit to a lesser extent) when mental age was included in the analysis. The observation that younger children with ASD do not seem to be impaired on these executive function tasks resonates with similar findings reported by Griffith, Pennington, Wehner and Rogers (1999) and by McEvoy, Rogers and Pennington (1992), and prompts us to re-evaluate the role of executive dysfunction as a cause of ASD.

The observation by all these investigators of a correlation between some executive measures and the capacity for joint attention (especially the initiation of joint attention) may well, as Mundy (2003) speculates, be due to executive functioning being a consequence rather than a cause of autistic difficulties with joint attention. Starting from the premise that joint attention behaviours are the first observable markers of a child's ability to understand others as persons with mental states, Mundy draws together several strands of literature. The first is of studies of typical infants, which shows that activity measured at 14 months in certain areas of the medial frontal lobes as well as some dorsolateral and orbitofrontal regions is correlated with degree of initiation of joint attention at 18 months (Henderson, Yoder, Yale & McDuffie, 2002). He then considers the literature on brain correlates of theory of mind in older individuals and notes that the areas activated in these studies show considerable overlap with those implicated in the development of joint attention in typical children. Mundy's conclusion is that dorso-medial frontal cortex (DMFC) and the anterior cingulate gyrus (AC) are regions that are common to joint attention behaviours in infancy and to understanding mental states in later childhood and in adulthood, and as such are candidate areas to be impaired in ASD. However, Mundy is careful not to draw simplistic conclusions that impaired joint attention and theory of mind are the consequence of damage to or atypical functioning of these regions. He is careful to argue that the processes that are mediated by these regions (e.g. planning, self-initiation and self-monitoring of goal-directed behaviours), impairment of which may well give rise to a range of behaviours that are characteristic of ASDs such as repetitive behaviours, are phenomena that can be loosely grouped under the heading of WCC or the processing of complex information, but most importantly, the regulation of attention 'depending on the motivational context of the task' (p. 803). For Mundy, it is this aspect of DMFC/AC functioning that mediates social orienting and ultimately the development of representations of the self. In addition, these areas integrate information on the goal-directed activities of others and enable comparisons with the child's own self-directed activity that ultimately enables a more sophisticated understanding of others' mental states. Thus, behavioural capacities made possible by the DMFC/AC complex may provide the child with an entry into the kinds of intersubjective activities that Hobson (2002) argues are so important for the child's development (see Chapter 3 and the discussion of the self in ASD in Chapter 10). Mundy also draws on Dawson et al.'s (1998) argument that the impaired social orienting that follows from dysfunction of the DMFC/AC may itself compromise further brain development in ways that impair later-developing socio-cognitive abilities. In short, impairments of later, higher-order socio-cognitive and socio-emotional capacities, although a consequence of early brain dysfunction, may not be directly caused by it but follow as a result of brain dysfunction in other areas that arises because of the absence of certain behavioural and experiential inputs normally made possible by intact functioning of areas such as the DMFC/AC. This scenario may seem rather convoluted and invite a 'so what?' response. But it has important implications for remediation, in that it makes plausible the hypothesis that if the kinds of experiences made possible by intact DMFC/AC functioning are elicited through intervention, then later socio-cognitive impairment may be circumvented.

To recapitulate, the current state of evidence on the development of executive functions in ASD is that they appear to be intact in younger individuals, with impairment not appearing until later childhood. However, even in early childhood, performance on tasks that tap functioning of dorsal frontal and anterior cingulate cortex correlates with impairments in the initiation of joint attention, a capacity that is generally agreed to be a precursor to an understanding of mental states in self and others. This leads theorists such as Mundy (see Mundy, 2003) to argue for a key role of the DMFC/AC in the regulation of joint attention and the eventual development of an understanding of mental states in others. Although arguments like Mundy's are powerful and compelling, we should reflect on the current evidence base for these claims. Relatively few studies have been carried out in this area, and so far, none has been longitudinal. In particular, longer-term follow-up studies are needed to explore the predictive power of early executive measures on later measures of mental state understanding. Until we have evidence of this kind, we have no way of evaluating the necessity of the causal connections hypothesised in accounts like Mundy's. The advantage of such accounts, however, is that they adopt a genuinely developmental account of psychological processing, avoiding a simplistic reference to brain maturation. Brain maturation, in particular the delayed maturation of the frontal lobes, may well play a role in the evolution of executive functioning and joint attention capacity, but the different timing of the emergence of abnormal function on these different measures suggests that a simple maturational account may not be the whole story. The advantage of accounts such as Mundy's is that they provide a framework within which to generate testable hypotheses in relation to this story.

DEVELOPMENTAL THEORY AND ASD

Thus far, our discussion of developmental change in ASD has been descriptive. We have covered a range of focus from broad behavioural and psychological functions such as social adaptation to more restricted competences such as performance on tasks like DNMS that are thought on the one hand to reflect functioning of specific brain regions and on the other to constitute components of the other, broader categories of adaptive function. Some investigators have attempted to model potential interactions among descriptive measures, both longitudinally and cross-sectionally. But if these modelling exercises are to be more than just the simple documentation of behavioural change over time and the descriptions of relations among factors, they need to embody some form of theoretical framework not only as a tool to help us to organise the existing findings but also to help us to think about them in new and potentially productive ways. In short, we need to consider the role of developmental theory in our understanding of ASD.

For many decades, the psychology of typical development revolved around a small number of what we might call 'grand theories', most notably those of Piaget (1952; 1962; 1970), Vygotsky (1962; 1978) and Werner (1948). (There are other theorists, such as Bühler, 1947 and Wallon, 1973, but these authors are less widely known in the English-speaking world.) In the broadest terms, these theorists have attempted to give accounts of how an individual moves from a state of being a helpless, speechless organism to one that possesses the capacity for independent, intelligent, adaptive action in its environment. All recognise that such development is not simply a question of the unfolding of a genetic blueprint; individual circumstances affect development to too great an extent for this to be the case. Nor can behavioural evolution in an individual be entirely a product of circumstances, because there are marked similarities in development across individuals. Different theorists place different emphasis on the respective importance of regularity and variability or of internal and external factors, but all recognise the need to encompass the two in a way that captures the reality of individual psychological development. Piaget was concerned with specifying the abstract, logico-mathematical properties of a child's representational system at different points in development. Possession of a representational system enabled the child to engage with the world in a way that accumulated information, which both confirmed (through a process he called *assimilation*) and disconfirmed the child's existing knowledge base. Accumulated disconfirmations resulted in a systematic reorganisation (or *accommodation*) of the representational system to enable further assimilation of new information and better adaptation to the environment. This periodic reorganisation of the child's conceptual system gave rise to what is perhaps the most famous aspect of Piaget's account of development, namely his sequence of stages of cognitive development. Vygotsky, by contrast, was more concerned with the ways in which knowledge developed through social

DEVELOPMENT

interactions and with the way that culturally determined forms of knowledge were transmitted to the child through social interactions. And Werner saw psychological change over time in terms of his *orthogenetic principle of development* which states that '. . . whenever development occurs, it proceeds from a state of relative globality and lack of differentiation to a state of increasing differentiation, articulation and hierarchic integration' (Werner, 1948, p. 126). Developing individuals move from a stage of indifferentiation between subject and object to one where they become polarised. This, in turn, entails an increasing freedom from reliance on the here-and-now and a greater facility with the use of internal representations as a regulator of behaviour. Werner argues that these changes make possible planned action as well as enhanced understanding of others in psychological terms.

Two themes common to all grand theories of development are those of internalisation of action and abstraction, or distancing, from the here-and-now properties of stimuli. Internalisation involves the development of mental representations of entities and events, representations that can be used to guide future behaviour. Distancing is the capacity to become freed from the idiosyncratic nature of a particular stimulus while at the same time retaining an awareness of the properties it shares with other, similar stimuli. The material covered in earlier chapters demonstrates how both these themes have echoes in the behaviour profiles of individuals with ASD.

Although theories such as those of Piaget and Vygotsky (and to a lesser extent, that of Werner) dominated the field of developmental psychology up to the 1970s, since then research in the field has tended to become more focused on individual aspects of development, such as language, number and mathematical understanding, attention, executive functions or socio-cognitive understanding with little reference to overarching systems to tie these together. This state of affairs has resulted in a fragmentation of the discipline of developmental psychology and a reduction of the notion of developmental change to what Van Geert (1998) has termed a 'sociology of ages'. Rather than seeing developmental change as something to be first described and then explained, the tendency has been just to describe it and leave things at that. However, explanations of developmental change are important, especially in the context of developmental psychopathological conditions such as ASD because, as we have seen in the example of Mundy's (2003) speculations above, they give us clues about which psychological (and possibly brain) processes might be causes and which might be consequences of particular aspects of symptomatology. Mundy's analysis serves to remind us that in the context of trying to understand ASD, there are still lessons to be learned from the approach embodied in the grand theories of psychological development (see Burack, Charman, Yirmiya & Zelazo, 2001 for further elaboration). All organisms end up making some kind of sense of their environments and eventually achieve some stable equilibrium, in the process of which they become changed. The task for the observer of these adaptations is not to take too linear a view of possible underlying processes, nor to become overly fixated on a small number of the pieces of the explanatory jigsaw. Understanding different developmental trajectories involves a consideration of factors within as well as outside the individual, and of how these reciprocally interact over time. But this must be done with a view to systematic, principled understanding, not merely with the aim of gathering collections of facts in an ad-hoc, unstructured manner.

CONNECTIONISM AND DEVELOPMENT

The grand theories of typical psychological development were conceived at a time when techniques for neuropsychological investigation were considerably less sophisticated than they are today. But with developments in imaging techniques and the rise of neural network and connectionist modelling (see Chapter 8), new theoretical accounts aimed at not just describing but also explaining development have begun to make their appearance. A recent issue of the journal *Trends in Cognitive Science* (2005, Volume 9, issue 3) has been devoted to what it refers to the crossroads faced by the scientific study of cognitive development and the new paradigms that are emerging as a consequence of the new methodologies. Increasing understanding of brain structure, together with increasingly sophisticated models of brain functioning, have placed constraints on the kinds of psychological theorising that reached its zenith in the work of Piaget. However, this increasing need to take account of the brain in accounts of development should not, as the example of Mundy (2003) described above elegantly shows, lead us to think that everything in development – whether typical or atypical – is determined by brain functioning, with little room for experience. The brain may well constrain what experiences an individual has, but these experiences in turn change the way the brain organises itself. In Chapter 8 we briefly discussed connectionist models of brain function. Connectionist models that employ back-propagation of error algorithms use feedback from the environment to alter the weights of connections between elements of a network, thereby altering the structure and functioning of the system. Self-organising networks arrange themselves in configurations that optimally satisfy internal and external constraints. But in either case, although brain structure can determine behaviour, it is not immune from being, in turn, determined by the experiences brought about by behaviour. It is perhaps worth noting that this dialogue or interchange between a biologically given structure and the feedback from its effects on the environment, together with the subsequent adaptive change in the whole system, lies at the core of the whole of Piaget's research enterprise. But it is only with the development of connectionist-like models that we can begin to marry behavioural and cognitive conceptualisations along the lines of those of Piaget to actual brain function.

As yet, there have been very few attempts to apply connectionist thinking to the case of ASD (see McClelland, 2000 and Chapter 8), but this is a situation that is likely to change as the possibility of enacting connectionist models becomes more widespread. The seductive nature of connectionist systems both as models of brain functioning and as potential accounts of the development of ASD raises the issue of a trap that needs to be avoided when analysing ASD (or any other form of developmental psychopathology) in neural network or connectionist terms. This is what Thomas and Karmiloff-Smith (2002) call *residual normality*, or the tendency to assume that systems that develop atypically are atypical only in respect to those aspects of function that register as abnormal and are, in all other respects, normal and typical. Thomas and Karmiloff-Smith take issue with standard neuropsychological accounts of the consequences of acquired brain damage, which tend to take a modularist view of psychological function, seeing impairments as the result of malfunctioning of encapsulated modules dedicated to the kinds of processing that are impaired as a result of the brain damage. They argue that in the case of developmental disorders, damage to the system is usually present at the outset, so that any explanation of abnormal functioning must take developmental processes into account and cannot assume that processing in areas outside those of obvious malfunction is taking place normally, that is to say as a result of processes that are indistinguishable from someone without the developmental pathology. In short, anything that does not appear superficially abnormal must be normal and by implication, undamaged. Thomas and Karmiloff-Smith develop their critique of this position by means of a series of simulations carried out using neural networks. In one of these simulations, they taught the neural network illustrated in Figure 9.1 to learn the past tense of four categories of English verb. These were verbs that added -ed (walk – walked), that remained the same (hit – hit) and two types of exception verbs: those that changed an internal vowel sound (hide – hid) and those where there was no relation between the present and the past form (go – went). Damage to the neural network was implemented in three different ways: by 'lesioning', which involved setting a proportion of the connections to a strength of zero (analogous to cutting a nerve fibre so that it transmits no information), by adding noise to the hidden layer of the network or by changing the discriminability function by which each unit classified input.

The results of the simulation showed that the amount of lesion damage required to produce a given level of impaired performance was far greater at the outset than after learning had taken place. This suggests that in the case of the 'mature' network (where learning has already taken place), severing connections involves losing already acquired information, whereas lesioning the same connections in a naive network still leaves the system with the capacity to acquire what knowledge it can, but in an obviously different manner from the way in which the unlesioned network acquired it. The effects of adding

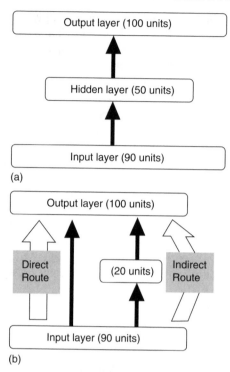

Figure 9.1. Diagram of neural network used by Thomas and Karmiloff-Smith (2002). Reproduced by kind permission of Cambridge University Press.

noise were the reverse of those brought about by lesioning the network. The levels of noise that needed to be added at the start in order to produce a given level of impairment were substantially less than those needed to impair the performance of the trained network. Finally, reducing discriminability either before or after training did not affect the performance of the network, and increasing discriminability had no effect if applied at the start of training. But increasing discriminability at the end of training severely disrupted performance on irregular, exception pattern verbs, suggesting that the system cannot compensate for the effects of this kind of change, once it has established a pattern for processing inputs.

Although abstract, and seemingly far removed from the phenomena of ASD, this example serves to highlight the importance of the process of development in the organisation of a system that takes input and transforms it into output. In particular, it shows us the complex relationship that can exist between damage that occurs before and after a particular set of developmental events and eventual atypical performance, as well as on typical performance. We cannot, for example, conclude that a network that can still generate the correct past-tense form of regular and irregular verbs even though it has been lesioned before training is functioning in a similar way to an undamaged network. We cannot, in the terms used by Thomas and Karmiloff-Smith, assume residual normality. These demonstrations concretise speculations such as those made by Bowler (1992), Happé (1995) and Hermelin and O'Connor (1985), who used terms like 'logico-affective state' or 'hacking out' to describe the good performance of some individuals with ASD on socio-cognitive measures such as false-belief tasks.

MODELLING DISCONTINUOUS CHANGE: NON-LINEAR DYNAMIC SYSTEMS THEORY AND CATASTROPHE THEORY

Our discussion of connectionism, both here and in Chapter 8, has introduced the notion that representations of objects and events may not be specifically localised at particular points in the brain, but rather, distributed across networks of nerve cells. Brain lesions will therefore rarely have precise or catastrophic effects, because only part of a system underlying a particular representation or process will be damaged, and the very nature of networks is such that they can compensate for damage, at least to some extent. This shift in conceptualisation represents a move away from the kinds of one-to-one correspondences that have characterised not only certain types of neuropsychological theories that have seen representations of objects and events as highly localised in specific brain structures but also have seen psychological processes (such as mental state understanding) as underpinned by specific neural architectures, to one where such entities are seen as emergent properties of the operation of a whole system.* This kind of abstraction is analogous to the sorts of explanations for development advocated by the 'grand theorists' such as Piaget and Vygotsky. Their view of developmental change in particular domains such as understanding space, number, mass, etc. was that it was an emergent property of very general, non-specific processes such as assimilation and accommodation or of forms of social interaction within the zone of proximal development. Such abstraction in the form of increased distancing is a feature of other attempts to model developmental change that have appeared in the literature in recent decades. As yet these have not been applied to the topic of ASD, but given the increasing attention devoted to them, coupled with the increasing recognition of the need to take a more systematically developmental approach to understanding ASD (see Burack et al., 2001), such application will surely come about.

Non-linear dynamic systems theory (NLDST) is a branch of mathematics that has been used by developmental biologists to account for developmental change in terms of shifting patterns of parameters that contribute to the functioning of a particular aspect of a complex system. In the context of

*Some theorists who take a strongly systems-oriented view acknowledge that neural systems may become 'modularised' through development (see Karmiloff-Smith, 1992).

developmental psychology, NDLST has received its fullest exposition by Esther Thelen, Brenda Smith and their colleagues (see Smith & Thelen, 1993; 2003; Thelen & Smith, 1994; Thelen, Schöner, Scheler & Smith, 2001). The core of their position is that although we can see regularities in behaviour change when we look at data from large groups of individuals (typical children pass false-belief tasks late in their fourth or early in their fifth year; children with ASD do so much later, if at all), these 'typical' or mean values hide a great deal of variability that in conventional scientific methodology has been treated as undesirable noise and consigned to error variance in statistical analyses. The NLDST approach, however, takes this variability as its starting point and looks for ways to manipulate it systematically. Such manipulations and their effects on patterns of variability (not on mean level of performance, as would be done in more conventional approaches) enable us to model processes of developmental change. An example (taken from Smith & Thelen, 2003) will make this clearer.

There is a task that was described by Piaget (1963) and which he used to determine when infants developed an awareness of the existence of objects that was independent of their own action on them. The task is illustrated in Figure 9.2 and involves the experimenter hiding an object in location A and

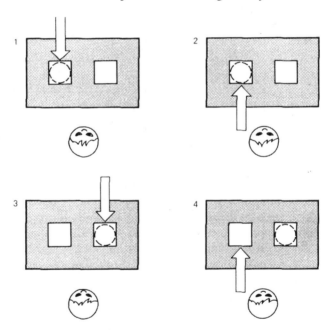

Figure 9.2. Test procedure to demonstrate the 'A-not-B error' in children. The child initially retrieves an object hidden in the left hand location. When the object is then hidden in the right hand location, children who commit the error continue to look in the left hand hiding place. Reproduced from Bremner, G. (1994) *Infancy*, Oxford: Blackwell by kind permission of Blackwell Publishing.

getting the child to reach for the object. After several repetitions, the experimenter hides the object in location B, and after a short delay, the child is allowed to reach for the object. Children aged younger than 10 months typically reach back to location A, and not to B, where they saw the object disappear. By 12 months of age on average, children can solve the task correctly. Many explanations have been offered for this developmental change. Piaget saw it as a manifestation of a profound change in the child's knowledge of objects, but other researchers have argued, for example, that it reflects the maturation of the prefrontal cortex that enables the child to inhibit a well-learned situational response (Diamond, 1998). Thelen, Smith and colleagues argue that most attempts to explain the A-not-B error attempt to do so in terms of a single cause, when in fact there are multiple causes. Instead, they propose a field theory in which activation states corresponding to the two locations are activated to different levels depending on the state of input parameters and the state of other areas within the field. So if a point in the field becomes highly activated, this will inhibit activity in neighbouring areas, with the result that the activation–inhibition pattern can be maintained without further input. Figure 9.3 is taken from Smith and Thelen (2003) and represents different configurations of the field at different times in the task. In Figure 9.3a, the child has just seen an object hidden in location A, and thus has a highly activated area of the field corresponding to location A (one could say that the child is representing location A, although Smith and Thelen try to avoid this terminology), which is further strengthened by the child's reaching to location A. When the experimenter switches the location of the hidden object to location B, activity in the area of the field is correspondingly activated (see Figure 9.3b), but not as strongly or as persistently as the activation in A, and so responding continues to be under the control of the high level of activation at A.

So far, Smith and Thelen's analysis of the A-not-B problem appears to be merely a re-description of the problem that could just as easily be summarised along the lines that the child has a better memory for or representation of the object in location A and that this temporarily overrides the new and weaker knowledge that it is now in location B. But, they argue, their formulation permits the error to be understood in terms of a range of parameters that, when manipulated, should push rates of commission of the error up or down. Thus, by manipulating the number of trials at location A, Smith, Thelen, Titzer and McLin (1999) showed how an infant could be made to commit or not to commit the error. Smith et al. (1999) also caused the error to disappear by changing the context in which A and B hidings occurred. During hidings at location A infants were seated, whereas for hidings at location B they were stood up on their mother's lap. Thelen et al. (2001) also made the error disappear by altering the physical dynamics of the child's reach in the two types of trial by adding wrist weights in one condition and not in the other. Findings like these lead the advocates of NLDST to argue that we cannot meaningfully

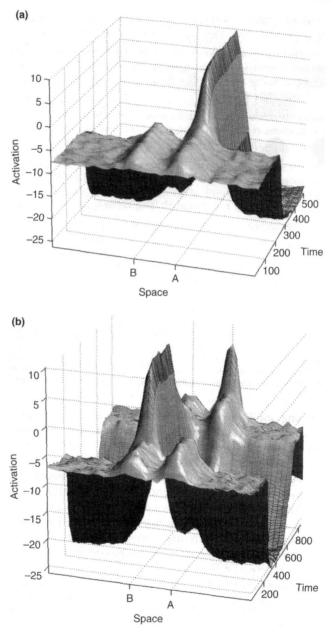

Figure 9.3. NLDST analysis of A-not-B task performance. Reproduced from Smith and Thelen (2003) by kind permission of Elsevier.

speak of developmental changes in terms of single causes, but in terms of constellations of dynamic interactions among a range of different factors that operate differently at different times across individuals. The similarity of change that we see when we aggregate data across large numbers of children is most likely due to a common biological heritage and to an environment that in many respects is common across individuals. But NLDST theorists strongly argue that such similarities hide marked individual variability, the understanding of which gives the key to understanding developmental change.

So far, there have been no applications of NLDST to ASD, but it is possible to speculate on how it might be applied. The work of Dawson and colleagues described in an earlier section (Dawson et al., 2002) showed that in very young children with ASD, performance on tasks like Delayed Non-Matching to Sample, which is in many respects similar to the A-not-B task, is relatively unimpaired, and that it is not until children are older that an ASD-related deficit in performance becomes evident. The task could be re-conceptualised in terms of a field of activity which reorganises itself both in response to changes to internal and external factors, and this re-description could form the basis for systematic testing of hypotheses relating to the effects of different control parameters. Different patterns of response to such manipulations could tell us a great deal about how individuals with ASD organise their responses to changes in their environment in the context of adaptive action. Understanding these differences could eventually form the basis of intervention strategies. Our understanding of repetitive behaviour could also benefit from the kinds of conceptualisations advocated by NLDST. We would need to think of why the behavioural field organises itself in ways that tend to fall back into a single or small set of ruts, which channel behaviour along highly predictable lines (such as repeatedly spinning the wheels of a car, or talking at length about the architecture of town hall facades in different countries).

Many developmental theorists – most famously, Piaget – argue that cognitive development takes place as a sequence of stages, each of which is characterised by a qualitatively different form of thought. Transitions between stages are thought of as being abrupt, in contrast to other forms of developmental change such as memory capacity or vocabulary where change is smoother, even if the slope of the developmental curve varies at different time periods. In the ASD literature, the most widely studied developmental change is the transition from an inability to understand the representational nature of mental states in others to a state where such understanding is readily in evidence. Although some theorists have begun to argue that this might be a more gradual affair (see e.g. Tager-Flusberg, 2001), it is nonetheless a transition that is markedly delayed in ASD. Developmental theorists have long puzzled over the question of how discontinuous change (stepwise or stage-like development) can emerge as a function of linear changes in other developmental variables (see Hartelman, van der Maas & Molenaar, 1998). One way to model such interactions has borrowed ideas from a branch of mathematics known as catastrophe theory (Thom, 1989), and which was originally developed to model and explain how discontinuous events in the physical world (such as a concrete platform bending under a load and suddenly breaking) could be accounted for in terms of continuous change in other parameters (such as applied load). Theorists such as van der Maas and Molenaar (1992) have applied this theory to model discontinuous change in children's development. We know for example that if you show a 5 year old typical child two identical balls of plasticine and then roll one of them into a sausage shape, the child will typically judge there to be less plasticine in the sausage because it is thinner. But if we repeat this test on a 7 year old, the child will judge the two to contain the same quantity of material. This is Piaget's famous conservation task. This shift from an overreliance on the appearance of the world to a more conceptual understanding of the relationship between objects and the actions performed on them is an example of the kinds of abrupt stage transitions in understanding that are amenable to an analysis in terms of catastrophe theory. We can pose the question of how variables like attentional capacity or short-term memory capacity, which do not mature in abrupt changes, interact to produce step-like changes in measures such as conservation (see van der Maas & Molenaar, 1992 for more discussion).

Although as yet there have not been any empirical tests of catastrophe theory in the context of ASD, it has been explored in this context in two theoretical papers by Mottron (Mottron, 1987; 1988). Mottron draws on Thom's analysis of semiotics in terms of one-term, two-term and three-term relations and uses it to explain the diminished use of semantic relationships by individuals with ASD as well as their atypical development of understanding mental states in others. Although not containing any prediction-driven empirical findings, Mottron's interpretation of Thom resonates with other research discussed at various points in this book, most notably Bowler et al.'s (2005) interpretation of performance on false-belief tasks in terms of the ternary relations put forward by Halford (1992), and Minshew's invocation of complexity as an explanation of information-processing atypicalities in ASD (see Minshew, Johnson & Luna, 2001).

Both catastrophe theory and NLDST have the potential to address some of the questions that are not adequately answered by existing approaches in the field. In Chapter 4 we discussed the 'homunculus problem' in relation to executive dysfunction in ASD. The problem is how to conceptualise a system that can monitor and correct its own activity without having an infinite regress of executive processes, each controlling the one below it. Both NLDST and catastrophe theory get around this problem by positing the notion of self-organisation, whereby the configuration of a system of psychological processes establishes itself in such a way that it will have a number of 'preferred' ways of dealing with a particular set of inputs (these are often called 'attractor

states', because activity is attracted towards them) but under certain circumstances, activity can be shifted out of a given attractor state and into a different way of functioning, which, in turn, alters the configuration of the system
and changes the way it responds to new patterns of input. This way of thinking about development has a long pedigree, going back to Waddington's (1966)
idea of an *epigenetic landscape* (see Figure 9.4) in which the child's activity is
likened to a ball that rolls over a piece of ground, which represents cognitive
structures that change over time. This change results in increasing undulations
in the ground that constrain and channel the direction of the ball. The deeper
the undulation, the more force (i.e. the stronger the environmental input) is
needed to push the ball out of it and into another trajectory. In the case of
ASD, we could speculate that the undulations become particularly deep, thus
channelling the child's behaviour into a narrow and restricted repertoire,
which gives rise to a picture of repetitive and executively dysfunctional behaviour. Catastrophe theory may help us to understand the mixed findings on the
role of semantic relatedness in memory for individuals with ASD discussed
in Chapter 7. Some studies have shown sensitivity to such relatedness (e.g.
Bowler et al., 2000b; Leekam & Lopez, 2003), whereas others have not (e.g.
Bowler et al., 1997; Tager-Flusberg, 1991). Clearly there is some factor that
at a certain level triggers semantic sensitivity in this group. A clue to what
this might be can be had from the findings of a study by Bowler, Gaigg and
Gardiner (under review), based on a study by Tulving (1962). Adults with high-
functioning ASD and a typical comparison group were asked to recall a list of
16 unrelated words presented one by one on a computer screen. The same
words were re-presented in a different order on 15 subsequent trials, with free
recall on each trial. The results showed that both groups organised the way

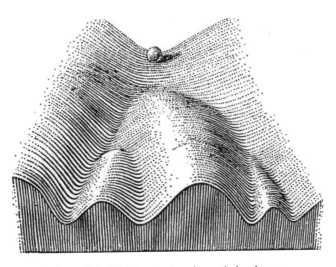

Figure 9.4. Waddington's epigenetic landscape.

they recalled the material but that whereas the pattern of organisation in the typical group tended to converge across participants, that of the ASD participants did not. This means that the ASD participants were organising the material in an idiosyncratic manner – they differed not only from the typical participants but also from each other. We can speculate that the typical participants were probably mostly using semantic relatedness to organise their recall, whereas the ASD participants may well have used this feature, but may also have used other features such as the phonology of the words, their shape on the screen or the number of syllables they contained. These observations are reminiscent of those of Wang and Mottron (2005) who found that whereas typical participants tended to opt for global processing of hierarchical stimuli, participants with ASD were as likely to use a local as a global strategy. Catastrophe theory could contribute to the investigation of such phenomena by providing a formal framework to model why and how people with ASD opt for particular styles of processing when typical individuals do not.

The advantage of NLDST and catastrophe theory is that they provide a formalism and a means of modelling different kinds of developmental landscapes that can be used as a basis for hypothesis testing and thus take descriptions of behaviour beyond metaphor and speculation and into the realm of empirical test. A further advantage of these two approaches to conceptualising development is that they are what can be termed *emergentist* accounts, that is to say that they see complex psychological functions as arising out of interactions of simpler ones in response to particular environmental contingencies. Such a view contrasts with many of the ideas discussed in earlier chapters, where particular processes are seen as the behavioural manifestations of dedicated neural systems. Neither NLDST nor catastrophe theory denies a role to the nervous system, but they differ from extreme biological reductionist accounts in that they do not see everything as being specified in advance either by means of modular brain systems or in the organism's genes. Piaget (1970) observed that 'that which is inevitable is not necessarily innate',* which is to say that just because a complex process (for example, understanding mental states in other people) may inevitably follow from the possession of certain attentional and memory capacities and an upbringing in a certain kind of caregiving environment, does not mean that mental state understanding *per se* is innately specified. The example often given, taken from D'Arcy Thompson (see Elman et al., 1996; Thompson, 1917), is that of bees, who typically build honeycombs that are hexagonal in structure. But bees are not programmed to build hexagons. Rather, they build cylinders of wax, and then in concert, push these together. The physics of flexible cylinders being subjected to radial forces does the rest; the hexagonal structure emerges as the best solution to contiguous flexible cylinders being pushed together. Similarly, we can argue that although at some level, psychological processing is innately specified, at any

*I am grateful to the late Elizabeth Bates for drawing this quote to my attention.

given level of analysis this specification is incomplete, and that structure in behaviour at this level is a consequence of this specification and aspects of experience. The research programme that derives from the foregoing account requires a shift in emphasis from cross-sectional to longitudinal studies, especially to the kind of longitudinal studies that manipulate variables to assess their effects over time. Studies such as those of Howlin et al. and Sigman and Ruskin described in the first part of this chapter are an important first step, in that they describe contingencies across time between changes in one measure and changes in another. But these investigations now need to be extended to assess the extent to which the consequences of naturally occurring variability in one measure on level of functioning in another area can be systematically manipulated. (Although there are obvious ethical issues here relating to the direction of experimental manipulation; we could not, for example, hinder a child's language development in order to see if impaired social adjustment resulted at a later date.)

CONCLUSION

Although ASD has long been characterised as a set of developmental disorders, the systematic study of change over time in ASD has tended to occupy a relatively small proportion of research activity. This is a situation that is changing, and we now have a considerable body of research that provides descriptions of development and is beginning to chart possible causal mechanisms that drive different patterns of change. What is less in evidence is a theoretical framework within which to generate hypotheses to guide further investigation. The theoretical frameworks exist, to a large extent. What is needed is their application to ASD.

10 Whence and Whither: Glimpses of the Tapestry, Paths Through the Jungle

The first part of the title to this chapter is self-evident: where have we come from, and where are we going? Has psychological research in any way enhanced our understanding of ASD? Any reader who has made it as far as here might reasonably be forgiven for concluding that all they have read is a series of necrologies. It seems as though each theoretical approach has been described and then dissected only to find that the entrails may not be that informative after all and that burial of the carcass might be the best option. Dissection there certainly has been; but I hope that it is a dissection that has enhanced our understanding of the psychological anatomy of ASD. I hope too that I have not fallen into the all-too-easy trap of being critical of others' work and not providing any positive suggestions or ideas of my own. All through the book I have offered comments and observations about how our thinking might be developed either by refining existing empirical approaches or by developing new ones. But these comments are scattered throughout the text and linked more or less closely to one or other of the theoretical positions reviewed. What has been lacking is a distanced view of the issues.

One of the problems in ASD research is that particular theoretical positions are often presented (usually not by their proponents, it must be said) as if they contained *the* key to understanding the condition. The true situation, however, is somewhat different. If we imagine a richly coloured medieval tapestry such as *La Dame à la Licorne* at the Musée de Cluny in Paris, we can see that it is made up of areas of many different colours. Imagine that ASD is a tapestry like this, but that it is covered by an opaque film. Scientists who want to describe what is behind the film can only do so by making small holes in it and shining a light through the hole. Some scientists loudly proclaim that the tapestry is blue, and others that it is red, or gold and some are even unaware that the colour of the light might affect what they see behind the film. But the truth is that the tapestry is all of these and that to understand it properly we need to punch lots of holes and then stand back to try to get an impression of the patterning of what lies behind each hole. Hence the first metaphor in the title.

The second metaphor refers to a talk at the 2001 meeting of the Society for Research in Child Development in Minneapolis where Alison Gopnik described her experiences as editor of the prestigious journal *Child Development*. She likened the field of developmental psychology research, and ASD research in particular, to a vast expanse of jungle that has some roads and pathways through it. The roads tend to carry a great deal of traffic, the paths somewhat less, but what is striking is the fact that there is so much jungle that no one seems keen to explore. What I propose in this chapter is to summarise what I see as the current state of play in the psychology of ASD and then to step out, if not into the jungle, at least on to some less worn paths in order to try to identify cross-domain themes that might help to direct future research.

HOW FAR HAVE WE REALLY COME?

In researching this book, I came across a volume edited by J. K. Wing (1966) entitled *Early Childhood Autism: Clinical, Educational and Social Aspects*. It was published barely two decades after Kanner's original description and not long after diagnoses of autism started to become common in the United Kingdom. The book consists in the main of a series of accounts by clinicians, educators and parents, all of whom had had extensive experience of what were then called 'autistic children'. What is remarkable about these accounts is their insightfulness and their resonance with the kinds of debates covered in this book. This resonance with later work is remarkable given that much of what the authors had to say was based on uncontrolled observations and an almost non-existent research base. But now, even after four decades that have witnessed an explosion of research into ASD, it is tempting to ask whether our understanding has changed to any significant extent since the publication of Wing's book. Having read most of the research that has been done over this period, I tend towards the conclusion that even if we have not had any major breakthroughs, we have come a long way not least in that we have backed up many of the insights contained in Wing's book by controlled observations.

It is now known that ASD is no longer a condition confined to childhood, but one that persists throughout the lifespan. We also know that it comprises a range or spectrum of conditions, including Asperger's syndrome. In parallel with this enlarged conception of the autism spectrum, we have a more refined understanding of the symptomatology of the conditions that make it up. The work of Lorna Wing and Judy Gould has highlighted the fact that core features of all manifestations of the spectrum lie in the areas of reciprocal social interactions and repetitive behaviours. And it is these two features that have driven much of the psychological research on ASD. The broader conception of autism embodied in a spectrum approach has also resulted in revised epidemiological estimates of the prevalence of ASD. Whereas Kanner-type autism was thought to be found in 4 per 10000 of the population, prevalence of the broader spectrum is much greater, representing about 8 in every 1000 people. This shift in our understanding both of the symptomatology and the prevalence of ASD has had important implications for service provision – it has made agencies more aware of the extent of the need for care as well as of the amount of science funding needed in order to enhance our understanding what can no longer be considered an extremely rare condition. But apart from redefining and reassessing the prevalence of the syndrome, has our psychological understanding of ASD changed since the publication of Wing's book?

From our current perspective, it can easily be forgotten that when the book was published, accounts of the causes and treatment of ASD that blamed parents and advocated psychoanalytically oriented treatment approaches were still widespread. The book's contributors all dissented from this view and shared the notion that ASD was a biologically based condition that needed appropriate management and educational intervention. The increased volume of research activity on ASDs over the past two decades has justified that shared view and has brought us closer to understanding the precise nature of its neurobiological underpinnings. Perhaps somewhat ironically, the fact that we now know that ASD includes individuals with good language and normal or supranormal levels of intelligence, together with the fact that, as we shall see shortly, the sense of self appears to be constructed differently in such individuals, means that we must return to considering the development of appropriate forms of psychotherapeutic intervention to help such individuals understand and come to terms with their own feelings about the sense of difference they feel in relation to the typical population.

The characterisation of ASD as being a disorder of social, symbolic and communicative functioning led, as we saw in Chapters 2 and 3, to a plethora of research into social and interpersonal understanding. This research was driven initially by the observations of Wing and Gould (1979) on social impairment but rapidly became dominated by particular and often opposing theoretical frameworks drawn from mainstream psychology and philosophy. On the one hand, the work derived from the seminal study by Baron-Cohen et al. (1985) demonstrating delayed understanding of false belief in children with ASD posited an impaired brain system that mediated the understanding of other people's minds. On the other hand was the work of Hobson (see Hobson, 2002, but also e.g. Sigman et al., 1992), which took Kanner's observation of impairments in affective contact as its starting point. This line of work saw ASD as an impairment in the understanding of emotions in others with consequent knock-on effects for those aspects of development that depend crucially on emotionally charged interactions between children and their caregivers. Debate also centred on the question of whether or not any underlying atypical processes were modular and domain-specific (i.e. dedicated to the processing of information relevant to social functioning and no other) or were a by-product of more widely spread atypical functioning. Although this particular question is by no means settled, there is now considerable evidence that atypical psychological functioning in ASD goes far beyond the realms of social interaction and social understanding and that impairments in these domains are likely to be an emergent aspect of atypical functioning that is not social-specific.

The theme of more domain-general psychological atypicalities was taken up by researchers interested in executive dysfunction (see Chapter 4) and in atypical perceptual and attentional functions, particularly a tendency to concentrate on detail of complex stimulus arrays rather than their global configurations (see Chapters 5 and 6). The current state of our understanding of these domains is that the invocation of overarching concepts like 'executive function' or 'central coherence' may not have been as helpful as had initially been hoped. Considerable empirical evidence has shown that these two constructs are at once too broad and make assumptions that are not borne out by the evidence. Yet the data from individual measures of executive function and WCC remain helpful in that they prompt us to consider which processes operate in a typical fashion and which atypically in the autistic population. On the basis of current evidence it would appear that people with ASD experience difficulties in regulating their behaviour when courses of action have to be chosen on the basis of a set of possibilities that first has to be generated and then selected from. It also seems to be the case that they are less likely to overlook the details of a complex situation in circumstances where an optimal response strategy calls for attention to the global configuration. This can lead to atypical patterns of responding, for example in face processing, where there is a tendency to look less at the eyes and more at other face regions, thus presumably compromising the ability to evaluate (among other things) the facial expressions of emotion that are thought by Hobson to play a role in general psychological development (see Chapter 3). A tendency to focus on details may also contribute to the fact that children with ASD are less likely to notice certain dynamic patterns of movement involving the coordinated action of two animate objects (Bowler & Thommen, 2000), which are important in the development of an understanding of interpersonal relations and social competence generally. We should also note, as Frith and Happé (1994) remind us, that these atypical patterns of processing can lead to enhancement of performance on tasks where typical global processing bias can be disadvantageous, thus confirming ASD as a set of conditions characterised by peaks as well as troughs of ability. Whether this patterning of abilities results from difficulties in seeing the whole or from the operation of enhanced lower-level perceptual processes that enable the parts to compete with the whole remains a hotly debated question (see Caron, Mottron, Berthiaume & Dawson, 2006; Mottron, Dawson, Soulières et al., 2006).

Research on low-level perceptual abilities of individuals with ASD (see Chapter 6) has shown a number of systematic differences from the typical population such as enhanced pitch perception, atypical brain responses to human speech sounds and atypical processing of static and dynamic complex visual stimuli. If we adopt a linear notion of information processing, in which low-level perception provides the building blocks for higher-level perceptual and conceptual processes that drive adaptive action, then it is tempting to conclude that the 'core difficulty' experienced by people with ASD lies in atypical low-level perceptual functioning. But, as we also discussed in that chapter, the way we perceive the world is not entirely a one-way process; what we see or hear is determined as much by the incoming stimulation as by how perception of this information is modulated by our existing knowledge of the world – so-called 'top-down' processing. We saw in Chapter 5 that individuals with ASD seem to engage in less top-down processing when making perceptual judgments, that is to say, their reactions to the world are based on information that is closer to the properties of the incoming stimulus. We can speculate that this shift in balance between top-down (conceptually driven) and bottom-up (stimulus driven) processing will affect any permanent representations of a particular stimulus that may be laid down, which in turn will affect future top-down processing. This dynamic interaction between existing understanding and new information sets up a situation whereby infants and children with ASD embark on different developmental trajectories, which lead to atypical behavioural outcomes later in life.

The theme of developmental trajectories was taken up in Chapter 9, where it emerged that truly developmental studies of ASD – that is to say, theoretically driven attempts to account for the patterns of symptomatology over time – are still fairly thin on the ground. Yet the characterisation of ASDs as a set of pervasive *developmental* disorders requires us to take the question of development more seriously. We need to shift focus from considering ASD as a static disorder defined by numerous deficits (possibly accompanied by islets or peaks of ability as WCC theory does) to one where it is seen as a dynamic adaptation to a world that is sometimes perceived differently. Such a shift in focus requires us to think of ASD as a different adaptation (see Bowler, 2001), which, precisely because it is based on a dynamic interplay between the organism and its environment, offers possibilities for intervention, both at the level of the organism and at the level of the environment.

At the risk of stating the obvious, the most plausible locus of organism-related factors in ASD is the brain. We saw in Chapter 8 that despite considerable research activity over the last decade, and despite remarkable improvements in the technology available for functional brain research, we still know remarkably little about how the brains of people with ASD differ from those with typical development. We know that they have larger brains, that parts of the temporal lobe are characterised by immature and densely packed nerve cells, and that the maturational trajectory of the whole brain – but in particular, the frontal lobes – is atypical. Some authors have speculated that the cells in the immature parts of the brains of people with ASD may have too many dendrites, resulting in too much communication between cells. This view is consistent with the behavioural data on enhanced processing of low-level perceptual detail in this population. Yet, paradoxically, recent studies show that activity in different regions of the brains of people with ASD is less coordinated, suggesting diminished long-distance connectivity, which is consistent with the behavioural evidence on diminished top-down processing. But it should be constantly borne in mind that brain research is in its infancy. Research methods are still relatively crude and investigations of brain–behaviour relations rely crucially on theoretical formulations of the organisation of behaviour. If these are flawed or inadequate, then so will be our interpretations of brain function.

Coming back to the question of how far we have come since the publication of Wing (1966), we now have a clearer picture of the extent and diversity of ASD. We also have sets of controlled observations of functioning in a number of domains, observations that can begin to give us a glimpse of the world as experienced by individuals who are on the spectrum. We are also in a position to be more sceptical of claims to have found the 'key' that unlocks the 'secret' of ASD. The core characteristics of autism are a complex set of phenomena, with a core set of manifestations that are often accompanied by other attributes – such as severe global cognitive or language difficulties – that may have greater consequences for the individual than the autism itself.

STEPPING BACK TO MOVE FORWARD? EMERGING THEMES

Many of the increases in our understanding of ASD that have emerged in the past few decades – difficulties in social understanding as an emergent property of domain-general processes, atypical responses to locally complex and globally coherent stimuli – can be thought of within the framework of the theoretical systems within which they were conceived. This is the view that is generally taken by the advocates of a particular deficit being fundamental to ASD, and tends to foster an adversarial approach that sees different theoretical accounts as being mutually incompatible. But we can step back and take a broader survey of findings across the different theoretical frameworks. Doing this allows us to discern new classes of phenomena that transcend the traditional theoretical boundaries.

THE SELF AT THE CORE OF EXPERIENCE*

A recurrent theme that crops up in much of the research that was discussed in earlier chapters is the notion that people with ASD experience a different

*I would like to thank Sophie Lind for her help in preparing this section.

sense of themselves in relation to the world. This was given great prominence by Hobson, whose work is discussed in Chapter 3 and has also been discussed extensively by U. Frith (2003) and by Happé (2003). Hobson places great emphasis on the importance of a sense of self that enables the child to see other people as being like themselves. According to Hobson (see Hobson, 2002), it is this identification with the other that forms the bedrock of subsequent psychological development, and which operates atypically in people with ASD. There is a wealth of empirical evidence that shows that individuals with ASD have difficulties with self-awareness. Pronominal reversal (Lee, Hobson & Chiat, 1994), diminished imitation of self-oriented actions (Hobson & Lee, 1999), fewer descriptions of self in social or interpersonal terms (Lee & Hobson, 1998), diminished autonoetic awareness in recognition memory (Bowler et al., 2000a; in press) all suggest that the 'me' that most people experience as being at the centre of their existence operates differently in this population. As U. Frith (2003) observed, this contention is supported by findings from areas of research that less explicitly address the notion of a self. The work on executive functions, discussed in Chapter 4, as well as the concept of attention, both contain components that involve the making of decisions about whether or not to orient to a particular aspect of the environment. Sometimes, orientation or responding is automatic and determined solely by the nature of the external stimulus, but sometimes it involves conscious processes, raising the 'homunculus question' – the question of who, in an executive account of adaptive behaviour, executes the commands, makes the decision to respond or not to respond to a given stimulus. It is probably a mistake to dichotomise automatic and controlled executive and attentional processes, but in both cases, there needs to be an account of how such control is exercised without positing an infinite regress of controlling agents when dealing with the question of who controls the controller. In Chapter 4, we came across Pennington's attempt to model a system that could exert executive control without falling into the trap of infinite regress (Pennington, 1994). This account represents an attempt to deal with the technical issue of how executive control can be implemented within a system. But from an individual person's perspective, executive control (and attentional control, episodic recall, appropriate pronoun use) is a more subjective matter than this. When I refer to myself as 'I' or 'me', or when I say 'I went to Paris for New Year', I am expressing a subjective sense of self that is at the heart of experience and that I feel to be at the heart of what I do and what I experience. On the evidence discussed at various points in this book, this sense of 'me' at the heart of experience is diminished in people with ASD.

Although, intuitively, our experience of self seems to be a unitary sense of a 'me' that is distinct from other people and which is both at the core of our experience and is the source of our voluntary actions (for example, when I reach out for a cup of coffee, I feel as if it is I who does the reaching, whereas when a doctor tests my knee reflex, I do not experience my self as responsible for the jerking of the lower leg that follows from the tap just below the kneecap). However, our sense of self can be thought of as having a number of dimensions. Neisser (1988) proposes five ways of knowing the self, two of which are implicit and three explicit. What he terms ecological and interpersonal self-awareness are implicit and are perceptually based and emerge early on in development. Ecological self-awareness refers to children's understanding that they can exert influence over their environment. There is a wealth of behavioural evidence to show that newborn babies can use their actions to influence events – for example by varying their sucking rate to maintain a picture of their mother in view (Siqueland & DeLucia, 1969; DeCasper & Fifer, 1980). When we can see behavioural indicators of the child's exerting influence on and being influenced by other people, such as vocal and gesture turn-taking and imitation (Trevarthen & Aitken, 2001), we infer an interpersonal sense of self.

Neither ecological nor interpersonal self-awareness requires any concept of an enduring representation of the self in order to operate. But when the child develops an enduring concept of 'I' and 'me' that can be reflected upon, the self then becomes an object of thought, a development that makes possible more sophisticated forms of self-related behaviour. Children begin to use personal pronouns appropriately and to recognise themselves in mirrors. For example if we surreptitiously place a red mark on the face of an 18-month-old child and then ask her to look at her reflection in a mirror, she will reach to the mark to try to rub it off (Amsterdam, 1972). It is this milestone that marks the onset of what Neisser calls the 'conceptual self'. However, although the rouge test shows that a child can entertain multiple representations of the self ('me' without the red smudge; 'me' with it), in order to develop what Neisser calls the *temporally extended self*, the child must incorporate a temporal dimension along which to organise these different conceptions of themself. It is this temporally extended self that enables the child to recall themself in past events (i.e. have episodic memories) and to imagine themself in future situations (i.e. engage in planning). Thus, the temporally extended self entails the adequate development of multiple representations of self and an adequate conception of time (see Lind & Bowler, in press; in preparation for further discussion). Neisser also talks about the *private self* which encompasses those experiences that are not available to others. He also argues that it is not just the fact that we have these experiences but also the fact that we can do such things as remember that we had them (and, by implication, that others did not) that also forms part of the private self.

I have already mentioned some evidence – difficulties with personal pronoun use, planning tasks and diminished autonoetic awareness in memory – that individuals from the autism spectrum may have atypical self-awareness. There is also evidence that they are less likely to grasp that another person who has not witnessed what they themselves have witnessed will not know about this event (Perner, Frith, Leslie & Leekam, 1989). And Hurlburt, Happé and Frith (1994) found that self-reports of the inner experiences of people with ASD were composed mainly of static visual images frozen in time, which contrasted with those of typical individuals, which were more varied, mentalistic and experiential in nature. These two sets of observations suggest a diminished private self in ASD. People with ASD also have difficulty in telling apart their own intended and unintended actions (Philips, Baron-Cohen & Rutter, 1998), suggesting that they have a diminished ecological sense of self. An important systematic theoretical analysis of the sense of self acting in the world as a possible source of autistic psychological functioning is that of Russell (1996) who invoked the concept of agency – akin to Neisser's ecological self – in an attempt to explain, among other things, why individuals with ASD perform poorly on some executive tasks. Russell bases his arguments on those of the philosopher Schopenhauer (1844/1966 cited in Russell 1996) and the developmental psychologist James Mark Baldwin (Baldwin, 1906). Starting from the idea that a child's bodily experience is both internal or subjective and external or objective, Russell argues that the experiences of bodily actions that cause external events to happen result in the development of a first-person experience of agency that eventually leads to a sense of self as the source of one's own action. This sense of self forms the basis of distinctions between self and other that lead to the elaboration of the kinds of knowledge of other people that are often loosely referred to as a theory of mind. People with ASD, according to this account, experience difficulties in understanding consequences of actions as resulting from the agency of the self and as a consequence have problems in differentiating self and other with knock-on consequences for their understanding of others.

Despite the evidence for an atypical sense of private and ecological self-awareness in ASD, there are some indications that people with ASD have developed at least some form of self-awareness. Indeed, it would be difficult to imagine how someone who had not developed such awareness could reach the levels of adaptation that most people with ASD manage to achieve. Despite Russell (1996) having argued for an impaired sense of agency as a cause of ASD, some of his experimental work shows an intact ecological self. Russell and Hill (2001) found that children with ASD were able to identify which of a set of moving dots on a screen were under their own control. There is also evidence that children with ASD develop a conceptual sense of self, albeit later than in typical children. Successful performance on the rouge task has been demonstrated by several studies (Dawson & McKissick, 1984; Neuman & Hill, 1978; Spiker & Ricks, 1984). It can, however, be argued that this task can be solved at a perceptual level and that only tasks with a social component are a valid indicator of conceptual self-awareness. Recent work by Hobson and colleagues (Hobson & Meyer, 2005; Meyer & Hobson, 2004), however, suggests that children with ASD do have a conceptual difficulty with the self. When children were asked by an experimenter where she (the experimenter) should place a sticker on her own body, children without ASD mostly pointed to a place on their own body whereas children with ASD indicated somewhere on the experimenter's body. Hobson and Meyer conclude from these findings that the ASD children had difficulty in grasping that another person would understand that the child's own point to herself indicated a corresponding point on the other's body. To grasp this correspondence requires conception of self that goes beyond perceptual mapping of similar points on the child's and experimenter's bodies. This argument is further supported by consideration of the emotional components of tasks such as the mirror recognition procedure. In the rouge task, typical children can be seen to exhibit self-conscious emotional behaviours – they appear embarrassed or coy in response to finding out that they have a red mark on their faces. Children with ASD do not show such emotions (nor do they share expressions of pride when successfully completing a task, see Kasari, Sigman, Baumgartner and Stipek, 1993), suggesting that they have a diminished sense of self in relation to others. Whether this is due to difficulties with the concept of self or with emotions or the relations between the two remains an open question.

The fact that there appears to be some degree of diminished self-awareness in people with ASD should alert us to the fact that they have a different phenomenology, that their subjective experience is different from that of typical individuals. This conclusion is the subjective counterpart of Mottron's notion of *une autre intelligence* – a different intelligence (Mottron, 2004). If, as Mottron argues, a large proportion of the observable behaviour of people with ASD is arrived at through the operation of mechanisms that are different from those found in typical individuals, then it is not surprising that their subjective world is also different. The implications for such a position are profound. Earlier on in this chapter, I commented that our enlarged conception of the autism spectrum to include individuals of normal intelligence and good language has raised the need for psychotherapeutic interventions. The aim of such interventions would not be to 'cure' the ASD, but to help individuals make sense of their own experience of the world in order to adapt better to it. At the heart of any psychotherapeutic process is the notion of a therapeutic alliance in which therapist and client establish a shared view of the world that is used as the basis for conceptualising difficulties in a way that leads to their resolution or management. It is clear from the ideas discussed in these paragraphs that in order to be effective, therapists working with individuals with ASD need to be aware of the very different subjective experiences that these individuals have, and that assumptions and strategies that work in the typical case may not do so with this group of clients.

THE FLICKERING LIGHT BULB

Intermittent replication of findings is a frequent occurrence in ASD research. For example, although many investigators have reported unimpaired recognition memory in high-functioning individuals with ASD (see Chapter 7),

Bowler et al. (2004) found a small but significant impairment in a large sample of adolescents and adults with Asperger's syndrome. Also in the memory literature, although Tager-Flusberg (1991) and Bowler et al. (1997) observed that children with ASD and adults with Asperger's syndrome were less likely than typical comparison participants to use semantic relations among words to aid their free recall, other researchers such as Leekam & Lopez (2003) could replicate these findings only if they used the same word lists as the earlier investigators. And we also saw in Chapter 7 how Bowler et al. (2000b) found that adults with Asperger's syndrome were subject to associatively generated illusory memories but that Beversdorf et al. (2000) using a slightly different method did not (see p. 158). Similarly variable findings can be found in other domains of inquiry. The literature on false-belief understanding (see Chapter 2) shows failure rates of children with ASD on false-belief tasks that are often quite inconsistent across studies (see Happé, 1995). Similarly, many of the phenomena of WCC have not stood the test of replication (see Chapter 5).

Failure to replicate findings can be explained in a number of ways. Either the phenomenon does not exist and the initial, positive finding was a random event. Or perhaps there were differences in the samples used; one study may have tested higher-functioning or older individuals while another used those with lower IQ. Many studies have small sample sizes and as a consequence have insufficient statistical power to reveal between-group differences. Procedural differences may also yield different outcomes. In a review of the research on recognition memory in ASD, Bowler et al. (2004) concluded that impairment was more likely if forced choice rather than yes/no procedures were used, although this was also confounded by issues of developmental level, where reduced recognition was more likely in individuals with some degree of intellectual disability. There remains, however, another possibility, namely that variability in performance on similar tasks across different studies is a genuine phenomenon that is characteristic of at least some people with ASD. Such performance can be likened to that of the unpredictable, intermittent, on–off flickering of a poorly seated light bulb. If intermittent success and failure on similar tasks is a genuine characteristic of people with ASD, then it is something to be explained, rather than explained away by relegation to error variance in our statistical analyses.

A pattern of intermittent success and failure to replicate should prompt us to seek out parameters that modulate variable findings. For example, we now know that individuals with ASD are more likely than typical individuals to respond to the local features of a complex stimulus and that they are differentially sensitive to certain kinds of low-level perceptual stimuli (see Chapters 5 and 6 for details). In contexts where stimuli are defined with reference to the psychological functioning of individuals without ASD, it is perhaps not surprising, then, that they may respond differently. But we should be careful about rushing to conclude that on the basis of having available alternative processing strategies, an individual must respond in a manner that is different from typical individuals. They may respond differently some of the time and similarly on others. Thus, in memory illusion experiments, participants will be subject to an illusory memory only if they notice that studied items are related to a non-presented item. If they do not notice this relatedness, then they will not produce an illusory memory. Thus, rather than asking ourselves whether or not people with ASD are subject to illusory memories, we need to think in terms of which circumstances are likely to produce such illusions and which not. In this example, noticing or not noticing semantic or associative relations among items dramatically influences outcome, but it is possible that differential responding to aspects of the experimental situation that are not those intended by the investigator may influence overall outcome only slightly or not at all. An experiment from our own laboratory illustrates this (Bowler, Gaigg & Gardiner, under review).

This experiment was based on one by Tulving (1962) in which participants were asked to study and then to free recall the same list of 16 semantically unrelated words on 16 consecutive trials. On each trial the words were presented in a different order. Tulving (1962) observed that recall increases over trials and that participants increasingly organise their output, i.e. they tend to cluster specific items together irrespective of where they are placed in the study list. He also observed that recall and subjective organisation were correlated. We also observed learning in a group of adults with Asperger's syndrome, albeit at a slightly lower rate than in typical comparison participants. The Asperger participants also exhibited subjective organisation that correlated with their rate of learning of the studied material. What was most remarkable, however, was the observation that whereas the subjective organisation of the typical participants tended to converge towards a common pattern over trials, that of the Asperger participants did not. In other words, although the Asperger group did organise the material subjectively, each member of the group did so in their own way. What is also striking is that these idiosyncratic ways of organising material had only a relatively small effect on learning across trials, suggesting that typical or near-typical levels of performance on a particular measure is no guarantee that the mechanisms that typically drive such performance are operating in any particular instance or with any particular group. Although our experiment does not allow us to specify the basis for the idiosyncratic organisation of the Asperger participants, we can speculate that in addition to meaning-based connections, they may also have used phonological, visual or structural aspects of the words or combinations of these. The overall behavioural outcome of such a strategy – in this case, free recall performance – is only marginally lower than that found in the comparison group, except for the fact that the groups did not establish a shared structuring of the material that would provide the basis for easier communication with others. In this respect, the findings suggest a link between a tendency to structure behaviour on the basis of an idiosyncratic set of stimulus properties (rather than one – semantic relatedness – that typical individuals tend to use) and difficulties in establishing social relations because of an impoverished set of shareable social representations of the environment.

The possibility that individuals with ASD might respond to aspects of their environment differently from their typical peers and that the resulting different representations may sometimes yield test performance that is similar to that of typical individuals is a recurrent theme in ASD research and goes back to the 'hacking out' argument that has been made by Happé (1995) and by Bowler (1992) in relation to the successful performance by some individuals with ASD on false-belief tasks. Both these authors observed that despite passing such tests, the social behaviour of individuals with ASD was still atypical, suggesting that we should be cautious when inferring intact underlying processes from intact test performance.

Two major implications follow from the observations just made. The first echoes one from Chapter 9 in relation to non-linear dynamic systems theory (NLDST). Rather than regarding individual difference as noise in the data, to be consigned to the error term in an analysis of variance, NLDST uses variability *as* data and advocates a research strategy that attempts to map the parameters that alter patterns of variability. Such an exercise requires us not just to show that lower-level impairments exist and to assert that these must compromise development in some unspecified way so as to yield higher-level atypicalities. We must try to demonstrate how this happens. As part of this exercise, we also need to draw a more detailed map of atypical functioning at all levels from low-level perception to the highest level cognition in order to tell a more complete developmental story. This process needs to be carried out both at a molar level, where broad-brush developmental trajectories need to be specified (e.g. Hobson, 2002), and also at the level of interactions among different psychological functions. Some of the research outlined at the start of Chapter 9 begins to address the first part of this question, by attempting to map developmental changes in different psychological domains such as language and communication and developmental level and to establish which early measures predict later development. A greater level of precision is exemplified by the work of Jarrold, Butler, Cottington and Jimenez (2000), who found that measures of perceptual central coherence (e.g. block design and embedded figures, see Chapter 5) and mental state understanding correlated both in typical children and in children with ASD when differences in developmental level were taken into account. This finding suggests that the mechanisms that tie development in these two areas together are similar in both groups although the way in which they contribute to those processes that drive performance on tests of general intellectual development may differ. Bowler et al.'s (2005) observation that development of mature performance on Sally–Anne type false-belief tasks correlates to a similar extent to the development of performance on mechanical analogues of such tasks in children with and without ASD raises a similar possibility. Although both tasks correlate to a similar extent in both populations, the age at which they are correctly solved is greater in children with ASD. Once again, this suggests that the relationship between the development of the variables thought to mediate performance on both these tasks and those variables that underlie general intellectual development differs in children with and without ASD.

The second, related set of implications is that we need to reconsider the ways in which we interpret the patterning of behaviours we see in ASD. Traditionally descriptions and explanations of ASD have been couched in terms of abnormalities and deficits. The behaviour of typically developed individuals is seen as the benchmark against which that of individuals with ASD is compared. The argument made here is that since ASD is the result of a different developmental trajectory with a different behavioural outcome (albeit one that has considerable overlap with that of typical individuals), we cannot readily make the assumption that the mechanisms underlying any particular behaviour in this population are the same as those that underlie the same behaviour in the typical population. This position was set out by Baron-Cohen (2000) and Bowler (2001) and closely mirrors that of Mottron (2004) and Mottron and Soulières (in press). These last two authors argue ASD results from the operation of a different intelligence (*une autre intelligence* – Mottron, 2004) and that we should try to avoid what they call 'normocentrism' – the explanation of ASD-specific patterns of functioning in terms of impaired typical functioning. Rather, we should attempt to see ASD as a phenomenon to be explained in its own terms. It is important to be clear about what is being advocated here. None of the authors who have touched on these ideas is arguing that there is nothing abnormal or potentially disadvantageous about some of the behaviours of individuals with ASD. In the statistical sense, to spend virtually the whole of one's time hand-flapping, spinning objects or compiling lists of dinosaur names is highly unusual. And to do so can literally crowd out other activities that are necessary for survival. Even when such statistically abnormal activities do not monopolise the whole of a person's waking hours, the fact that they occupy most of them, and do so in a rigid and inflexible manner, makes the kinds of flexible adaptation to the uncertainties of the physical and social environment very difficult, often resulting in considerable disadvantage for the individual concerned. But the disadvantage that results from abnormal behaviour patterns in a particular physical and social environment should not unquestioningly be used as the basis for inferring abnormal internal processes in the individual concerned. In other words, the language of deficit and damage should be used carefully, if at all. An example will help to illustrate this.

Human eyes typically respond to light waves from a very narrow part of the electromagnetic spectrum (from wavelength 400 nm to 700 nm). Bees, by contrast, can see well beyond violet, down to wavelength 350 nm or less. Bees also have compound eyes that see very little in the way of detail, whereas humans have single eyes that are very well adapted to see detail. Bees and humans are social animals, and they cooperate and communicate among each other in order, for example, to let each other know where food is located so that a food supply can be secured for the group. But they do this in very different ways. Because bees can see ultraviolet light and the way it is polarised, they use this information on cloudy days to determine the position of the sun, which is then used as the basis for a dance that indicates to other members of the hive where a particular food source is located. By contrast, the same end is achieved by humans through the use of language, which is used to communicate the details (defined by what their visual system can detect) of where food is located. In terms of understanding where food is located, an individual human is as disadvantaged in a beehive as a bee is in a human community. Yet it makes no sense to say that humans have deficient vision any more than to say that bees are visually impaired. The two species are different from each other and these differences have consequences for the ways in which they interact with the world. Of course, people with and without ASD are not as different from each other as are humans and bees, and because both belong to the same species, they have to get along together in ways that humans and bees do not. In this respect, people with ASD find themselves in a world where they are a tiny minority – less than 1% of the population – and in which typical action patterns tend to be defined by the majority. This sociological majority–minority relationship tends to confer power on the majority and places the minority in a position of having to adapt. However, unlike many social minorities, who can create their own community which either explicitly or implicitly negotiates an accommodation with the majority, we have seen that individuals with ASD may show greater individual differences in the way they build a model of the world from their experience (Bowler, Gaigg & Gardiner, under review), thus making it harder to create a minority sense of community amongst themselves. This set of processes reinforces the sense of difference that the typical population experiences when encountering people with ASD and tends to foster a discourse couched in terms of abnormality and deficit.

Shifting our focus from one of abnormality to one of difference carries with it a number of other implications for the way future investigators might work. If patterns of adaptation shown by people with ASD result from different underlying processes from those operating in the typical population, then a large number of the assumptions that underlie the way we go about conducting research are called into question. In Chapters 1 and 9 we discussed the issue of matching participants when carrying out research. When researching people with ASD who have normal levels of intelligence, we typically match on standard psychometric measures of intelligence. If we are investigating people with some level of global impairment, then we compare performance with that of people without ASD but who have a comparable level of cognitive impairment. Leaving aside the question of what measure of cognitive impairment we should choose (see Chapter 1 and the special issue of the

Journal of Autism and Developmental Disorders, 2004, Volume 34, issue 1), we also need to reflect on the validity of the assumptions upon which such matching strategies are based. The arguments made in the preceding paragraph suggest that we should be very careful when assuming that similar levels of performance on a psychometric test (whether a single test or a battery) reflect the operation of similar underlying processes in a manner that justifies matching in the way that it has been traditionally done. Such scepticism also prompts us to ask the question of how we should go about doing research in the future. Calling into question the matched groups approach to research raises the related issue of how we define the groups that we are matching. Once again, we saw in Chapter 1 how the classification of people with ASD into groups such as 'autistic disorder', 'Asperger disorder', etc. is becoming increasingly unsatisfactory, and that a dimensional approach, whereby functioning is evaluated along different dimensions of adaptive functioning is gaining acceptance. But rather than then matching on the basis of scores falling within particular bands on a given dimension, we should consider adopting research procedures such as multiple regression, factor analysis or cluster analysis that are more appropriate to a dimensional approach. Continuing with current matched-group strategies would merely compound the felony. Apart from anything else, recruiting sufficient numbers of individuals that could be matched on even a small number of dimensions would be time consuming and would result in large numbers of potential participants being rejected for lack of suitable comparison participants. We must look for other ways to tackle research questions.

Exploring developmental change using microgenetic studies of individual participants within a framework of newer developmental theories such as nonlinear dynamic systems theory or catastrophe theory (see Chapter 9 for fuller discussion) is one way to work around the twin problems highlighted in the last paragraph. Microgenetic studies explore how an individual's behaviour changes over short periods of time in response to shifting environmental demands and can provide a detailed picture of the parameters that control developmental change (see Smith & Thelen, 2003). We could also adopt an approach that takes large groups of individuals from the autism spectrum and other groups and explores group-level patterns of correlations among a wide range of measures with a view to delineating causal relations at a group rather than an individual level. Taking these approaches together would help to provide a clearer picture of how specific behavioural end points (what in some contexts might be described using the language of symptoms) can emerge out of different clusters of functions on a variety of measures and how some measures (such as age, memory span, or characteristic attentional strategy) might operate to alter the timing of the emergence of these behavioural end points. In the almost total absence of any such studies, we can do little more than speculate about what kinds of findings might emerge. But we can ground our speculations in some existing work. For example, Happé's (1995) observations on the relationship between language development and false-belief under-standing were supported by Bowler et al. (2005), who also noted that a measure of complex systems understanding added predictive power in typical children, children with intellectual disabilities and with ASD. But the ages at which false-belief understanding emerged in these groups differed. Future research operating within the framework outlined above would attempt to determine, both at an individual and a group level, what factors affected the age at which the capacity to pass false-belief tasks emerged in different groups of participants. The choice of factors to investigate would initially have to be made on a speculative basis – memory span, attentional capacities such as ability to zoom out (Mann & Walker, 2003) and level of grammatical language development appear to be good candidates. Adopting this approach to iden-tifying how a range of measures interacted in different groups to produce particular behavioural outcomes would have two consequences. First, it would provide a map of how more basic psychological processes co-acted over time to yield (or to fail to yield) particular behavioural outcomes and develop-mental milestones. Second, it would open possibilities for intervention that went beyond mere training in the 'missing behaviours', in the hope that once the child started doing a particular thing (e.g. performing correctly on a false-belief task), everything else that typically follows from this would do so. The training studies reviewed in Chapter 9 have shown that this is usually not what happens (or is predicted on theoretical grounds not to follow from it).

SEDUCED BY THE HERE-AND-NOW: THE TASK SUPPORT HYPOTHESIS

Continuing with the metaphor of stepping back from the tapestry or the flight over Gopnik's jungle, another pattern of findings that my colleagues and I initially observed in the context of memory research, but which may have far wider implications for understanding ASD, has given rise to what we have called the *task support hypothesis* (Bowler et al., 1997; 2004). This states that in any task, performance of individuals with ASD, will be better under con-ditions where information for successful resolution is physically present at the time of testing. When elements necessary for solving the task have to be recalled, generated or inferred from other elements that are present, then per-formance will be impaired. A very clear example of this phenomenon can be seen in memory, where success on tasks that require recall of items tends to be diminished whereas on tasks such as cued recall, it is not, even for inci-dentally encoded material (see Bowler et al. 2004).

Examples of task support can be seen in many studies from a wide range of topics in the psychological literature. For example, Baron-Cohen and Good-hart (1994) carried out an experiment to test whether children with ASD could understand that someone who had looked inside a box knew what it contained whereas someone who had not looked inside did not. As a control task, they took two story characters and placed a red counter in front of one and a blue counter in front of the other and asked the children which character had the red and which the blue counter. The inclusion of the control task is a necessary methodological device that helps us to rule out the possibility that children's difficulty in the looking task is not simply the result of a general difficulty with remembering any temporary attribute of a story character or of problems with understanding questions about specific attributes of the protagonists. But whereas the experimental condition requires the child to recall a transient event, the visible evidence for which has passed, the control task asks the child which character has which counter *when both counters are still present in front of the characters and visible to the child*. To be certain that this study demonstrates what it claims to demonstrate, we need a further control task containing a non-mentalistic procedure that is transient and that does not leave evidence to cue the child to the correct answer. We can infer a difficulty in understanding seeing-leads-to-knowing only if children fail the seeing task and pass the new control task. If they fail the new task, then the difficulty with the seeing task is merely a specific aspect of recalling elements of the story that are no longer present. In a similar vein, Peterson and Bowler (2000) found that when the question in a false-belief task of the Sally–Anne type was changed from one of the form 'where will Sally look for her marble?' to one along the lines of 'if the marble had not been moved, where would Sally look for it?', the performance of children with ASD improved significantly. Although the authors did not explain their findings in terms of task support, they did argue that the second form of the question made fewer demands on the child in terms of having to come up with the information needed to provide a correct solution to the problem.

At a more general level, many of the characteristics used to describe people with ASD are consistent with the task support hypothesis. Individuals with classic Kanner-type autism usually show poorer performance on language-based psychometric tests than on those that do not involve language. Language is the perfect example of a human activity that is universally used to regulate behaviour yet when spoken leaves little physical trace. When we ask someone a question, the respondent has to hold the question in mind while formulating a response. This is the format of the majority of language-based psychometric tests. By contrast, tasks on which individuals with ASD usually perform well, such as Block Design (see Chapter 4) or Raven's Matrices (Raven, 1996), supply in a concrete, non-transient form, all the information the testee requires for successful resolution of the task. Other defining characteristics of ASD – inflexible and repetitive routines and diminished generativity – can also be interpreted in terms of task support in that they both involve the application of absent possibilities to the task currently in hand. If an object lends itself to being spun, and an attempt at spinning it is successful, that physical evidence (the spinning object) of something to do with that object will take precedence over absent possibilities such as pretending the object is a car. The work of

Boucher, Jarrold, Lewis and colleagues (see Chapter 1) showing that more flexible play routines can be prompted in children with ASD is also consistent with a task support analysis. When a child with ASD is shown – provided with concrete evidence – that an object can be used in a range of (often counter-factual) ways, it can engage in a wider range of behaviours towards that object, some of which we might regard as symbolic. But when the prompting ceases, the object-directed behaviour of the children usually comes back under the control of the here-and-now.

Although it is possible to gather evidence that is consistent with the task support hypothesis, we should be careful of falling into the trap identified by Popper (1965) of developing a theory that explains everything and predicts nothing. The hypothesis, in order to be plausible, needs supporting evidence, but it also needs evaluation by means of investigations that test predictions that can be falsified. Like any theory, it will advance our understanding only if we can establish circumstances where it holds and where it does not hold. Although such systematic studies have yet to be done, the hypothesis is at present a plausible one that accounts for many of the findings in the experimental literature on ASD and may contribute to an explanation of the flickering light bulb effect described earlier on. The inconsistent findings that are characteristic of this effect can be thought of as the result of control tasks that are poorly designed from a task support perspective or a failure by investigators to take account of atypical perceptual processes when designing tasks. These observations take us back to Mottron's (2004) notion of a different intelligence and to Happé's (1995) notion of 'hacking out' solutions to tasks using mechanisms different from those of typical individuals and to my own observations in the context of theory of mind that adults with Asperger's syndrome, although capable of passing quite sophisticated tests of false belief, did not use such understanding in their everyday social interactions (Bowler, 1992).

It is also possible to use the task support hypothesis as the basis for speculations about the development of children with ASD. The psychological development of children* depends on a complex, iterative process of building up representations of the world on the basis of children's sensory and perceptual experiences as well as the modulation of these experiences on the basis of feedback from their actions on their environments. These modified experiences (or representations of experiences) in turn make further kinds of actions possible, which then further change the child's representation of the world thereby enhancing the field of possibilities for action. In the information-processing language used in Chapters 5 and 6, there is a reciprocal interaction

---

*This is an extremely condensed conflation of Piagetian and Vygotskian accounts of children's development. Interested readers should consult either some original sources (e.g. Piaget, 1952; 1963; Vygotsky, 1962; 1978) or a good introductory textbook on child development such as Valsiner and Connolly (2003).

of bottom-up (perceptually driven) and top-down (conceptually driven) processing. All this takes place within a social context in which caregivers direct the child to different aspects of her environment. Typically, children follow the gaze or the points of another person, and can themselves direct the attention of another person by means of their own object-directed actions. However, we have seen that children with ASD experience difficulty in shifting attention in response to cues, that they may have difficulty in understanding pointing (or, indeed any contingent relations that occur at a distance) and that they often perceive complex aspects of their environments in a more detail-focused manner. We can speculate that all these atypicalities of engagement with their physical and social world mean that the aspects of the environment that these children come to rely on are different from those of typical children. The resulting different representational base will have considerable knock-on effects, particularly for those actions that require the child to draw on internal representational resources. Such an account links together atypical perceptual experience with the need to rely more on environmental support as a regulator of behaviour. It is possible to go even further by speculating that this reliance on the external world would yield a phenomenology – an experience of the world – that was rooted more in the external here-and-now than in inner experience, which would in turn diminish the experience of self. But this is speculation.

FINAL THOUGHTS

The speculations in the last paragraph bring us back to the question of what it must be like to be autistic (see Frith & Happé, 1999). Ultimately, the psychology of ASD must provide an answer to this question. But it must also provide an explanation. Readers who have made it this far (as well as those who have skipped straight to here) may be expecting such descriptions and explanations as well as a punchy take-home message. Without wishing to be unkind to colleagues in the field (or perhaps, wishing to be unkind to those who often misinterpret their ideas), the message is probably that we are sometimes too quick to generate quick, snappy messages and that we are often too uncritical of the work we ourselves do. Autism spectrum disorder is now known to be a set of conditions that should not be reduced to a simple dichotomy of presence or absence. When present, the conditions are multidimensional and complex, and although they share the common characteristics of social impairment and repetitive behaviours (at least from the perspective of a typically developed person) they often exhibit additional features that are not necessarily defining features of the spectrum. Such complexity requires a more subtle explanation than a simple reduction to an absent theory of mind, a failure of affective appreciation, diminished sense of self or fragmented perception. The complexity of ASD requires us to take a more distanced view and to go beyond simply trying to find new ways of describing the fact that people with ASD are autistic. Science is about the reduction of complexity to simpler sets of entities and processes that interact in ways that are somehow lawful and predictable. We now have a wealth of controlled descriptions of the behavioural manifestations of ASD. The challenge that faces us now is to step outside our own, narrow conception of the issue and to work out how they fit together and why.

References

Abell, F., Krams, M., Ashburner, J., Passingham, R., Friston, K., Frackowiak, R. et al. (1999). The neuroanatomy of autism: A voxel-based whole brain analysis of structural scans. *Neuroreport, 10*, 1647–1651.

Adolphs, R., Baron-Cohen, S., & Tranel, D. (2002). Impaired recognition of social emotions following amygdala damage. *Journal of Cognitive Neuroscience, 14*, 1264–1274.

Adolphs, R., Sears, L., & Piven, J. (2001). Abnormal processing of social information from faces in autism. *Journal of Cognitive Neuroscience, 13*, 232–240.

Adolphs, R., & Tranel, D. (2000). Emotion recognition and the human amygdala. In J. P. Aggleton (Ed.), *The amygdala: A functional analysis* (2nd ed., pp. 587–630). Oxford: Oxford University Press.

Adolphs, R., Tranel, D., & Damasio, A. R. (1998). The human amygdala in social judgement. *Nature, 393*(6684), 470–474.

Adolphs, R., Tranel, D., Damasio, H., & Damasio, A. R. (1994). Impaired recognition of emotion in facial expressions following bilateral damage to the human amygdala. *Nature, 372*(6507), 669–672.

Akshoomoff, N., Pierce, K., & Courchesne, E. (2002). The neurobiological basis of autism from a developmental perspective. *Development and Psychopathology, 14*, 613–634.

Allen, G., & Courchesne, E. (2001). Attention function and dysfunction in autism. *Frontiers in Bioscience, 6*, 105–119.

Altgassen, M., Kliegel, M., & Williams, T. (2005). Pitch perception in children with autistic spectrum disorders. *British Journal of Developmental Psychology, 23*, 543–558.

Amaral, D. G., Bauman, M. D., & Schumann, C. M. (2003). The amygdala and autism: Implications from non-human primate studies. *Genes, Brain, & Behavior, 2*, 295–302.

Ameli, R., Courchesne, E., Lincoln, A., Kaufman, A. S., & Grillon, C. (1988). Visual memory processes in high-functioning individuals with autism. *Journal of Autism and Developmental Disorders, 18*, 601–615.

American Psychiatric Association (1980). *Diagnostic and statistical manual of mental disorders* (3rd ed.). Washington, DC: APA.

American Psychiatric Association (1987). *Diagnostic and statistical manual of mental disorders* (4th ed.). Washington, DC: APA.

American Psychiatric Association (2000). *Diagnostic and statistical manual of mental disorders* (4th ed. – Text Revision). Washington, DC: APA.

Amsterdam, B. (1972). Mirror self-image reactions before age two. *Developmental Psychobiology, 5*, 297–305.

Asperger, H. (1944). Die 'autistische Psychopathen' im Kindesalter. *Archiv für Psychiatrie und Nervenkrankheiten, 117*, 76–136.

Asperger, H. (1991). Autistic psychopathy in childhood (trans. U. Frith). In U. Frith (Ed.), *Autism and Asperger syndrome* (pp. 37–92). Cambridge, UK: Cambridge University Press.

Atkinson, R. C., & Shiffrin, R. M. (1968). Human memory: A control system and its control processes. In K. W. Spence & J. T. Spence (Eds.), *The psychology of learning and motivation: Advances in research and theory* (Vol. 2, pp. 89–195). New York: Academic Press.

Aylward, E. H., Minshew, N. J., Goldstein, G., Honeycutt, N. A., Augustine, A. M., Yates, K. O. et al. (1999). MRI volumes of amygdala and hippocampus in non-mentally retarded autistic adolescents and adults. *Neurology, 53,* 2145–2150.

Bachevalier, J. (1994). Medial temporal lobe structures and autism: A review of clinical and experimental findings. *Neuropsychologia, 32,* 627–648.

Baddeley, A. D. (1986). *Working memory.* Oxford: Clarendon Press.

Baddeley, A. D., & Hitch, G. (1974). Working memory. In G. H. Bower (Ed.), *The psychology of learning and motivation* (Vol. 8, pp. 47–90). New York, Academic Press.

Bailey, A., Luthert, P., Dean, A. F., Harding, B., Janota, I., Montgomery, M. et al. (1998). A clinicopathological study of autism. *Brain, 121,* 889–905.

Baird, G., Charman, T., Baron-Cohen, S., Cox, A., Swettenham, J., Wheelwright, S., & Drew, A. (2000). A screening instrument for autism at 18 months of age: A 6-year follow-up study. *Journal of the American Academy of Child and Adolescent Psychiatry, 39,* 694–702.

Baird, G., Charman, T., Cox, A., Baron-Cohen, S., Swettenham, J., Wheelwright, S., & Drew, A. (2001). Screening and surveillance for autism and pervasive developmental disorders. *Archives of Disease in Childhood, 84,* 468–475.

Baldwin, D. A. (1993). Early referential understanding: Infants' ability to recognize referential acts for what they are. *Developmental Psychology, 29,* 832–843.

Baldwin, J. M. (1906). *Thought and things* (3 volumes). London: Swann & Sonnenschein.

Baranek, G. T. (1999). Autism during infancy: A retrospective video analysis of sensory-motor and social behaviors at 9–12 months of age. *Journal of Autism and Developmental Disorders, 29,* 439–484.

Baranek, G. T., Barnett, C. R., Adams, E. M., Wolcott, N. A., Watson, L. R., & Crais, E. R. (2005). Object play in infants with autism: Methodological issues in retrospective video analysis. *American Journal of Occupational Therapy, 59,* 20–30.

Baron-Cohen, S. (1987). Autism and symbolic play. *British Journal of Developmental Psychology, 5,* 139–148.

Baron-Cohen, S. (1989a). Perceptual role-taking and protodeclarative pointing in autism. *British Journal of Developmental Psychology, 7,* 113–127.

Baron-Cohen, S. (1989b). The autistic child's theory of mind: A case of specific developmental delay. *Journal of Child Psychology and Psychiatry, 30,* 285–297.

Baron-Cohen, S. (1992). Out of sight or out of mind: Another look at deception in autism. *Journal of Child Psychology and Psychiatry, 33,* 1141–1155.

Baron-Cohen, S. (1995). *Mindblindness.* Cambridge, MA: MIT Press.

Baron-Cohen, S. (1997). Hey! It was just a joke! Understanding propositions and propositional attitudes by normally developing children and children with autism. *Israel Journal of Psychiatry, 34,* 174–178.

Baron-Cohen, S. (2000). Is Asperger syndrome/high-functioning autism necessarily a disability? *Development and Psychopathology, 12,* 489–500.

Baron-Cohen, S. (2002a). *The essential difference: men, women and the extreme male brain.* London: Allen Lane.

Baron-Cohen, S. (2002b). The extreme male brain theory of autism. *Trends in Cognitive Sciences, 6,* 248–254.

Baron-Cohen, S. (2002c). Is autism an extreme of the male brain? *Journal of Neurology, Neurosurgery and Psychiatry, 72,* 826–826.

Baron-Cohen, S., Allen, J., & Gillberg, C. (1992). Can autism be detected at 18 months? The needle, the haystack and the CHAT. *British Journal of Psychiatry, 161,* 839–843.

Baron-Cohen, S., Baldwin, D. A., & Crowson, M. (1997a). Do children with autism use the speaker's direction of gaze strategy to crack the code of language? *Child Development, 68,* 48–57.

Baron-Cohen, S., Campbell, R., Karmiloff-Smith, A., Grant, J., & Walker, J. (1995). Are children with autism blind to the mentalistic significance of the eyes? *British Journal of Developmental Psychology, 13,* 379–398.

Baron-Cohen, S., & Cross, P. (1992). Reading the eyes: Evidence for the role of perception in the development of a theory of mind. *Mind and Language, 6,* 173–186.

Baron-Cohen, S., & Goodhart, F. (1994). The seeing-leads-to-knowing deficit in autism: The Pratt and Bryant probe. *British Journal of Developmental Psychology, 12,* 397–401.

Baron-Cohen, S., Jolliffe, T., Mortimore, C., & Robertson, M. (1997b). Another advanced test of theory of mind: Evidence from very high functioning adults with autism or Asperger syndrome. *Journal of Child Psychology and Psychiatry and Allied Disciplines, 38,* 813–822.

Baron-Cohen, S., Leslie, A., & Frith, U. (1985). Does the autistic child have a 'theory of mind'? *Cognition, 21,* 37–46.

Baron-Cohen, S., Leslie, A., & Frith, U. (1986). Mechanical, behavioural and intentional understanding of picture stories in autistic children. *British Journal of Developmental Psychology, 4,* 113–125.

Baron-Cohen, S., O'Riordan, M., Stone, V., Jones, R., & Plaisted, K. (1999a). Recognition of faux pas by normally developing children and children with Asperger syndrome or high-functioning autism. *Journal of Autism and Developmental Disorders, 29,* 407–418.

Baron-Cohen, S., Richler, J., Bisarya, D., Gurunathan, N., & Wheelwright, S. (2003). The Systemising Quotient (SQ): An investigation of adults with Asperger syndrome or high functioning autism and normal sex differences. *Philosophical Transactions of the Royal Society,* Series B. Special issue on 'Autism: Mind and brain', *358,* 361–374.

Baron-Cohen, S., Ring, H. A., Bullimore, E. T., Wheelwright, S., Ashwin, C., & Williams, S. C. R. (2000). The amygdala theory of autism. *Neuroscience and Biobehavioral Reviews, 24,* 355–364.

Baron-Cohen, S., Ring, H., Moriarty, J., Schmitz, B., Costa, D., & Ell, P. (1994). Recognition of mental state terms. Clinical findings in children with autism and a functional neuroimaging study of normal adults. *British Journal of Psychiatry, 165,* 640–649.

Baron-Cohen, S., Ring, H., Wheelwright, S., Bullimore, E., Brammer, M., Simmons, A., & Williams, S. (1999b). Social intelligence in the normal and autistic brain: An fMRI study. *European Journal of Neuroscience, 11,* 1891–1898.

Baron-Cohen, S., Tager-Flusberg, H., & Cohen, D. (Eds.) (1993). *Understanding other minds: Perspectives from autism.* Oxford: Oxford Medical Publications.

Baron-Cohen, S., Tager-Flusberg, H., & Cohen, D. (Eds.) (1999). *Understanding other minds: Perspectives from developmental cognitive neuroscience* (2nd ed.). Oxford: Oxford University Press.

Baron-Cohen, S., Wheelwright, S., Hill, J., Raste, Y., & Plumb, I. (2001). The 'Reading the Mind in the Eyes' test revised version: A study with normal adults, and adults with Asperger syndrome or high-functioning autism. *Journal of Child Psychology and Psychiatry and Allied Disciplines*, 42, 241–251.

Baron-Cohen, S., Wheelwright, S., Scott, F., & Bolton, P. (1997). Is there a link between engineering and autism? *Autism*, 1, 101–109.

Bartak, L., Rutter, M., & Cox, A. (1975). A comparative study of infantile autism and specific developmental receptive language disorder. I. The children. *British Journal of Psychiatry*, 126, 127–145.

Bartak, L., Rutter, M., & Cox, A. (1977). A comparative study of infantile autism and specific receptive language disorders. III. Discriminant function analysis. *Journal of Autism and Childhood Schizophrenia*, 7, 383–396.

Bates, E. (1979). *The emergence of symbols: Cognition and communication in infancy.* New York: Academic Press.

Bates, E. (1993). Address to annual conference of Developmental Section of the British Psychological Society, University of Birmingham, Sept. 1993.

Bates, E., Camaioni, L., & Volterra, V. (1975). The acquisition of performatives prior to speech. *Merrill-Paimer Quarterly*, 27, 205–216.

Bauman, M., & Kemper, T. L. (1985). Histoanatomic observations of the brain in early infantile autism. *Neurology*, 35, 866–874.

Bauman, M. D., Lavenex, P., Mason, W. A., Capitanio, J. P., & Amaral, D. G. (2003). Persistence of social fear and evidence of social interest in rhesus monkeys with neonatal amygdala lesions. Abstract Viewer, Society for Neuroscience, New Orleans.

Bauminger, N., & Kasari, C. (1999). Brief report: Theory of mind in high-functioning children with autism. *Journal of Autism and Developmental Disorders*, 29, 81–86.

Bayley, N. (1993). *Bayley scales of infant development, Manual* (2nd ed.). New York: The Psychological Corporation/Harcourt Brace & Company.

Bechtel, W. (1988). *Philosophy of mind: An overview for cognitive science.* Hillsdale, NJ: Erlbaum.

Beckett, C., Bredenkamp, D., Castle, J., Groothues, C., O'Connor, T. G., & Rutter, M. (2002). Behavior patterns associated with institutional deprivation: A study of children adopted from Romania. *Journal of Developmental and Behavioral Pediatrics*, 23, 297–303.

Belmonte, M. K., Allen, G., Beckel-Mitchener, A., Boulanger, L. M., Carper, R. A., & Webb, S. J. (2004). Autism and abnormal development of brain connectivity. *Journal of Neuroscience*, 24, 9228–9231.

Bender, L. (1947). One hundred cases of childhood schizophrenia treated with electric shock. *Transactions of the American Neurological Society*, 7, 65–169.

Bennetto, L., Pennington, B. F., & Rogers, S. J. (1996). Intact and impaired memory function in autism. *Child Development*, 67, 1816–1835.

Bertenthal, B. I., Proffitt, D. R., Kramer, S. J., & Spetner, N. B. (1987). Infants' encoding of kinetic displays varying in relative coherence. *Developmental Psychology*, 23, 171–178.

Bertone, A., Mottron, L., Jelenic, P., & Faubert, J. (2003). Motion perception in autism: A 'complex' issue. *Journal of Cognitive Neuroscience*, 15, 218–225.

Bertone, A., Mottron, L., Jelenic, P., & Faubert, J. (2005). Enhanced and diminished visuo-spatial information processing in autism depends on stimulus complexity. *Brain, 128,* 2430–2441.

Beversdorf, D. Q., Smith, B. W., Crucian, G. P., Anderson, J. M., Keillor, J. M., Barrett, A. M. et al. (2000). Increased discrimination of 'false memories' in autism spectrum disorder. *Proceedings of the National Academy of Sciences of the USA, 97,* 8734– 8737.

Biró, S., & Russell, J. (2001). The role of arbitrary procedures in means-end behaviour in autism. *Development and Psychopathology, 13,* 96–108.

Bishop, D. V. M. (1989). Autism, Asperger's syndrome and semantic-pragmatic disorder: Where are the boundaries? *British Journal of Disorders of Communication, 24,* 107–121.

Bishop, D. V. M., & Norbury, C. F. (2002). Exploring borderlands of autistic disorder and specific language impairment: A study using standardised diagnostic instruments. *Journal of Child Psychology and Psychiatry, 43,* 917–929.

Blake, R., Turner, L. M., Smoski, M. J., Pozdol, S. L., & Stone, W. L. (2003). Visual recognition of biological motion is impaired in children with autism. *Psychological Science, 14,* 151–157.

Blakemore, S.-J., Winston, J., & Frith, U. (2004). Social cognitive neuroscience: Where are we heading? *Trends in Cognitive Science, 8,* 216–222.

Bleuler, E. (1911). *Dementia Praecox oder Gruppe der Schizophrienien.* Leipzig: Deuticke.

Boddaert, N., Belin, P., Chabane, N., Poline, J.-B., Barthélémy, C., Mouren-Simeoni, M.-C. et al. (2003). Perception of complex sounds: Abnormal patterns of cortical activation in autism. *American Journal of Psychiatry, 160,* 2057–2060.

Boddaert, N., Chabane, N., Belin, P., Bourgeois, M., Royer, V., Barthélémy, C. et al. (2004). Perception of complex sounds in autism: Abnormal cortical processing in autism. *American Journal of Psychiatry, 161,* 2117–2120.

Bonnel, A., Mottron, L., Peretz, I., Trudel, M., Gallun, E., & Bonnel, A.-M. (2003). Enhanced pitch sensitivity in individuals with autism: A signal detection analysis. *Journal of Cognitive Neuroscience, 15,* 226–235.

Bosch, G. (1970). *Infantile autism: A clinical and phenomenological-anthropological approach taking language as the guide.* New York: Springer-Verlag.

Boucher, J. (1978). Echoic memory capacity in autistic children. *Journal of Child Psychology and Psychiatry, 19,* 161–166.

Boucher, J. (1981). Immediate free recall in early childhood autism: Another point of behavioural similarity with the amnesic syndrome. *British Journal of Psychology, 72,* 211–215.

Boucher, J. (2001). Lost in a sea of time. In T. McCormack & C. Hoerl (Eds.), *Time and memory: Issues in philosophy and psychology.* Oxford: Oxford University Press.

Boucher, J., & Lewis, V. (1989). Memory impairments and communication in relatively able autistic children. *Journal of Child Psychology and Psychiatry, 30,* 99– 122.

Boucher, J., & Lewis, V. (1992). Unfamiliar face recognition in relatively able autistic children. *Journal of Child Psychology and Psychiatry, 33,* 843–859.

Boucher, J., & Warrington, E. K. (1976). Memory deficits in early infantile autism: Some similarities to the amnesic syndrome. *British Journal of Psychology, 67,* 73–87.

Bowler, D. M. (1992). 'Theory of mind' in Asperger's syndrome. *Journal of Child Psychology and Psychiatry, 33*, 877–893.

Bowler, D. M. (1997). Reaction times for mental-state and non mental-state questions in 'theory of mind tasks': Evidence against logico-affective states in Asperger's syndrome. *European Child and Adolescent Psychiatry, 6*, 160–165.

Bowler, D. M. (2001). Autism: Specific cognitive deficit or emergent end-point of multiple interacting systems. In J. Burack, T. Charman, P. R. Zelazo, & N. Yirmiya (Eds.), *Development of autism: Perspectives from theory and research*. Mahwah, NJ: Erlbaum.

Bowler, D. M., & Briskman, J. A. (2000). Photographic cues do not always facilitate performance on false belief tasks in children with autism. *Journal of Autism and Developmental Disorders, 30*, 305–316.

Bowler, D. M., Briskman, J. A., & Grice, S. (1999). Experimenter influence and children's understanding of false drawings and false beliefs. *Journal of Genetic Psychology, 160*, 443–460.

Bowler, D. M., Briskman, J. A., Gurvidi, N., & Fornells-Ambrojo, M. (2005). Autistic and non-autistic children's performance on a non-social analogue of the false belief task. *Journal of Cognition and Development, 6*, 259–283.

Bowler, D. M., Gaigg, S. B., & Gardiner, J. M. (under review). Subjective organisation in the free recall of adults with Asperger's syndrome.

Bowler, D. M., Gardiner, J. M., & Berthollier, N. (2004). Source memory in Asperger's syndrome. *Journal of Autism and Developmental Disorders, 34*, 533–542.

Bowler, D. M., Gardiner, J. M., & Gaigg, S. B. (in press). Factors affecting conscious awareness in the recollective experience of adults with Asperger's syndrome. *Consciousness and Cognition*.

Bowler, D. M., Gardiner, J. M., & Grice, S. (2000a). Episodic memory and remembering in adults with Asperger's syndrome. *Journal of Autism and Developmental Disorders, 30*, 305–316.

Bowler, D. M., Gardiner, J. M., Grice, S., & Saavalainen, P. (2000b). Memory illusions: False recall and recognition in high functioning adults with autism. *Journal of Abnormal Psychology, 109*, 663–672.

Bowler, D. M., Matthews, N. J., & Gardiner, J. M. (1997). Asperger's syndrome and memory: Similarity to autism but not amnesia. *Neuropsychologia, 35*, 65–70.

Bowler, D. M., & Strom, E. (1998). Elicitation of first-order 'theory of mind' in children with autism. *Autism, 2*, 33–44.

Bowler, D. M., & Thommen, E. (2000). Attribution of mechanical and social causality to animated displays by children with autism. *Autism, 4*, 147–171.

Braeutigam, S., Bailey, A. J., & Swithenby, S. J. (2001). Task-dependent early latency (30–60 ms) visual processing of human faces and other objects. *Neuroreport, 12*, 1531–1536.

Braverman, M., Fein, D., Lucci, D., & Waterhouse, L. (1989). Affect comprehension in children with pervasive developmental disorders. *Journal of Autism and Developmental Disorders, 19*, 301–316.

Brent, E., Rios, P., Happé, F., & Charman, T. (2004). The performance of children with autism spectrum disorder on advanced theory of mind tests. *Autism, 8*, 283–299.

Bretherton, I., McNew, S., & Beeghly-Smith, M. (1981). Early person knowledge as expressed in gestural and verbal communication: When do infants acquire a 'theory of mind.' In M. Lamb & L. Sherrod (Eds.), *Infant social cognition: Empirical and theoretical considerations* (pp. 333–373). Hillsdale, NJ: Erlbaum.

Brock, J., Brown, C. C., Boucher, J., & Rippon, G. (2002). The temporal binding deficit hypothesis of autism. *Development and Psychopathology, 14*, 209–224.

Brosnan, M., Scott, F., Fox, S., & Pye, J. (2004). Gestalt processing in autism: Failure to process perceptual relations and the implications for contextual understanding. *Journal of Child Psychology and Psychiatry, 45*, 459–469.

Brothers, L. (1990). The social brain: A project for integrating primate behavior and neuropsychology in a new domain. *Concepts in Neuroscience, 1*, 27–51.

Brown, R., Hobson, R. P., Lee, A., & Stevenson, J. (1997). Are there 'autistic-like' features in congenitally blind children? *Journal of Child Psychology and Psychiatry, 38*, 693–703.

Bruinsma, Y., Koegel, R. L., & Koegel, L. K. (2004). Joint attention and children with autism: A review of the literature. *Mental Retardation and Developmental Disabilities Research Reviews, 10*, 169–173.

Brüne, M., Ribbert, H., & Shiefenhövel, W. (2003). *The social brain.* Wiley Interscience Online Books, htttp://www3.interscience.wiley.com/cgi-bin/booktoc/104557685.

Bruneau, N. B., Bonnet-Brilhault, F., Gomot, M., Adrien, J.-L., & Barthélémy, C. (2003). Cortical auditory processing and communication in children with autism: Electrophysiological/behavioural relations. *International Journal of Psychophysiology, 51*, 17–25.

Bruner, J. (1975). From communication to language: A psychological perspective. *Cognition, 3*, 255–287.

Bruner, J. S. (1983). *Child's talk: Learning to use language.* New York: W. W. Norton.

Bühler, C. M. (1947). *From birth to maturity: An outline of the psychological development of the child.* London: K. Paul Trench.

Burack, J. A. (1994). Selective attention deficits in persons with autism: Preliminary evidence of an inefficient attentional lens. *Journal of Abnormal Psychology, 103*, 535–543.

Burack, J. A., Charman, T., Yirmiya, N., & Zelazo, P. R. (2001). *The development of autism: Perspectives from theory and research.* Mahwah, NJ: Erlbaum.

Burack, J. A., Enns, J. T., Stauder, J. E. A., Mottron, L., & Randolph, B. (1997). Attention and autism: Behavioural and electrophysiological evidence. In D. J. Cohen & F. R. Volkmar (Eds.), *Handbook of autism and pervasive developmental disorders* (pp. 226–247). New York: Wiley.

Burack, J. A., Iarocci, G., Flanagan, T. D., & Bowler, D. M. (2004). On mosaics and melting pots: Conceptual considerations of comparison and matching questions and strategies. *Journal of Autism and Developmental Disorders, 34*, 65–73.

Bzoch, K., & League, R. (1971). *Assessing language skills in infancy.* Baltimore, MD: University Park Press.

Campos, J., & Sternberg, C. (1981). Perception, appraisal, and emotion: The onset of social referencing. In M. Lamb & L. Sherrod (Eds.), *Infant social cognition: Empirical and theoretical considerations* (pp. 273–314). Hillsdale, NJ: Erlbaum.

Cantwell, D., Baker, L., Rutter, M., & Mawhood, L. (1989). Infantile autism and developmental receptive dysphasia: A comparative follow-up into middle childhood. *Journal of Autism and Developmental Disorders, 19*, 19–32.

Caron, M.-J., Mottron, L., Berthiaume, C., & Dawson, M. (2006). Cognitive mechanisms, specificity and neural underpinnings of visuospatial peaks in autism. *Brain,* in press.

Carpenter, M., Nagell, K., Tomasello, M., Butterworth, G., & Moore, C. (1998). Social cognition, joint attention and communicative competence from 9 to 15 months of age. *Monographs of the Society for Research in Child Development*, *63*, 1–174.

Carper, R. A., & Courchesne, E. (2000). Inverse correlation between frontal lobe and cerebellum sizes in children with autism. *Brain*, *123*, 836–844.

Carper, R. A., & Courchesne, E. (2005). Localized enlargement of the frontal cortex in early autism. *Biological Psychiatry*, *57*, 126–133.

Carper, R. A., Moses, P., Tigue, Z. D., & Courchesne, E. (2002). Cerebral lobes in autism: Early hyperplasia and abnormal age effects. *Neuroimage*, *16*, 1038–1051.

Carruthers, P. (1996). Simulation and self-knowledge: A defence of theory-theory. In P. Carruthers & P. K. Smith (Eds.). *Theories of theories of mind* (pp. 22–38). Cambridge, UK: Cambridge University Press.

Casanova, M. F., Buxhoeveden, D. P., Switala, A. E., & Roy, E. L. (2002). Minicolumnar pathology in the brains of autistic and Asperger's patients. *Neurology*, *58*, A2–A3, Suppl. 3.

Casey, B. J., Gordon, C. T., Mannheim, G., & Rumsey, J. M. (1993). Attentional dysfunction in calendar calculating savants. *Journal of Clinical and Experimental Neuropsychology*, *15*, 933–946.

Castelli, F., Frith, C., Happé, F., & Frith, U. (2002). Autism, Asperger syndrome and brain mechanisms for the attribution of mental states to animated shapes. *Brain*, *125*, 1839–1849.

Castelli, F., Happé, F., Frith, U., & Frith, C. (2000). Movement and mind: A functional imaging study of perception and interpretation of complex intentional movement patterns. *Neuroimage*, *12*, 314–325.

Celani, G., Battacchi, M. W., & Arcidiacono, L. (1999). The understanding of the emotional meaning of facial expressions in people with autism. *Journal of Autism and Developmental Disorders*, *29*, 57–66.

Ceponiené, R., Lepistö, T., Shestakova, A., Vanhala, R., Alko, P., Näätänen, R., & Yaguchi, K. (2003). Speech-sound-selective auditory impairment in children with autism: they can perceive but they do not attend. *Proceedings of the National Academy of Sciences of the USA*, *100*, 5567–5572.

Charlesworth, W. R., & Dzur, C. (1987). Gender comparisons of preschoolers' behavior and resource utilization in group problem-solving. *Child Development*, *58*, 191–200.

Charman, T., & Baron-Cohen, S. (1992). Understanding drawings and beliefs: A further test of the metarepresentation theory of autism. *Journal of Child Psychology and Psychiatry*, *33*, 1105–1112.

Charman, T., Swettenham, J., Baron-Cohen, S., Cox, A., Baird, G., & Drew, A. (1997). Infants with autism: An investigation of empathy, pretend play, joint attention and imitation. *Developmental Psychology*, *33*, 781–789.

Charman, T., Taylor, E., Drew, A., Cockerill, H., Brown, J. A., & Baird, G. (2005). Outcome at 7 years of children diagnosed with autism at age 2: Predictive validity of assessments conducted at 2 and 3 years of age and pattern of symptom change over time. *Journal of Child Psychology and Psychiatry*, *46*, 500–513.

Clark, A. (1997). *Being there: Putting brain, body and world together again*. Cambridge, MA: MIT Press.

Cody, H., Pelphrey, K., & Piven, J. (2002). Structural and functional magnetic resonance imaging of autism. *International Journal of Developmental Neuroscience*, *20*, 421–438.

Cohen, I. L. (1998). An artificial neural network analogue of learning in autism. *Biological Psychiatry*, *36*, 5–20.

Cohen, J. D., & Servan-Schreiber, D. (1992). Context, cortex, and dopamine – a connectionist approach to behavior and biology in schizophrenia. *Psychological Review*, *99*, 45–77.

Collins, D. W., & Kimura, D. (1997). A large sex difference on a two-dimensional mental rotation task. *Behavioral Neuroscience*, *111*, 845–849.

Colvert, E., Custance, D., & Swettenham, J. (2002). Rule-based reasoning and theory of mind in autism: A comment on the work of Zelazo, Jacques, Burack and Frye. *Infant and Child Devlopment*, *11*, 197–200.

Corona, R., Dissanayake, C., Arbelle, S., Wellington, P., & Sigman, M. (1998). Is affect aversive to young children with autism? Behavioral and cardiac responses to experimenter distress. *Child Development*, *69*, 1494–1502.

Courchesne, E., Karns, C. M., Davis, H. R., Ziccardi, R., Carper, R. A., Tigue, Z. D. et al. (2001). Unusual brain growth patterns in early life in patients with autistic disorder: An MRI study. *Neurology*, *57*, 245–254.

Courchesne, E., Yeung-Courchesne, R., Press, G., Hesselink, J., & Jernigan, T. (1988). Hypoplasia of cerebellar vermal lobules VI and VII in autism. *New England Journal of Medicine*, *318*, 1349–1354.

Craik, F. I. M., & Anderson, N. D. (1999). Applying cognitive research to the problems of ageing. *Attention and Performance*, *17*, 583–615.

Craik, F. I. M., Morris, L. W., Morris, R. G., & Loewen, E. R. (1990). Relations between source amnesia and frontal lobe functioning in older adults. *Psychology and Aging*, *5*, 148–151.

Creak, M. (1963). Childhood psychosis: A review of 100 cases. *British Journal of Psychiatry*, *109*, 84–89.

Cromer, R. (1974). The development of language and cognition: The cognition hypothesis. In B. Foss (Ed.), *New Perspectives in Child Development*. Harmondsworth, Middlesex: Penguin Books.

Cutting, A. L., & Dunn, J. (1999). Theory of mind, emotion understanding, language, and family background: Individual differences and interrelations. *Child Development*, *70*, 853–865.

Cycowicz, Y. M., Friedman, D., & Snodgrass, J. G. (2001). Remembering the color of objects: An ERP investigation of source memory. *Cerebral Cortex*, *11*, 322–334.

Dahlgren, S. O., & Trillingsgaard, A. (1996). Theory of mind in non-retarded children with autism and Asperger's syndrome. *Journal of Child Psychology and Psychiatry*, *37*, 759–763.

Damasio, A. R. (1994). Time-locked multiregional retroactivation: A systems-level proposal for the neural substrates of recall and recognition. *Cognition*, *33*, 25–62.

Damasio, A. R., & Van Hoesen, G. W. (1983). Emotional disturbances associated with focal lesions of the limbic frontal lobe. In K. M. Heilman & P. Satz (Eds.), *Neuropsychology of human emotion* (pp. 85–110). New York: Guilford Press.

Damon, W., & Hart, D. (1982). The development of self-understanding from infancy through adolescence. *Child Development*, *53*, 841–864.

Davidson, R. J., & Slagter, H. A. (2000). Probing emotion in the developing brain: Functional neuroimaging in the assessment of the neural substrates of emotion in normal and disordered children and adolescents. *Mental Retardation and Developmental Disabilities Research Reviews*, *6*, 166–170.

Dawson, G., Finley, C., Phillips, S., & Galpert, L. (1986). Hemispheric specialisation and the language abilities of autistic children. *Child Development, 57*, 1440–1453.

Dawson, G., & Lewy, A. (1989). Arousal, attention and the socioemotional impairments of individuals with autism. In G. Dawson (Ed.), *Autism: Nature, diagnosis, and treatment* (pp. 49–74). New York: Guilford.

Dawson, G., & McKissick, F. C. (1984). Self-recognition in autistic children. *Journal of Autism and Developmental Disorders, 14*, 383–394.

Dawson, G., Meltzoff, A. N., Osterling, J., & Rinaldi, J. (1998). Neuropsychological correlates of early symptoms of autism. *Child Development, 69*, 1276–1285.

Dawson, G., Munson, J., Estes, A., Osterling, J., McPartland, J., Toth, K. et al. (2002). Neurocognitive function and joint attention ability in young children with autism spectrum disorder. *Child Development, 73*, 345–358.

DeCasper, A., & Fifer, W. (1980). Of human bonding: Newborns prefer their mothers' voices. *Science, 208*, 1174–1176.

Deese, J. (1959). On the prediction of occurrence of particular verbal intrusions in immediate recall. *Journal of Experimental Psychology, 58*, 17–22.

Delis, D. C., Kramer, J. H., Kaplan, E., & Ober, B. A. (1986). *The California verbal learning test – research edition*. New York: The Psychological Corporation.

DeLong, G. R. (1992). Autism, amnesia, hippocampus and learning. *Neuroscience and Biobehavioral Reviews, 16*, 63–70.

DeLong, G. R., Bean, S. C., & Brown, F. R. (1981). Acquired reversible autistic syndrome in acute encephalopathic illness in children. *Archives of Neurology, 38*, 191–194.

DeLong, G. R., & Heinz, E. R. (1997). The syndrome of early-life bilateral hippocampal sclerosis. *Annals of Neurology, 42*, 11–17.

DeMeyer, M., Barton, S., Alpern, G. D., Kimberlin, C., Allen, J., Yang, E., & Steele, R. (1974). The measured intelligence of autistic children. *Journal of Autism and Childhood Schizophrenia, 4*, 42–60.

Dennett, D. C. (1987). *The intentional stance*. Cambridge, MA: MIT Press.

Deruelle, C., Rondan, C., Gepner, B., & Tardif, C. (2004). Spatial frequency and face processing in children with autism and Asperger's syndrome. *Journal of Autism and Developmental Disorders, 34*, 199–210.

De Sanctis, S. (1906). Sopra alcune varieta della demenza precoce. *Rivista Sperimentale de Freniatria di Medicina Legale, 32*, 141–165.

De Sanctis, S. (1908). Dementia praecocissima catatonica oder Katatonie des fruheren Kindesalters? *Folia Neurobiologica, 2*, 9–12.

Deutsch, C. K., Folstein, S. E., Gordon-Vaughn, K., Tager-Flusberg, H., Schmid, C., Martino, B., & Sherman, D. (in press). Macrocephaly and cephalic disproportion in autistic probands and their first-degree relatives. *American Journal of Medical Genetics*. Cited in Deutch & Joseph 2003.

Deutsch, C. K., & Joseph, R. M. (2003). Brief report: Cognitive correlates of enlarged head circumference in children with autism. *Journal of Autism and Developmental Disorders, 33*, 209–215.

de Villiers, J. G. (2000). Language and theory of mind: What are the developmental relationships? In S. Baron-Cohen, H. Tager-Flusberg, & D. Cohen (Eds.), *Understanding other minds: Perspectives from autism and developmental cognitive neuroscience* (pp. 83–123). Cambridge, UK: Cambridge University Press.

Diamond, A. (1998). Understanding the A-not-B error: Working memory vs. reinforced response, or active vs. latent trace. *Developmental Science, 1*, 185–189.

DiPietro, J. A. (1981). Rough and tumble play: A function of gender. *Developmental Psychology, 17*, 50–58.

Dissanayake, C., Sigman, M., & Kasari, C. (1996). Long-term stability of individual differences in the emotional responsiveness of children with autism. *Journal of Child Psychology and Psychiatry, 37*, 461–467.

Donaldson, M. (1984). *Children's minds*. London: Fontana.

Donnelly, N., & Hadwin, J. A. (2003). Children's perception of the Thatcher illusion: Evidence for development in configural face processing. *Visual Cognition, 10*(8), 1001–1017

Drewe, E. (1975). Go-no-go learning after frontal lobe lesion in humans. *Cortex, 11*, 8–16.

Dumas, J. A., & Hartman, M. (2003). Adult age differences in temporal and item memory. *Psychology and Aging, 18*, 573–586.

Dunbar, R. I. M. (1998). The social brain hypothesis. *Evolutionary Anthropology, 6*, 178–190.

Dunn, L. M., Dunn, L. M., Whetton, C., & Burley, J. (1997). *The British Picture Vocabulary Scale.* London: NFER-Nelson.

Dunn, M., Gomes, H., & Sebastian, M. (1996). Prototypicality of responses of autistic, language disordered, and normal children in a word fluency task. *Child Neuropsychology, 2*, 99–108.

Dunn, M., Vaughan, H., Kreuzer, J., & Kurtzberg, D. (1999). Electrophysiologic correlates of semantic classification in autistic and normal children. *Developmental Neuropsychology, 16*, 79–99.

Edelman, G. M. (1987). *Neural darwinism: The theory of neuronal group selection.* New York: Basic Books.

Ehlers, S., & Gillberg, C. (1993). The epidemiology of Asperger's syndrome: A total population study. *Journal of Child Psychology and Psychiatry, 34*, 1327–1350.

Ekstrom, R. B., French, J. W., & Harman, H. H. (1976). *Manual for kit of factor-referenced cognitive tests.* Princeton, NJ: Educational Testing Service.

Elman, J. L., Bates, E. A., Johnson, M. H., Karmiloff-Smith, A., Parisi, D., & Plunkett, K. (1996). *Rethinking innateness: A connectionist perspective on development.* Cambridge, MA: MIT Press.

Emery, N. J., Capitanio, J. P., Mason, W. A., Machado, C. J., Mendoza, S. P., & Amaral, D. G. (2001). The effects of bilateral lesions of the amygdala on dyadic social interactions in rhesus monkeys (*Macaca mulatta*). *Behavioral Neuroscience, 115*, 515–544.

Farrant, A., Blades, M., & Boucher, J. (1998). Source monitoring in children with autism. *Journal of Autism and Developmental Disorders, 28*, 43–50.

Fatemi, S. H., Halt, A. R., Realmuto, G., Earle, J., Kist, D. A., Thuras, P., & Merz, A. (2002). Purkinje cell size is reduced in autism. *Cellular and Molecular Neurobiology, 22*, 171–175.

Filipek, P. A. (1999). Neuroimaging the developmental disorders: The state of the science. *Journal of Child Psychology and Psychiatry, 40*, 113–128.

Fletcher, P. C., Happé, F., Frith, U., Baker, S. C., Dolan, R. J., Frackowiak, R. S. J., & Frith, C. D. (1995). Other minds in the brain: A functional imaging study of theory of mind in story comprehension. *Cognition, 57*, 109–128.

Fodor, J. (1983). *The modularity of mind*. Cambridge, MA: MIT Press.

Foxton, J. M., Stewart, M. E., Barnard, L., Rodgers, J., Young, A. H., O'Brien, G., & Griffiths, T. D. (2003). Absence of auditory 'global interference' in autism. *Brain*, *126*, 2703–2709.

Frith, C. (2003). What do imaging studies tell us about the neural basis of autism? *Autism: Neural Basis and Treatment Possibilities. Novartis Foundation Symposium*, *251*, 149–176.

Frith, U. (1989). *Autism: Explaining the enigma*. Oxford: Blackwell.

Frith, U. (2001). Mind blindness and the brain in autism. *Neuron*, *32*, 969–979.

Frith, U. (2003). *Autism: Explaining the enigma* (2nd ed.). Oxford: Blackwell.

Frith, U., & Happé, F. (1994). Autism – beyond theory of mind. *Cognition*, *50*, 115–132.

Frith, U., & Happé, F. (1999). Theory of mind and self-consciousness: what is it like to be autistic? *Mind and Language*, *14*, 1–22.

Frith, U., Happé, F., & Siddons, F. (1994). Autism and theory of mind in everyday life. *Social Development*, *3*, 108–124.

Frith, U., & Snowling, M. (1983). Reading for meaning and reading for sound in autistic and dyslexic children. *British Journal of Developmental Psychology*, *1*, 329–342.

Frye, D., Zelazo, P. D., & Burack, J. A. (1998). Cognitive complexity and control: I. theory of mind in typical and atypical development. *Current Directions in Psychological Science*, *7*, 116–121.

Frye, D., Zelazo, P. D., & Palfai, T. (1995). Theory of mind and rule-based reasoning. *Cognitive Development*, *10*, 483–547.

Fuster, J. M. (1997). *The pre-frontal cortex: Anatomy, physiology and neuropsychology of the frontal lobe*. Philadelphia: Lippincott-Raven.

Gaigg, S. B., Bowler, D. M., & Gardiner, J. M. (2004). Free recall in Asperger's syndrome: The role of relational and item-specific encoding. Paper presented at the International Meeting for Autism Research, Sacramento, CA.

Gardiner, J. M. (in press). Concepts and theories of memory. In J. Boucher and D. M. Bowler (Eds.), *Memory in autism*. Cambridge, UK: Cambridge University Press.

Garretson, H. B., Fein, D., & Waterhouse, L. (1990). Sustained attention in autistic children. *Journal of Autism and Developmental Disorders*, *20*, 101–114.

Gauthier, I., Skudlarski, P., Gore, J. C., & Anderson, A. W. (2000). Expertise for cars and birds recruits brain areas involved in face recognition. *Nature Neuroscience*, *3*, 191–197.

Gauthier, I., Tarr, M. J., Anderson, A. W., Skudlarski, P., & Gore, J. C. (1999). Activation of the middle fusiform 'face area' increases with expertise in recognising novel objects. *Nature Neuroscience*, *2*, 568–573.

Gepner, B., Deruelle, C., & Grynfeltt, S. (2001). Motion and emotion: A novel approach to the study of face processing by young autistic children. *Journal of Autism and Developmental Disorders*, *31*, 37–45.

Gepner, B., Mestre, D., Masson, G., & de Schonen, S. (1995). Postural effects of motion vision in young autistic children. *Neuroreport*, *6*, 1211–1214.

Gershberg, F. (1997). Implicit and explicit conceptual memory following frontal lobe damage. *Journal of Cognitive Neuroscience*, *9*, 105–116.

Gervais, H., Belin, P., Boddaert, N., Leboyer, M., Coez, A., Sfaello, I. et al. (2004). Abnormal cortical voice processing in autism. *Nature Neuroscience*, *7*, 801–802.

Ghaziuddin, M., Tsai, L. Y., & Ghaziuddin, N. (1992). A comparison of the diagnostic criteria for Asperger syndrome. *Journal of Autism and Developmental Disorders*, *22*, 643–649.

Gibson, E., & Walk, R. D. (1960). The visual cliff. *Scientific American*, *202*(4), 64–71.

Gibson, J. J. (1968). *The senses considered as perceptual systems*. London: Allen and Unwin.

Gillberg, C. (1983). Perceptual, motor and attentional deficits in Swedish primary-school children – some child psychiatric aspects. *Journal of Child Psychology and Psychiatry*, *24*, 377–403.

Gillberg, I., Bjure, J., Uvebrant, P., Vestergren, E., & Gillberg, C. (1993). SPECT in 31 children and adolescents with autism and autistic like syndromes. *European Child and Adolescent Psychiatry*, *2*, 50–59.

Goldman, A. I. (1993). The psychology of folk psychology. *Behavioral and Brain Sciences*, *16*, 15–28.

Goldman-Rakic, P. S. (1988). Topography of cognition: Parallel distributed networks in primate association cortex. *Annual Review of Neuroscience*, *11*, 137.

Goldstein, G., Johnson, C., & Minshew, N. J. (2001). Attentional processes in autism. *Journal of Autism and Developmental Disorders*, *31*, 433–440.

Gopnik, A. (1993). How we know our minds: The illusion of first-person knowledge of intentionality. *Behavioral and Brain Sciences*, *16*, 1–14.

Gordon, R. M. (1995). Sympathy, simulation, and the impartial spectator. *Ethics*, *105*, 727–742.

Grandin, T., & Scariano, M. (1986). *Emergence: Labelled autistic*. Novato, CA: Arena.

Grant, C., Riggs, K., & Boucher, J. (2004). Counterfactual and mental state reasoning in children with autism. *Journal of Autism and Developmental Disorders*, *34*, 177–188.

Gray, J. M., Fraser, W. L., & Leudar, I. (1983). Recognition of emotion from facial expression in mental handicap. *British Journal of Psychiatry*, *142*, 566–571.

Green, B. F. (1956). A method of scalogram analysis using summary statistics. *Psychometrica*, *21*, 79–88.

Green, S., Pring, L., & Swettenham, J. (2004). An investigation of first-order false belief understanding of children with congenital profound visual impairment. *British Journal of Developmental Psychology*, *22*, 1–17.

Grelotti, D. J., Klin, A. J., Gauthier, I., Skudlarski, P., Cohen, D. J., Gore, J. C. et al. (2005). fMRI activation of the fusiform gyrus and amygdala to cartoon characters but not to faces in a boy with autism. *Neuropsychologia*, *43*, 373–385.

Grice, S. J., Spratling, M. W., Karmiloff-Smith, A., Halit, H., Csibra, G., de Haan, M., & Johnson, M. H. (2001). Disordered visual processing and oscillatory brain activity in autism and Williams syndrome. *NeuroReport*, *12*, 2697–2700.

Griffith, E. M., Pennington, B. F., Wehner, E. A., & Rogers, S. J. (1999). Executive functions in young children with autism. *Child Development*, *70*, 817–832.

Grossman, J. B., Klin, A., Carter, A. S., & Volkmar, F. R. (2000). Verbal bias in recognition of emotions in children with Asperger's syndrome. *Journal of Child Psychology and Psychiatry*, *41*, 369–379.

Gusnard, D. A., Akbudak, E., Shulman, G. L., & Raichle, M. E. (2001). Medial prefrontal cortex and self-referential mental activity: Relation to a default mode of brain function. *Proceedings of the National Academy of Sciences of the USA*, *98*, 4259–4264.

Gustafsson, L., & Paplinski, A. P. (2004). Self-organization of an artificial neural network subjected to attention shift impairments and familiarity preference, characteristics studied in autism. *Journal of Autism and Developmental Disorders, 34*, 189–198.

Hadjikhani, N., Joseph, R. M., Snyder, J., Chabris, C. F., Clark, J., Steele, S. et al. (2004). Activation of the fusiform gyrus when individuals with autism spectrum disorder view faces. *Neuroimage, 22*, 1141–1150.

Haist, F., Adamo, M., Westerfield, M., Courchesne, E., & Townsend, J. (2005). The functional neuroanatomy of spatial attention in autism spectrum disorder. *Developmental Neuropsychology, 27*, 425–458.

Halford, G. S. (1992). *Children's understanding: The development of mental models.* Hillsdale, NJ: Erlbaum.

Hamlyn, D. W. (1974). Person perception and our understanding of others. In T. Mischel (Ed.), *Understanding other persons* (pp. 1–36). Oxford: Blackwell.

Happé, F. G. E. (1994). An advanced test of theory of mind: Understanding of story characters' thoughts and feelings by able autistic, mentally handicapped and normal children and adults. *Journal of Autism and Developmental Disorders, 24*, 129–154.

Happé, F. G. E. (1995). The role of age and verbal ability in the Theory of Mind task: Performance of subjects with autism. *Child Development, 66*, 843–855.

Happé, F. G. E. (1996). Studying weak central coherence at low levels: Children with autism do not succumb to visual illusions: A research note. *Journal of Child Psychology and Psychiatry, 37*, 873–877.

Happé, F. G. E. (1997). Central coherence and theory of mind in autism: Reading homographs in context. *British Journal of Developmental Psychology, 15*, 1–12.

Happé, F. (1999). Autism: Cognitive deficit or cognitive style? *Trends in Cognitive Sciences, 3*, 216–222.

Happé, F. (2003). Theory of mind and the self. *Autism: Neural Basis and Treatment Possibilities. Novartis Foundation Symposium, 251*, 134–144.

Happé, F., Ehlers, S., Fletcher, P., Frith, U., Johansson, M., Gillberg, C. et al. (1996). 'Theory of mind' in the brain. Evidence from a PET scan study of Asperger syndrome. *Neuroreport, 8*, 197–201.

Hardan, A. Y., Minshew, N. J., Mallikarjuhn, M., & Keshavan, M. S. (2001). Brain volume in autism. *Journal of Child Neurology, 16*, 421–424.

Harris, P. (2000). *The work of the imagination.* Oxford: Blackwell.

Hartelman, P. A. I., van der Maas, H. L. J., & Molenaar, P. C. M. (1998). Detecting and modelling developmental transitions. *British Journal of Developmental Psychology, 16*, 97–122.

Haznedar, M. M., Buchsbaum, M. S., Wei, T. C., Hof, P. R., Cartwright, C., Bienstock, C. A., & Hollander, C. (2000). Limbic circuitry in patients with autism spectrum disorders studied with positron emission tomography and magnetic resonance imaging. *American Journal of Psychiatry, 157*, 1994–2001.

Heaton, P. (2003). Pitch memory, labeling and disembedding in autism. *Journal of Child Psychology and Psychiatry, 44*, 543–551.

Heaton, P., Hermelin, B., & Pring, L. (1998). Autism and pitch processing: A precursor for savant musical ability? *Music Perception, 15*, 291–305.

Heaton, R. K., Chelune, G. J., Talley, J. L., Kay, G. G., & Curtis, G. (1993). *Wisconsin Card Sorting Test manual: Revised and expanded.* Odessa, FL: Psychological Assessment Resources.

Hebb, D. O. (1949). *The organization of behavior: A neuropsychological theory.* New York: Wiley.

Heider, F., & Simmel, M. (1944). An experimental study of apparent behavior. *American Journal of Psychology, 57,* 243–249.

Heller, T. (1908). Über Dementia infantilis. *Zeitschrift für die Erforschung und Behandlung des Jugendlichen Schwachsinns, 2,* 17–28.

Henderson, L., Yoder, P., Yale, M., & McDuffie, A. (2002). Getting the point: Electrophysiological correlates of proto-declarative pointing. *International Journal for Developmental Neuroscience, 20,* 449–458.

Hendriks-Jansen, H. (1996). *Catching ourselves in the act.* Cambridge, MA: MIT Press.

Herbert, M. R., Ziegler, D. A., Deutsch, C. K., O'Brien, L. M., Lange, A., Bkardjiev, A. et al. (2003). Dissociations of cerebral cortex, subcortical and cerebral white matter volumes in autistic boys. *Brain, 126,* 1182–1192.

Hermelin, B. (1978). Images and language. In M. Rutter & E. Schopler (Eds.). *Autism: A reapprisal of concepts and treatment.* New York: Plenum.

Hermelin, B., & O'Connor, N. (1967). Remembering of words by psychotic and subnormal children. *British Journal of Psychology, 58,* 213–218.

Hermelin, B., & O'Connor, N. (1970). *Psychological experiments with autistic children.* Oxford: Pergamon Press.

Hermelin, B., & O'Connor, N. (1985). Logico-affective states and nonverbal language. In E. Schopler & G. B. Mesibov (Eds.), *Communication problems in autism* (pp. 283–310). New York: Plenum Press.

Hill, E. L. (2004a). Executive dysfunction in autism. *Trends in Cognitive Sciences, 8,* 26–32.

Hill, E. L. (2004b). Evaluating the theory of executive dysfunction in autism. *Developmental Review, 24,* 189–233.

Hill, E. L., & Russell, J. (2002). Action memory and self-monitoring in children with autism: Self versus other. *Infant and Child Development, 11,* 159–170.

Hines, M. (2004). *Brain gender.* Oxford: Oxford University Press.

Hobson, R. P. (1986a). The autistic child's appraisal of expressions of emotion. *Journal of Child Psychology and Psychiatry, 27,* 321–342.

Hobson, R. P. (1986b). The autistic child's appraisal of expressions of emotion: A further study. *Journal of Child Psychology and Psychiatry, 27,* 671–680.

Hobson, R. P. (1990a). On acquiring knowledge about people and the capacity to pretend: Response to Leslie (1987). *Psychological Review, 97,* 114–121.

Hobson, R. P. (1990b). On psychoanalytic approaches to autism. *American Journal of Orthopsychiatry, 60,* 324–336.

Hobson, R. P. (1991a). Methodological issues for experiments on autistic individuals' perception and understanding of emotion. *Journal of Child Psychology and Psychiatry, 32,* 1135–1158.

Hobson, R. P. (1991b). Against the theory of theory of mind. *British Journal of Developmental Psychology, 9,* 33–51.

Hobson, R. P. (1993). *Autism and the development of mind.* Hove: Erlbaum.

Hobson, R. P. (2002). *The cradle of thought.* Oxford: Oxford University Press.

Hobson, R. P., & Lee, A. (1989). Emotion-related and abstract concepts in autistic people: Evidence from the British Picture Vocabulary Scale. *Journal of Autism and Developmental Disorders, 19,* 601–623.

Hobson, R. P., & Lee, A. (1999). Imitation and identification in autism. *Journal of Child Psychology and Psychiatry, 40*, 649–659.

Hobson, R. P., & Meyer, J. A. (2005). Foundations of self and other: A study in autism. *Developmental Science, 8*, 481–491.

Hobson, R. P., Ouston, J., & Lee, A. (1988a). Emotion recognition in autism: Coordinating faces and voices. *Psychological Medicine, 18*, 911–923.

Hobson, R. P., Ouston, J., & Lee, A. (1988b). What's in a face? The case of autism. *British Journal of Psychology, 79*, 441–453.

Hodapp, R. M. (2004). Studying interactions, reactions and perceptions: Can genetic disorders serve as behavioral proxies. *Journal of Autism and Developmental Disorders, 34*, 29–34.

Holland, P. A. (2005). *Arbitrariness, attention and memory: Alternative explanations for false belief failure in autism.* Unpublished Doctoral Dissertation, Department of Psychology, City University, London.

Holland, P. A., & Bowler, D. M. (2005). *The effect of cues on false belief performance of children with autism.* Paper presented at the International Meeting for Autism Research, Boston, MA, May 2005.

Holroyd, S., & Baron-Cohen, S. (1993). Brief report: How far can people with autism go in developing a theory of mind? *Journal of Autism and Developmental Disorders, 23*, 379–385.

Hongwanishkul, D., Happaney, K. R., Lee, W., & Zelazo, P. D. (2005). Hot and cool executive function: Age-related changes and individual differences. *Developmental Neuropsychology, 28*, 617–644.

Howard, M. A., Cowell, P. E., Boucher, J., Broks, P., Mayes, A., Farrant, A., & Roberts N. (2000). Convergent neuroanatomical and behavioural evidence of an amygdala hypothesis of autism. *Neuroreport, 11*, 2931–2935.

Howlin, P., Goode, S., Hutton, J., & Rutter, M. (2004). Adult outcome for children with autism. *Journal of Child Psychology and Psychiatry, 45*, 212–229.

Howlin, P., Mawhood, L. M., & Rutter, M. (2000). Autism and developmental receptive language disorder: A follow-up comparison in early adult life: II. Social, behavioural and psychiatric outcomes. *Journal of Child Psychology and Psychiatry, 41*, 561–578.

Hoy, J. A., Hatton, C., & Hare, D. (2004). Weak central coherence: A cross-domain phenomenon specific to autism? *Autism, 8*, 268–281.

Hughes, C. (1996). Brief report: Planning problems in autism at the level of motor control. *Journal of Autism and Developmental Disorders, 26*, 101–109.

Hughes, C. H., & Russell, J. (1993). Autistic children's difficulties with mental disengagement from an object: Its implications for theories of autism. *Developmental Psychology, 29*, 498–510.

Hughes, C., Russell, J., & Robbins, T. W. (1994). Evidence for executive dysfunction in autism. *Neuropsychologia, 32*, 477–492.

Hunt, R. R., & Seta, C. E. (1984). Category size effects in recall: The role of relational and item-specific information. *Journal of Experimental Psychology: Learning, Memory and Cognition, 10*, 454–464.

Hurlburt, R. T., Happé, F., & Frith, U. (1994). Sampling the form of inner experience in three adults with Asperger syndrome. *Psychological Medicine, 24*, 385–395.

Hutt, C., Hutt, S. J., Lee, D., & Ounsted, C. (1964). Arousal and childhood autism. *Nature, 204*, 908–909.

Hutt, C., & Ounsted, C. (1966). The biological significance of gaze aversion with particular reference to the syndrome of infantile autism. *Behavioral Science, 11*, 346–356.

Iarocci, G., & Burack, J. A. (2004). Intact covert orienting to peripheral cues among children with autism. *Journal of Autism and Developmental Disorders, 34*, 257–264.

Jacoby, L. L. (1991). A process dissociation framework: Separating automatic from intentional uses of memory. *Journal of Memory and Language, 30*, 513–541.

Jarrold, C. (2003). A review of research into pretend play in autism. *Autism, 7*, 379–390.

Jarrold, C., Boucher, J., & Smith, P. K. (1993). Symbolic play in autism: A review. *Journal of Autism and Developmental Disorders, 23*, 281–307.

Jarrold, C., Boucher, J., & Smith, P. K. (1996). Generativity deficits in pretend play in autism. *British Journal of Developmental Psychology, 14*, 275–300.

Jarrold, C., Butler, C. W., Cottington, E. M., & Jimenez, F. (2000). Linking theory of mind and central coherence bias in autism and in the general population. *Developmental Psychology, 36*, 126–138.

Jarrold, C., & Routh, D. A. (1998). Is there really a link between engineering and autism? A reply to Baron-Cohen et al., *Autism, 1997, 1*(1), 101–9. *Autism, 2*, 281–289.

Jemel, B., Mottron, L., & Dawson, M. (2006). Impaired face processing in autism: Fact or artefact? *Journal of Autism and Developmental Disorders, 36*, 91–106.

Jitsumori, M., Siemann, M., Lehr, M., & Delius, J. D. (2002). A new approach to the formation of equivalence classes in pigeons. *Journal of the Experimental Analysis of Behavior, 78*, 397–408.

Jolliffe, T., & Baron-Cohen, S. (1997). Are people with autism and Asperger syndrome faster than normal on the embedded figures test? *Journal of Child Psychology and Psychiatry, 38*, 527–534.

Jolliffe, T., & Baron-Cohen, S. (1999). The Strange Stories Test: A replication with high-functioning adults with autism or Asperger's syndrome. *Journal of Autism and Developmental Disorders, 29*, 395–406.

Jolliffe, T., & Baron-Cohen, S. (2000). Linguistic processing in high-functioning adults with Asperger's syndrome: Is global coherence impaired? *Psychological Medicine, 30*, 1169–1187.

Jones-Gotman, M., & Milner, B. (1977). Design fluency: The invention of nonsense drawings after focal cortical lesions. *Neuropsychologia, 15*, 653–674.

Jordan, R. (2003). Social play and autistic spectrum disorders: A perspective on theory, implications and educational approaches. *Autism, 7*, 347–360.

Joseph, R. M., & Tanaka, J. (2003). Holistic and part-based face recognition in children with autism. *Journal of Child Psychology and Psychiatry, 44*, 529–542.

Just, M. A., Cherkassky, V. L., Keller, T. A., & Minshew, N. J. (2004). Cortical activation and synchronization during sentence comprehension in high-functioning autism: evidence of underconnectivity. *Brain, 127*, 1811–1821.

Kaland, N., Møller-Nielsen, A., Callesen, K., Mortensen, E. L., Gottlieb, D., & Smith, L. (2002). A new 'advanced' test of theory of mind: Evidence from children and adolescents with Asperger syndrome. *Journal of Child Psychology and Psychiatry, 43*, 517–528.

Kanner, L. (1943). Autistic disturbances of affective contact. *Nervous Child, 2*, 217–250.

Kanner, L. (1973). *Childhood psychosis: Initial studies and new insights.* New York: Winston/Wiley.

Kanwisher, N. (2000). Domain specificity in face perception. *Nature Neuroscience, 3,* 759–763.

Kanwisher, N., McDermott, J., & Chun, M. M. (1997). The fusiform face area: A module in extrastriate cortex specialised for face perception. *Journal of Neuroscience, 17,* 4302–4311.

Kapur, N. (1996). Paradoxical functional facilitation in brain-behaviour research: A critical overview. *Brain, 119,* 1779–1790.

Karmiloff-Smith, A. (1992). *Beyond modularity: A developmental perspective on cognitive science.* Cambridge, MA: MIT Press.

Kasari, C., Sigman, M. D., Baumgartner, P., & Stipek, D. J. (1993). Pride and mastery in children with autism. *Journal of Child Psychology and Psychiatry, 34,* 353–362.

Kawakubo, Y., Maekawa, H., Itoh, K., Hashimoto, O., & Iwanami, A. (2004). Spatial attention in individuals with pervasive developmental disorders using the gap overlap task. *Psychiatry Research, 125,* 269–275.

Kemper, T. L., & Bauman, M. (1998). Neuropathology of infantile autism. *Journal of Neuropathology and Experimental Neurology, 57,* 645–652.

Klein, S. B., Chan, R. L., & Loftus, J. (1999). Independence of episodic and semantic self-knowledge: The case from autism. *Social Cognition, 17,* 413–436.

Klin, A. (1991). Young autistic children's listening preferences in regard to speech: A possible characterization of the symptom of social withdrawal. *Journal of Autism and Developmental Disorders, 21,* 29–42.

Klin, A., Jones, W., Schultz, R., Volkmar, F., Cohen, D. (2002). Visual fixation patterns during viewing of naturalistic social situations as predictors of social competence in individuals with autism. *Archives of General Psychiatry, 59,* 809–816.

Klin, A., Volkmar, F. R., Sparrow, S. S., Cicchetti, D. V., & Rourke, B. P. (1995). Validity and neuropsychological characterization of Asperger syndrome: Convergence with nonverbal learning-disabilities syndrome. *Journal of Child Psychology and Psychiatry, 36,* 1127–1140.

Klinger, L. G., & Dawson, G. (2001). Prototype formation in autism. *Development and Psychopathology, 13,* 111–124.

Klüver, H., & Bucy, P. C. (1938). Analysis of certain effects of temporal lobectomy in the rhesus monkey with special reference to 'psychic blindness'. *Journal of Psychology, 5,* 33–54.

Klüver, H., & Bucy, P. C. (1939). Preliminary analysis of the functioning of the temporal lobes in monkeys. *Archives of Neurology and Psychiatry, 42,* 979–1000.

Koshino, H., Carpenter, P. A., Minshew, N. J., Cherkassky, V. L., Keller, T. A., & Just, M. A. (2005). Functional connectivity in an fMRI working memory task in high-functioning autism. *NeuroImage, 24,* 810–821.

Krug, D. A., Arick, J. R., & Almond, P. J. (1980). *Autism screening instrument for education planning.* Portland, Oregon: AISEP Educational Company.

Kylliäinen, A., & Hietanen, J. K. (2004). Attention orienting by another's gaze direction in children with autism. *Journal of Child Psychology and Psychiatry, 45,* 435–444.

Lahaie, A., Mottron, L., Arguin, M., Berthiaume, C., Jemel, B., & Saumier, D. (2006). Face perception in high functioning autistic adults: Evidence for superior processing of face parts, not for a configural face processing deficit. *Neuropsychology*, *20*, 30–41.

Landry, R., & Bryson, S. E. (2004). Impaired disengagement of attention in young children with autism. *Journal of Child Psychology and Psychiatry*, *45*, 1115–1122.

Lane, H. (1977). *The wild boy of Aveyron*. London: Allen & Unwin.

Langdell, T. (1978). Recognition of faces: An approach to the study of autism. *Journal of Child Psychology and Psychiatry*, *19*, 255–268.

Lavoie, M. E., & Charlebois, P. (1994). The discriminant validity of the Stroop Color and Word Test: Toward a cost-effective strategy to distinguish subgroups of disruptive preadolescents. *Psychology in the Schools*, *31*, 98–107.

Lawson, J., Baron-Cohen, S., & Wheelwright, S. (2004). Empathizing and systemizing in adults with and without Asperger syndrome. *Journal of Autism and Developmental Disorders*, *34*, 301–310.

LeCouteur, A., Lord, C., & Rutter, M. (2003). *The Autism Diagnostic Instrument – Revised (ADI-R)*. Los Angeles, CA: Western Psychological Services.

LeCouteur, A., Rutter, M., Lord, C., Rios, P., Robertson, S., Hgrafer, M., & McLennan, M. (1989). Autism Diagnostic Interview: A standardised investigator-based instrument. *Journal of Autism and Developmental Disorders*, *19*, 363–387.

Lee, A., & Hobson, R. P. (1998). On developing self-concepts: a controlled study of children and adolescents with autism. *Journal of Child Psychology and Psychiatry*, *39*, 1131–1144.

Lee, A., Hobson, R. P., & Chiat, S. (1994). I, you, me and autism: an experimental study. *Journal of Autism and Developmental Disorders*, *24*, 155–176.

Leekam, S., Hunnisett, E., & Moore, C. (1998). Targets and cues: Gaze-following in children with autism. *Journal of Child Psychology and Psychiatry*, *39*, 951–962.

Leekam, S., & Lopez, B. (2003). Do children with autism fail to process information in context? *Journal of Child Psychology and Psychiatry*, *44*, 285–300.

Leekam, S., Lopez, B., & Moore, C. (2000). Attention and joint attention in preschool children with autism. *Developmental Psychology*, *36*, 261–273.

Leekam, S. R., & Moore, C. (2001). The development of attention and joint attention in children with autism. In J. A. Burack, T. Charman, N. Yirmiya & P. R. Zelazo (Eds.), *The development of autism: Perspectives from theory and research* (pp. 105–129). Mahwah, NJ: Erlbaum.

Leekam, S., & Perner, J. (1991). Does the autistic child have a metarepresentational deficit? *Cognition*, *40*, 203–318.

Leslie, A. M. (1987). Pretense and representation: The origins of 'theory of mind'. *Psychological Review*, *94*, 412–426.

Leslie, A. M., & Frith, U. (1988). Autistic children's understanding of seeing, knowing and believing. *British Journal of Developmental Psychology*, *6*, 315–324.

Leslie, A. M., & Frith, U. (1990). Prospects for a cognitive neuropsychology of autism: Hobson's choice. *Psychological Review*, *97*, 122–131.

Leslie, A., & Roth, D. (1993). What autism teaches us about metarepresentation. In S. Baron-Cohen, H. Tager-Flusberg & D. Cohen (Eds.), *Understanding other minds: Perspectives from autism* (pp. 83–111). Oxford: Oxford Medical Publications.

Leslie, A. M., & Thaiss, L. (1992). Domain specificity in conceptual development: Neuropsychological evidence from autism. *Cognition*, *43*, 225–251.

Lewis, V., & Boucher, J. (1995). Generativity in the play of young children with autism. *Journal of Autism and Developemental Disorders*, 25, 105–121.

Lincoln, A. J., Allen, M. H., & Kilman, A. (1995). The assessment and interpretation of intellectual abilities in people with autism. In E. Schopler & G. Mesibov (Eds.), *Language and cognition in autism* (pp. 88–117). New York: Plenum.

Lind, S. E., & Bowler, D. M. (in press). Episodic memory, mental time travel and self-awareness in autism. In J. Boucher & D. M. Bowler (Eds.), *Memory in autism*. Cambridge, UK: Cambridge University Press.

Lind, S. E., & Bowler, D. M. (in preparation). Autism and the self: A review.

Linn, M. C., & Petersen, A. C. (1985). Emergence and characterization of sex differences in spatial ability: A meta-analysis. *Child Development*, 56, 1479–1498.

Lister Brook, S., & Bowler, D. M. (1992). Autism by another name? – semantic-pragmatic difficulties in children. *Journal of Autism and Developmental Disorders*, 22, 61–81.

Litrownik, A. J., McInnis, E. T., Wetzel-Pritchard, A. M., & Filipelli, D. L. (1978). Restricted stimulus control and inferred attentional deficits in autistic and retarded children. *Journal of Abnormal Psychology*, 87, 554–562.

Lockyer, L., & Rutter, M. (1969). A five- to fifteen-year follow-up study of infantile psychosis. *British Journal of Psychiatry*, 115, 865–882.

Lockyer, L., & Rutter, M. (1970). A five to fifteen year follow-up study of infantile psychosis: IV. patterns of cognitive ability. *British Journal of Social and Clinical Psychology*, 9, 152–163.

Lord, C., & Bailey, A. (2002). Autism spectrum disorders. In M. Rutter & E. Taylor (Eds.), *Child and adolescent psychiatry* (4th ed., pp. 664–681). Oxford: Blackwell.

Lord, C., Risi, S., Lambrecht, L., Cook, E. H. Jr., Leventhal, B. L., DiLavore, P. C. et al. (2000). The Autism Diagnostic Observation Schedule–Generic: A standard measure of social and communication deficits associated with the spectrum of autism. *Journal of Autism and Developmental Disorders*, 30, 205–223.

Lord, C., Rutter, M., Goode, S., Heemsbergen, J., Jordan, J., Mawhood, L., & Schopler, E. (1989). Autism Diagnostic Observation Schedule: a standardised observation of communicative and social behavior. *Journal of Autism and Developmental Disorders*, 19, 185–212.

Lord, C., Rutter, M., & LeCouteur, A. (1994). Autism Diagnostic Interview – Revised: A revised version of a diagnostic interview for caregivers of individuals with possible pervasive developmental disorders. *Journal of Autism and Developmental Disorders*, 24, 659–685.

Losh, M., & Capps, L. (2003). Narrative ability in high-functioning children with autism or Asperger's syndrome. *Journal of Autism and Developmental Disorders*, 33, 239–251.

Lotter, V. (1966). Epidemiology of autistic conditions in young children: I. Prevalence. *Social Psychiatry*, 1, 124–137.

Lotter, V. (1967). Epidemiology of autistic conditions in young children: II. Some characteristics of the parents and children. *Social Psychiatry*, 1, 163–173.

Lovaas, O. I., Koegel, R. L., & Schreibman, L. (1979). Stimulus overselectivity in autism: A review of research. *Psychological Bulletin*, 86, 1236–1254.

Lovaas, O. I., Schreibman, L., Koegel, R. L., & Rehm, R. (1971). Selective responding by autistic children to multiple sensory input. *Journal of Abnormal Psychology*, 77, 211–222.

Loveland, K., & Landry, S. (1986). Joint attention and language in autism and developmental language delay. *Journal of Autism and Developmental Disorders, 16*, 335–349.

Luna, B., Minshew, N. J., Garver, K. E., Lazar, N. A., Thulborn, K. R., Eddy, W. F., & Sweeney, J. A. (2002). Neocortical system abnormalities in autism. An fMRI study of spatial working memory. *Neurology, 59*, 834–840.

Luria, A. R. (1966). *Higher cortical functions in man.* New York: Basic Books.

Machado, C. J., & Bachevalier, J. (2003). Non-human primate models of childhood psychopathology: The promise and the limitations. *Journal of Child Psychology and Psychiatry, 44*, 64–87.

Macintosh, K. E., & Dissanayake, C. (2004). Annotation: The similarities and differences between autistic disorder and Asperger's disorder: A review. *Journal of Child Psychology and Psychiatry, 45*, 421–434.

Manjiviona, J., & Prior, M. (1999). Neuropsychological profiles of children with Asperger syndrome and autism. *Autism, 3*, 327–356.

Mann, T., & Walker, P. (2003). Autism and a deficit in broadening the spread of visual attention. *Journal of Child Psychology and Psychiatry, 44*, 274–284.

Martinot, J. L., Allilaire, J. F., Mazoyer, B. M., & Hantouche, E. (1990). Obsessive-compulsive disorder: A clinical, neuropsychological and positron emission topography study. *ActaPsychiatrica Scandinavica, 82*, 233–242.

Maurer, D., Le Grand, R., & Mondloch, C. (2002). The many faces of configural processing. *Trends in Cognitive Sciences, 6*, 255–260.

Maurer, H., & Newbrough, J. R. (1987). Facial expressions of mentally retarded and non-retarded adults. *American Journal of Mental Deficiency, 91*, 505–510.

Mawhood, L. M., Howlin, P., & Rutter, M. (2000). Autism and developmental receptive language disorder: A follow-up comparison in early adult life: I. Cognitive and language outcomes. *Journal of Child Psychology and Psychiatry, 41*, 547–599.

Mayes, S. D., Calhoun, S. L., & Crites, D. L. (2001). Does *DSM-IV* Asperger's disorder exist? *Journal of Abnormal Child Psychology, 29*, 263–271.

McClelland, J. L. (2000). The basis of hyperspecificity in autism: A preliminary suggestion based on properties of neural nets. *Journal of Autism and Developmental Disorders, 30*, 497–502.

McEvoy, R. E., Rogers, S. J., & Pennington, B. F. (1992). Executive function and social communication in young autistic children. *Journal of Child Psychology and Psychiatry, 34*, 563–578.

McGarrigle, J., & Donaldson, M. (1975). Conservation accidents. *Cognition, 3*, 341–350.

McGregor, E., Whiten, A., & Blackburn, P. (1998). Teaching theory of mind by highlighting intention and illustrating thoughts: A comparison of their effectiveness with three-year-olds and autistic subjects. *British Journal of Developmental Psychology, 16*, 281–300.

Medin, D. L., & Smith, E. E. (1984). Concepts and concept formation. *Annual Review of Psychology, 35*, 113–138.

Merleau-Ponty, M. (1964). The child's relations with others. In M. Merleau-Ponty (Ed.), *The primacy of perception* (pp. 96–155). Evanston, IL: Northwestern University Press.

Meyer, J. A., & Hobson, R. P. (2004). Orientation in relation to self and other: The case of autism. *Interaction Studies, 5*, 221–244.

Miller, J. N., & Ozonoff, S. (1997). Did Asperger's cases have Asperger disorder? A research note. *Journal of Child Psyhology and Psychiatry*, *38*, 247–251.

Miller, J. N., & Ozonoff, S. (2000). The external validity of Asperger disorder: Lack of evidence from the domain of neuropsychology. *Journal of Abnormal Psychology*, *109*, 227–238.

Miller, L. K. (1999). The savant syndrome: Intellectual impairment and exceptional skill. *Psychological Bulletin*, *125*, 31–46.

Millward, C., Powell, S., Messer, D., & Jordan, R. (2000). Recall of self and other in autism: Children's memory for events experienced by themselves and their peers. *Journal of Autism and Developmental Disorders*, *30*, 15–28.

Milne, E., Swettenham, J., Hansen, P., Campbell, R., Jeffries, H., & Plaisted, K. (2002). High motion coherence thresholds in children with autism. *Journal of Child Psychology and Psychiatry*, *43*, 255–263.

Milner, B., Corsi, P., & Leonard, G. (1991). Frontal lobe contribution to recency judgments. *Neuropsychologia*, *29*, 601–618.

Minshew, N., Goldstein, G., Muenz, L. R., & Payton, J. (1992). Neuropsychological functioning in nonmentally retarded autistic individuals. *Journal of Clinical and Experimental Neuropsychology*, *14*, 749–761.

Minshew, N. J., Johnson, C., & Luna, B. (2001). The cognitive and neural basis of autism: A disorder of complex information processing and dysfunction of neocortical systems. *International Review of Research in Mental Retardation*, *23*, 111–138.

Minshew, N. J., Luna, B., & Sweeney, J. A. (1999). Oculomotor evidence for neocortical systems but not cerebellar dysfunction in autism. *Neurology*, *52*, 917–922.

Minter, M., Hobson, R. P., & Bishop, M. (1998). Congenital visual impairment and 'theory of mind'. *British Journal of Developmental Psychology*, *16*, 183–196.

Mirenda, P. L., & Donellan, A. M. (1987). Issues in curriculum development. In D. J. Cohen, A. M. Donnellan, & R. Paul (Eds.), *Handbook of autism and pervasive developmental disorders*. (pp. 211–226) New York: John Wiley & Sons.

Mitchell, P., & Lacohée, H. (1991). Children's early understanding of false belief. *Cognition*, *39*, 107–127.

Mitchell, P., & Ropar, D. (2004). Visuo-spatial abilities in autism: A review. *Infant and Child Development*, *13*, 185–198.

Mitchell, P., & Taylor, L. M. (1999). Shape constancy and theory of mind: Is there a link? *Cognition*, *70*, 167–190.

Molesworth, C. J., Bowler, D. M., & Hampton, J. A. (2005). Memory for modal prototypes in high-functioning children with autism. *Journal of Child Psychology and Psychiatry*, *46*, 661–672.

Moore, D. G., Hobson, R. P., & Lee, A. (1997). Components of person perception: An investigation with autistic and non-autistic retarded and typically developing children and adolescents. *British Journal of Developmental Psychology*, *15*, 401–423.

Mottron, L. (1987). La diffusion de prégnance de R. Thom: Une application à l'ontogenèse des conduites sémiotiques normales et pathologiques. *Semiotica*, *67*, 233–244.

Mottron, L. (1988). René Thom's semiotics: An application to the pathological limitations of semiosis. In T. A. Sebeok & J. Umiker-Sebeok (Eds.), *The semiotic web*. (pp. 91–127) Berlin: Mouton de Gruyter.

Mottron, L. (2004). *Autisme: Une autre intelligence*. Brussels: Mardaga.

Mottron, L., & Belleville, S. (1993). A study of perceptual analysis in a high-level autistic subject with exceptional graphic abilities. *Brain and Cognition*, *23*, 279–309.

Mottron, L., Belleville, S., & Ménard, E. (1999a). Local bias in autistic subjects as evidenced by graphic tasks: Perceptual hierarchization or working memory deficit? *Journal of Child Psychology and Psychiatry*, *40*, 743–755.

Mottron, L., & Burack, J. A. (2001). Enhanced perceptual functioning in the development of autism. In J. Burack, T. Charman, P. R. Zelazo, & N. Yirmiya (Eds.), *The development of autism: Perspectives from theory and research* (pp. 131–148). Mahwah, NJ: Erlbaum.

Mottron, L., Burack, J., Iarocci, G., Belleville, S., & Enns, J. (2003). Locally-oriented perception with intact global processing among adolescents with high-functioning autism: Evidence from multiple paradigms. *Journal of Child Psychology and Psychiatry*, *44*, 904–913.

Mottron, L., Burack, J., Stauder, J., & Robaey, P. (1999b). Perceptual processing among high-functioning persons with autism. *Journal of Child Psychology and Psychiatry*, *40*, 203–212.

Mottron, L., Dawson, M., Soulières, I., Hubert, B., & Burack, J. (2006). Enhanced perceptual functioning in autism: An update, and eight principles of autistic perception. *Journal of Autism and Developmental Disorders*, *36*, 27–43.

Mottron, L., Morasse, K., & Belleville, S. (2001). A study of memory functioning in individuals with autism. *Journal of Child Psychology and Psychiatry*, *42*, 253–260.

Mottron, L., Peretz, I., Belleville, S., & Rouleau, N. (1999c). Absolute pitch in autism: A case study. *Neurocase*, *5*, 485–502.

Mottron, L., Peretz, I., & Ménard, E. (2000). Local and global processing of music in high-functioning persons with autism: Beyond central coherence. *Journal of Child Psychology and Psychiatry*, *41*, 1057–1065.

Mottron, L., & Soulières, I. (in press). How useful are distinctions build for people without autism in describing autistic memory? In J. Boucher & D. M. Bowler (Eds.), *Memory in autism*. Cambridge, UK: Cambridge University Press.

Mueser, K. T., Doonan, R., Penn, D. L., Blanchard, J. J., Bellack, A. S., Nishith, P., & DeLeon, J. (1996). Emotion recognition and social competence in chronic schizoprhrenia. *Journal of Abnormal Psychology*, *105*, 271–275.

Muller, R.-A., Behen, M. E., Rothermel, R. D., Chugani, D. C., Muzik, O., Mangner, T. J., & Chugani, H. T. (1999). Brain mapping of language and auditory perception in high-functioning autistic adults: A PET study. *Journal of Autism and Developmental Disorders*, *29*, 19–31.

Mundy, P. (2003). Annotation: The neural basis of social impairments in autism: The role of the dorsal medial-frontal cortex and anterior cingulate system. *Journal of Child Psychology and Psychiatry*, *44*, 793–809.

Mundy, P., Sigman, M., & Kasari, C. (1993). The theory of mind and joint-attention deficits in autism. In S. Baron-Cohen, H. Tager-Flusberg, & D. Cohen (Eds.), *Understanding other minds: Perspectives from autism* (pp. 181–203). Oxford: Oxford University Press.

Mundy, P., Sigman, M., Ungerer, J., & Sherman, T. (1986). Defining the social deficits of autism: The contribution of non-verbal communication measures. *Journal of Child Psychology and Psychiatry*, *27*, 647–655.

Murphy, G. (2002). *The big book of concepts*. Cambridge, MA: MIT Press.

REFERENCES

Navon, D. (1977). Forest before trees: The precedence of global features in visual perception. *Cognitive Psychology, 9,* 353–383.

Neath, I., & Surprenant, A. M. (2003). *Human memory: An introduction to research, data and theory.* Belmont, CA: Thomson/Wadsworth.

Neisser, U. (1988). Five kinds of self-knowledge. *Philosophical Psychology, 1,* 35–59.

Neuman, C. J., & Hill, S. D. (1978). Self-recognition and stimulus preference in autistic children. *Developmental Psychobiology, 11,* 571–578.

Norman, D. A., & Shallice, T. (1986). Attention to action: Willed and automatic control of behaviour. In G. E. Schwartz & D. Shapiro (Eds.), *Consciousness and self-regulation* (Vol. 4, pp. 1–18). New York: Plenum.

Nosofsky, R. M. (1991). Tests of an exemplar model for relating perceptual classification and recognition memory. *Journal of Experimental Psychology: Human Perception and Performance, 17,* 3–27.

Novak, M. F., & Sackett, G. P. (1997). Pair-rearing infant monkeys (*Macaca nemestrina*) using a 'rotating peer' strategy. *American Journal of Primatology, 41,* 141–149.

Nyberg, L., Cabeza, R., & Tulving, E. (1996). PET studies of encoding and retrieval: The HERA model. *Psychonomic Bulletin and Review, 3,* 135–148.

Nyden, A., Gillberg, C., Hjelmquist, E. U., & Heiman, M. (1999). Executive/attention deficits in boys with Asperger syndrome, attention disorder and reading/writing disorder. *Autism, 3,* 213–228.

O'Connor, N., & Hermelin, B. (1967). The selective visual attention of autistic children. *Journal of Child Psychology and Psychiatry, 8,* 167–179.

O'Connor, N., & Hermelin, B. (1973). Spatial or temporal organisation of short-term memory. *Quarterly Journal of Experimental Psychology, 25,* 335–343.

O'Neill, M., & Jones, R. S. P. (1997). Sensory-perceptual abnormalities in autism: a case for more research? *Journal of Autism and Developmental Disorders, 27,* 279–289.

O'Riordan, M. A. F. (2004). Superior visual search in adults with autism. *Autism, 8,* 229–248.

O'Riordan, M. A. F., & Plaisted, K. C. (2001). Enhanced discrimination in autism. *Quarterly Journal of Experimental Psychology, Section A, 54,* 961–979.

Ornitz, E. M. (1969). Disorders of perception common to early infantile autism and schizophrenia. *Comprehensive Psychiatry, 10,* 259–274.

Ornitz, E. M., & Ritvo, E. R. (1968). Perceptual inconstancy in early infantile autism. *Archives of General Psychiatry, 18,* 76–98.

Osterling, J., Dawson, G., & Munson, J. (2002). Early recognition of one year old infants with autism spectrum disorder versus mental retardation: A study of first birthday party home videotapes. *Development and Psychopathology, 14,* 239–252.

Ozonoff, S. (1997). Components of executive function in autism and other disorders. In J. Russell (Ed.), *Autism as an executive disorder,* (pp. 179–211) Oxford: Oxford University Press.

Ozonoff, S., & Jensen, J. (1999). Specific executive function profiles in three neurodevelopmental disorders. *Journal of Autism and Developmental Disorders, 29,* 171–177.

Ozonoff, S., & McEvoy, R. (1994). A longitudinal study of executive function and theory of mind development in autism. *Development and Psychopathology, 6,* 415–431.

Ozonoff, S., & Miller, J. N. (1995). Teaching theory of mind: A new approach to social skills training for individuals with autism. *Journal of Autism and Developmental Disorders, 25.*

Ozonoff, S., Pennington, B. F., & Rogers, S. J. (1990). Are there emotion perception deficits in young autistic children? *Journal of Child Psychology and Psychiatry, 31,* 343–361.

Ozonoff, S., Pennington, B. F., & Rogers, S. J. (1991a). Executive function deficits in high-functioning autistic individuals: Relationship to theory of mind. *Journal of Child Psychology and Psychiatry, 32,* 1081–1105.

Ozonoff, S., Rogers, S. J., & Pennington, B. F. (1991b). Asperger's syndrome: Evidence of an empirical distinction from high-functioning autism. *Journal of Child Psychology and Psychiatry, 32,* 1107–1122.

Ozonoff, S., South, M., & Miller, J. N. (2000). DSM-IV-defined Asperger Syndrome: Cognitive, behavioral, and early history differentiation from high-functioning autism. *Autism, 4,* 29–46.

Ozonoff, S., & Strayer, D. L. (1997). Inhibitory function in nonretarded children with autism. *Journal of Autism and Developmental Disorders, 27,* 59–77.

Ozonoff, S., Strayer, D. L., McMahon, W. M., & Filloux, F. (1994). Executive function abilities in autism and Tourette Syndrome: An information processing approach. *Journal of Child Psychology and Psychiatry, 35,* 1015–1032.

Palmen, S. J., & van Engeland, H. (2004). Review on structural neuroimaging findings in autism. *Journal of Neural Transmission, 111,* 903–929.

Parsons, L. M. (2003). Superior parietal cortices and varieties of mental rotation. *Trends in Cognitive Sciences, 7,* 515–517.

Parsons, S., & Mitchell, P. (2002). The potential of virtual reality in social skills training for people with autistic spectrum disorders. *Journal of Intellectual Disability Research, 46,* 430–443.

Pascualvaca, D. M., Fantie, B. D., Papageorgiou, M., & Mirsky, A. F. (1998). Attentional capacities in children with autism: Is there a general deficit in shifting focus? *Journal of Autism and Developmental Disorders, 28,* 479–485.

Peeters, T. (1997). *Autism: From theory to practice.* London: Whurr.

Pelphrey, K. A., Sasson, N. J., Reznick, J. S., Paul, G., Goldman, B. N., & Piven, J. (2002). Visual scanning of faces in adults with autism. *Journal of Autism and Developmental Disorders, 32,* 249–261.

Pennington, B. F. (1994). The working memory function of the prefrontal cortices: Implications for developmental and individual differences in cognition. In M. M. Haith, J. Benson, R. Roberts, & B. F. Pennington (Eds.), *The development of future oriented processes* (pp. 243–289). Chicago: University of Chicago Press.

Pennington, B. F., & Ozonoff, S. (1996). Executive function and developmental psychopathology. *Journal of Child Psychology and Psychiatry, 37,* 51–87.

Perner, J. (1991). *Understanding the representational mind.* Cambridge, MA: MIT Press.

Perner, J. (1993). The theory of mind deficit in autism; rethinking the metarepresentation theory. In S. Baron-Cohen, H. Tager-Flusberg, & D. Cohen (Eds.), *Understanding other minds: Perspectives from autism* (pp. 83–111). Oxford: Oxford Medical Publications.

Perner, J. (2001). Episodic memory: Essential distinctions and developmental implications. In C. Moore & K. Lemmon (Eds.), *The self in time: Developmental issues* (pp. 181–202). Hillsdale, NJ: Erlbaum.

Perner, J., Frith, U., Leslie, A. M., & Leekam, S. R. (1989). Exploration of the autistic child's theory of mind: Knowledge, belief and communication. *Child Development, 60,* 689–700.

288

REFERENCES

Perner, J., Leekam, S., & Wimmer, H. (1987). Three-year-olds' difficulty with false belief: The case for a conceptual deficit. *British Journal of Developmental Psychology, 5,* 125–137.

Perner, J., & Wimmer, H. (1986). 'John *thinks* that Mary *thinks* that . . .' attribution of second-order beliefs by 5–10year old children. *Journal of Experimental Child Psychology, 39,* 437–471.

Peterson, C. C., & Siegal, M. (2000). Insights into a theory of mind from deafness and autism. *Mind and Language, 15,* 123–145.

Peterson, C. C., Wellman, H. M., & Liu, D. (2005). Steps in theory-of-mind development for children with deafness or autism. *Child Development, 76,* 502–517.

Peterson, D., & Bowler, D. M. (2000) Counterfactual reasoning and false belief understanding in children with autism, children with severe learning difficulties and children with typical development. *Autism, 4,* 391–405.

Peterson, D. M., & Riggs, K. J. (1999). Adaptive modelling and mindreading. *Mind and Language, 14,* 80–112.

Philips, W., Baron-Cohen, S., & Rutter, M. (1998). Understanding intention in normal development and in autism. *British Journal of Developmental Psychology, 16,* 337–348.

Piaget, J. (1952). *The origins of intelligence in children.* New York: International Universities Press.

Piaget, J. (1962). *Play, dreams and imitation in childhood.* London: Routledge & Kegan Paul.

Piaget, J. (1963). *The psychology of intelligence.* London: Routledge.

Piaget, J. (1970). *Structuralism.* New York: Basic Books.

Pierce, K., Haist, F., Sedaghat, F., & Courchesne, E. (2004). The brain response to personally familiar faces in autism: Findings of fusiform activity and beyond. *Brain, 127,* 2703–2716.

Pierce, L., Müller, R.-A., Ambrose, J., Allen, G., & Courchesne, E. (2001). Face processing occurs outside the 'face area' in autism: evidence from functional MRI. *Brain, 124,* 2059–2073.

Piggot, J., Kwon, H., Mobbs, D., Blasey, C., Lotspeich, L., Menon, V. et al. (2004). Emotional attribution in high-functioning individuals with autistic spectrum disorder: A functional imaging study. *Journal of the American Academy of Child and Adolescent Psychiatry, 43,* 473–480.

Piven, J., Saliba, K., Bailey, J., & Arndt, S. (1997). An MRI study of autism: The cerebellum revisited. *Neurology, 49,* 546–551.

Plaisted, K. C. (2001). Reduced generalization: An alternative to weak central coherence. In J. A. Burack, A. Charman, N. Yirmiya, & P. R. Zelazo (Eds.), *Development and autism: Perspectives from theory and research* (pp. 149–169). Mahwah, NJ: Erlbaum.

Plaisted, K. C., O'Riordan, M., & Baron-Cohen, S. (1998a). Enhanced discrimination of novel, highly similar stimuli by adults with autism during a perceptual learning task. *Journal of Child Psychology and Psychiatry, 39,* 765–775.

Plaisted, K. C., O'Riordan, M. A. F., & Baron-Cohen, S. (1998b). Enhanced visual search for a conjunctive target in autism: A research note. *Journal of Child Psychology and Psychiatry, 39,* 777–783.

Plaisted, K., Saksida, L., Alcántara, J., & Weisblatt, E. (2003). Towards an understanding of the mechanisms of weak central coherence effects: Experiments in visual configural learning and auditory perception. *Philosophical Transactions of the Royal Society, Series B, 358*(1430), 375–386.

Plaisted, K, Swettenham, J., & Rees, L. (1999). Children with autism show local precedence in a divided attention task and global precedence in a selective attention task. *Journal of Child Psychology and Psychiatry, 40*, 733–742.

Plunkett, K., & Elman, J. L. (2000). *Exercises in rethinking innateness.* Cambridge, MA: MIT Press.

Poirier, M., Gaigg, S. B., & Bowler, D. M. (2004). Digit span in adults with Asperger's syndrome. Poster presented at the International Meeting for Autism Research, Sacramento, CA.

Polleux, F., & Lauder, J. M. (2004). Toward a developmental neurobiology of autism. *Mental Retardation and Developmental Disabilities Research Reviews, 10*, 303–317.

Popper, K. (1965). *Conjectures and refutations: The growth of scientific knowledge.* New York: Basic Books.

Posner, M. I. (1980). Orienting of attention. *Quarterly Journal of Experimental Psychology, 32*, 3–25.

Posner, M. I. (1988). Structures and functions of selective attention. In T. Boll & B. Bryant (Eds.), *Master lectures in clinical neuropsychology and brain function: Research, measurement, and practice* (pp. 171–202). Wahsington, DC: American Psychological Association.

Prather, M. D., Lavenex, P., Mauldin-Jourdain, M. L., Mason, W. A., Capitanio, J. P., Mendoza, S. P., & Amaral, D. G. (2001). Increased social fear and decreased fear of objects in monkeys with neonatal amygdala lesions. *Neuroscience, 106*, 653–658.

Premack, D., & Woodruff, G. (1978). Does the chimpanzee have a theory of mind? *Behavioral and Brain Sciences, 4*, 515–526.

Prior, M., & Bradshaw, J. (1979). Hemisphere functioning in autistic children. *Cortex, 15*, 73–81.

Prior, M. Eisenmajer, R., Leekam, S., Wing, L., Gould, J., Ong, B., & Dowe, D. (1998). Are there subgroups within the autistic spectrum? A cluster analysis of a group of children with autistic spectrum disorders. *Journal of Child Psychology and Psychiatry, 39*, 893–902.

Ramondo, N., & Milech, D. (1984). The nature and specificity of the language coding deficit in autistic children. *British Journal of Psychology, 75*, 95–103.

Rapin, I. (1996). Preschool children with indadequate communication: developmental language disorders, autism or low IQ? *Clinics in Developmental Medicine*, No. 139. London: MacKeith Press.

Raven, J. C. (1996). *Standard progressive matrices.* Oxford: Oxford Psychologists Press.

Reynell, J. K. (1977). *Reynell developmental language scales.* Windsor, UK: NFER.

Richardson-Klavehn, A., Lee, M. G., Joubran, R., & Bjork, R. A. (1994). Intention and awareness in perceptual identification priming. *Memory & Cognition, 22*, 293–312.

Riggs, K., J., Peterson, D. M., Robinson, E. J., & Mitchell, P. (1998). Are errors in false belief tasks symptomatic of a broader difficulty with counterfactuality? *Cognitive Development, 13*, 73–90.

Rimland, B. (1964). *Infantile autism: The syndrome and its implications for a neural theory of behavior.* New York: Appleton-Century-Crofts.

Rinehart, N. J., Bradshaw, J. L., Moss, S. A., Brereton, A. V., & Tonge, B. J. (2000). Atypical interference of local detail on global processing in high-functioning autism and Asperger's syndrome. *Journal of Child Psychology and Psychiatry, 41*, 769–778.

Ritvo, E. R., Freeman, B. J., Scheibel, A. B., Duong, T., Robinson, H., Guthrie, D., & Ritvo, A. (1986). Lower Purkinje cell counts in the cerebella of four autistic subjects: Initial findings of the UCLA-NSAC autopsy research report. *American Journal of Psychiatry, 146*, 862–866.

Robel, L., Ennouri, K., Piana, H., Vaivre-Douret, L. Perier, A., Flament, M. F., & Mouren-Simeoni, M.-C. (2004). Discrimination of face identities and expressions in children with autism: Same or different? *European Child and Adolescent Psychiatry, 13*, 227–233.

Rodriguez, E., George, N., Lachaux, J. P., Martinere, J., Renault, B., & Varela, F. J. (1999). Perception's long shadow: Long-distance synchronization of human brain activity. *Nature, 397*, 430–433.

Roediger, H. L. III., & McDermott, K. B. (1995). Creating false memories: Remembering words not presented in lists. *Journal of Experimental Psychology: Learning, Memory and Cognition, 21*, 803–814.

Ropar, D., & Mitchell, P. (1999). Are individuals with autism and Asperger's syndrome susceptible to visual illusions? *Journal of Child Psychology and Psychiatry, 40*, 1283–1293.

Ropar, D., & Mitchell, P. (2001). Susceptibility to illusions and performance on visuospatial tasks in individuals with autism. *Journal of Child Psychology and Psychiatry, 42*, 539–549.

Ropar, D., & Mitchell, P. (2002). Shape constancy in autism: The role of prior knowledge and perspective cues. *Journal of Child Psychology and Psychiatry, 43*, 647–653.

Ropar, D., Mitchell, P., & Ackroyd, K. (2003). Do children with autism find it difficult to offer alternative interpretations to ambiguous figures? *British Journal of Developmental Psychology, 21*, 387–395.

Rosch, E. (1975). Cognitive representations of semantic categories. *Journal of Experimental Psychology: General, 104*, 192–233.

Rosen, W. G. (1980). Verbal fluency in aging and dementia. *Journal of Clinical Neuropsychology, 2*, 135–146.

Rosenhall, U., Nordin, V., Sandström, M., Ahlsén, G., & Gillberg, C. (1999). Autism and hearing loss. *Journal of Autism and Developmental Disorders, 29*, 349–357.

Rosvold, H. E., Mirsky, A. F., Sarason, I., Bronsome, E. D., & Beck, L. H. (1956). A continuous performance test of brain damage. *Journal of Consulting Psychology, 20*, 343–350.

Rourke, B. P. (1989). *Nonverbal learning disabilities: The syndrome and the model*. New York: Guilford Press.

Rouse, H., Donnelly, N., Hadwin, J. A., & Brown, T. (2004). Do children with autism perceive second-order relational features? The case of the Thatcher illusion. *Journal of Child Psychology and Psychiatry, 45*, 1246–1257.

Rumelhart, D. E., & McClelland, J. L. (1986). *Parallel distributed processing: Explorations in the microstructure of cognition*. Vol. 1. Cambridge, MA: MIT Press.

Rumsey, J. M., Rapoport, J. L., & Sceery, W. R. (1985). Autistic children as adults: Psychiatric, social, and behavioral outcomes. *Journal of the American Academy of Child Psychiatry, 24*, 465–473.

Russell, J. (1992). The theory-theory: So good they named it twice? *Cognitive Development, 7*, 485–519.

Russell, J. (1996). *Agency: Its role in mental development*. Hove: Taylor & Francis.

REFERENCES

Russell, J. (1997a). *Autism as an executive disorder*. Oxford: Oxford University Press.

Russell, J. (1997b). How executive disorders can bring about an inadequate 'theory of mind'. In J. Russell (Ed.), *Autism as an executive disorder* (pp. 256–304). Oxford: Oxford University Press.

Russell, J., & Hill, E. L. (2001). Action-monitoring and intention reporting in children with autism. *Journal of Child Psychology and Psychiatry, 42*, 317–328.

Russell, J., & Jarrold, C. (1998). Error-correction problems in autism: Evidence for a monitoring impairment. *Journal of Autism and Developmental Disorders, 28*, 177–188.

Russell, J., & Jarrold, C. (1999). Memory for actions in children with autism: Self versus other. *Cognitive Neuropsychiatry, 4*, 303–331.

Russell, J., Jarrold, C., & Henry, L. (1996). Working memory in children with autism and with moderate learning difficulties. *Journal of Child Psychology and Psychiatry, 37*, 673–686.

Russell, J., Jarrold, C., & Hood, B. (1999). Two intact executive capacities in children with autism: Implications for the core executive dysfunctions in the disorder. *Journal of Autism and Developmental Disorders, 29*, 103–112.

Russell, J., Mauthner, N., Sharpe, S., & Tidswell, T. (1991) The 'windows task' as a measure of strategic deception in preschoolers and autistic subjects. *British Journal of Developmental Psychology, 9*, 331–349.

Rutter, M. (2005). Incidence of autism spectrum disorders: Changes over time and their meaning. *Acta Paediatrica, 94*, 2–15.

Rutter, M., Andersen-Wood, L., Beckett, C., Bredenkamp, D., Castle, J., Groothues, C. et al. (1999). Quasi-autistic patterns following severe global privation. *Journal of Child Psychology and Psychiatry, 40*, 537–549.

Rutter, M., Greenfield, D., & Lockyer, L. (1967). A five- to fifteen-year follow-up study of infantile psychosis. II: Social and behavioral outcome. *British Journal of Psychiatry, 113*, 1187–1199.

Rutter, M., Krepner, J. M., & O'Connor, T. G. (2001). Specificity and heterogeneity in children's responses to profound institutional privation. *British Journal of Psychiatry, 179*, 97–103.

Rutter, M., & Lockyer, L. (1967) A five to fifteen year follow-up study of infantile psychosis. I: Description of sample. *British Journal of Psychiatry, 113*, 1169–1182.

Ryle, G. (1949). *The concept of mind*. London: Hutchinson.

Schopler, E., Reichler, R. J., & Renner, B. R. (1986). *The childhood autism rating scale*. Austin, TX: Pro-Ed Inc.

Schover, L. R., & Newsom, C. D. (1976). Overselectivity, developmental level, and over-training in autistic children. *Journal of Experimental Child Psychology, 4*, 289–298.

Schultz, R. T. (2005). Developmental deficits in social perception in autism: The role of the amygdala and the fusiform face area. *International Journal of Developmental Neuroscience, 23*, 125–141.

Schultz, R. T., Gauthier, I., Klin, A., Fulbright, R. K., Anderson, A. W., Volkmar, F. et al. (2000). Abnormal ventral temporal cortical activity during face discrimination among individuals with autism and Asperger syndrome. *Archives of General Psychiatry, 57*, 344–346.

Schultz, R. T., Grelotti, D. J., Klin, A., Kleinman, J., van der Gaag, C., Marois, R., & Skudlarski, P. (2003). The role of the fusiform face area in social cognition:

Implications for the pathobiology of autism. *Philosophical Transactions of the Royal Society of London, Series B, 358*, 415–427.

Segalowitz, S. J., & Schmidt, L. A. (2003). Developmental psychology and the neurosciences. In J. Valsiner and K. Connolly (Eds.), *Handbook of developmental psychology* (pp. 48–71). London: Sage.

Shah, A., & Frith, U. (1983). An islet of ability in autism: A research note. *Journal of Child Psychology and Psychiatry, 24*, 613–620.

Shah, A., & Frith, U. (1993). Why do autistic individuals show superior performance on the block design task? *Journal of Child Psychology and Psychiatry, 34*, 1351–1364.

Shallice, T. (1982). Specific deficits in planning. *Philosophical Transactions of the Royal Society of London, 298*, 199–209.

Shallice, T. (1988). *From neuropsychology to mental structure*. Cambridge, UK: Cambridge University Press.

Shallice, T. (1994). Multiple levels of control processes. In C. Umilta & M. Moscovitch (Eds.), *Attention and performance 15: Conscious and nonconscious information processing* (pp. 395–420). Cambridge, MA: MIT Press.

Shallice, T., & Burgess, P. W. (1991). Deficits in strategy application following frontal lobe damage in man. *Brain, 114*, 727–741.

Shamay-Tsoory, S. G., Tomer, R., Yaniv, S., & Aharon-Peretz, J. (2002). Empathy deficits in Asperger syndrome: A cognitive profile. *Neurocase, 8*, 245–252.

Shimamura, A. P. (1996). The control and monitoring of memory function. In L. M. Reder (Ed.), *Implicit memory and metacognition* (pp 259–274). Mahwah, NJ: Erlbaum.

Shulman, C., Yirmiya, N., & Greenbaum, C. W. (1995). From categorization to classification: A comparison among individuals with autism, mental retardation, and normal development. *Journal of Abnormal Psychology, 104*, 601–609.

Siebert, J. M., Hogan, A. M., & Mundy, P. C. (1982). Assessing interactional competencies: The Early Social-Communication Scales. *Infant Mental Health Journal, 3*, 244–245.

Sigman, M., Dijamco, A., Gratier, M., & Rozga, A. (2004). Early detection of core deficits in autism. *Mental Retardation and Developmental Disabilities Research Reviews, 10*, 221–233.

Sigman, M., Dissanayake, C., Corona, R., & Espinosa, M. (2003). Social and cardiac responses of young children with autism. *Autism, 7*, 205–216.

Sigman, M. D., Kasari, C., Kwon, J. H., & Yirmiya, N. (1992). Responses to the negative emotions of others by autistic, mentally retarded, and normal children. *Child Development, 63*, 796–807.

Sigman, M., Mundy, P., Sherman, T., & Ungerer, J. (1986). Social interactions of autistic, mentally retarded and normal children and their caregivers. *Journal of Child Psychology and Psychiatry, 27*, 647–655.

Sigman, M., & Ruskin, E. (1999). Continuity and change in the social competence of children with autism, Down syndrome and developmental delays. *Monographs of the Society for Research in Child Development, 64*, 1–119.

Siqueland, E. R., & DeLucia, C. A. (1969). Visual reinforcement of nonnutritive sucking in human infants. *Science, 165*, 1144–1146.

Skinner, B. F. (1938). *The behavior of organisms*. New York: Appleton-Century.

Skuse, D., Warrington, R., Bishop, D., Chowdhury, U., Lau, J., Mandy, W., & Place, M. (2004). The Developmental and Diagnostic Interview (3di): A novel computerized assessment for autism spectrum disorders. *Journal of the American Academy of Child and Adolescent Psychiatry, 43,* 548–558.

Smith, B. J., Gardiner, J. M., & Bowler, D. M. (in press). Further evidence of a relational deficit in adults with Asperger's syndrome. *Journal of Autism and Developmental Disorders.*

Smith, L. B., & Thelen, E. (1993) *A dynamic systems approach to development: Applications.* Cambridge, MA: MIT Press.

Smith, L. B., & Thelen, E. (2003). Development as a dynamic system. *Trends in Cognitive Science, 7,* 343–348.

Smith, L. B., Thelen, E., Titzer, R., & McLin, D. (1999). Knowing in the context of acting: The task dynamics of the A-not-B error. Psychological Review, *106,* 235–260.

Smith, M., Apperly, I. A., & White, V. (2003). False belief reasoning and the acquisition of relative class sentences. *Child Development, 74,* 1709–1719.

Snowling, M., & Frith, U. (1986). Comprehension in hyperlexic readers. *Journal of Experimental Chld Psychology, 42,* 392–415.

Sodian, B., & Frith, U. (1992). Deception and sabotage in autistic, retarded and normal children. *Journal of Child Psychology and Psychiatry, 33,* 591–606.

Sparks, B. F., Friedman, S. D., Shaw, D. W., Aylward, E. H., Echelard, D., Artru, A. A. et al. (2002). Brain structural abnormalities in young children with autism spectrum disorder. *Neurology, 59,* 184–192.

Sparrevohn, R., & Howie, P. (1995). Theory of mind in children with autistic disorder: Evidence of developmental progression and the role of verbal ability. *Journal of Child Psychology and Psychiatry, 36,* 249–263.

Sparrow, S., Balla, D., & Cicchetti, D. (1984). *Vineland Adaptive Behavior Scales.* Circle Pines, MN: American Guidance Service.

Spencer, J., O'Brien, J., Riggs, K., Braddick, O., Atkinson, J., & Wattam-Bell, J. (2000). Motion processing in autism: Evidence for a dorsal stream deficiency. *Neuroreport, 11,* 2765–2767.

Spiker, D., & Ricks, M. (1984). Visual self-recognition in autistic children: developmental relationships. *Child Development* 55: 214–225.

Spreen, O., & Benton, A. L. (1977). *Neurosensory Center Comprehensive Examination for Aphasia.* Victoria, BC: University of Victoria Neuropsychology Laboratory.

Steele, S., Joseph, R. M., & Tager-Flusberg, H. (2003). Brief report: Developmental change in theory of mind abilities in children with autism. *Journal of Autism and Developmental Disorders, 33,* 461–467.

Strawson, P. F. (1962). Persons. In V. C. Chappell (Ed.), *The philosophy of mind* (pp. 127–146). Englewood-Cliffs, NJ: Prentice-Hall.

Strayer, F. F. (1980). Child ethology and the study of preschool social relations. In H. C. Foot, A. J. Chapman, & J. R. Smith (Eds.), *Friendship and social relations in children* (pp. 235–266). Chichester: Wiley.

Stroop, J. R. (1935). Studies of interference in serial verbal reactions. *Journal of Experimental Psychology, 18,* 643–662.

Stuss, D. T., & Knight, R. T. (2002). *Principles of frontal lobe function.* Oxford: Oxford University Press.

Summers, J. A., & Craik, F. I. M. (1994). The effects of subject-performed tasks on the memory performance of verbal autistic children. *Journal of Autism and Developmental Disorders, 24,* 773–783.

REFERENCES

Swettenham, J. (1996). Can children with autism be taught to understand false belief using computers? *Journal of Child Psychology and Psychiatry, 37*, 157–165.

Swettenham, J., Baron-Cohen, S., Gomez, J.-C., & Walsh, S. (1996). What's inside a person's head? Conceiving of the mind as a camera helps children with autism develop an alternative to a theory of mind. *Cognitive Neurospychiatry, 1*, 73–88.

Swettenham, J., Condie, S., Campbell, R., Milne, E., & Coleman, M. (2003). Does the perception of moving eyes trigger reflexive visual orienting in autism? *Philosophical Transactions of the Royal Society, Series B, 358*, 325–334.

Szatmari, P., Bartolucci, G., Bremner, R. S., Bond, S., & Rich, S. (1989). A follow-up study of high-functioning autistic children. *Journal of Autism and Developmental Disorders, 19*, 213–226.

Szatmari, P., Bremner, R., & Nagy, J. (1989). Asperger's syndrome: A review of clinical features. *Canadian Journal of Psychiatry, 34*, 554–560.

Tager-Flusberg, H. (1985a). Basic level and superordinate level categorization by autistic, mentally retarded, and normal children. *Journal of Experimental Child Psychology, 40*, 450–469.

Tager-Flusberg, H. (1985b). The conceptual basis for referential word meaning in children with autism. *Child Development, 56*, 1167–1178.

Tager-Flusberg, H. (1991). Semantic processing in the free recall of autistic children: Further evidence for a cognitive deficit. *British Journal of Developmental Psychology, 9*, 417–430.

Tager-Flusberg, H. (1995). 'Once upon a ribbit': Stories narrated by autistic children. *British Journal of Developmental Psychology, 13*, 45–60.

Tager-Flusberg, H. (2001). A re-examination of the theory of mind hypothesis of autism. In J. Burack, T. Charman, N. Yirmiya, & P. Zelazo (Eds.), *The development of autism: Perspectives from theory and research* (pp. 173–193). Mahwah, NJ: Erlbaum.

Tager-Flusberg, H., & Sullivan, K. (1994). A 2nd look at 2nd-order belief attribution in autism. *Journal of Autism and Developmental Disorders, 24*, 577–586.

Tantam, D., Monaghan, L., Nicholson, H., & Stirling, J. (1989). Autistic children's ability to interpret faces: A research note. *Journal of Child Psychology and Psychiatry, 30*, 623–630.

Teunisse, J. P., & de Gelder, B. (2003). Face processing in adolescents with autistic disorder: The inversion and composite effects. *Brain and Cognition, 52*, 285–294.

Thelen, E., Schöner, G., Scheler, C., & Smith, L. B. (2001). The dynamics of embodiment: a field theory of infant perseverative reaching. *Behavioral and Brain Sciences, 24*, 1–86.

Thelen, E., & Smith, L. B. (1994). *A dynamic systems approach to the development of cognition and action.* Cambridge, MA: MIT Press.

Thom, R. (1989). *Structural stability and morphogenesis.* Boulder, CO: Westview Press.

Thomas, M. S. C., & Karmiloff-Smith, A. (2002). Are developmental disorders like cases of adult brain damage? Implications from connectionist modelling. *Behavioral and Brain Sciences, 25*, 727–788.

Thommen, E. (1992) *Causalité et intentionnalité chez l'enfant.* Bern: Peter Lang.

Thompson, D. W. (1917). *On growth and form.* Cambridge, UK: Cambridge University Press.

Thompson, P. (1980). Margaret Thatcher: A new illusion. *Perception, 9*, 483–484.

Tipper, S. P. (1985). The negative priming effect: Inhibitory priming by ignored objects. *Quarterly Journal of Experimental Psychology, 37A*, 571–590.

Toichi, M., & Kamio Y. (2002). Long-term memory and levels-of-processing in autism. *Neuropsychologia, 40*, 964–969.

Tomasello, M. (1988). The role of joint attentional processes in early language development. *Language Sciences, 10*, 69–88.

Tomasello, M., & Rakoczy, H. (2003). What makes human cognition unique? From individual to shared to collective intentionality. *Mind and Language, 18*, 121–147.

Townsend, J., & Courchesne, E. (1994). Parietal damage and narrow 'spotlight' spatial attention. *Journal of Cognitive Neuroscience, 6*, 220–232.

Townsend, J., Courchesne, E., & Egaas, B. (1996). Slowed orienting of covert visual-spatial attention in autism: Specific deficits associated with cerebellar and parietal abnormality. *Development and Psychopathology, 8*, 563–584.

Townsend, J., Westerfield, M., Leaver, E., Makeig, S., Jung, T. P., Pierce, K., & Courchesne, E. (2001). Event-related brain response abnormalities in autism: Evidence for impaired cerebello-frontal spatial attention networks. *Cognitive Brain Research, 11*, 127–145.

Tranel, D., Damasio, H., & Damasio, A. R. (1995). Double dissociation between overt and covert face recognition. *Journal of Cognitive Neuroscience, 7*, 425–432.

Trevarthen, C., & Aitken, K. J. (2001). Infant intersubjectivity: Research, theory and clinical applications. *Journal of Child Psychology and Psychiatry, 42*, 3–48.

Tulving, E. (1962). Subjective organisation in the free recall of 'unrelated' words. *Psychological Review, 69*, 344–354.

Tulving, E. (1995). Organization of memory: Quo vadis? In M. S. Gazzaniga (Ed.), *The cognitive neurosciences* (pp. 839–847). Cambridge, MA: MIT Press.

Tulving, E. (2001). Episodic memory and common sense: How far apart? *Philosophical Transactions of the Royal Society, Series B, 356*, 1505–1515.

Turner, M. (1999). Annotation: Repetitive behaviour in autism: a review of psychological research. *Journal of Child Psychology and Psychiatry, 40*, 839–849.

Ungerer, J. A., & Sigman, M. (1987). Categorization skills and receptive language development in autistic children. *Journal of Autism and Developmental Disorders, 17*, 3–16.

Valsiner, J., & Connolly, K. (2003). *Handbook of developmental psychology*. London: Sage.

van der Geest, J. N., Kemner, C., Camfferman, G., Verbaten, M. N., & van Engeland, H. (2002a). Eye-movements, visual attention and autism: A saccadic reaction time study using the gap and overlap paradigm. *Biological Psychiatry, 50*, 614–619.

van der Geest, J., Kemner, C., Verbaten, M., & van Engeland, H. (2002b). Gaze behavior of children with pervasive developmental disorder toward human faces: A fixation time study. *Journal of Child Psychology and Psychiatry, 43*, 669–678.

van der Maas, H. L. J., & Molenaar, P. C. M. (1992). Stagewise cognitive development: an application of catastrophe theory. *Psychological Review, 99*, 395–417.

Van Geert, P. (1998). We almost had a great future behind us: The contribution of non-linear dynamics to developmental-science-in-the-making. *Developmental Science, 1*, 143–159.

Van Krevelen, D. A. (1971). Early infantile autism and autistic psychopathy. *Journal of Autism and Childhood Schizophrenia, 1*, 82–86.

Vargha-Khadem, F., Gadian, D. G., Watkins, K. E., Connelly, A., Van Paesschen, W., & Mishkin, M. (1997). Differential effects of early hippocampal pathology on episodic and semantic memory. *Science, 277*, 376.

Venter, A., Lord, C., & Schopler, E. (1992). A follow-up study of high-functioning autistic children. *Journal of Child Psychology and Psychiatry, 33*, 489–507.

Vygotsky, L. S. (1962). *Thought and language.* Cambridge, MA: MIT Press.

Vygotsky, L. S. (1978). *Mind in society.* Cambridge, MA: Harvard University Press.

Waddington, C. H. (1957). *The strategy of the genes.* London: Allen & Unwin.

Waddington, C. H. (1966). *Principles of development and differentiation.* New York: Macmillan.

Wainwright, J. A., & Bryson. S. E. (1996). Visual-spatial orienting in autism. *Journal of Autism and Developmental Disorders, 26*, 423–438.

Wainwright-Sharp, J. A., & Bryson, S. E. (1993). Visual orienting deficits in high functioning people with autism. *Journal of Autism and Developmental Disorders, 23*, 1–13.

Wallon, H. (1973). *Les origines de la pensée chez l'enfant.* Paris: Presses Universitaires de France.

Wang, L., & Mottron, L. (2005). Free choice condition with hierarchical stimuli demonstrates intact global processing, faster local response and random level preference in persons with autism. Poster presented at the International Meeting for Autism Research, Boston, MA, May 2005.

Wang, T. A., Dapretto, M., Hariri, A. R., Sigman, M., & Bookheimer, S. Y. (2004). Neural correlates of facial affect processing in children and adolescents with autism spectrum disorder. *Journal of the American Academy of Child and Adolescent Psychiatry, 43*, 48–490.

Waterhouse, L., Fein, D., & Modahl, C. (1996). Neurofunctional mechanisms in autism. *Psychological Review, 103*, 457–489.

Watson, N. V., & Kimura, D. (1991). Nontrivial sex differences in throwing and intercepting: Relation to psychometrically-defined spatial functions. *Personality and Individual Differences, 12*, 375–385.

Weeks, S. J., & Hobson, R. P. (1987). The salience of facial expression for autistic children. *Journal of Child Psychology and Psychiatry, 28*, 137–152.

Weintraub, S., & Mesulam, M.-M. (1983). Developmental learning disabilities of the right hemisphere: Emotional, interpersonal, and cognitive components. *Archives of Neurology, 40*, 463–468.

Welch-Ross, M. (1997). Mother–child participation in conversations about the past: Relations to preschoolers' theory of mind. *Developmental Psychology, 33*, 618–629.

Wellman, H. M., & Liu, D. (2004). Scaling theory of mind tasks. *Child Development, 75*, 523–541.

Welsh, M. C., & Pennington, B. F. (1988). Assessing frontal lobe functioning in children: views from developmental psychology. *Developmental Neuropsychology, 4*, 199–230.

Werner, H. (1948). *The comparative psychology of mental development.* New York: International Universities Press.

Werner, H., & Kaplan, B. (1963). *Symbol formation.* New York: Wiley.

Wheeler, M. A., & Stuss, D. T. (2003). Remembering and knowing in patients with frontal lobe injuries. *Cortex, 39*, 827–846.

Wheelwright, S., & Baron-Cohen, S. (1998). The link between autism and skills such as engineering, maths, physics and computing – A reply to Jarrold and Routh. *Autism, 5*, 223–227.

Williams, D. (1994). *Somebody somewhere.* London: Doubleday.

Williams, D. (1996). *Autism: An inside-out approach.* London: Jessica Kingsley.

Williams, J. H. G., Whiten, A., & Singh, T. (2004). A systematic review of action imitation in autistic spectrum disorder. *Journal of Autism and Developmental Disorders*, *34*, 285–299.

Wimmer, H., & Perner, J. (1983). Beliefs about beliefs: Representation and constraining function of wrong beliefs in young children's understanding of deception. *Cognition*, *13*, 103–128.

Wing, J. K. (1966). Diagnosis, epidemiology, aetiology. In J. K. Wing (Ed.), *Early childhood autism: Clinical, educational and social aspects* (pp. 3–49). Oxford: Pergamon.

Wing, L. (1981). Asperger's syndrome: A clinical account. *Psychological Medicine*, *11*, 115–129.

Wing, L. (1993). The definition and prevalence of autism: A review. *European Child and Adolescent Psychiatry*, *2*, 61–74.

Wing, L. (1996). *The autistic spectrum: A guide for parents and professionals*. London: Constable.

Wing, L. (2006). Editorial comment. *Autism*, *10*, 9–10.

Wing, L., & Gould, J. (1979). Severe impairments of social interaction and associated abnormalities in children: Epidemiology and classification. *Journal of Autism and Developmental Disorders*, *9*, 11–29.

Wing, L., Gould, J., Yeates, S. R., & Brierly, L. M. (1977). Symbolic play in severely mentally retarded and in autistic children. *Journal of Child Psychology and Psychiatry*, *18*, 167–178.

Wing, L., Leekam, S. R., Libby, S. J., Gould, J., & Larcombe, M. (2002). The diagnostic interview for social and communication disorders: Background, inter-rater reliability and clinical use. *Journal of Child Psychology and Psychiatry*, *43*, 307–325.

Winston, J. S., Strange, B. A., O'Doherty, J., & Dolan, R. J. (2002). Automatic and intentional brain responses during evaluation of trustworthiness of faces. *Nature Neuroscience*, *5*, 277–83.

Witkin, H. A., Oltman, P. K., Raskin, E., & Karp, S. (1971). *A Manual for the Embedded Figures Test*. Palo Alto, CA: Consulting Psychologists Press, California.

Wittgenstein, L. (1980). *Remarks on the philosophy of psychology* (Vol. 2). G. H. von Wright & H. Nyman (Eds.), C. G. Luckhardt & M.A.E. Aue (Trans.). Oxford: Blackwell.

Wolff, S. (1995). *Loners: The life path of unusual children*. London: Routledge.

Wolff, S. B. (1985). The symbolic and object play of children with autism: A review. *Journal of Autism and Developmental Disorders*, *15*, 139–148.

Wolff, S., & Barlow, A. (1979). Schizoid personality in childhood: A comparative study of schizoid, autistic and normal children. *Journal of Child Psychology and Psychiatry*, *20*, 29–46.

Wolff, S., & Chick, J. (1980). Schizoid personality in childhood: A controlled follow-up study. *Psychological Medicine*, *10*, 85–100.

World Health Organization (1993). *International classification of diseases* (10th ed.). Geneva: WHO.

Yirmiya, N., Erel, O., Shaked, M., & Solomonica-Levi, D. (1998). Meta-analyses comparing theory of mind abilities of individuals with autism, individuals with mental retardation, and normally developing individuals. *Psychological Bulletin*, *124*, 283–307.

Yoshino, A., Inoue, M., & Suzuki, A. (2000). A topographic electrophysiologic study of mental rotation. *Cognitive Brain Research*, *9*, 121–124.

Zaitchik, D. (1990). When representations conflict with reality: The pre-schooler's problem with false beliefs and 'false' photographs. *Cognition, 35*, 41–68.

Zelazo, P. D., Burack, J. A., Benedetto, E., & Frye, D. (1996). Theory of mind and rule use in individuals with Down syndrome: A test of the uniqueness and specificity claims. *Journal of Child Psychology and Psychiatry, 37*, 479–484.

Zelazo, P. D., Burack, J. A., Boseovski, J., Jacques, S., & Frye, D. (2001). A cognitive complexity and control framework for the study of autism. In J. A. Burack, T. Charman, N. Yirmiya & P. R. Zelazo (Eds.), *The development of autism: Perspectives from theory and research* (pp. 195–217). Mahwah, NJ: Erlbaum.

Zelazo, P. D., & Frye, D. (1998). Cognitive complexity and control: II. The development of executive control in childhood. *Current Directions in Psychological Science, 47*, 121–126.

Zelazo, P. D., Jacques, S., Burack, J. A., & Frye, D. (2002). The relation between theory of mind and rule use: Evidence from persons with autism-spectrum disorders. *Infant and Child Development, 11*, 171–195.

Zilbovicius, M., Garreau, B., Samson, Y., Remy, P., Barthélémy, C., Syrota, A., & Lelord, G. (1995). Delayed maturation of the frontal cortex in childhood autism. *American Journal of Psychiatry, 152*, 248–252.

Index